THE ECONOMIC APPROACH TO LAW

The Economic Approach to Law

edited by

Paul Burrows
Cento G. Veljanovski

Butterworths
London Boston Sydney Wellington Durban Toronto

First published 1981

British Library Cataloguing in Publication Data

The Economic approach to law.
1. Law – Economic aspects
I. *Burrows, Paul* II. *Veljanovski, Cento G.*
340'.115 K487.E3

ISBN 0–408–10686–7
ISBN 0–408–10685–9 Pbk

Typeset by Scribe Design, Gillingham, Kent
Printed in England by Billing & Sons Ltd,
London & Guildford

Acknowledgements

We would like to thank the authors of the papers for their co-operation in keeping to fairly tight deadlines, and the editors and staff of Butterworths for their patience and encouragement throughout.

The opinions expressed by us in the Introduction should not be attributed to the contributors, although we believe that there is *some* overlap between our view of law and economics and theirs.

We are grateful to the editors of the Journal of Law and Economics for permission to reprint portions of Professor Williamson's article 'Transaction-Cost Economics: the Governance of Contractual Relations', as part of his chapter in this volume.

Paul Burrows
Cento G. Veljanovski

Contributors

Richard P. Adelstein Wesleyan University

William Bishop London School of Economics

Roger A. Bowles University of Bath

Paul Burrows University of York

D.N. Dewees University of Toronto

J. Feldman The Institute for Fiscal Studies, London

Paul T. Fenn Centre for Socio-Legal Studies, Oxford

Werner Z. Hirsch University of California, Los Angeles

J.A. Kay The Institute for Fiscal Studies, London

Ian R. Macneil Northwestern University

Anthony I. Ogus University of Newcastle-upon-Tyne

M.J. Trebilcock University of Toronto

Cento G. Veljanovski Centre for Socio-Legal Studies, Oxford

Christopher J. Whelan Centre for Socio-Legal Studies, Oxford

Oliver E. Williamson University of Pennsylvania

Contents

CHAPTER ONE

Introduction: the economic approach to law[1]

Paul Burrows and Cento G. Veljanovski

A major development in North American legal scholarship over the last decade has been the increasing use of economics. This is evident not only in the type of article that is finding its way into legal journals but also in the teaching of law in some universities, in the appointment of full time economists to law schools, and more recently in the establishment of research centres in law and economics[2]. In Britain the situation is quite different, although there are signs that the study of law and economics is beginning to develop[3].

While the economic approach to law has firmly established itself in North America it has not been without its critics (e.g. Leff, 1974), some of whom have been hostile to the whole idea, whereas others have objected to the particular variety of law and economics known as the 'Chicago approach'[4]. 'Economic analysis of central legal issues', observes Krier, 'seems to forment storms where otherwise mild breezes blow' (Krier, 1974, p.1665). While some of the criticisms constitute attacks on economics in general, rather than specifically on its application to law, others draw attention to problems that the economic approach to law has encountered and that have been ignored or inadequately treated by those doing research in this area.

The purpose of this introduction is to examine the present state of the art and to draw attention to the strengths and weaknesses of the economic approach to law[5]. We would emphasize that the critical perspective adopted here is not intended to imply that the economic approach has failed; rather it is motivated by the belief that any new intellectual endeavour is enhanced rather than retarded by moderately critical appraisal[6]. In law and economics the endeavour hinges on the expectation among both lawyers and economists that the disciplines are complementary and that collaboration is potentially fruitful. It is a sustainable point of view that such collaboration will ultimately be discouraged if an influential group of the practitioners of one of the disciplines is apparently intent on the hard-sell, on adopting a colonizing posture to bring the 'right' methodology to those unfortunate enough not to have been born with it, or at least to have been weaned on to it at an early age. The danger of the hard-sell is that the potential buyers will divide into one group which rapidly loses interest in the collaborative endeavour, and another which succumbs and adopts the typically uncritical attitude of the new convert, the born-again economist. It is difficult to say which of these two reactions is likely to be the more damaging to the progress of law and economics.

Our intention is first to introduce the reader who is unfamiliar with the economic analysis of law to the central tenets of the analysis and its main applications, and secondly to describe the main trends in the literature and to highlight the difficulties that are encountered when lawyers use economics to provide descriptive theories of the law.

This introduction is organized as follows. Section 1.1 outlines the positive and normative types of economic analysis, and section 1.2 compares the main advantages and disadvantages of the economic studies of law. Section 1.3 concentrates on recent attempts by lawyers to use economic theory as a basis for a descriptive theory of law. The difficulties which this theory of law involves justify the examination, in section 1.4, of an alternative methodology for the descriptive theory of law. Section 1.5 briefly mentions some recent developments in the use of economics to evaluate the operation of statutory controls in areas of the law that hitherto have not been subject to such scrutiny.

1.1 The economic approach to law

1.1.1 Basic ideas in the economics of law

The marrying of economics and law is not new. 'Economic' approaches can be found in the works of Beccaria-Bonesara (1764), Bentham (1789), Marx (1867) and in the turn-of-the-century work of the American Institutionalist school, particularly the writing of Commons (1924). For a considerable period (1920–1960) the economic study of law and institutions fell into disrepute, although the intersection between law and economics continued in areas where the law had obvious economic objectives and/or effects, e.g. antitrust, competition and trade policy and regulation. The resurgence in the economic analysis of law came from a number of sources. The work of Becker (1957) on discrimination, although not specifically law related, provided the initial step in generalizing neoclassical economics to non-market behaviour. The early work of Alchian (1961) and Demsetz (1969) on property rights, Calabresi (1961) on tort, and Coase (1966) on nuisance represent the building blocks on which the new law and economics now rest. Mention should also be made of the *Journal of Law and Economics*, which, under the general editorship of Ronald Coase, provided an outlet for much of the new work in the field[7].

The 'new' economic approach to law differs from its precursors both in the rigour of its theoretical approach and in its subject matter, namely non-market law[8]. Economics has been increasingly applied to a variety of non-market activities, ranging from rioting (Chalmers and Shelton, 1975;

Buchanan, 1971), church attendance (Azzi and Ehrenberg, 1975) and suicide (Hammermesh and Soss, 1974) to abortion reform (Deyak and Smith, 1976; Coelen and McIntyre, 1978), the family (Becker, 1976), marriage (Becker, 1973), divorce (Becker, Landes and Michael, 1977; Landes, 1978) and extra-marital affairs (Fair, 1978). The economic approach to law is part of this wider development which has resulted from the belief held by some (but not all) economists that the core of economics, the theory of choice, is in principle applicable to all human and institutional behaviour[9]. As Robbins (1932) states 'when time and means for achieving ends are limited and capable of alternative applications, and the ends are capable of being distinguished in order of importance then behaviour necessarily assumes the form of choice . . . it has an economic aspect'[10]. The restriction of economics to the study of prices, money and material welfare no longer applies, although the study of this subject matter in the past has contributed to the growth of economics as 'science' and will continue to do so in the future. Contemporary economics is probably better described as a methodological approach than as a discipline defined by its subject matter.

The basic ideas contained in the economic approach to law are those of maximizing behaviour (utility maximization), stable preferences and opportunity cost[11]. The economic approach takes the individual as the basic unit of analysis and pictures him as a self-interested egoist who maximizes utility. Its assumptions of utility maximization and rationality have given rise to much criticism and confusion. When an economist says that an individual is acting rationally or maximizing his utility he is saying no more than that the individual is making consistent choices, and that he chooses the preferred alternative(s) from those available to him. The modern economic theory of utility/rationality attempts to describe rigorously the choice process and to draw out the implications of that process for behaviour under different conditions. It does not attempt to explain why individuals prefer particular things, or to show that the choices made are 'good' in any other sense than as subjectively assessed by the individuals concerned[12]. That is, the individual is regarded as the best judge of his own welfare, and tastes are assumed to be given and stable. The latter assumption prevents the economist from using taste changes to rationalize observed inconsistencies between theory and experience.

The economic approach does *not* contend that all individuals are rational nor that these assumptions are necessarily realistic. The economist's model of man as a rational actor is a fiction, but one that has proved extremely useful in analysing the behaviour of groups. Although much of economics is framed in terms of individual behaviour there is no belief among economists that all people behave in this way. Rather 'economic man' is some weighted average of the individuals under study in which the non-uniformities and extremes in behaviour are evened out. The theory allows for irrationality but argues that *groups* of individuals behave as if their members are rational.

Related to this 'as if' approach is that the utility maximizing postulate is not one concerned with the psychology of man or his actual thought process. It does not assert that individuals consciously calculate the costs and benefits of all actions, only that their behaviour can be explained 'as if' they did so. Admittedly this is not the only view of rationality[13], but it is the one that forms the basis of what will later be referred to as positive, or predictive, economics.

A corollary to the rationality postulate is that individuals react to changes in the net benefits received from the alternatives which confront them. In their market activities individuals are assumed to trade with each other in order to maximize their perceived welfare, and this trading will cease when all have achieved the best they can do given their initial endowment of resources and innate talents. If there is a change in the net benefits of the various alternatives available, then rational individuals will respond by acquiring more of those goods which have become relatively cheaper and fewer of those which have become relatively dearer. This inverse relationship between the price (cost) and the quantity demanded of a good is perhaps the most frequent prediction of economics.

Perhaps the most pervasive notion in economic theory is that of opportunity cost. This says simply that the use of resources for any purpose incurs a cost which is equal to the value of the best forgone alternative use. This cost is clearly fundamental to the choice between competing uses for resources, and it is equally central to those choices which are made through market transactions and those made through non-market operations. The emphasis placed by economists on the need to make choices based upon opportunity cost is not, therefore, to be thought the same as an insistence on the relevance or importance of markets. An analysis of public sector decision-making, for example, might well eschew any significant reference to markets, yet it would be based on the characteristics of non-market choices and costs. The relevance of this point to the economic analysis of law is that it means that it is consistent to argue that *any* law is likely to have economic implications (if only because the imposition of a law involves resources) even if it bears little relation to market activities and relates to behaviour that is not at all similar to market behaviour. It emphatically does not mean, however, that it is necessarily fruitful to describe non-market behaviour in terms of the language of a market analogy. For example, it is undoubtedly true that the enforcement of the law against rape involves the use of scarce resources which have alternative uses. It is also true that when a decision is made as to how many resources should be devoted to such enforcement, either implicitly or explicitly a comparison is being made between that use and alternative uses of those resources. In addition, a decision must be made on the most effective way of utilizing the resources that are to be devoted to the enforcement of the law against rape. These are issues into which economic analysis can provide some insight. But this does not mean that the lawyer-economist is well advised to view rape as a 'transaction', the penalties for rape as 'the price the law sets for participating in the transaction as a rapist', or the ideal penalty as 'the optimal pricing scheme which balances the social benefits and costs of the activity and clears the market for rape'. When it comes to winning friends and influencing people some economists have a good deal to learn!

In some legal contexts, of course, market behaviour is very relevant to the impact of law simply because the law regulates market behaviour. Thus, it is hard to gain an insight into the implications of contract law without an understanding of the market context of contract formation. In the analysis of markets economists have found a concept of equilibrium helpful to the task of predicting the consequences for market outcomes of changes in the attitudes of the participants, as well as of changes in the legally determined rules of the market game. In an ideal market competitive pressures ensure that goods are produced at least cost and the market is cleared at a price that reflects the marginal costs to society of their production. The function performed by prices is to clear the market by making participants' plans mutually consistent (equilibrium) and to signal to producers and consumers the need to change their actions when supply and demand are not in balance. Price is, from an economic perspective, solely an allocative device that provides information to the market, and in equilibrium the economic value (price) of a commodity will equal its opportunity cost[14].

There are two other features of the economic approach. First, it is a marginal approach, it is concerned with analysing incremental changes in a system that is otherwise stable. It therefore cannot deal with dramatic changes in legal/social systems. But once the change has occurred, economic marginalism can again be used to examine the efficiency of incremental legal/social changes from the new status quo. Secondly, it is an *ex ante* approach. It focuses on incentives and on people's predicted responses to changes in the law given their expectations for the future. This is best illustrated by the way uncertainty is incorporated into economic models. Individuals are assumed to maximize their expected utility on the basis of their beliefs about uncertain events. On the basis of these beliefs individuals will make choices that *ex ante* will be efficient but *ex post* may not be if beliefs are not confirmed by experience. The *ex ante* nature of the economic approach is perhaps the major difference between it and orthodox legal analysis which looks at past events and actual cases i.e. is an *ex post* approach. For the economist the past is a 'sunk' cost and he views the law as an incentive system affecting future actions.

1.1.2 Positive economic analysis

Building upon this basic framework, economics can be divided into two traditions of discourse, positive and normative analysis. Positive economics views economics exclusively as an empirical science[15]. It is based on a methodology that sees economic analysis solely as a means of deriving a set of testable (i.e. potentially refutable) predictions that can be verified by empirical evidence. This approach judges the usefulness of a piece of analysis (or model) by its ability to predict the behavioural responses to a change in the situation under investigation more accurately than any competing theory. If the model is successful in predicting then the negative judgment can be made that the model has not been falsified and is preferable to those that have been falsified. Positive economic analysis is therefore used largely to make qualitative predictions and organize data for the empirical testing of these predictions.

The predictions of positive economic models must be interpreted with some care. First, such models only establish partial relationships. For example, one of the most common predictions in economics is the inverse relationship between the price of a good and the quantity demanded. However, the statement must be read with an important caveat; it says that in practice the quantity demanded will decrease as price increases only if all other things remain constant in the system. Thus the predictions of positive economic models are in the nature of conditional statements 'if *A* — then *B*, given *C*', but *B* may never be observed to occur because other influences (*C*) have also changed. Secondly, the *partial* nature of the model does not imply that the relationships studied are the most important ones. An economist may argue, for example, that people will respond to cost-pressures (such as liability for damages) in the care they take in an activity which places others at risk, and he may empirically establish this proposition. But this is not to say that pecuniary incentives are the only, or even the best, means of achieving an increase in the level of safety.

The methodology of positive economics as described above is one that lawyers find difficult to accept. The main criticism which they are inclined to make is that the models are too simplistic and do not capture the full complexity of the legal phenomena which they seek to explain. This view usually expresses itself in the form of an attack on the unrealistic assumptions of the economists' model. In response, the economists will argue that models are by their nature 'unrealistic' — they are abstractions from, not descriptions of, reality — and that furthermore, it is not the model's assumptions that are to be verified but its predictions. We shall argue in section 1.3 that the force of this criticism, and of its rebuttal, depends on the intended use of the model.

The techniques of positive economics are most relevant to *legal impact studies* or what Hirsch has called 'effect evaluation' (Hirsch, 1979, p. 6). Legal impact studies seek to identify and quantify the effects of law on measurable variables[16]. A good, though not uncontroversial, example of this application is the positive economic analysis of crime[17].

The economic analysis of crime treats the decision to engage in crime as an example of occupational choice[18]. An individual participates in criminal activity because it provides a greater stream of net benefits than any alternative legitimate occupation. The fundamental assumption of the economic approach is 'that offenders and those who attempt to control crime on the whole respond to measurable opportunities and incentives' (Ehrlich, 1979, p. 25). The criminal is characterized as a rational individual with stable preferences who maximizes not wealth but expected utility. It is a common misconception that the economic theory of occupational choice asserts that individuals choose jobs solely on the basis of pecuniary wage comparisons. On the contrary, the theory predicts that individuals will be influenced in their job choices by the net advantages of the jobs i.e. by the total bundle of their pecuniary and non-pecuniary characteristics. Thus the hypothesis is that the decision to engage in crime will be determined both by the wealth that can be gained and by more intangible characteristics such as the risk and life-style. Naturally the type of behaviour predicted from the economic model of a utility-maximizing potential criminal is likely to fit some types of crime better than others. For example, crimes which are substantially motivated by the prospect of monetary gain are more likely to display a pattern predicted by the maximization model than the crimes motivated by personal hatred, jealousy or lust. Even those of us who are unenthusiastic about the style of argument of this literature may concede that the only way to find out whether this is so is to test empirically the relationships predicted by the theory for different types of crime.

The principal focus of the economics literature on crime is the theoretical and empirical investigation of the deterrence hypothesis. A corollary to the economic theory of crime as a rational act is that any factor that reduces the expected return to a crime will, other things being equal, reduce the criminal's level of participation in it. The punishment meted out by the criminal law will decrease the potential criminal's expected return from engaging in a crime. The *ex ante* expected level of punishment is the product of two elements, the severity of the sanction and the frequency with which it is imposed on offenders, and the theory predicts not only that an increase in the severity or in the frequency of sanctions will decrease the number of offenders, but which of these two elements will have the greater deterrent effect.

The model of crime serves not only to provide these predictions but to organize the data to test them and is concerned with 'verifying' the deterrence hypothesis. Using sophisticated statistical techniques the evidence so far accumulated does, at least, provide tentative support for the deterrence hypothesis. A particularly sensitive area of empirical research has been the examination of the deterrence effects of capital punishment[19]. The work of Isaac Erlich has generated a considerable academic and public debate, not only because of its finding in support of deterrence but because it yields very specific estimates of the magnitude by which capital punishment reduces the homocide rate[20]. Although the debate has been vigorous

(Ehrlich, 1979, pp.50–54) it has not been about theory or approach but rather about statistical methodology, e.g. the appropriate statistical technique, the sensitivity of the results to the form of the estimating equation and the time periods chosen, and the nature of the data used[21].

To the economist legal impact studies are a natural application of economic theory and empirical methods. They ask and attempt to answer the questions: What are the likely effects of the law? Have they actually occurred? Have the objectives of the law been attained? Moreover, the economist currently has a comparative advantage over the lawyer, because of his statistical training, in answering these questions. Lawyers, when they venture into this area, all too frequently discuss the effects of law in language and arguments which are based on unsupported empirical assumptions, and their empirical research is often of dubious validity and lacks statistical rigour. But to many lawyers, the prediction and quantification of the effects of laws, while of interest, is not seen as having particular legal relevance. As a result there is a tendency to adopt a dismissive attitude to the economists' work in this area. But there can be no doubt that impact studies have an important role to play in legal analysis; for surely the law must ultimately be evaluated in terms of its success in achieving its goals, and not purely in terms of its formal legalistic structure.

1.1.3 Normative economic analysis

Normative or welfare economics is concerned with the goals of private and social allocative efficiency. The aim is to identify situations in which these are not achieved and to prescribe corrective solutions[22]. The analysis begins with the assumption that *perfectly* competitive markets achieve private efficiency, that is an allocation of resources which is efficient from the point of view of the participants in the transactions. The relationship between the market and economic efficiency is often confused. The theory does not say that actual markets are efficient, only that a market operating under a set of restrictive assumptions is. The more important of these assumptions are conveniently summarized by one standard text:

> Perfect competition is an economic model possessing the following characteristics: each economic agent acts as if prices are given, that is each acts as a price-taker; the product is homogeneous; there is free mobility of all resources including entry and exit of business firms; and all economic agents in the market possess complete and perfect knowledge (Ferguson and Gould, 1975, p.225).

It is on the basis of these assumptions that the economist's theorems concerning the private efficiency of the market and freedom of contract are based.

A privately efficient allocation of resources will imply an allocation that is efficient from the point of view of society as a whole, i.e. that will be socially efficient, only if *all* of the consequences of reallocations of resources between uses are taken into account by the participants in the transactions. In other words privately efficient allocations will be socially efficient as long as there are no external costs, or benefits, of a transaction (we shall define an external cost more explicitly below). In the absence of externalities a perfectly competitive market system is socially efficient because it 'place[s] every productive resource in that position in the productive system where it can make the greatest possible contribution to the total social dividend measured in price terms; and tends to reward every participant in production by giving it the increase in the social dividend which its co-operation makes possible' (Knight, 1935, p. 48). That is, society's resources are allocated to their highest competitively valued uses, and are sold at prices that reflect their marginal cost to society. In essence, social efficiency is a technical concept of unimprovability; there is no rearrangement of productive activity that would improve the welfare of society as measured by the competitive market place *given the distribution of income* upon which the market transactions are based (a point to which we return later).

The prescriptive ability of welfare economics is based on the concept of market failure[23]. When the assumptions underlying the perfectly competitive market are not met the market will either operate inefficiently or fail to exist. This departure from the ideal outcome of the perfectly competitive market is referred to as market failure and it provides the social efficiency rationale for legal intervention. Although market failure may result from many imperfections (monopoly, imperfect information, etc.), the most important one for legal analysis is an external cost. An external cost is an uncompensated loss that is imposed on individuals (or firms) by some harmful activity. The most significant examples of external cost relate to pollution, crime, and road accidents. The existence of external costs leads to excessively high levels of the harm-imposing activities; the socially efficient amount of avoidance or care will not be undertaken.

The existence of harmful activities is not, however, necessarily sufficient for market failure to occur. In an influential paper Ronald Coase (1960) demonstrated that perfectly competitive markets could in principle control harmful activities efficiently. Take the case of pollution. In a perfect market the loss that pollution imposes on individuals would provide them with an incentive to bargain for a reduction in its level if they had no legal rights to compensation by the polluter. If the payment offered by the victims exceeded the costs to the polluter of reducing the level of pollution then the polluter would accept the victims' payment and decrease the pollution, because this would increase his profits. Voluntary bargaining of this type would continue until all the mutual gains were exhausted, which would occur at the socially efficient level of pollution (Burrows, 1979, ch.2–3). Moreover, this bargaining process would be unaffected by a change in the law. If the law required the firm to compensate the victims for the harm it imposed on them, the firm would continue to pollute up to the point at which the profit from an increment of pollution is exceeded by the increased compensation payment. When *all* of the profit from an increment in pollution has to be paid to victims as compensation the firm would cease to increase the level of pollution, and at that point he would be inflicting the socially efficient level of harm. This elegant piece of analysis, known as the *Coase Theorem*, implies that the choice of legal (property) rights would not affect the social efficiency of the final outcome. But the analysis relies on a set of highly restrictive assumptions, which includes the assumption that the cost of the transactions (bargains) is zero. Even in the context of zero transactions costs, however, the choice of legal rights would be expected to alter the distribution of income and this, in turn, would determine the particular socially efficient resource allocation that the bargaining process would bring about (*see* Mishan, 1967; Burrows, 1970).

The Coase Theorem has had a significant influence on the economic approach to law. Its popularity has been due to the fact that by describing an idealized market situation it focuses attention on the *obstacles* to socially efficient markets, the causes of market failure. These causes tend to be grouped under one heading, transactions costs, but they include a variety of frictions that impede the exchange of the kind envisaged by the model of the perfectly competitive market. These frictions include the costs of obtaining information, and of searching, negotiating, and enforcing agreements[24].

When transactions costs exist the law is unlikely to be allocatively neutral: it has an efficiency role to play. This is true whether the law in effect provides a legal rights basis for the market (bargaining) process to operate upon to determine the level of external costs, or whether the law directly determines the level of external costs by establishing legal rights (to pollute or to be protected from pollution) where the market is not operative with respect to such costs. In principle, the Coase Theorem can be interpreted merely as the statement that socially efficient levels of external costs depend, in the case of pollution for example, on the balance of the costs of polluting (damage costs) and the costs of not polluting (abatement costs). This says nothing about the operability of markets, but perhaps because Coase originally presented the theorem in the context of bargaining over external costs many economists and lawyers have since explored the implications of the theorem in the context of the analysis of market solutions[25]. Much of this literature has been neoclassical in style and pro-market in conviction, and has tended to favour common law and damages measures designed to give the ever-willing market a gentle nudge in the direction of social efficiency. More recently there has developed a considerable degree of scepticism concerning both the suitability of the neoclassical model of the behaviour of firms for the analysis of many problems in law and economics, and the relevance of the free market to the control of external costs in the real world of poor information and uncertainty. This scepticism has led first to the presentation of analyses, which we shall refer to as neo-institutional, that focus primarily on the organization of transactions when transactions costs are significant (e.g. Williamson, 1975; Goldberg, 1976b), and secondly to the investigation of statutory methods of control intended to deal with market failure or to achieve other social objectives[26].

Before dealing with these approaches the normative approach to the economics of law will be illustrated by looking first at the work of Calabresi, on accident law, and then at a recent attempt to use the notion of efficiency to provide a theory of legal rights and duties.

The efficiency approach to law usually proceeds by stating as the objective the minimization of the total social costs of an activity. According to Calabresi 'the principal function of accident law is to reduce the sum of the cost of accidents and the cost of avoiding accidents'[27]. This goal presupposes three things: that all losses can be expressed in monetary terms[28], that accidents can be reduced by devoting more resources to accident prevention, and that those (potentially) involved in accidents are sensitive to cost pressures.

The efficiency goal of negligence is to deter uneconomical accidents by placing liability on the 'cheapest cost avoider'[29]. The aim is to use damages awards after the event to replace 'unfeasible agreements'[30] that would have occurred had an accident market been possible. Although many people would accept the proposition that accidents can be reduced by committing more resources to preventive measures, there is a lively controversy over whether the type of cost pressures which are generated by damages awards will be effective in encouraging greater care. However, unlike the economics of crime, very little empirical research has been undertaken, although several recent studies do suggest that changes in the liability rules do have an impact on the accident rate[31].

The development of the normative economic approach to tort is also interesting for the more general trend it reflects. Economics has been used in two distinct areas that correspond to the two dominant functions of tort, namely compensation and deterrence. The 'older' economic approach examined in great detail the operation of the tort system as an imperfect compensation scheme (e.g. Conard *et al.*, 1964). This literature is generally marred by its tendency to identify economics with purely financial considerations, and to assess the efficiency of accident law solely in terms of minimizing the administrative costs of providing compensation. It also ignores the fact, which it has been primarily responsible for revealing, that very few victims are compensated by tort. The 'new' economic approach, on the other hand, ignores the compensation goal and assumes that the aim of tort is to promote the efficient allocation of resources to accident prevention. The work of Calabresi uses economics to provide a general framework for a coherent, albeit efficiency-based, appraisal of tort. It presents a comprehensive treatment of the efficiency dimensions by specifying the components of social cost to include not only the direct accident-related losses, but also the (legal) administrative costs and the costs which are generated by uncompensated losses in society. The more recent literature has retreated from this wide ranging approach to provide a more analytically rigorous (though simplistic) treatment, and the economists' contribution here has been limited almost exclusively to attempting to 'set Calabresi to mathematics' (Diamond, 1974, p.107) in the area of tort doctrine[32]. In order to provide this highly abstract representation of doctrinal issues, the analysts have been forced to assume away all the empirically important (i.e. complicating) features, in particular the costs involved in using the tort action as a loss-internalizing device. Thus, their models frequently assume that the legal system is costless, that individuals are aware of the law, and that the court is capable of divining all of the information required to make the efficiency calculation. These limitations notwithstanding, the literature has made an important contribution to doctrinal analysis by demonstrating that legal standards embodying cost–benefit type comparisons have a clear economic rationale. What it has not convincingly shown is that the real-world common law rules are efficient. In fact, it conveys to the reader the erroneous impression that efficient doctrine in an abstract world necessarily means efficient law in some empirically relevant sense (Posner, 1977, ch.6). This question of rationalizing the law in terms of economic efficiency will be taken up in section 1.3.

A disappointing feature of the economic approach to law to date has been the tendency of many studies to ignore the relationship between *social efficiency* and the distribution of income and wealth[33]. If a perfectly competitive market is to operate we require, in addition to the assumptions listed below, a clearly defined initial distribution of income and wealth which is legally protected by a set of property rights. The characteristics of a socially efficient market outcome are in part dependent on the initial distribution, because for each different distribution of income there is a different socially efficient outcome. Theoretically, therefore, there are an infinite number of socially efficient outcomes, each of which is just as good as any other in terms of efficiency alone. The desirability of social efficiency as a goal requires a value judgment as to the justness of the underlying distribution of income and property rights. As Sen stresses, efficiency itself is not such 'a momentous achievement from the point of view of social welfare. A person who starts off ill-endowed may stay poor and deprived even after . . . [trading] and if being . . . [efficient] . . . is all that competition offers, the propertyless may be forgiven for not regarding the achievement as a "big deal"'[34].

It is worth pursuing this point because of the confusion that has recently arisen in the literature. It has been asserted that legal rights should be assigned to those who value them most highly. This dictum is seen as establishing efficiency as a 'comprehensive and unitary theory of rights and duties'[35]. But this claim fails for a number of reasons. First, the valuation of rights in terms of money is itself determined by the bundle of rights the individual already possesses, which in turn determines the individual's wealth. The willingness-to-pay criterion depends on the legal rights possessed by the individual, so that it is circular to argue that it can determine the 'efficient' set of rights. Secondly, the contention that corrective rights should mimic perfect market outcomes begs the question. If rights are to be assigned to mimic perfect market outcomes we must know what structure of rights that outcome was based on. The Coase Theorem tells us that *any* assignment of rights is efficient in the abstract, so that in the most favourable setting efficiency does not provide a theory of rights. The situation is not remedied by market failure, and an efficiency theory of rights is not possible unless some value judgment is made about the distribution of rights that defines the hypothetical market outcome one is attempting to replicate.

An efficiency theory of legal rights is admitted by its advocates to be a very limited theory: 'it [is] a theory that the law seeks to optimize the use and exchange of whatever rights people start out with' (Posner, 1979a, p.108). Yet even this is an exaggerated claim because it is not theory of rights at all, but a definition of allocative efficiency which assumes a pre-existing set of rights!

The exclusive concentration on efficiency in much of this literature associated with the 'Chicago school' clearly has normative connotations. It implies that efficiency is desirable, although this interpretation has been vigorously denied, for example by Posner: '"more efficient" is not a synonym for "better"' (Posner, 1973b, p.113). But this statement only elicits the reasonable response: if efficient does not necessarily mean better what is the use of an analysis which makes no attempt to specify the conditions under which it does[36]? And should not analysts who are admittedly restricting their attention to only one of the objects of the legal system be a good deal more circumspect in the claims they make for their theory? Moreover, it is not surprising if people read into these analyses a total and unquestioning commitment to the market when the logical sequence 'the law pursues an efficiency objective → markets are efficient → the law should (and does!) seek to sustain and/or mimic the market' is relentlessly employed.

1.2 The benefits and costs of the economic approach

Let us now consider a possible balance sheet of the main advantages and disadvantages of the economic analysis of law, beginning with an economist's eye view of the merits of economic analysis relative to purely legal analysis.

The major source of disagreement between the economist and academic lawyer over the economic analysis of the law relates to the nature and value of model building. Lawyers and economists approach problems in different ways[37]. The lawyer is concerned with the particular, with factual details and with formal legal propositions supported by argument. The economist, on the other hand, is concerned with generalities, prefers to sweep away details as obscuring key relationships, and his analysis tends either to be partial or to stress the numerous considerations which apply to a particular problem. The economic approach seeks to connect ends to means, to provide generalizations that can be used to frame policy and to evaluate legal doctrine and procedure, to reveal the trade-offs between goals, and to trace through the interrelationships between different laws and private behaviour. From an economist's perspective the lawyer's analysis is often *ad hoc*; the economist likes to see a framework in which the assumptions are clearly stated and used to derive a consistent analysis of the issue under examination. When the lawyer brings his formal legal training to bear on the wider issues surrounding law the result can be anecdotal, pragmatic and lacking formal analytical structure. The economist in return is attacked either for being too theoretical or for addressing wrong or irrelevant issues, and his assumptions are criticised as being unrealistic and leading to conclusions that are subject to overwhelming qualifications. In part the lawyer's aversion to the intrusion of economics also embodies an irritation with its 'mechanical, hedonistic analysis of legal relationships' (Lowry, 1972, p.111) and its overt 'calculatedness' to all human activity.

To some extent these differences of opinion arise from the lawyer's unfamiliarity with the methodology of scientific inquiry. The attack on economics because it uses abstractions which are necessarily 'unrealistic' is in many respects misguided. One can always point to examples where the model appears not to apply, or relate a story where economic considerations were irrelevant. But the correct choices are between competing approaches to legal analysis and between different levels of abstraction (a question to which we shall return later) and not, as often seems to be argued, between an approach which is based on theory and one which is not.

Not only is the theoretical framework of economics the best-developed among the social sciences, but there is widespread acceptance among economists of its fundamental concepts and techniques, though not necessarily the conclusions to be derived from them. This is not the case for, say, sociological approaches to law. The economic approach cannot provide a comprehensive treatment of law — it is partial and complementary to other perspectives, and it necessarily emphasizes those aspects of law that it has comparative advantage in dealing with. Undeniably there is a danger, well illustrated in some of the literature, that some may take simplified theoretical models as representing reality and be over-zealous in applying the conclusions of these models. But the value of abstraction and theory should not be obscured by such excesses. The major considerations are recognized by Calabresi and Melamed (1972, p. 1128).

> Framework or modelbuilding has two short-comings. The first is that models can be mistaken for the total view of phenomena, like legal relationships which are too complex to be painted in any one picture. The second is that models generate boxes into which one then feels compelled to force situations which do not truly fit. There are, however, compensating advantages. Legal scholars, precisely because they have tended to eschew model building, have often proceeded in an *ad hoc* way, looking at cases and seeing what categories emerged. But this approach also affords only one view . . . It may neglect some relationships among the problems involved in the cases which model building can perceive, precisely because it does generate boxes, or categories.

The economic approach places at the forefront of discussion the need to choose and the costs and benefits of alternative choices, which must always be a relevant consideration where resources are limited. All too often lawyers discuss the law in language that implies that costs are irrelevant or that a goal can be achieved at no cost and with no sacrifice of other goals. Economics tells us that nothing is free from society's viewpoint. Increasing access to the courts, for example, consumes resources that will then be unavailable for other uses, and the economic approach can assist in determining whether in allocating resources for this purpose rather than another society is 'getting value for money'. As Leff has succinctly put it, 'the central tenet and most important operative principle of economic analysis is to ask of every move (1) how much will it cost; (2) who pays; and (3) who ought to decide both questions' (Leff, 1974, p.460).

A common criticism, and one that holds wide currency, is that the utility maximization hypothesis is tautological and therefore it should not be surprising that its apparent 'explantory' power is great (Leff, 1974, 457–459; Kelman, 1979). People maximize utility and what they do is utility maximizing! In a purely formal sense this criticism is incorrect. The utility maximization hypothesis is based on a set of axioms that requires preferences to exhibit certain properties which if they do not will refute the *assumption* that choice is rational. In its predictive use the utility maximization hypothesis is capable of falsification if the predictions derived from it do not conform to experience. But it is true that the utility maximization hypothesis can be rendered into a sterile truism, particularly when used normatively, if actual choices are accepted without qualification as rational and therefore 'good'.

The rationality assumption has been responsible for revealing some important consequences of legal change. People do not respond passively to the law, nor mindlessly obey it, but they adapt to the changed costs and benefits that it brings about. This may be in the desired direction, but it may also lead to perverse effects that subvert the objectives of the law. The most obvious example is tax evasion and avoidance, but the phenomenon is more widespread. Recently Peltzman has shown the subtlety of the adaptive responses that can occur in his investigation of the impact of compulsory seat belts legislation in the U.S. (Peltzman, 1975; Manne and Miller, 1976; Robertson, 1977). Peltzman develops and tests a model in which one of the responses of motorists to the increased safety brought about by seat belts is to drive faster, thereby increasing pedestrian fatalities and injuries. Similarly the responses to legally imposed price controls can be quite complex. Whether they relate to commodities or rented accommodation, or take the form of minimum wage legislation, they not only have distributional effects but they also can reduce the quantity and quality of the activity and increase the total costs to society by encouraging greater search and transaction costs[38]. The economic approach not only provides an integrated treatment of these side-effects, but has also been responsible for drawing attention to the more subtle and hitherto unrecognized effects.

Another attractive feature of economics is the sophisticated level of its statistical analysis and its ability to quantify the impact of law. Although not all legal questions are susceptible to statistical analysis, those that are can be examined with more rigour and statistical validity in the context of an explicitly formulated theory. The lawyer's approach to empirical analysis is mostly confined to the examination of trends, the citing of statistics or bivariate comparisons which are potentially misleading, especially where the data are subject to influences from many sources.

Against these attractive features of the economic approach must be set some of its deficiencies as displayed in the literature to date.

The first is the concentration on efficiency previously discussed. This conveys the misleading impression that the sole contribution of economics is to analyse the law in terms of efficiency whereas economics has elsewhere been applied fruitfully to the discussion of justice (equity), distributional and political questions. It must be remembered that the efficiency/equity distinction is only an aid to analytical tractability and not one that can be sustained in practice. Indeed, as Tideman states 'the most controversial questions of public policy can be stated usefully as questions of what losses should go uncompensated' (Tideman, 1972, p.202–203; *see also* Michelman, 1967; Samuels, 1974). While the economist may be able to contribute more to discussions of efficiency this does not justify or support the suppression (or as Thurow (1973) puts it the 'undiscussability') of the ethical basis and implications of legal decisions, and one of his tasks should be to make these clear. If there is a conflict between efficiency and justice the nature of the trade-offs can be illuminated by economic analysis; and since the attainment of justice involves the use of resources the economic approach can contribute to normative discussions by providing information on the cost of justice.

The alternative view has been stated by several prominent exponents of the economic approach to law, that efficiency and justice are synonymous. 'A second meaning of "justice", and the most common,' argues Posner (1975, p.777) 'is simply efficiency'. While this conventionally removes the need to consider questions of justice, it does so by refusing to acknowledge that there are widely held notions of justice and of just protection from interference that do not coincide with efficiency.

The efficiency approach focuses exclusively on the efficiency of *outcomes*, and assumes that the processes by which they are achieved are not valued by individuals[39]. The law is treated as a factor of production, like a machine, which is efficient if it maximizes the economic value of goods and services. The suppression of processes and other intangible factors in economics is largely the result of the economist's urge to make things commensurable in terms of the common denominator of money. But at a conceptual level the efficiency calculus cannot sustain this distinction between means and ends if both are independent sources of utility. If legal processes or the way of doing a thing yield utility, then individuals will be willing to pay for these (through the reduced efficiency of the outcome), and if they are not incorporated into the efficiency calculation it will be both incomplete and misleading. This is a very important point[40]. It implies that if there are reasons to believe that a law or regulation is valued in itself because it is just, one cannot comment on its 'efficiency' by merely doing a cost–benefit analysis of its impact on the economic value of goods and services. The value people place on the legal processes must also be included in the efficiency calculus, despite the difficulties involved in placing monetary values on them. In cases where procedural considerations are important the role of the usual efficiency analysis is elegantly summed up by Liebhafsky: 'A benefit–cost study ought to be recognized for what it is . . . a piece of evidence presented by one side or the other. In an adjudicative or legislative adversary proceeding, evidence is not a substitute for the proceeding itself' (Liebhafsky, 1973, p.623).

We turn now to the peculiar problems encountered with lawyers' idiosyncratic use of economic analysis for the purpose of describing and explaining the law.

1.3 Positive economic theories of law – prediction v description

Lawyers tend to use economics to provide descriptive and comprehensive theories of law. This is a 'separate branch of positive economic analysis of law [which] seeks to explain . . . the structure of the legal system itself' (Posner, 1976b, p. 287). This endeavour gives rise to numerous methodological difficulties that have been neither clearly recognized nor adequately resolved. An attempt will be made to isolate the difficulties that this descriptive use of economics encounters and to outline (in section 1.4) an alternative approach that deals with some of these difficulties in a more satisfactory way.

The restriction of positive economics to the derivation of predictions is not universally accepted, nor is this type of analysis the most frequently found positive economics of law in the literature. The economics of crime, it is true, has been largely predictive, but this is probably a declining research area for economists and it has had a minimal impact on legal thinking about the criminal law. There are two reasons for this lack of impact. First, the question it addresses — do criminal sanctions deter crime? — is one that many lawyers do not regard as relevant to the operation of the criminal justice system, or to the legal issues surrounding the treatment of individual offenders and procedural and substantive criminal law. Secondly, the literature on the economics of crime is about enforcement and deterrence, not about the law. Moreover, when the economic theory of crime is used to explain the structure of the criminal law it performs poorly[41].

In contrast to the experience with criminal law, economics has had a considerable impact on legal scholarship on tort and contract. Today one rarely finds a substantial piece of North America tort scholarship which does not make extensive reference to economics. The major reasons for this are that the bulk of this literature does address questions that are central to legal scholarship, and that it uses economics not to predict the impact of law, but to describe and explain the law — to provide it with an economic rationale.

That the lawyer should use economics in a way different from the economist, and for a different purpose, should not be surprising. However, the lawyer's use of economics to provide descriptive theories of the economic content and consistency of legal systems raises both a methodological and an empirical problem. Descriptive models of law involve a different methodology to those which are designed solely for prediction. It was stated earlier that the assumptions of economic models purporting to provide predictions need not be 'realistic' or subject to empirical verification. This was because the criterion by which the model was to by judged was the degree to which it provided accurate predictions. The intrinsic deficiency of the predictive approach is that it lacks descriptive content, and hence as a conceptual system to analyse specific laws it has severe limitations. 'Viewed as a language', says Friedman, '[predictive economic] theory has no substantive content. It is a set of tautologies. Its function is to serve as a filing system for organizing empirical material and facilitating our understanding of it; and the criteria by which it is to be judged are those appropriate to a filing system' (Friedman, 1953, p.26).

The descriptive use of economics must be judged by a different criterion, for two reasons. First, since its purpose is to *describe* the existing system of law, rather than to predict the impact of changes in the law, it must be given substantive descriptive content. The assumptions used must bear a strong resemblance to observed phenomena, and these assumptions need to be subject to empirical verification[42]. In practice, however, the descriptive analyses have tended instead to adopt assumptions concerning the efficiency of the market which are not empirically verified propositions at all. They have, in other words, retained the descriptive unrealism of assumptions which characterizes predictive economics. Secondly, as shown later the descriptive theories have not been subject to the type of rigorous empirical testing that is deemed appropriate to predictive economics, and there are serious doubts as to whether the descriptive theories are even potentially refutable in this way. The difficulty of testing the theories strengthens the need for descriptive accuracy; otherwise how can any descriptive theory be rejected if the assumptions do not need to be realistic and an empirical test of the end product of the logical process is infeasible?

Let us try to substantiate this point of view by considering the descriptive use of economics to provide an efficiency theory of the common law. Note that although the notion of efficiency is used, the analysis is supposed to be positive rather than normative because the aim is not to discover the nature of a hypothetical legal structure that would satisfy the requirements of efficiency and use it as a standard by which to judge real law, but rather to see to what extent the existing law is consistent with (can be explained by) the notion of efficiency. It has to be admitted that the borderline between positive and normative theory would become decidedly fuzzy if any implicit or explicit disapprobium were to be attached to those parts of the law that did not seem to fit the efficiency explanation.

The efficiency theory of the common law, which was first advanced by Posner (1972) in a paper entitled 'A Theory of Negligence', centres on the hypothesis that the (implicit) goal of the common law is to promote an efficient allocation of resources. In a largely descriptive analysis Posner attributes to the doctrines, remedies and procedures of the common law economic interpretations that suggest that the efficiency content of the law is high. In the area of tort the common law's choice of negligence, and the defence of contributory negligence, are seen as seeking to encourage efficiency in safety production; and the dominance of damages as a remedy and the calculation of damages are seen to be based on 'economic logic', as are the doctrines in a wide range of the common law (contract law, the law relating to rescue at sea, and procedure)[43]. Although the proponents of this interpretation of the common law consider that the evidence provides considerable support for it, a more balanced evaluation suggests that in fact the interpretation has a very meagre empirical backing and that the evidence itself is subject to conflicting interpretations and often is of dubious validity[44].

A major problem with the efficiency explanation is that it is slippery to handle and hard to refute. In the abstract, any law can be made to look efficient, since there is always *some* configuration of costs, including transactions costs, that if it were to exist would mean that the observed law is efficient. Thus, imposing liability for any pollution abatement costs on the pollutee would be efficient if either pollutees were the lower cost abaters, or bargaining costs were negligible so that abatement would be undertaken by the lower cost abater (as the result of a bargain) even if that party were not liable to bear the cost. So that if we observe pollutee liability in the common law, we could conclude that the law is efficient because it is consistent with this configuration of costs. Of course, it is not consistent with other cost configurations, but no matter: we assume that people are acting rationally and thus real world institutions must be efficient or they wouldn't have been so devised would they?

The problem is that, as Goldberg (1980, p.342) states, 'efficiency is contextual'. It only has a clear definition if the actual circumstances surrounding, and by implication the consequences of, the law are known. If we do not know the existing cost configuration the law cannot be judged to be efficient or inefficient. The researcher may make some impressionistic estimate of the cost configuration, but unless objective cost measures are used there is a danger that he will assume that which he sets out to prove. The alleged success of the efficiency explanations of the law is in fact attributable largely to their 'pseudo-empirical' nature (Calabresi, 1978a, p.11). Unlike predictive economics the data used to verify the hypothesis are qualitative data, i.e. the law itself. The efficiency theory uses a market-based model to derive propositions about the law that, curiously, ignore the factor that the theory argues gives rise to the need for legal intervention — transaction costs. Instead transaction costs are drawn into the discussion at the hypothesis testing stage, not as one would expect in a separate empirical analysis, but *by inferring their nature and magnitude from the law itself*. That is, the law is rationized as efficient by assuming a configuration of transaction (and other) costs that makes it so, without any attempt to investigate whether these costs exist in practice[45]. This method of 'testing' the theory often amounts to little more than a restatement of the hypothesis that the common law is efficient by using transaction costs in a way that makes the whole approach a tautology[46]. As Fried (1977, p. 176) has commented often 'there is almost no distance between the conclusions and the premises'.

Another example of the efficiency explanation of the law is Landes and Posner's (1978) study of the law relating to rescues of people and property. Briefly, the authors attempt to provide a unified treatment of a diverse range of legal responses to the problem of rescue by arguing that 'the major doctrines and case outcomes . . . have been shaped by a concern with promoting efficiency' (ibid. p.85) The common law achieves efficiency by using compensation to rescuers to encourage 'rescues in settings of high transactions costs by simulating the conditions and outcomes of a competitive market'[47]. Two comments will be made on this analysis.

First, to say that the common law is efficient is not the same as saying that it seeks to simulate an ideal market. Ideal market outcomes are only efficient under conditions (such as zero transactions costs) that obviously do not prevail, otherwise there would be no need for 'efficient' law. The correct definition of efficient law when markets fail is the encouragement of rescues to the level that maximizes the net benefits, where 'net' means in excess of all costs including transactions costs. *This* efficient outcome need bear little resemblance to that which would be generated in a hypothetical ideal market. Secondly, the authors recognize that a perusal of the rescue law shows that it cannot be explained in terms of an attempt to simulate markets. In order to cope with the anomalies (referred to as 'puzzles') a model of altruistic rescue is formulated. Altruistic rescue is defined as rescue 'devoid of all expectation of any form of compensation', and it is expected that 'a legal system concerned with maximizing efficiency would refuse to grant compensation in rescue situations where altruism provides a strong inducement to rescue attempts' (Landes and Posner, 1978, pp.94–95). The introduction of altruism forces a redefinition of 'efficiency'. The 'efficient' level of rescue when altruism is present exceeds the market level, and this higher level is 'efficient' because although social costs are higher this is counterbalanced by the increase in utility of altruistic rescuers[48]. Whatever the validity of this proposition, it amounts to a rejection of the hypothesis that the common law seeks to simulate ideal markets[49]. As Landes and Posner are forced to concede '[A]ltruism . . . has negative survival value under competition and would tend to be weeded out of competitive markets' (ibid. pp.97–98). Thus two mutually inconsistent models are posited to 'explain' the law[50], and it is clear that whenever the law is rationalized in altruistic terms this amounts to a rejection of the hypothesis that 'rescue' law's 'fundamental [economic] purpose [is] simulating the market' (ibid. p.118). The implication which we draw from all this is that the term 'efficient' is sufficiently elastic to explain *any* law if one is searching for an efficiency rationalization; and a theory which 'explains' any and every observed phenomenon explains nothing.

If the efficiency rubric is so elastic as to be able to rationalize any law as being efficient then, clearly, speculating on the nature of costs and benefits that relate to a law is not a valid empirical test of the efficiency theory. This is particularly so when the analyst has an apparent urge to provide a *comprehensive* theory of the law based on the concept of efficiency[51].

These difficulties with the descriptive efficiency theory of law can be overcome in one of two ways: either the 'hard' data must be collected to identify the *existing* configuration of costs, so that the efficiency of the law can be judged in context (e.g. *see* Burrows, Rowley and Owen, 1974), or it must be accepted that a different methodology is needed. These are not mutually exclusive possibilities, but in this paper we shall consider only the second.

1.4 Towards an economic approach of the third kind

An alternative methodology for the descriptive theory of law must be based on an explicit recognition that the models are not going to be predictive and that they will deal with 'data' that are not quantifiable but which constitute a web of interrelated legal processes that are not amenable to elegant theorizing or empirical analysis.

A conceptual framework that recognizes these requirements has been evolving in recent years in an approach based on the neglected institutional economics of John Commons[52] and the work of Hayek on market processes. This neo-institutionalist resurgence follows Commons by making not the individual but the transaction the basic unit of analysis. For Commons (1932, p.4) the transaction represented the 'unit of activity' that possessed the three essential 'principles of conflict, mutuality and order' that he saw as necessary to 'correlate' law and economics (and also ethics). Although the transactional approach, alternatively called neo-institutional, relational or transaction cost approach, is still in its formative stages, the work of Williamson (1979; *see* chapter two in this volume), Goldberg (1976a, 1976b), the related legal discussions of MacNeil on contract (1974, 1975; *see* chapter three in this volume), Calabresi on tort and several Austrian economic critiques, (*see* Littlechild, 1978; Rizzo, 1980) all provide a complementary framework that deals explicitly with the difficulties of the neoclassical market approach.

The neo-institutional approach eschews models based on the fiction of frictionless, ideal markets, and views them as a special case and useful for reference purposes only. Instead it focuses directly on transaction cost considerations (the frictions) in an attempt to explain the choice between market and various non-market modes of organizing production, and interprets institutions and their evolution as arising from attempts to economize on transaction costs. The approach develops a more complex conceptual picture of the economic and non-economic factors relevant to legal/institutional analysis; and its models tend, as a consequence, to be less elegant, less precise than, and not given to the same deterministic predictions as market-based models.

The neo-institutional approach embodies the following characteristics. First, it is taxonomical. It lists a set of economically relevant categories that are useful for examining the law. It thus remedies one of the failings of neo-classical market approaches, that of being over-general and incapable of dealing convincingly with specific legal phenomena. As Markovits (1978, p.728) notes: '[A]t least in part, the failings of conventional economics reflect a simplistic vocabulary that fails to distinguish a large number of phenomena that need to be analysed separately'. And hence we see a new vocabulary being developed, particularly by Williamson, for this purpose. Secondly, and related to this, the approach is more microanalytical. It focuses on the details of the environment in which transactions take place, and it suggests an empirical approach that requires the collection of more detailed data on individual transactions rather than data on quantitative aggregates. It is able, for example, to integrate and use constructively the sociological evidence on how businessmen contract and use contract law, originally provided by Macaulay (1968; *see also* Beale and Dugdale, 1975). Thus, while the market approach focuses on impersonal, aggregative forces, the neo-institutional approach focuses on individual or small number transactions where personality, relations and power are important. Thirdly, in terms of methodology it comes closer to qualitative biology than to the physical sciences that have greatly influenced neoclassical economics. It is therefore process-orientated, dynamic, tends to be evolutionary, and seeks to identify the principal factors that have been responsible for institutional development. Stated somewhat differently it rejects (market) equilibrium analysis and instead places emphasis on the adaption to disequilibrium, hypothesizing that 'inefficiency' gives rise to adaptive efforts to minimize costs. Lastly, it investigates specifically legal/institutional phenomena, and uses these to develop conceptual categories rather then evidence to verify an efficiency-type hypothesis.

The differences between market and neo-institutional approaches are best illustrated by their respective treatment of contractual relations. The evolving economics of contractual relations recognizes that it is the inherently temporal character of contract that gives rise to the need for contract law. In situations where the exchange of obligations and performance is not simultaneous, and extends over periods of varying duration, there is a need for some enforcement mechanism. The temporal element of these contracts, and the fact that many contracts are formed with less than complete information and much uncertainty, gives rise to the possibility that one party may breach the contract even when it is inefficient to do so. In the neoclassical framework the allocative goal of contract law is to promote the efficient allocation of resources. Thus contract law is seen as having a set of efficiency-related purposes[53]. The first is the provision of remedies that will discourage inefficient breaches. Thus if the breach is avoidable, the breaching party should make good the other's loss thereby providing a test of the breach's efficiency. If in anticipation of paying the victim's (net) loss the breaching party still decides to breach, the implication is that the resources thereby released are being allocated to more efficient uses. Where the breach is due to mistake or is unavoidable because of events beyond the control of the parties to the contract, the loss should be imposed on the superior information producer in the former case and on the superior risk-bearer in the latter case. The economic function of contract law is also to reduce transaction costs and uncertainty by supplying a set of standard (implied) terms, thereby avoiding the costs of explicit negotiation and alerting the parties to potential difficulties that will assist them in contract planning. Finally, contract law provides a framework for the regulation of abuses in the contracting process such as fraud, misrepresentation and duress, that impede or are poorly controlled by market forces.

Although this market-based approach has provided a number of excellent analyses of contract law, it does not come to grips with many issues relevant to a large subset of contractual activity[54]. While the market-based approach recognizes that it is the temporal element that necessitates contract law, it is nonetheless based on a timeless model of contract and treats the sale of goods contract as the paradigm case. The neo-institutional approach emphasizes time, uncertainty and the frictions associated with sale of goods contracts, which it regards as a special and not particularly interesting case, and non-market (or relational[55]) contracts. The transactions costs of writing and executing contracts are interpreted as emanating from two related sources: uncertainty and bounded rationality[56] on the one hand, and lack of competitive pressures (small number of contractors) on the other. The combination of these factors gives rise to 'opportunism', which is 'effort(s) to realise individual gains through lack of candour or honesty in transactions' (Williamson, Wachter and Harris, 1975, p.258) and to the need for 'governance structures' (law, arbitration, the market) that will discourage parties from being opportunistic. The emphasis of this approach is not on a utility maximizing contract where the 'law' fills in terms that the parties would have agreed to had they addressed the problem at the contract formation stage, but on adjustment processes that will preserve continuing contractual relations in the face of opportunism and deal with cases where contracts are incompletely specified.

The neo-institutional approach, it will be recalled, stems partially from the same basis as the market-based analysis and it therefore should not be surprising if it is vulnerable to some of the same criticisms. It also attempts to 'explain' everything in terms of 'efficiency'. However, the concept of efficiency used is quite different — it is not that of replicating ideal market results, but *procedural* efficiency in adjusting to an uncertain and changing environment. The approach is in fact less committed to the market than it would appear, and often provides persuasive economic reasons why activities should be sheltered from market forces. The neo-institutional approach is also susceptible, and possible more so, to providing a tautologous treatment of the 'efficiency' of real world institutions and law. One can always think of another (unobservable) transaction cost category that will rationalize observed outcomes as being efficient. This calls for a 'disciplined treatment' of transaction costs both in theoretical discussion and the interpretation of institutional phenomena. But because the neo-institutional approach begins with a comprehensive discussion of all the relevant cost considerations this problem may tend to be less serious, particularly in view of the task the approach has set itself. Unlike the market-based approach it does not assert that the law or institutions are efficient, but usually only attempts to identify the efficiency attributes of various institutional arrangements, and to hypothesize that there is a tendency for institutions to evolve to exploit opportunities for improving the efficiency with which market and non-market goals are pursued.

1.5 Statutory control

It says a good deal for the industry of the pro-market economists and lawyers that such a large proportion of the economics of law literature has, until recently at least, related to methods of fostering markets rather than finding alternatives to them when they have failed. A classic example of this is the amazingly extensive debate on liability rules and bargaining solutions to external cost problems, when most of the serious external costs relate to air and water pollution (affecting large groups), which are virtually certain to offer no prospect of solution by a 'market in externalities'.

There has been developing, however, an increasing interest in the scrutiny and evaluation of the operation and impact of statute laws in a number of areas: for example, pollution control, safety at work legislation, consumer protection, habitation law, planning and social security law[57]. In addition it has been recognized that the law in practice may diverge significantly from the law on the statute books, so that a greater emphasis has been placed on the performance of enforcement procedures[58].

While economists have long been accustomed to being involved in the analysis and empirical testing of the impact of regulations which relate to publicly owned or controlled enterprises[59], the techniques of regulatory impact analysis have not yet been widely extended to legislation of a less obviously 'economic' kind. But the statutory controls which are now so pervasive, influencing the behaviour of people and firms in a wide range of contexts, are ripe for evaluation. We anticipate that this endeavour will increase in the next decade, and that less will be heard of the prospects for bargaining between crop-producing and cattle-raising farmers and more will be heard of the basis, nature and impact of the public law regulation of social and economic activity[60].

1.6 Concluding remarks

It has not been possible in this survey to examine particular studies of the economics of law in much detail. Rather an attempt has been made to outline some of the trends in the literature, and some of the strengths and weaknesses of the work to date. A good deal of criticism has been offered, but we should not like this to conceal our belief that the economics of law can provide insights in places where traditional legal analysis fails to penetrate.

It is the essentially complementary nature of the two disciplines that makes us optimistic that collaboration between lawyers and economists will be increasingly fruitful in the future (cf. Coase, 1978 and Nutter, 1979).

Notes to chapter one

1 This introductory survey incorporates material from Veljanovski (1980a).
2 For a somewhat dated overview see Lovett (1974). The newsletter, *Lexecon*, published by University of Miami's Law and Economics Center provides information on current developments.
3 In recent years several articles applying economics to law have appeared in English law journals; Phillips and Hawkins (1976), Phillips (1976), Ogus and Richardson (1977), Harris, Ogus and Phillips (1979) and Bishop (1980). Also see Atiyah (1975) ch.25 and Beale (1980).
The Social Science Research Council has for some time financed research seminars in law and economics, held a summer school in economics for lawyers, and financed the Oxford Centre for Socio-Legal Studies whose research projects include topics in law and economics.
4 Particularly as exemplified by the work of Posner (1977). See the reactions of Liebhafsky (1976), Cranston (1977) and Bloustein (1978).
5 For general discussion of the interrelationship between law and economics by English commentators see Parry (1931), Robinson (1939), Wilberforce (1978), Williams (1975) and Ogus (1980).
6 As one legal scholar has commented '. . . it is exactly because so many . . . [lawyers] . . . are inclined to take economics so seriously that one feels impelled to search for . . . [its] . . . limitations' Schwartz (1979) p. 813.
7 Since the establishment of the *Journal of Law and Economics*, in 1972 the University of Chicago began publishing the *Journal of Legal Studies*, devoted to the economic analysis of the legal system. On going to press a third specialized journal, the *International Review of Law and Economics*, based in Britain and published by Butterworths, is due to begin publication.
8 For two selective surveys of this work see Posner (1975) and (1976).
9 For general methodological discussions of this development see Tullock (1973), McKenzie (1978), Dales (1975), Coase (1978) and Nutter (1979).
10 Compare Buchanan's (1964) view that 'gains from trade' is the essential concept of economics.
11 According to Becker the trilogy of assumptions of maximizing behaviour, market equilibrium and stable preferences 'used relentlessly and unflinchingly, form the heart of the economic approach as I see it', Becker (1976) p. 5. We are perplexed as to why market equilibrium is a necessary ingredient. Also see Hirshleifer (1977) for another 'unqualified' definition of the economic approach.
12 For an excellent collection of essays on the methodological and philosophical underpinnings of economics see Hahn and Hollis (1979).
13 An increasing emphasis has been placed on a view of rationality that takes account of the complexity of decision making. As Simons states 'economics has traditionally been concerned with what decisions are made rather than how they are made – with substantive rationality rather than procedural rationality', Simons (1978) p. 494. Also see his essay in Hahn and Hollis (1979).
14 A more complete treatment of this can be found in Posner (1977) ch. 1.
15 This approach to positive economics began with Friedman (1953).
16 Examples of such impact studies are Landes (1968), Ehrlich (1972), Peltzman (1975) and Hirsch (1975).
17 The literature effectively begins with Becker's (1968) classic essay and the empirical work of Ehrlich (1970).
18 For an introduction and survey see Ehrlich (1979).
19 See Ehrlich (1975) and Wolpin's (1978a and 1978b) work for England and Wales.
20 Ehrlich's statistical analysis *tentatively* suggested that each execution in the US over the period 1935–1969 deterred 7–8 murders.

21 See debate in the pages of the *Yale Law Journal* (1975 and 1976), Cook (1977) and Blumstein, Cohen and Nagin (1978).
22 For a clear exposition of welfare theory see Bator (1957).
23 See Arrow (1970) for an excellent discussion of market failure.
24 Although transaction costs play a central role in the economic approach to law they have not as yet received rigorous theoretical or empirical treatment.
25 See Posner (1977) and references surveyed in Veljanovski (1979c) Part I.
26 See, for example, Baumol and Oates (1979), Kneese and Schultze (1975), Kneese (1977) and Burrows (1979) on pollution; Komesar (1973) and Markovits (1976) on housing standards; and Ellickson (1973, 1977) on zoning.
27 Calabresi (1970) p. 24. Also see Calabresi (1975), Calabresi and Hirschoff (1972) and references cited in Veljanovski's essay in this volume (ch. 5).
28 For an introduction to the literature on valuing a statistical life, and on economic damage valuation in general, see Zeckhauser (1975) and Mooney (1977). For a survey of the empirical work see Smith (1979b). Also see Needleman (1976).
29 The 'cheapest cost avoider' is defined by Calabresi as 'which of the parties to the accident is in the best position to make the cost benefit analysis between accident and accident avoidance and to act on that decision once it is made'. Calabresi and Hirschoff (1972) p. 1060.
30 Calabresi (1978b) p. 529. See Veljanovski in this volume (ch. 5) for a more detailed discussion of liability rules and accident bargains.
31 For impact studies of liability rule changes see Chelius (1976), Higgins (1978), Canon and Jaros (1979) and Veljanovski (1980b). There is also evidence that industrial accident rates respond to cost pressures, Smith (1973).
32 E.g. Brown (1973). For an annotated bibliography see Veljanovski (1979c).
33 For an excellent discussion of social efficiency and normative economics see Graaf (1957).
34 Sen in Hahn and Hollis (1979) pp. 89–90.
35 Posner (1979a) p. 140. Compare Samuels (1974) and Fried (1978) pp. 86–131.
36 As Thurow (1973) argues. Also see Baker (1975).
37 For a discussion of the differences between legal and social science approaches see Aubert (1973).
38 Price controls tend to increase the time costs (queues) associated with purchases, thereby imposing differential costs on intending purchasers, and they encourage sellers to practice discrimination among classes of consumers. See Becker (1965) and Cheung (1974).
39 The neoclassical economic approach can be contrasted to the neo-institutionalist approach which does not maintain a sharp ends–means distinction. The neo-institutionalists, following the philosophy of John Dewey, take an 'ends-in-view' perspective and see issues in terms of processes rather than outcomes. Ends are not viewed as given or clearly defined but emerge from the problem at hand in an evolutionary process. For a short introduction see Gruchy (1973). The *Journal of Economics Issues* is devoted to this type of economic analysis.
40 Clearly 'justice' involves more than wealth distribution preferences i.e. distributive justice. As Tribe stresses 'one simply cannot . . . assign rights so as to maximize efficiency while relying on lump-sum transfers to achieve a proper distribution of wealth, for the very concept of a proper distribution must be defined . . . with respect to the enjoyment of these rights as such'. Tribe (1972a) p. 88. Also see Tribe (1972b), and the discussion by Rawls (1971) of 'basic liberties', pp. 60–61, 243–248 and 541–548.
41 Posner is one of the few who have attempted to explain the criminal law in economic terms, Posner (1977) ch. 7. Much of his analysis is unconvincing as pointed out by Buchanan (1974) p. 485 and Adelstein (1980). For a different, but at times equally strained, economic analysis of the criminal law see Adelstein (1979) and (1980).
42 For criticisms of Posner's work along these lines see Polinsky (1974) and Hirsch (1975). Also see Morgenstern's (1972) comments on the role of competitive market models in descriptive economics.
43 Much of this work, mostly by Posner, is summarized in Posner (1977). Also see references cited in Posner (1979).

44 For critiques of this efficiency theory see Michelman (1977, 1978 and 1979), Bloustein (1978), Rizzo (1979) and Veljanovski (1979a).

45 For a forceful critique of this type of analysis see Cheung (1979), whose main criticism is that it fails to investigate real world situations and hence arrives at 'policy implications out of sheer imagination', ibid, p. 65.

46 This interpretation is also shared by some economists: 'transaction costs have a well-deserved bad name as a theoretical device . . . [partly] because there is a suspicion that almost anything can be rationalised by invoking suitably specified transaction costs'. Fischer (1977) p. 322, note 5.

47 Landes and Posner (1978) p. 100. The theory is really better described as a market based approach. For example, Posner hypothesizes 'that the common law tends to simulate market outcomes – to mimic how [an ideal] market would operate if a market were feasible' in Goldberg (1979) p. 368.

48 This definition of 'efficiency' is tucked away in a footnote, Landes and Posner (1978), p. 95, note 27.

49 Ibid, p. 98. Duncan Kennedy (1976) has analysed the common law in terms of these two 'opposed rhetorical modes' which he terms individualism and altruism. We are not of course suggesting that altruism cannot be analysed in economic terms, see for example the readings in Phelps (1975).

50 More recently Posner has revealed a certain unease with the role of altruistic explanations in his market-based theory, see Posner (1979) pp. 123–124.

51 This point has been made by Backhaus (1979). It is illustrated by Posner's tendency to refer to any laws that cannot be explained in terms of his model as 'puzzles', thereby implicitly assuming that efficiency *is* in fact the guiding norm of the common law. Previously, rescue law was one of these 'puzzles' — 'the law is out of phase with economic analysis in the matter of . . . rescues', Posner (1973a) p. 220. But as we have seen the theory is so elastic that eventually even the 'puzzles' can be rationalized as consistent with the efficiency viewpoint.

52 See Commons (1924, 1925 and 1934), Mitchell (1935) and Gonce (1971).

53 Summaries of this approach can be found in Posner (1977) pp. 65–69, and Kronman and Posner (1979) ch. 1.

54 See the collection of readings in Kronman and Posner (1979), and the bibliography by Veljanovski (1979b).

55 Particularly by MacNeil. See his essay in this volume (ch. 3).

56 Bounded rationality refers to the cognitive limits of individuals to deal comprehensively with the complex decisions they are required to make. See references above.

57 E.g. Smith (1979a), Viscusi (1980), Miller and Yandle (1979), Grabowski (1976), Peltzman (1973), Swan (1979), Smith and Swann (1979) and Weisbrod (1978).

58 See references cited in Richardson, Ogus and Burrows (1981).

59 See for example Kahn (1971), and most issues of the *Bell Journal of Economics*.

60 For reviews of the theoretical and empirical work that has been done in North America see Posner (1974), Joskow and Noll (1978) and Trebilcock, Waverman and Prichard (1978).

References

ADELSTEIN, R. P. (1979), Informational paradox and the pricing of crime: capital sentencing standards in economic perspective, *Journal of Criminal Law and Criminology*, **70**, no. 3, 281–298.

ADELSTEIN, R. P. (1980), Institutional function and evolution in the criminal process, *Research Study No. 2*, Oxford: Centre for Socio-Legal Studies.

ALCHIAN, A.A. (1961). Some economics of property rights, *Rand Paper No. 2316*, Santa Monica: Rand Corporation.

ARROW, K.T. (1970) The organization of economic activity: issues pertinent to the choice of market versus non-market allocation, in *The Analysis of Public Output* (J. Margolis, ed.) Columbia University Press, New York.

ATIYAH, P. S. (1977), *Accidents, Compensation and the Law*, 2nd ed., London: Weidenfeld.

AUBERT, V. (1973), Researches in the sociology of law, in *Law and the Social System* (M. Barken, ed.).

AZZI, C. and EHRENBERG, R. (1975), Household allocation of time and church attendance, *Journal of Political Economy*, **83**, no. 1, 27–56.

BACKHAUS, J. (1979), Lawyers' economics

vs. economic analysis of law, *Munich Social Science Review*, **1**.
BAKER, C. E. (1975), The ideology of the economic analysis of law, *Philosophy and Public Policy*, **5**, no. 1, 3–48.
BATOR, F. M. (1957), The simple analytics of welfare maximization. *American Economic Review*, **47**, no. 1, 22–59.
BAUMOL, W. J. and OATES, W. E. (1975), *The Theory of Environmental Policy*, Englewood Cliffs, NJ: Prentice-Hall.
BEALE, H. (1980), *Remedies for Breach of Contract*, London: Sweet & Maxwell.
BEALE, H. and DUGDALE, T. (1975), Contracts between businessmen: planning and the use of contractual remedies, *British Journal of Law and Society*, **2**, no. 1, 45–60.
BECCARIA-BONESARA, C. (1958), *An Essay in Crime and Punishment* (1764), New York: Oceania Pub.
BECKER, G. S. (1957), *The Economics of Discrimination*, University of Chicago Press.
BECKER, G. S. (1965), A theory of the allocation of time, *Economic Journal*, **75**, no. 299, 493–517.
BECKER, G. S. (1968), Crime and punishment: an economic approach, *Journal of Political Economy*, **76**, no. 1. 169–217.
BECKER, G. S. (1973), A theory of marriage, part I, *Journal of Political Economy*, **81**, no. 4, 813–846.
BECKER, G. S. (1976), *The Economic Approach to Human Behaviour*, University of Chicago Press.
BECKER, G. S., LANDES, E. M. and MICHAEL, R. T. (1977), An economic analysis of marital instability, *Journal of Political Economy*, **85**, no. 6, 1141–1187.
BENTHAM, J. (1789), *An Introduction to the Principles of Morals and Legislation*, Oxford: Clarendon Press, 1892.
BISHOP, W. (1980), Negligent misrepresentation through economists' eyes, *Law Quarterly Review*, **96**, 360–379.
BLOUSTEIN, E. J. (1978), Privacy is dear at any price: a response to Professor Posner's economic theory, *Georgia Law Review*, **12**, no. 3, 421–495.
BLUMSTEIN, A., COHEN, J. and NAGIN, D. (eds.) (1978), *Deterrence and Incapacitation: Estimating the Effects of Criminal Sanctions on Crime Rates*, Washington DC: National Academy of Science.
BROWN, J. P. (1973), Toward an economic theory of liability, *Journal of Legal Studies*, **2**, no. 2, 323–349.
BUCHANAN, J. M. (1964), Is economics the science of choice?, in *Roads to Freedom* (E. Stressler, ed.), London: Routledge and Kegan.
BUCHANAN, J. M. (1971), Violence, law and equilibrium in the university, *Public Policy*, **18**, no. 1, 1–18.
BUCHANAN, J. M. (1974), Good economics—bad law, *Virginia Law Review*, **60**, no. 4, 483–492.
BURROWS, P. (1970), On external costs and the visible arm of the law, *Oxford Economic Papers*, **22**, no. 1, 39–56.
BURROWS, P., ROWLEY, C. K. and OWEN, D. (1974), Operational dumping and the pollution of the sea by oil: an evaluation of preventative measures, *Journal of Environmental Economics and Management*, 1, no. 2, 202–218.
BURROWS, P. (1979), *The Economic Theory of Pollution Control*, Oxford: Martin Robertson; Cambridge, Mass.: MIT Press.
CALABRESI, G. (1961), Some thoughts on risk distribution and the law of torts, *Yale Law Journal*, **70**, no. 4, 499–553.
CALABRESI, G. (1970), *The costs of accidents: a legal and economic analysis*, New Haven: Yale University Press.
CALABRESI, G. (1975), Optimal deterrence and accidents, *Yale Law Journal*, **84**, no. 4, 656–671.
CALABRESI, G. (1978a), On the general state of law and economics research today and its current problems and prospects, in *Law and Economics* (G. Skogh, ed.), Lund, Sweden: Juridisha Foreningen i Lund.
CALABRESI, G. (1978b), Torts — the law of a mixed society, *Texas Law Review*, **56**, no. 3, 519–536.
CALABRESI, G. and HIRSCHOFF, J. T. (1972), Toward a test for strict liability in torts, *Yale Law Journal*, **81**, no. 6, 1054–1085.
CALABRESI, G. and MELAMED, A. D. (1972), Property rules, liability rules and inalienability: one view of the cathedral, *Harvard Law Review*, **85**, no. 6, 1089–1128.
CANON, B. C. and JAROS, D. (1979), The impact of changes in judicial doctrine: the abrogation of charitable immunity, *Law and Society Review*, **13**, no. 4, 969–986.
CARR-HILL, R. A. and STERN, H. H. (1979), *Crime, the police and criminal statistics*, London: Academic Press.
CHALMERS, J. A. and SHELTON, R. B. (1975), An economic analysis of riot participation, *Economic Inquiry*, **13**, no. 3, 322–336.
CHELIUS, R. S. (1976), Liability for industrial accidents: a comparison of negligence and strict liability system, *Journal of Legal Studies*, **5**, no. 2, 293–309.
CHEUNG, S. N. S. (1974), A theory of price control, *Journal of law and economics*, **17**, no. 1, 52–72.
CHEUNG, S. N. S. (1979), *The Myth of*

Social Cost, London: Institute of Economic Affairs.
COASE, R. H. (1960), The problem of social cost, *Journal of Law and Economics*, **3**, no. 1, 1–44.
COASE, R. H. (1978), Economics and contiguous disciplines, *Journal of Legal Studies*, **7**, no. 2, 201–211.
COELEN, S. P. and MACINTYRE, R. J. (1978), An econometric model of pronatalist and abortion policies, *Journal of Political Economy*, **86**, no. 6, 1077–1101.
COMMONS, J. R. (1924), *Legal Foundations of Capitalism*, New York: Macmillan.
COMMONS, J. R. (1925), Law and economics, *Yale Law Journal*, **34**, no. 4, 371–382.
COMMONS, J. R. (1932), The problem of correlating law, economics and ethics, *Wisconsin Law Review*, **8**, no. 1, 3–26.
COMMONS, J. R. (1934), *Institutional Economics*, New York: Macmillan.
CONARD, A.F., MORGAN, J.N., PRATT, R.W., VOLTZ, C.E. and BOMBAUGH, R.L. (1964), Automobile accidents costs and payments — studies in the economics of injury reparation, Ann Arbor: Univerity of Michigan Press.
COOK, P.J. (1977), Punishment and crime: a critique of current findings concerning the preventative effects of punishment, *Law and Contemporary Problems*, **41**, no. 1, 164–209.
CRANSTON, R. (1977), Creeping economism: some thoughts on law and economics, *British Journal of Law and Society*, **4**, no. 1, 103–115.
DALES, J. H. (1975), Beyond the marketplace, *Canadian Journal of Economics*, **8**, no. 4, 483–503.
DEMSETZ, H. (1964), Some aspects of property rights, *Journal of Law and Economics*, **9**, no. 1, 61–70.
DEMSETZ, H. (1969), Toward a theory of property rights, *American Economic Review (papers and proceedings)*, **57**, no. 2, 347–359.
DEYAK, T. A. and SMITH, V. K. (1976), The economic value of statute reform: the case of liberalized abortion, *Journal of Political Economy*, **84**, no. 6, 83–99.
DIAMOND, P. A. (1974), Single activity accidents, *Journal of Legal Studies*, **3**, no. 1, 107–164.
EHRLICH, I. (1972), The deterrence effect of criminal law enforcement, *Journal of Legal Studies*, **1**, no. 2, 259–276.
EHRLICH, I. (1973), Participation in illegitimate activities: a theoretical and empirical investigation, *Journal of Political Economy*, **81**, no. 3, 521–565.
EHRLICH, I. (1975), The deterrent effect of capital punishment: a question of life and death, *American Economic Review*, **65**, no. 3, 397–417.
EHRLICH, I. (1979), The economic approach to crime — a preliminary assessment, in *Criminological Review Yearbook*, vol. 1 (S. L. Messinger and E. Brittiner, eds.), Beverly Hills: Sage Publications.
ELLICKSON, R. C. (1973), Alternatives to zoning: covenants, nuisance rules and fines as land use controls, *University of Chicago Law Review*, **40**, no. 4, 681–781.
ELLICKSON, R. C. (1977), Suburban growth controls: an economic and legal analysis, *Yale Law Journal*, **86**, no. 3, 385–511.
FAIR, R. C. (1978), A theory of extramarital affairs, *Journal of Political Economy*, **86**, vol. 1, 45–61.
FERGUSON, C. E. and GOULD, J. P. (1975), *Microeconomic Theory*, 4th ed., Homewood, Ill: Irwin.
FISCHER, S. (1977), Long term contracting, sticky prices and monetary policy: comment, *Journal of Monetary Economics*, **3**, 312–323.
FRIED, C. (1977), Difficulties in the economic analysis of rights, *Markets and Morals* (G. Dworkin *et al.*, eds.), Washington: Hemisphere.
FRIED, C. (1978), *Right and Wrong*, Cambridge, Mass: Harvard University Press.
FRIEDMAN, M. (1953), The methodology of positive economics, in *Essays in Positive Economics*, University of Chicago Press.
GOLDBERG, V.P. (1976a), Regulation and administered contracts, *Bell Journal of Economics*, **7**, no. 2, 426–448.
GOLDBERG, V.P. (1976b), Toward an expanded economic theory of contract, *Journal of Economic Issues*, **10**, no. 1, 45–61.
GOLDBERG, V. P. (ed.) (1979), Discussion by seminar participants, *Journal of Legal Studies*, **8**, no. 2, 323–378.
GOLDBERG, V. P. (1980), Relational exchange: economics and complex contracts, *American Behavioural Scientist*, **23**, no. 3, 337–352.
GONCE, R. A. (1971), John R. Commons' legal theory, *Journal of Economic Issues*, **5**, no. 1, 80–95.
V. GRAAF, J. (1957), *Theoretical Welfare Economics*, Cambridge University Press.
GRABOWSKI, H. G. (1976), *Drug Regulation and Innovation: Empirical Evidence and Policy*, Washington DC: American Enterprise Institute.
GRUCHY, A. (1973), Law, politics and institutionalist economics, *Journal of*

Economic Issues, **7**, no. 4, 623–643.
HAHN, F. and HOLLIS, M. (eds.) (1979), *Philosophy and Economic Theory*, Oxford University Press.
HAMMERMESH, D. S. and SOSS, N. M. (1974), An economic theory of suicide, *Journal of Political Economy*, **82**, no. 1, 83–98.
HARRIS, D., OGUS, A. I. and PHILLIPS, J. (1979), Contract remedies and the consumer surplus, *Law Quarterly Review*, **95**, 581–610.
HIGGINS, R. S. (1978), Producers' liability and product-related accidents, *Journal of Legal Studies*, **7**, no. 2, 299–301.
HIRSCH, W. Z. (1975), Review: economic analysis of law, *UCLA Law Review*, **22**, no. 4, 980–998.
HIRSCH, W. Z. (1979), *Law and Economics — An Introductory Analysis*, New York: Academic Press.
HIRSCH, W. Z., HIRSCH, J. G. and MARGOLIS, S. (1975), Regression analysis of the effects of habitability laws upon rent: an empirical observation on the Ackerman–Komesar debate, *California Law Review*, **63**, no. 5, 1095–1143 (1975).
HIRSHLEIFER, J. (1977), Economics from a biological viewpoint, *Journal of Law and Economics*, **20**, no. 3, 1–52.
JOSKOW, P. L. and NOLL, R. G. (1978), Regulation in theory and practice: an overview, unpublished manuscript, California Institute of Technology.
KAHN, A. (1971), *The Economics of Regulation*, New York: Wiley.
KELMAN, S. (1979), Choice and utility, *Wisconsin Law Review*, 797–814.
KENNEDY, D. (1976), Form and substance in private law adjudication, *Harvard Law Review*, **89**, no. 8, 1685–1778.
KNEESE, A. V. (1977), *Economics and the Environment*, Penguin, Harmondsworth.
KNEESE, A. V. and SCHULTZE, C. L. (1975), *Pollution, Prices and Public Policy*, Washington DC: Brookings.
KNIGHT, F. H. (1935), The ethics of competition, in *The Ethics of Competition and Other Essays*, London: Allen & Unwin.
KOMESAR, N. K. (1973). Return to slumville: a critique of the Ackerman analysis of housing code enforcement and the poor, *Yale Law Journal*, **82**, no. 6, 1175–1193.
KRIER, J. (1974), Economics in the law school, *University of Pennsylvania Law Review*, **122**, 1664–1705.
KRONMAN, A. T. and POSNER, R. A. (eds.) (1979), *The Economics of Contract Law*, Boston: Little-Brown.
LANDES, E. M. (1978), Economics of alimony, *Journal of Legal Studies*, **7**, no. 1, 35–64.
LANDES, W. M. (1968), The economics of fair employment laws, *Journal of Political Economy*, **76**, no. 3, 507–559.
LANDES, W. M. and POSNER, R. A. (1978), Salvers, finders, good samaritans, and other rescuers: an economic study of law and altruism, *Journal of Legal Studies*, **7**, no. 1, 83–128.
LEFF, A. A. (1974), Economic analysis of law: some realism about nominalism, *Virginia Law Review*, **60**, no. 4, 451–482.
LIEBHAFSKY, H. H. (1973), The problem of social cost — an alternative approach, *Natural Resources Journal*, **13**, no. 4, 615–676.
LIEBHAFSKY, H. H. (1976), Price theory as jurisprudence: law and economics Chicago style, *Journal of Economic Issues*, **10**, no. 1, 23–43.
LITTLECHILD, S. C. (1978), The problem of social cost, in *New Directions in Austrian Economics* (L. M. Spadaro, ed.), Kansas City: Sheed Andrews and McMeel.
LOVETT, W.A. (1974), Economic analysis and its role in legal education, *Journal of Legal Education*, **26**, no. 4, 385–421.
LOWRY, T. S. (1972), Review: Posner's economic analysis of law, *Journal of Economic Issues*, **6**, no. 1, 111–114.
MACNEIL, I. R. (1974), The many futures of contracts, *Southern California Law Review*, **47**, no. 3, 691–816.
MACNEIL, I. R. (1978), Contracts: adjustments of long-term economic relations under classical, neoclassical and relational contract law, *Northwestern University Law Review*, **72**, no. 2, 854–965.
McKENZIE, R. B. (1978), On the methodological boundaries of economic analysis, *Journal of Economic Issues*, **12**, no. 3. 627–645.
MACAULAY, S. (1976), Non-contractual relations in business: a preliminary study, *American Sociological Review*, **25**, no. 1, 55–69.
MANNE, H. G. and MILLER, R. M. (eds.) (1976) *Auto Safety Regulation: The Cure or the Problem?*, New Jersey: Horton.
MARKOVITS, R. S. (1976), The distributive impact, allocative efficiency, and overall desirability of ideal housing codes: some theoretical clarifications, *Harvard Law Review*, **89**, no. 8, 1817–1846.
MARKOVITS, R. S. (1978), Predicting the competitive impact of horizontal mergers in a monopolistically competitive world: a non-market-oriented proposal and critique of the

market-definition—market-share—market-concentration approach. *Texas Law Review*, **56**, no. 4, 587–731.
MARX, K. (1867), *Capital*, London: Dent, 1962.
MICHELMAN, F. I. (1967), Property, utility and fairness: comments on the ethical foundations of 'just compensation' law, *Harvard Law Review*, **80**, no. 6, 1165–1258.
MICHELMAN, F. I. (1977), Political markets and community self determination: competing judicial models of local government legitimacy, *Indiana Law Journal*, **53**, no. 2, 145–206.
MICHELMAN, F. I. (1978), Norms and normativity in the economic theory of law, *Minnesota Law Review*, **62**, no. 6, 1015–1048.
MICHELMAN, F. I. (1979), A comment on some uses and abuses of economics in law, *University of Chicago Law Review*, **46**, no. 2, 307–315.
MILLER, J. C. and YANDLE, B. (eds.) (1979), *Benefit-Cost Analysis of Social Regulation*, Washington DC: American Enterprise Institute.
MISHAN, E. J. (1967), Pareto optimality and the law, *Oxford Economic Papers*, **19**, no. 3, 247–287.
MITCHELL, W. C. (1935), Commons on institutional economics, *American Economics Review*, **25**, no. 4, 635–652.
MOONEY, G. (1977), *The Valuation of Human Life*, London: Macmillan.
MORGENSTERN, O. (1972), Thirteen critical points in contemporary economic theory, *Journal of Economic Literature*, **10**, no. 4, 1163–1180.
NEEDLEMAN, L. (1976), Valuing other people's lives, *Manchester School*, **44**, no. 4, 309–342.
NUTTER, W. (1979), On economism, *Journal of Law and Economics*, **22**, no. 2, 263–268.
OGUS, A. I. (1980), Economics, liberty and the common law, *Journal of Society of Public Teachers of Law*, **18**, no. 1. 42–57.
OGUS, A. I. and RICHARDSON, G. (1977), Economics and the environment: a study of private nuisance, *Cambridge Law Journal*, **36**, no. 2, 284–325.
PARRY, D. H. (1931), Economic theories in English case law, *Law Quarterly Review*, **47**, 183–196.
PELTZMAN, S. (1973), An evaluation of consumer protection legislation: the 1962 drug amendments, *Journal of Political Economy*, **81**, no. 5, 1049–1091.
PELTZMAN, S. (1975), The effects of automobile safety regulation, *Journal of Political Economy*, **83**, no. 4, 677–725.
PHELPS, E. S. (ed.) (1975), *Altruism, Morality, and Economic Theory*, New York: Russell Sage Foundation.
PHILLIPS, J. (1976), Economic deterrence and the prevention of industrial accidents, *Industrial Law Journal*, **5**, no. 3, 148–163.
PHILLIPS, J. and HAWKINS, K. (1976), Some economic aspects of the settlement process: a study in personal injury claims, *Modern Law Review*, **39**, no. 5, 497–515.
PIGOU, A. C. (1932), *The Economics of Welfare*, 4th ed., London: Macmillan.
POLINSKY, A. M. (1974), Economic analysis as a potentially defective product: a buyer's guide to Posner's economic analysis of law, *Harvard Law Review*, **87**, no. 8, 1655–1687.
POSNER, R. A. (1972), A theory of negligence, *Journal of Legal Studies*, **1**. no. 1, 28–96.
POSNER, R. A. (1973a), Strict liability: a comment, *Journal of Legal Studies*, **2**, no. 1, 205–221.
POSNER, R. A. (1973b), Economic justice and the economist, *Public Interest*, **33**, 109–113.
POSNER, R. A. (1974), Theories of economic regulation, *Bell Journal of Economics and Management Science*, **5**, no. 2, 335–358.
POSNER, R. A. (1975), The economic approach to law, *Texas Law Review*, **53**, no. 4, 757–782.
POSNER, R. A. (1977), *Economic Analysis of Law*, 2nd ed., Boston: Little-Brown.
POSNER, R. A. (1979a), Utilitarianism, economics, and legal theory, *Journal of Legal Studies*, **8**, no. 1, 103–140.
POSNER, R. A. (1979b), Some uses and abuses of economics in law, *University of Chicago Law Review*, **46**, no. 2, 281–306.
RAWLS, J. (1971), *A Theory of Justice*, Cambridge, Mass: Harvard University Press.
RICHARDSON, G., OGUS, A.I. and BURROWS, P. (1981), *Policing Pollution*, London: Macmillan.
RIZZO, M. J. (1979), Uncertainty, subjectivity and the economic analysis of law, in *Time, Uncertainty, and Disequilibrium* (M. J. Rizzo, ed.), Lexington: Lexington Books.
RIZZO, M.J. (1980), Law amid flux — the economics of negligence and strict liability in tort, *Journal of Legal Studies*, **10**, no. 2, 291–318.
ROBERTSON, L. S. (1977), A critical analysis of Peltzman's 'the effects of automobile safety regulations', *Journal of Economic Issues*, **11**, no. 3, 587–600.
ROBBINS, L. (1932), *An Essay on the*

Nature and Significance of Economic Science, London: Macmillan.
ROBINSON, H. W. (1939), Law and economics, *Modern Law Review*, **11**, no. 4, 257–265.
SAMUELS, W. J. (1974), Commentary: an economic perspective on the compensation problem, *Wayne Law Review*, **21**, no. 1, 113–134.
SAMUELS, W.J. (1974). The Coase Theorem and the study of law and economics, *Natural Resources Journal*, **14**, no. 1, 1–33.
SCHWARTZ, G. T. (1979), Economics, wealth distribution, and justice, *Wisconsin Law Review*, no. 3, 799–813.
SEN, A. K. (1976/77), Rational fools: a critique of the behavioural foundations of economic theory, *Philosophy and Public Affairs*, **6**, 317–344. Reprinted in Hahn and Hollis (1979).
SIMONS, H. A. (1978), On how to decide on what to do, *Bell Journal of Economics*, **9**, no. 2, 494–507.
SIMONS, H. A. (1979), From substantive to procedural rationality, in Hahn and Hollis. (1979).
SMITH, P. and SWANN, D. (1979), *Protecting the Consumer – An Economic and Legal Analysis*, Oxford: Martin Robertson.
SMITH, R. S. (1973), The feasibility of an 'injury tax' approach to occupational safety, *Law and Contemporary Problems*, **38**, no. 4, 730–744.
SMITH, R. S. (1979a), Compensating wage differentials and public policy: a review, *Industrial and Labor Relations Review*, **32**, no. 3, 339–351.
SMITH, R. S. (1979b), The impact of OSHA inspections on manufacturing injury rates, *Journal of Human Resources*, **14**, no. 2, 145–170.
SWANN, D. (1979), *Competition and Consumer Protection*, London: Penguin.
THUROW, L. (1973), Economic justice and the economist: a reply, *Public Interest*, **33**, 120–129.
TIDEMAN, N. (1972), Property as a moral concept, in *Perspective on Property*, pp. 202–203. (G. Wunderlich and W.L. Gibson eds.) Pennsylvania State University.
TREBILCOCK, M. J., WAVERMAN, L. and PRICHARD, J. R. S. (1978), Markets for regulation: implications for performance standards and institutional design, in *Government Regulation – Issues and Alternatives 1978*, Ontario: Ontario Economic Council.
TRIBE, L. H. (1972a), Policy science: analysis or ideology?, *Philosophy and Public Affairs*. **2**, no. 1, 66–110.
TRIBE, L. H. (1972b), Technological assessment and the fourth discontinuity: the limits of instrumental rationality, *Southern California Law Review*, **46**, no. 3, 617–660.
TULLOCK, G. (1978), Economic imperialism, in *Theory of Public Choice: Political Applications of Economics*, (J.M. Buchanan and R.D. Tollison, eds.) Ann Arbor: University of Michigan Press.
VELJANOVSKI, C. G. (1979a), *Economic Myths about Common Law Realities – Economic Efficiency and the Law of Torts*, Oxford: Centre for Socio-Legal Studies.
VELJANOVSKI, C. G. (1979b), *Bibliography in Law and Economics: Contract Analysis*, Oxford: Centre for Socio-Legal Studies.
VELJANOVSKI, C. G. (1979c), *Bibliography in Law and Economics – Legal Liability and Negligence*, Oxford: Centre for Socio-Legal Studies.
VELJANOVSKI, C. G. (1980a), The economic approach to law – a critical introduction, *British Journal of Law and Society*, **10**, no. 2.
VELJANOVSKI, C. G. (1980b), *An Economic and Empirical Analysis of the English Employers' Liability Act of 1980*, manuscript, Oxford: Centre for Socio-Legal Studies.
VISCUSI, W. K. (1979), The impact of occupational safety and health regulation, *Bell Journal of Economics*, **10**, no. 1, 117–140.
WACHTER, M. and WILLIAMSON, O. E. (1978), Obligational market and the mechanics of inflation, *Bell Journal of Economics*, **9**, no. 2, 549–571.
WEISBROD, B. A. (1978), *Public Interest Law: An Economic and Institutional Analysis*, Berkeley: University of California Press.
WILBERFORCE, Lord (1978), Law and economics, in *The Lawyer and Justice* (B. W. Harvey ed.), London: Sweet and Maxwell.
WILLIAMS, A. (1975), Collaboration between economists and lawyers in policy analysis, *Journal of Society of Public Teachers of Law*, **13**, no. 3, 212–218.
WILLIAMSON, O. E. (1975), *Markets and Hierarchies*, New York: Free Press.
WILLIAMSON, O. E. (1979), Transaction cost economics: the governance of contractual relations, *Journal of Law and Economics*, **22**, no. 2, 233–261.
WILLIAMSON, O. E., WACHTER, M. L. and HARRIS, J. F. (1975), Understanding the employment relation: the analysis of idiosyncratic exchange, *Bell Journal of Economics*, **6**, no. 2, 250–280.

WOLPIN, K.I. (1978a), Capital punishment and homicide in England: a summary of results, *American Economic Review (papers and proceedings)*, **62**, no. 2, 422–427.

WOLPIN, K.I. (1978b), An economic analysis of crime and punishment in England and Wales, 1894–1967, *Journal of Political Economy*, **86**, no. 5, 815–840.

WOLPIN, K.I. (1979), Capital punishment and homicide: The english experience, unpublished manuscript, Yale University.

ZECKHAUSER, R. A. (1975), Procedures for valuing lives, *Public Policy*, **23**, 419–464.

PART ONE
Contract

In his Rosenthal Lectures Professor Macneil stressed that contract law can only be analysed if the exchange process is understood. Both legal and economic models of exchange have until recently tended to be relatively simple, focusing mainly on the sale of goods contract, and indeed the legal model of contract is based on the economic model of market exchange (Horowitz, 1974; Atiyah, 1979). While market-type analyses have recently provided some excellent investigations of contract law[1], for a large number of non-market contracts the applicability of the model can be questioned. The essays by Williamson and Macneil attempt to develop a more detailed and descriptively plausible model of exchange that embraces both market and non-market contracts. Although Williamson and Macneil differ in emphasis and in the role they ascribe to economics, they agree that the crucial factor that gives rise to contract problems is uncertainty and the temporal nature of contract performance. Both essays provide a taxonomy of frictions to contractual activity. They contrast their approach to that of the market-based approach and (Williamson in particular) draw out the institutional significance of uncertainty by stressing both legal and non-legal methods of regulating contractual behaviour[2].

The essay by Trebilcock and Dewees provides a market-based analysis of standard form contracts and of recent attempts by the courts to regulate them[3]. The authors point out that a standard form contract *per se* tells us very little about its 'unfairness', and that such contracts are to be expected for transaction cost economizing reasons. Two factors may make such contracts 'unfair', namely inequality of bargaining power (monopoly) and imperfect information. Focusing on the latter, the essay argues that the effect of ignorance is more subtle than is generally appreciated, and the fact that many consumers have imperfect knowledge does not necessarily mean that the terms of standard form contracts are onerous. It is the marginal consumer that determines the nature of a contract in the market and the essay stresses that the investigation must consider whether those consumers who are contract searchers have adequate knowledge and are representative of the other consumers who are ignorant[4].

Notes to part one

1 Barton (1972), Goetz and Scott (1977), Kronman and Posner (1979), Clarkson, Miller and Muris (1978), Schwartz (1979), Perloff (1979) and Shavell (1980). See Veljanovski (1979) for other references.

2 Also see Williamson's analysis of labour contracts in transaction cost terms; Williamson (1980) and Williamson, Wachter and Harris (1975).

3 This joins a small body of literature analysing standard form contracts; Goldberg (1974), Coase (1974), Epstein (1975), Kornhauser (1976), Schwartz (1977), Trebilcock (1976 and 1979).

4 For an alternative approach in the same vein as Williamson's work see the comments of Klien (1980) on *Macaulay v Schroeder*.

References

ATIYAH, P. S. (1979), *The Rise and Fall of Freedom of Contract*, Oxford: Clarendon Press.

BARTON, J. H. (1972), The economic basis of damages for breach of contract, *Journal of Legal Studies*, **1**, no. 2, 277–304.

CLARKSON, K. W., MILLER, R. L. and MURIS, T. J. (1978), Liquidated damages v penalties: sense or nonsense?, *Wisconsin Law Review*, no. 2, 351–390.

COASE, R. H. (1974), The choice of the institutional framework: a comment, *Journal of Law and Economics*, **17**, no. 2, 493–496.

EPSTEIN, R. (1975), Unconscionability: a critical approach, *Journal of Law and Economics*, **18**, no. 2, 293–315.

GOETZ, C. J. and SCOTT, R. E. (1977), Liquidated damages, penalties, and just compensation principle: some notes on an enforcement model of efficient breach, *Columbia Law Review*, **77**, no. 4, 554–594.

GOLDBERG, V. P. (1974), Institutional change and the quasi-invisible hand, *Journal of Law and Economics*, **17**, no. 2, 461–492.

GOLDBERG, V.P. (1980), Relational exchange: economics and complex contracts, *American Behavioral Scientist*, **23**, no. 3, 337–352.

HARRIS, D., OGUS, A. I. and PHILLIPS, J. (1979), Contract remedies and the consumer surplus, *Law Quarterly Review*, **95**, 581–610.

HOROWITZ, M. J. (1974), The historical foundations of modern contract law, *Harvard Law Review*, **87**, no. 5, 917–956.

KLIEN, B. (1980), Transaction cost determinants of 'unfair' contractual arrangements, *American Economic Review (papers and proceedings)*, **70**, no. 2, 356–362.

KORNHAUSER, L. A. (1976), Unconscionability in standard forms, *California Law Review*, **64**, no. 5, 1151–1183.

KRONMAN, A. T. and POSNER, R. A. (1979), *The Economics of Contract*, Boston: Little Brown.

MACNEIL, I. R. (1980), *The New Social Contract: An Inquiry into Modern Contractual Relations*, New Haven: Yale University Press.

PERLOFF, J. M. (1979), *Breach of Contract and the Forseeability Doctrine of Hadley v Baxendale*, discussion paper no. 43, University of Pennsylvania: Center for the Study of Organizational Innovation.

SCHWARTZ, A. (1977), A reexamination of nonsubstantive unconscionability, *Virginia Law Review*, **63**, no. 6, 1053–1083.

SCHWARTZ, A. (1979), The case for specific performance, *Yale Law Journal*, **89**, no. 2, 271–307.

SHAVELL, S. (1980), Damage measures for breach of contract, *Bell Journal of Economics*, **11**, no. 2, 466–496.

TREBILCOCK, M. J. (1976), The doctrine of inequality of bargaining power: post-Benthamite economics in the House of Lords, *University of Toronto Law Journal*, **26**, no. 4, 359–385.

TREBILCOCK, M. J. (1979), An economic approach to the doctrine of unconscionability, in *Studies in Contract Law*, (B. J. Reiter and J. Swan, eds.), Toronto: Butterworths.

VELJANOVSKI, C. G. (1979), *Bibliography in Law and Economics — Contract Analysis*, Oxford: Centre for Socio-Legal Studies.

WILLIAMSON, O. E. (1980), The organisation of work: a comparative institutional assessment, *Journal of Economic Behaviour and Organization*, **1**, no. 1, 5–38.

WILLIAMSON, O. E., WACHTER, M. K. and HARRIS, J. F. (1975), Understanding the employment relation: the analysis of idiosyncratic exchange, *Bell Journal of Economics*, **6**, no. 1, 250–280.

CHAPTER TWO

Contract analysis: the transaction cost approach

Oiiver E. Williamson[1]

This chapter adopts a transaction cost approach to the study of contracting. While this approach has general application, it has special force for the study of commercial contracting, which is the main concern of this chapter. I argue that governance structures, including but not restricted to legal structures, need to be matched to transactions in a discriminating way if efficient and viable contractual relations are to emerge. This approach to the study of contracts is to be contrasted with alternative approaches in which either a single or predominant type of governance structure is emphasized or alternative structures are admitted but an economizing orientation is not employed.

What has been referred to as the 'market-based' approach to the study of contracts suffers in the first of these respects. Thus although it brings an economizing attitude to the subject, it restricts the domain of relevant governance structures unnecessarily. When compared, however, with unfocused legal studies of contracts in which 'everything matters', and thus anything goes and economizing barely surfaces, the narrow focus of the market-based approach has much to commend it. Indeed, I am prepared to assert that only when an economizing orientation is adopted and maintained will there be any prospect of developing a predictive and testable theory of commercial contracting.

The object, therefore, is to preserve economizing while simultaneously extending the inquiry to include nonmarket governance structures. This is what the transaction cost approach accomplishes.

Alternative economic approaches to the study of contracting are briefly sketched in section 2.1. Ian Macneil's recent three-way classification of contract is summarized in section 2.2. The essential transaction cost concepts and dimensions needed for matching governance structures with Macneil's contractual relations are developed in section 2.3. The differential match of governance structures with commercial contracting transactions is then accomplished in section 2.4. Other applications are briefiy sketched in section 2.5. Concluding remarks follow.

2.1 Economic approaches to contracting

Cento Veljanovski (1979) identifies two economic approaches to the study of contracting. He refers to the first of these as the market-based approach and associates it with the work of Richard Posner (1977, ch. 4). The second is the transaction-cost approach, which he identifies with the work of Ian Macneil, Victor Goldberg, and myself[2]. Each of these is briefly considered here, with emphasis on the last.

2.1.1 The market-based approach

The paradigm transaction for the market-based approach is the discrete transaction. Anthony Kronman and Richard Posner (1978) offer two examples, one very simple, the other more complex. The simple illustration has *A* buying a newspaper from news-vendor *B*. The more complex illustration involves *B* contracting to build a house for *A*. Whereas the first involves coincident exchange of money for goods of known quality, the second does not and requires more self-conscious attention to the structure of the exchange.

According to Posner, the law of contracts helps to facilitate exchanges of the latter kind in three respects. First, it imposes costs on those who would attempt to exploit such agreements, e.g., by accepting payment and refusing to deliver. Secondly, it reduces 'the complexity and hence cost of transactions by supplying a set of normal terms that, in the absence of the law of contracts, the parties would have to negotiate expressly' (Posner, 1977, p.69). Thirdly, it furnishes 'prospective contracting parties with information concerning the many contingencies that may defeat an exchange, and hence . . . [assists] them in planning their exchange sensibly. The parties, through their lawyers, are guided around the pitfalls in the process of exchange revealed by the opinions in decided contract cases' (ibid.).

Very simple transactions excepted, this market-based view of contracting suggests that commercial transactions are greatly dependent on and governed by legal forms and rules. The transactions cost approach sketched below relaxes this dependency and addresses itself to a wider set of transactions and governance structures than are captured by the discrete contracting approach.

2.1.2 The transaction cost approach

As Kenneth Arrow (1969, p.48) puts it, transaction costs are the 'costs of running the economic system'. Such costs 'impede and in particular cases completely block the formation of markets'. Nonmarket or market-assisted forms of organization arise on this account. Attention is thus focused less on technology than on the comparative costs of planning, adapting and monitoring task completion under alternative forms of contracting.

A wider conception of economic organization is contemplated by the transaction cost approach. Although market exchange remains important, it is only one of several governance structures. The importance of legal rules, moreover, varies with the nature of the transaction. This broader conception of contract owes its origins to a larger view of economics associated with the names of John R. Commons (1934), Ronald Coase (1937), and Friedrich Hayek (1945). Lawyers such as Karl Llewellyn (1931), Lon Fuller (1964), Stewart Macaulay (1963) and Ian Macneil (1974) have independently recognized the need to expand contract law beyond its technical features in order to include a more general concern with the contractual purposes to be served.

Commons took the position that the transaction rather than the commodity was the basic unit of analysis. Although conflicting interests among parties to a transaction were assumed to be natural, they were not taken as fixed. On the contrary, the object was to devise institutions that served to harmonize interests or at least to achieve order where otherwise there would be conflict. Legal institutions served these purposes, but so did other organizing structures.

Specifically, as Coase recognized, the business firm is an alternative to markets as a means for organizing transactions. The decision whether to organize transactions within a firm rather than across a market interface depends on the transaction costs that attend each. Coase also recognized that adapting transactions efficiently to changing circumstances easily gives rise to strain if the parties are autonomous and each appropriates a separate profit stream.

The importance of change and of the need to adapt effectively to uncertainty were even more prominently featured in Hayek's treatments of the economic problem. Rather than concentrate on equilibrium, Hayek emphasized disequilibrium and the need to understand the adaptation processes that were set in motion by disturbances. Comprehensive planning efforts were held to be ill-advised because human agents had limited capacities and, similarly, because specialized (idiosyncratic) knowledge of events and circumstances was in the possession of individuals and could not be costlessly disclosed to, much less apprehended by, central planners. These reasons, together with the 'marvel' of the price system — whereby changing economic opportunities are accurately signalled by relative prices — formed the basis for Hayek's preference for a market-based economy.

My transaction cost approach follows Commons by making the transaction the basic unit of analysis. Also, like Commons, I am interested in the design of institutions, legal and otherwise, that serve to promote the renewal or continuity of exchange relations. I follow Coase by regarding the firm as an important alternative to the market for governing economic activity, and I share Hayek's views on the limits of human agents and on the importance of organizing transactions in such a way as to realize more assuredly the productive values embedded in idiosyncratic human and physical assets. To be sure, legal rules and market processes remain important under this extended view of contract, but informal procedures and nonmarket organization also perform important governance functions. Moreover, and crucially to the exercise, *governance structures are matched with transactional attributes in a discriminating way* under the transaction cost approach to contracting set out here.

Not only does the transaction cost approach make allowance for a broader set of governance structures but it also makes allowance for a more diverse set of transactions than is admitted under the market-based model of contracting favored by Posner, which emphasizes relatively discrete trades between *A* and *B*. Both the attributes of human agents and of the trading environment come under scrutiny when this larger viewpoint is adopted. Given that contracts are negotiated and executed under conditions of uncertainty, the object is to assign governance structures to transactions so as to promote effective adaptation to changing circumstances without incurring unneeded costs.

2.2 A three-way classification of contracts

Although there is widespread agreement that the discrete-transaction paradigm — 'sharp in by clear agreement; sharp out by clear performance' (Macneil, 1974, p.738) — has served both law and economics well, there is increasing awareness that many contractual relations are not of this well-defined kind. A deeper understanding of the nature of contract has emerged as the legal-rule emphasis associated with the study of discrete contracting has given way to a more general concern with the contractual purposes to be served.

Ian Macneil, in a series of thoughtful and wide-ranging essays on contract, usefully distinguishes between discrete and relational transactions (*see* chapter 3; Macneil, 1974; 1978). He further supplies twelve different 'concepts' with respect to which these differ[3]. Serious problems of recognition and application are posed by such a rich classificatory apparatus. More useful for my purposes is the three-way classification of contracts that MacNeil offers in a more recent article, where classical, neoclassical and relational categories of contract law are recognized.

2.2.1 Classical contract law

As Macneil (1978) observes, any system of contract law has the purpose of facilitating exchange. What is distinctive about classical contract law is that it attempts to do this by enhancing discreteness and intensifying 'presentiation' (ibid., p.862), where the presentiation has reference to efforts to 'make or render present in place or time; to cause to be perceived or realized as present' (cf. note 2, ch. 3). The economic counterpart to complete presentiation is contingent-claims contracting, which entails comprehensive contracting in which all relevant future contingencies pertaining to the supply of a good or service are described and discounted with respect to both likelihood and futurity[4].

Classical contract law endeavours to implement discreteness and presentiation in several ways. For one thing, the identity of the parties to a transaction is treated as irrelevant. In this respect it corresponds exactly with the 'ideal' market transaction in economics[5]. Secondly, the nature of the agreement is carefully delimited and the more formal features govern when formal (for example, written) and informal (for example, oral) terms are contested. Thirdly, remedies are narrowly prescribed such that, 'should the initial presentiation fail to materialize because of nonperformance, the consequences are relatively predictable from the beginning and are not open-ended'. Additionally, third-party participation is discouraged (Macneil, 1978, p. 864). The emphasis, thus, is on legal rules, formal documents and self-liquidating transactions.

2.2.2 Neoclassical contract law

Not every transaction fits comfortably into the classical contracting scheme. In particular, long-term contracts executed under conditions of uncertainty are ones for which complete presentiation is apt to be prohibitively costly if not impossible. Problems of several kinds arise. First, not all future contingencies for which adaptations are required can be anticipated at the outset. Secondly, the appropriate adaptations will not be evident for many contingencies until the circumstances materialize. Thirdly, except where changes in states of the world are unambiguous, hard contracting between autonomous parties may well give rise to veridical disputes when state-contingent claims are made. In a world in which (at least some) parties are inclined to be opportunistic, whose representations are to be believed?

Faced with the prospective breakdown of classical contracting in these circumstances, three options are available. One would be to forego such transactions altogether. A second would be to remove these transactions from the market and organize them internally: adaptive, sequential decision making would then be implemented under common ownership and with the assistance of hierarchical incentive and control systems. Third, a different contracting relation that preserves trading but provides for additional governance structure might be devised. This last choice brings us to what Macneil refers to as neoclassical contracting.

As Macneil observes, 'two common characteristics of long-term contracts are the existence of gaps in their planning and the presence of a range of processes and techniques used by contract planners to create flexibility in lieu of either leaving gaps or trying to plan rigidly.' (ibid., p.865). Third-party assistance in resolving disputes and evaluating performance often has advantages over litigation in serving these functions of flexibility and gap filling. Lon Fuller's remarks (1964, pp. 11–12) on procedural differences between arbitration and litigation are instructive:

> . . . there are open to the arbitrator . . . quick methods of education not open to the courts. An arbitrator will frequently interrupt the examination of witnesses with a request that the parties educate him to the point where he can understand the testimony being received. This education can proceed informally, with frequent interruptions by the arbitrator, and by informed persons on either side, when a point needs clarification. Sometimes there will be arguments across the table, occasionally even within each of the separate camps. The end result will usually be a clarification that will enable everyone to proceed more intelligently with the case. There is in this informal procedure no infringement whatever of arbitrational due process.

A recognition that the world is complex, that agreements are incomplete and that some contracts will never be reached unless both parties have confidence in the settlement machinery thus characterizes neoclassical contract law. One important purposive difference in arbitration and litigation that contributes to the procedural differences described by Fuller is that whereas continuity (at least completion of the contract) is presumed under the arbitration machinery, this presumption is much weaker when litigation is employed (Friedman, 1965).

2.2.3 Relational contracting

The pressures to sustain continuing relations 'have led to the spin-off of many subject areas from the classical, and later the neoclassical contract law system, e.g., much of corporate law and collective bargaining' (Macneil, 1978, p.885). Thus, progressively increasing the 'duration and complexity' of contract has resulted in the displacement of even neoclassical adjustment processes by adjustment processes of a more throughly transaction-specific, ongoing-administrative kind (ibid., p.901). The fiction of discreteness is fully displaced as the relation takes on the properties of 'a minisociety with a vast array of norms beyond those centered on the exchange and its immediate processes' (ibid.). By contrast with the neoclassical system, in which the reference point for effecting adaptations remains the original agreement, the reference point under a truly relational approach is the 'entire relation as it has developed . . . [through] time. This may or may not include an "original agreement"; and if it does, may or may not result in great deference being given to it.' (ibid., p. 890).

2.3 Transaction cost economics

Macneil's three-way discussion of contracts discloses that contracts are a good deal more varied and complex than is commonly realized[6]. It furthermore suggests that governance structures — the institutional matrix within which transactions are negotiated and executed — vary with the nature of the transaction. But the critical dimensions of contract are not expressly identified, and the purposes of governance are not stated. The harmonizing of interests that would otherwise give away to antagonistic subgoal pursuits appears to be an important governance function but this is not explicit in his discussion

That simple governance structures should be used in conjunction with simple contractual relations and complex governance structures reserved for complex relations seems generally sensible. The use of a complex structure to govern a simple relation is apt to incur unneeded costs, whereas the use of a simple structure for a complex transaction invites strain. But what is simple and complex in contractual respects? Specific attention to the defining attributes of transactions is evidently needed.

Transaction cost economics is intended to be responsive to these needs. The transaction cost approach to the study of contracting is usefully developed in two parts. The behavioural assumptions to which transaction costs are ultimately traced are examined first. The critical dimensions for distinguishing between transactions are then considered.

2.3.1 Behavioural assumptions[7]

Bounded rationality and opportunism are the central behavioural assumptions upon which the transaction cost approach is based. Bounded rationality, which should not be confused with irrationality, refers to a condition in which human agents are '*intendedly* rational, but only *limitedly* so' (Simon, 1961). Put differently, it refers to rationality in the ordinary, dictionary sense of the term — 'agreeable to reason; not absurd, preposterous, extravagant, foolish, fanciful, or the like; intelligent, sensible'[8]—rather than in the hyperrational sense in which it is commonly used in microeconomics textbooks (Simon, 1978, pp.2–3). Thus economic agents who are boundedly rational are able to receive, store, retrieve and process only a limited amount of information. Such agents are routinely overwhelmed by the amount of information supplied to them in relation to their capacity to use it effectively. Accordingly, the economics of attention is an important but generally neglected item on the research agenda (ibid., p.13).

Opportunism extends the usual motivational assumption of self-interest to make allowance for self-interest with guile. Thus, whereas bounded rationality suggests decision-making less complex than the usual assumption of hyperrationality, opportunism suggests calculating behaviour that is more sophisticated than the usual assumption of simple self-interest. Opportunism refers to 'making false or empty, that is, self-disbelieved threats or promises' (Goffman, 1969), cutting corners for undisclosed personal advantage, covering-up tracks and the like. Although it is a central assumption, it is not essential that all economic agents behave in this way. What is crucial, however, is that some agents behave in this fashion and that it is costly to sort out those who are opportunistic from those who are not.

Organizational design issues arise by joining these two assumptions about the characteristics of human actors with the assertion that viable modes of organization (market, quasi-market or internal) are ones that serve to economize on transaction costs. Indeed, the basic organizational design issue essentially reduces to this: organize transactions in such a way as to economize on bounded rationality while simultaneously safeguarding the transactions in question against the hazards of opportunism.

2.3.2 Dimensionalizing

The puzzle of vertical integration is that under conventional assumptions it is an anomaly: if the costs of operating competitive markets are zero, 'as is usually assumed in our theoretical analysis' (Arrow, 1969, p.48) why integrate? Coase, in his 1937 paper (p.336), took exception to the usual assumption and argued that vertical integration permitted the firm to economize on the 'cost of negotiating and concluding' many separate intermediate product market contracts by substituting a flexible employment agreement. Inasmuch, however, as the factors that were responsible for differential transaction costs in the intermediate product market were not identified, the argument lacked testable implications. Why not use a flexible employment agreement to organize all transactions rather than just some? Until such time as the transaction cost argument was able to explain the organization of transactions in a discriminating way, it remained rather tautological (Alchian and Demsetz, 1972, p.783). Coase's observation (1972, p.63), some twenty-five years later, that his 1937 article was 'much cited and little used' is presumably explained by the failure to operationalize the issues over that interval.

As I have developed elsewhere (Williamson, 1979b), the critical dimensions for describing transactions, and hence for assigning some to markets and others to internal organization, are:

(1) uncertainty;
(2) the frequency with which transactions recur;
(3) the degree to which durable transaction-specific investments are required to realize least-cost supply.

The main governance modes to which transactions need to be matched are:

(1) markets (with varying degrees of adjudicatory support);
(2) internal organization;
(3) an intermediate form of bilateral exchange referred to as 'obligational market contracting'.

Transactions for which internal organization is well-suited are those that involve recurrent exchange in the face of a nontrivial degree of uncertainty and for which transaction-specific investments are incurred. Since internal organization requires the development of a specialized governance structure, the cost of which must be amortized across the transactions organized thereunder, it is rarely economical to organize infrequent (or occasional) transactions internally. Likewise, transactions for which uncertainty is low require little adaptation and hence little governance. Unspecialized market structures commonly work well for these. It should not be inferred, however, that markets function poorly wherever high frequency or great uncertainty, either individually or in combination, appear. On the contrary, except when *transaction-specific investments* are involved, neither frequency not uncertainty, individually or in combination, would justify the creation of internal organization (with its associated transaction-specific governance structure).

Considering the importance that I attach to transaction-specific investments, some explication is needed. The crucial issue is the degree to which durable, nonmarketable expenses are incurred. Items that are unspecialized among users pose few hazards, since buyers in these circumstances can easily turn to alternative sources, and suppliers can sell output intended for one buyer to other buyers without difficulty. Nonmarketability problems arise when the *specific identity* of the parties has important cost-bearing consequences. Transactions of this kind will be referred to as idiosyncratic.

Occasionally the identity of the parties is important from the outset, as when a buyer induces a supplier to invest in specialized physical capital of a transaction-specific kind. Inasmuch as the value of this capital in other uses is, by definition, much smaller than the specialized use for which it has been intended, the supplier is effectively 'locked into' the transaction to a significant degree. This is symmetrical, moreover, in that the buyer cannot turn to alternative sources of supply and obtain the item on favourable terms, since the cost of supply from unspecialized capital is presumably great. The buyer is thus committed to the transaction as well.

Ordinarily, however, there is more to idiosyncratic exchange than specialized physical capital. Human-capital investments that are transaction-specific commonly occur as well. Specialized training and learning-by-doing economies in production operations are illustrations. Except when these investments are transferable to alternative suppliers at low cost, which is rare, the benefits of the set-up costs can be realized only so long as the relationship between the buyer and seller of the intermediate product is maintained.

Additional transaction-specific savings can accrue at the interface between supplier and buyer as contracts are successively adapted to unfolding events, and as periodic contract-renewal agreements are reached. Familiarity here permits communication economies to be realized: specialized language develops as experience accumulates and nuances are signalled and received in a sensitive way. Both institutional and personal trust relations evolve.

In consideration of the value placed upon economies of these kinds, agents who engage in recurring, uncertain, idiosyncratic transactions have a strong interest in preserving the exchange relation. Autonomous contracting modes give way to internal organization as the value associated with exchange continuity increases. The continuity advantages of internal organization over markets in these circumstances are attributable to its more sensitive governance characteristics and its stronger joint profit maximizing features.

2.4 Commercial contracting

The discussion of commercial contracting begins with a brief statement on economizing. The proposed schema for characterizing transactions and their governance is then developed, including the relation of the schema with Macneil's three-way classification of contract.

2.4.1 Economizing

The criterion for organizing commercial transactions is assumed to be the strictly instrumental one of cost economizing. Essentially this takes two parts: economizing on production expense and economizing on transaction costs[9]. To the degree that transaction costs are negligible, buying rather than making will normally be the most cost-effective means of procurement[10]. Not only can static scale economies be more fully exhausted by buying rather than making, but the supplier who aggregates uncorrelated demands can realize collective pooling benefits as well. Since external procurement avoids many of the bureaucratic hazards of internal procurement (which hazards, are themselves of a transaction-cost kind)[11], external procurement is evidently warranted.

As indicated, however, the object is to economize on the sum of production and transaction costs. To the degree that production-cost economies of external procurement are small and/or the transaction costs associated with external procurement are great, alternative supply arrangements deserve serious consideration. Economizing on transaction costs essentially reduces to economizing on bounded rationality while simultaneously safeguarding the transactions in question against the hazards of opportunism. When the governance structure is held constant, these two objectives are in tension, since a reduction in one commonly results in an increase in the other[12].

Governance structures, however, are properly regarded as part of the optimization problem. For some transactions, a shift from one structure to another may permit a simultaneous reduction in both the expense of writing a complex contract (which economizes on bounded rationality) and the expense of executing it effectively in an adaptive, sequential way (by attenuating opportunism). Indeed, this is precisely the attraction of internal procurement for transactions of a recurrent, idiosyncratic kind. Not only are market-aggregation economies neglible for such transactions — since the requisite invesments are transaction-specific — but market trading in these circumstances is shot through with appropriable quasi-rent hazards. The issues here have been developed elsewhere[13]. The object of this chapter is to integrate them into a larger contractual framework.

Note in this connection that the prospect of recovering the set-up costs associated with specialized governance structures varies with the frequency with which transactions recur. Specialized governance structures are much easier to justify for recurrent transactions than for identical transactions that occur only occasionally.

2.4.2 Characterizing transactions

I asserted earlier (section 2.3.2) that the critical dimensions for describing contractual relations are uncertainty, the frequency with which transactions recur and the degree to which investments are idiosyncratic. To simplify the exposition, I will assume uncertainty exists in some intermediate degree and focus initially on frequency and the degree to which the expenses incurred are transaction-specific. The separate importance of uncertainty will then be developed in section 2.4.4. Three frequency and three investment categories will be recognized. Frequency can be characterized as one-time, occasional or recurrent, and investments are classed as nonspecific, mixed or idiosyncratic. To further simplify the argument, the following assumptions are made:

(1) Suppliers intend to be in business on a continuing basis; thus the special hazards posed by fly-by-night firms can be disregarded.
(2) Potential suppliers for any given requirement are numerous — which is to say that *ex ante* monopoly in ownership of specialized resources is assumed away.
(3) The frequency dimension refers strictly to buyer activity in the market[14].
(4) The investment dimension refers to the characteristics of investments made by suppliers[15].

Although discrete transactions are intriguing — for example, purchasing local spirits from a shopkeeper in a remote area of a foreign country which one never expects to visit again nor to refer his friends — few transactions have this totally isolated character. For those that do not, the difference between one-time and occasional transactions is not apparent. Accordingly, only occasional and recurrent frequency distinctions will be maintained. The two-by-three matrix shown in *Figure 2.1* thus describes the six types of transactions to which governance structures need to be matched. Illustrative transactions appear in the cells.

		Investment characteristics		
		Nonspecific	Mixed	Idiosyncratic
Frequency	Occasional	Purchasing standard equipment	Purchasing customized equipment	Constructing a plant
	Recurrent	Purchasing standard material	Purchasing customized material	Site-specific transfer of intermediate product across successive stages

Figure 2.1 *Illustrative commercial transactions*

2.4.3 Governance structures

Three broad types of governance structures will be considered: non-transaction-specific, semi-specific, and highly specific. The market is the classic nonspecific governance structure within which 'faceless buyers and sellers . . . meet . . . for an instant to exchange standardized goods at equilibrium prices' (Ben Porath, 1978). By contrast, highly specific structures are tailored to the special needs of the transaction. Identity here clearly matters. Semi-specific structures, naturally, fall in between. Several propositions are suggested immediately.

(1) Highly standardized transactions are not apt to require a specialized governance structure.
(2) Only recurrent transactions will support a highly specialized governance structure[16].
(3) Although occasional transactions of a nonstandardized kind will not support a transaction-specific governance structure, they require special attention nonetheless.

In terms of Macneil's three-way classification of contract, classical contracting presumably applies to all standardized transactions (whatever the frequency), relational contracting develops for transactions of a recurring and nonstandardized kind and neoclassical contracting is needed for occasional, nonstandardized transactions.

Market governance: classical contracting

Market governance is the main governance structure for nonspecific transactions of both occasional and recurrent contracting. Markets are especially efficacious when recurrent transactions are contemplated, since both parties need only consult their own experience in deciding to continue a trading relationship or, at little transitional expense, turn elsewhere. Being standardized, alternative purchase and supply arrangements are presumably easy to work out.

Nonspecific but occasional transactions are ones for which buyers (and sellers) are less able to rely on direct experience to safeguard transactions against opportunism. Often, however, rating services or the experience of other buyers of the same good can be consulted. Given that the good or service is of a standardized kind, such experience rating, by formal and informal means, will provide incentives for parties to behave responsibly.

To be sure, such transactions take place within and benefit from a legal framework. But such dependence is not great. As Lowry puts it, 'the traditional economic analysis of exchange in a market setting properly corresponds to the legal concept of *sale* (rather than contract), since sale presumes arrangements in a market context and requires legal support primarily in enforcing transfers of title' (Lowry, 1976, p.12). He would thus reserve the concept of contract for exchanges where, in the absence of standardized market alternatives, the parties have designed 'patterns of future relations on which they could rely' (Lowry, 1976, p.13).

The assumptions of the discrete-contracting paradigm are rather well satisfied for transactions where markets serve as a main governance mode. Thus the specific identity of the parties is of negligible importance, substantive content is determined by reference to formal terms of the contract and legal rules apply. Market alternatives are mainly what protect each party against opportunism by his opposite[17]. Litigation is strictly for settling claims; concentrated efforts to sustain the relation are not made because the relation is not independently valued[18].

Trilateral governance: neoclassical contracting

The two types of transactions for which trilateral governance is needed are occasional transactions of the mixed and highly idiosyncratic kinds. Once the principals to such transactions have entered into a contract, there are strong incentives to see the contract through to completion. Not only have specialized investments been made, the opportunity cost of which is much lower in alternative uses, but the transfer of these assets to a successor supplier would pose inordinate difficulties in asset valuation (Williamson, 1976). The interests of the principals in sustaining the relation are especially great for highly idiosyncratic transactions.

Market relief is thus unsatisfactory. Often the set-up costs of a transaction-specific governance structure cannot be recovered for occasional transactions. Given the limits of classical contract law for sustaining these transactions on the one hand, and the prohibitive cost of transaction-specific (bilateral) governance on the other, an intermediate institutional form is evidently needed.

Neoclassical contract law has many of the sought-after qualities. Thus rather than resort immediately to strict reliance on litigation — with its transaction-rupturing features — *third-party assistance* (arbitration) in resolving disputes and evaluating performance is employed instead. (The use of the architect as a relatively independent expert to determine the content of form construction contracts is an example; Macneil, 1978, p.866.) Also, the expansion of the specific-performance remedy in past decades is consistent with continuity purposes — though Macneil declines to characterize specific performance as the 'primary neoclassical contract remedy' (Macneil, 1978, p.879). The section of the Uniform Commercial Code that permits the 'seller aggrieved by a buyer's breach . . . unilaterally to maintain the relation'[19] is yet another example.

Transaction-specific governance: relational contracting

The two types of transactions for which specialized governance structures are commonly devised are recurring transactions of the mixed and highly idiosyncratic kinds. The nonstandardized nature of these transactions makes primary reliance on market governance hazardous, while their recurrent nature permits the cost of the specialized governance structure to be recovered.

Two types of transaction-specific governance structures for intermediate-production market transactions can be distinguished: bilateral structures, where the autonomy of the parties is maintained; and unified structures, where the transaction is removed from the market and organized within the firm, subject to an authority relation (vertical integration). Bilateral structures have only recently received the attention they deserve and their operation is least well understood.

Bilateral governance: obligational contracting. Highly idiosyncratic transactions are ones where the human and physical assets required for production are extensively specialized, so there are no obvious scale economies to be realized through interfirm trading that the buyer (or seller) is unable to realize himself through vertical integration. In the case, however, of mixed transactions, the degree of asset specialization is less complete. Accordingly, outside procurement for those components may be favoured for scale-economy considerations.

When compared with vertical integration, outside procurement is also good in eliciting cost control for steady-state supply. Problems, however, arise when adaptability and contractual expense are considered. Whereas internal adaptations can be effected by fiat, outside procurement involves effecting adaptations across the market. Unless the need for adaptations has been contemplated from the outset and expressly provided for by the contract, which often is impossible or prohibitively expensive, adaptations across a market interface can be accomplished only by mutual follow-on agreements. Inasmuch as the interests of the parties will commonly be at variance when adaptation proposals (originated by either party) are made, a dilemma is evidently posed.

On the one hand, both parties have an incentive to sustain the relationship rather than to permit it to unravel, the object being to avoid the sacrifice of valued transaction-specific economies. On the other hand, each party appropriates a separate profit stream and cannot be expected to accede readily to any proposal to adapt the contract. What is needed, evidently, is some way for declaring admissible dimensions for adjustment such that flexibility is provided under terms in which both parties have confidence. This can be accomplished partly by, first, recognizing that the hazards of opportunism vary with the type of adaptation proposed and, secondly, restricting adjustments to those where the hazards are least. But the spirit within which adaptations are effected is equally important[20].

Quantity adjustments have much better incentive-compatibility properties than do price adjustments. For one thing, price adjustments have an unfortunate zero-sum quality, whereas proposals to increase, decrease or delay delivery do not. Also price-adjustment proposals, except as discussed below, involve the risk that one's opposite is contriving to alter the terms within the bilateral monopoly trading gap to his advantage. By contrast, a presumption that exogenous events rather than strategic purposes are responsible for quantity adjustments is ordinarily warranted. Given the mixed nature of the exchange, a seller (or buyer) simply has little reason to doubt the representations of his opposite when a quantity change is proposed.

Thus buyers will neither seek supply from other sources nor divert products obtained (at favourable prices) to other uses (or users) — because other sources will incur high set-up costs and an idiosyncratic product is nonfungible across uses and users. Likewise, sellers will not withhold supply because better opportunities have arisen, because the assets in question have a specialized character. The result is that quantity representations for idiosyncratic products can ordinarily be taken at face value. Since inability to adapt both quantity and price would render most idiosyncratic exchanges nonviable, quantity adjustments occur routinely.

Unified governance: internal organization. Incentives for trading weaken as transactions become progressively more idiosyncratic. The reason is that as the specialized human and physical assets become more specialized to a single use, and hence less transferable to other uses, economies of scale can be as fully realized by the buyer as by an outside supplier. The choice of organizing mode then turns on which mode has superior adaptive properties[21]. As discussed elsewhere, vertical integration will invariably appear in these circumstances (Williamson, 1971).

The advantage of vertical integration is that adaptations can be made in a sequential way without the need to consult, complete or revise interfirm agreements. Where a single ownership entity spans both sides of the transactions, a presumption of joint profit maximization is warranted. Thus price adjustments in vertically integrated enterprises will be more complete than in interfirm trading. And quantity adjustments, of course, will be implemented at whatever frequency serves to maximize the joint gain to the transaction.

Unchanging identity at the interface coupled with extensive adaptability in both price and quantity is thus characteristic of highly idiosyncratic transactions that are vertically integrated. Obligational contracting is supplanted by the more comprehensive adaptive capability afforded by administration.

The match of governance structures with transactions that results from these economizing efforts is shown in *Figure 2.2*.

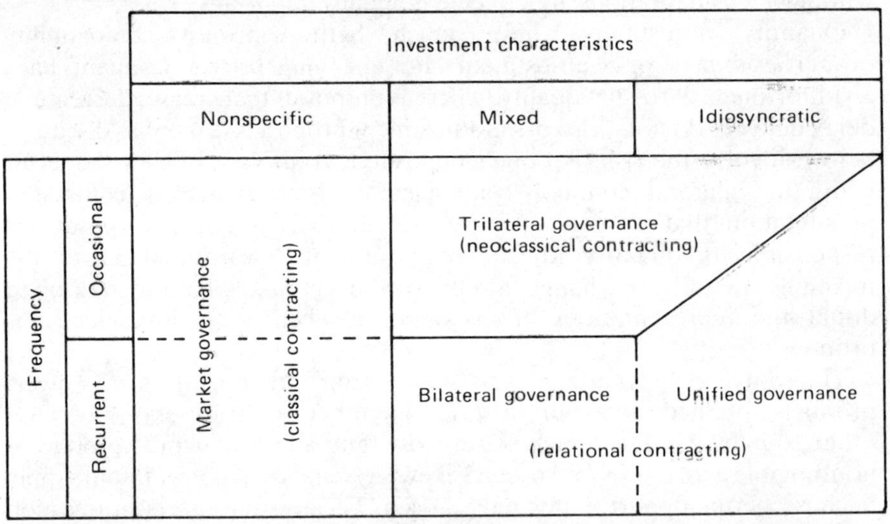

Figure 2.2 *Matching governanace structures with commercial transactions*

2.4.4 Uncertainty

Transactions conducted under certainty are relatively uninteresting. Except as they differ in the time required to reach an equilibrium-exchange configuration, any governance structure will do. More relevant are transactions where uncertainty is present to an intermediate or high degree. The foregoing has dealt with the first of these. The question here is how the governance of transactions is affected by increasing the degree of uncertainty.

Nonspecific transactions are ones for which continuity has little value, since new trading relations are easily arranged. Increasing the degree of uncertainty does not alter this. Accordingly, market exchange continues and the discrete-contracting paradigm (classical contract law) holds across standardized transactions of all kinds, whatever the degree of uncertainty.

Matters are different with transaction-specific investments. Whenever investments are idiosyncratic in nontrival degree, increasing the degree of uncertainty makes it more imperative that the parties devise a machinery to 'work things out', because contractual gaps will be larger and the occasions for sequential adaptations will increase in number and importance as the degree of uncertainty increases. This has special relevance for the organization of transactions with mixed investment attributes. Two possibilities exist. One would be to sacrifice valued design features in favour of a more standardized good or service. Market governance would then apply. The second would be to preserve the design but surround the transaction with an elaborate governance apparatus, thereby facilitating more effective adaptive, sequential decision-making. Specifically, a more elaborate arbitration apparatus is apt to be devised for occasional, nonstandard transactions. And bilateral governance structures will often give way to unified ones as uncertainty is increased for recurrent transactions.

Reductions in uncertainty, of course, warrant shifting transactions in the opposite direction. To the extent that uncertainty decreases as an industry matures, which is the usual case, the benefits that accrue to integration presumably decline. Accordingly, greater reliance on obligational market contracting is commonly feasible for transactions of recurrent trading in mature industries.

2.5 Other applications

Additional applications of the transaction cost approach are sketched out and/or detailed elsewhere (Williamson, 1979b, pp.254–259). These include the study of labour-contracting, the economics of regulation and aspects of family law. While the specifics differ, the spirit of the general approach set out above carries over.

Thus nonspecific labour market transactions are ones where the employer and employee are largely indifferent to the identity of each. Migrant farm labour is an example. From an efficiency (as contrasted to a power) point of view, there is little need to surround these transactions with a transaction-preserving infrastructure.

By contrast, transactions that involve an intermediate degree of transaction-specific investment are ones for which both employer and employee are interested in maintaining continuity. Collective organization, internal promotion ladders, restraints on entry and dispute settling machinery often contribute to these continuity purposes and service efficiency objectives.

Other applications are of this same kind. To wit, in the degree to which transaction-specific values are created, institutional supports that help to sustain these transactions are indicated. Again, since specialized governance structures are costly, they are reserved for the more idiosyncratic transactions for which frequency of exchange is high and the needs to adapt are great.

2.6 Concluding remarks

Although Commons (1934) located the study of governance at the very centre of the institutional research agenda some fifty years ago, institutional economics was then out of fashion and the call went unheeded. Economics, during the next forty years, was preoccupied with a single governance structure (the market) and with equilibrium rather than disequilibrium analysis. But matters have been changing. The past decade has witnessed a renewal of interest in nonmarket and market-assisted modes of organization. Nonfungible (idiosyncratic) transactions and disequilibrium conditions have attracted increasing attention. The study of governance has naturally reappeared as a crucial issue.

None of this is to say that more narrow conceptions of economics or of contract are not useful. On the contrary, the discrete transaction paradigm has been enormously instructive. The correspondence between frictionlessness in the physical sciences and the social sciences is noteworthy in this connection. Just as useful insights are often gleaned by assuming the absence of friction when studying physical systems, the assumed absence of transaction costs is likewise useful for studying many economic issues.

At the very least, the absence of friction (transaction costs) affords a useful standard. But there is more to it than this. There are numerous circumstances where the departure from ideal conditions is insufficient to warrant sacrificing the frictionless assumption when studying actual phenomena. Milton Friedman's discussion (1953, pp.16–19) of estimating the velocity of falling bodies by a simple formula ($s = \frac{1}{2}gt^2$) is illustrative. Whether this 'oversimplifies' or is quite adequate depends principally on what is being dropped (e.g., a steel ball or a feather), how close to a perfect vacuum has been attained and the precision of measurement required.

The corresponding contractual issue is to ascertain when the discrete transaction paradigm applies and when it needs to be augmented by a richer conception of contract. That the market-based paradigm is severly limited is evident from casual observation of the manner in which complex economies are organized and has been remarked upon in numerous essays on contract. But a predictive theory of contract requires more. The critical transaction cost dimensions for describing transactions need to be identified, and the resulting mix of transactions needs to be matched with governance structures in a discriminating (economizing) way.

This chapter attempts to be responsive to these needs and offers a *predictive theory* by identifying three critical dimensions for describing transactions, chief among which is the extent of transaction-specific investment. Uncertainty and the frequency with which transactions recur are the other two critical dimensions. Except in so far as uncertainty may be assumed away — which Robinson (1934, p.250) has characterized as 'Nirvana economics' and which are relatively uninstructive for comparative institutional purposes — market mediated transactions are placed under progressively greater strain as the degree of transaction-specific investment increases. Which governance structures come into play — in support of or to supplant market mediated exchange — is shown to vary systematically with these underlying transactional dimensions. Economizing on transaction costs is the main purpose being served. This interdisciplinary undertaking joins economics with organization theory and overlaps extensively with the work of those contract law specialists who adopt a relational approach to the study of contract.

Although this chapter has emphasized a particular class of contract — namely, commercial contract — the proposed framework for matching governance structures to transactions applies, with only modest changes, much more generally. The possibility that a unified approach to the study of contracting is beginning to emerge is at least suggested. This is encouraging, since a 'fundamental hypothesis of science is that appearances are deceptive and that there is a way of looking at or organizing the evidence that will reveal superficially disconnected and diverse phenomena to be manifestations of a more fundamental and relatively simple structure' (Friedman, 1953, p.33).

Notes to chapter two

1 Sections 2.2 and 2.4 of this paper draw extensively on my recent paper Transaction Cost Economics: The Governance of Contractual Relations, *Journal of Law and Economics*, **22**, October, 233–261 (1979).

2 See especially Macneil (1974; 1978), Goldberg (1976) and Williamson.

3 Macneil (1974) pp. 738–740; (1978) pp. 902–905; cf. section 3.2 in this volume.

4 For a discussion of complex contingent-claims contracting and its mechanics, see

Arrow (1971) pp. 121–134, Meade (1971) pp. 147–188 and Williamson (1975) pp. 20–40.

5 As Telser and Higinbotham put it: 'In an organized market the participants trade a standardized contract such that each unit of the contract is a perfect substitute for any other unit. The identities of the parties in any mutually agreeable transaction do not affect the terms of exchange. The organized market itself or some other institution deliberately creates a homogeneous good that can be traded anonymously by the participants or their agents.' (1977) p. 999.

6 To be sure, some legal specialists insist that all of this was known all along. There is a difference, however, between awareness of a condition and an understanding. Macneil's treatment heightens awareness and deepens the understanding.

7 The material in this subsection is from Williamson (1979a) pp. 856–957.

8 Webster's New International Dictionary of the English Language, 2nd ed., 1959, p. 2066.

9 More generally, the economizing problem includes choice between a special-purpose and a general-purpose good or service. A general-purpose item affords all of the advantages of market procurement, but possibly at the sacrifice of valued design or performance characteristics. A special-purpose item has the opposite features: valued differences are realized but market procurement here may pose hazards. For the purposes of this paper, intermediate product characteristics are mainly taken as given and I focus principally on production and transaction cost economies. A more general formulation would include product characteristics in the optimization.

10 This ignores transient conditions, such as temporary excess capacity. (In a zero-transaction-cost world, such excesses vanish as assets can be deployed as effectively by others as they can by the owner.)

11 On these hazards and their transaction-cost origins, see Williamson (1975) 117–31.

12 Thus a reduction in monitoring commonly gives rise to an increase in opportunism. Monitoring the employment relation, however, needs to be done with special care. Progressively increasing the intensity of surveillance can elicit resentment and have counterproductive (for example, work-to-rule) results. Such perversities are less likely for interfirm trading.

13 This assumes that it is costly for the incumbent supplier to transfer specialized physical assets to new suppliers. See Williamson (1976). Klein, Crawford and Alchian (1978) use the term 'appropriable quasi-rent' to refer to this condition.

14 This seems reasonable for most intermediate-product market transactions.

15 Production aspects are thus emphasized. Investments in governance structure are treated separately.

16 Defence contracting may appear to be a counter example, since elaborate governance structures are devised for many of these. This reflects in part, however, the special disabilities of the government as a production instrument. But for this, many of these contracts would be organized in-house. Also, contracts that are very large and of long duration, as many defence contracts are, do have a recurring character.

17 Although recurrent standard transactions are ones for which an active spot market commonly exists, term contracting may also be employed, especially as planning economies are thereby realized by the parties. The duration of these contracts will not be long, however, since the assets in question can be employed in other uses and/or in the service of other customers. The result is that changing market circumstances will be reflected relatively quickly in both price and quantity and relatively stringent contracting attitudes may be said to prevail.

18 'Generally speaking, a serious conflict, even quite a minor one such as an objection to a harmlessly late tender of the delivery of goods, terminates the discrete contract as a live one and leaves nothing but a conflict over money damages to be settled by a lawsuit. Such a result fits neatly the norms of enhancing discreteness and intensifying . . . presentiation.' Macneil (1978) p. 877.

19 Macneil (1978) p. 880. The rationale for this section of the Code is that 'identification of the goods to the contract will, within limits, permit the seller to recover the price of the goods

rather than merely damages for the breach . . ., ([where the] latter may be far less in amount and more difficult to prove).'

20 As Stewart Macaulay observes, 'disputes are frequently settled without reference to the contract or to potential or actual legal sanctions. There is a hesitancy to speak of legal right or to threaten to sue in . . . negotiations [where continuing business is valued]' Macaulay (1963) p. 61. The material which follows in this subsection was originally developed in connection with the study of inflation by Wachter and Williamson (1978).

21 This assumes that factor prices paid by buyer and outside supplier are identical. Where this is not true, as in some unionized firms, buyers may choose to procure outside because of a differential wage rate. This is a common problem in the automobile industry, which has a very flat and relatively high wage scale.

References

ALCHIAN, A.A. and DEMSETZ, H. (1972), Production, information costs, and economic organization, *American Economic Review*, **62**, no. 4, 777–795.

ARROW, K. J. (1969), The organization of economic activity, *The Analysis and Evaluation of Public Expenditure: The PPB System*, Joint Economic Committee, 91st Cong., 1st Sess., 47–64.

ARROW, K. J. (1971), *Essays in the Theory of Risk-Bearing*, Chicago: Markham.

BEN PORATH, Y. (1978), The F-connection: families, friends, and firms and the organization of exchange, *Population Development Review*, **6**, no. 1, 1–30.

COASE, R. H. (1937), The nature of the firm, *Economica N.S.*, **4**, 336–405, repr. in *Readings in Price Theory*(1952), (G. J. Stigler and K. E. Bouldings, eds.), Homewood, Ill: Richard D. Irwin, Inc.

COASE, R. H. (1972), Industrial organization: a proposal for research, in *Policy Issues and Research Opportunities in Industrial Organization*, 59–73, (V.R. Fuchs, ed.), New York: National Bureau of Economic Research.

COMMONS, J. R. (1934), *Institutional Economics*, Madison: University of Wisconsin Press.

FRIEDMAN, L. M. (1965), *Contract Law in America,* p. 205, Madison: University of Wisconsin Press.

FRIEDMAN, M. (1953), *Essays in Positive Economics*, University of Chicago Press.

FULLER, L. L. (1964), *The Morality of Law*.

GOFFMANN, I. (1969), *Strategic Interaction*, Philadelphia: University of Pennsylvania Press.

GOLDBERG, V.P. (1976), Toward an expanded theory of contract, *Journal of Economic Issues*, **10**, 45–61.

HAYEK, F. (1945), The use of knowledge in society, *American Economic Review*, **35**, 519–530.

KLEIN, B., CRAWFORD, R. G. and ALCHIAN, A. A. (1978), Vertical integration, appropriable rents, and the competitive contracting process, *Journal of Law and Economics*, **21**, 297–326.

KRONMAN, A. T. and POSNER, R. A. (1979), *The Economics of Contract Law*, Boston: Little-Brown.

LLEWELLYN, K. N. (1931), What price contract? – an essay in perspective, *Yale Law Journal*, **40**, 704–782.

LOWRY, S. T. (1976), Bargain and contract theory in law and economics, *Journal of Economic Issues*, **10**, No. 1, 1–22.

MACAULAY, S. (1963), Non-contractual relations in business, *American Sociological Review*, **28**, no. 2, 55–70.

MACNEIL, I. R. (1974), The many futures of contract, *Southern California Law Review*, **47**, 691–816.

MACNEIL, I. R. (1978), Contracts: adjustment of long-term economic relations under classical, neoclassical and relational contract law, *Northwestern university law review*, **72**, no. 6, 854–905.

MEADE, J. E. (1971), *The Controlled Economy*, London: George Allen & Unwin, Ltd.

POSNER, R. A. (1977), *Economic*

Analysis of Law, 2nd ed., Boston: Little-Brown.
ROBINSON, E. A. G. (1934), The problem of management and the size of the firms, *Economic Journal*, **44**, 240–54.
SIMON, H. A. (1961), *Administrative Behaviour*, 2nd ed., p. xxiv, New York: The Macmillan Company.
SIMON, H. A. (1978), Rationality and process and product of thought, *American Economic Review*, **68**, 1–16.
TELSER, L. G. and HIGINBOTHAM, H.N. (1977), Organized futures markets: costs and benefit, *Journal of Political Economy*, **85**, no. 6, 969–1000.
VELJANOVSKI, C. G. (1979), *Bibliography in Law and Economics—Contract Analysis*, Oxford: Centre for Socio-Legal Studies.
WACHTER, M. and WILLIAMSON, O. E. (1978), Obligational markets and the mechanics of inflation, *Bell Journal of Economics*, **9**, no. 2, 549–571.
WILLIAMSON, O. E. (1971), The vertical integration of production: market failure considerations, *American Economic Review*, **61**, no. 1, 112–123.
WILLIAMSON, O. E. (1975). *Markets and Hierarchies: Analysis and Antitrust Implications*, New York: Free Press.
WILLIAMSON, O. E. (1976), Franchise bidding for natural monopolies – in general and with respect to CATV, *Bell Journal of Economics*, **7**, 73–104.
WILLIAMSON, O. E. (1979a), Assessing vertical market restrictions: antitrust ramifications of the transaction cost approach, *University of Pennsylvania Law Review*, **127**, 953–993.
WILLIAMSON, O. E. (1979b), Transaction-cost economics: the governance of contractual relations, *Journal of Law and Economics*, **22**, no. 2, 233–261.

CHAPTER THREE

Economic analysis of contractual relations

Ian R. Macneil[1]

The paradigm for the conduct of exchange in the neoclassical micro-economic model is the discrete transaction. Victor Goldberg (1976, pp. 49, 51) summarizes this point:

> The paradigmatic contract of neoclassical economics . . . is a discrete transaction in which no duties exist between the parties prior to the contract formation and in which the duties of the parties are determined at the formation stage. Prior to their contract, Smith has no duty to Brown; at the time they enter their agreement, in a single joint exercise of their free choice, they determine their respective duties to each other for the duration of the agreement; completion of the promised performance terminates that party's obligations. . . .
>
> . . . the elegance (and, to be sure, practical merits in many contexts) of analytical models based on choice has led economists to suppress the relational aspects of contracts.
>
> . . . economists have treated all private sector exchange as presentiated[2] discrete transactions; firms equate marginal cost to marginal revenue, and how they do this is of no great concern to the analyst.

The paradigmatic contract of neoclassical economics may thus be viewed as 'nothing more than a sale with a time lag, a sale of futures, or, as Morris Cohen once put it, a system for distributing risk'[3].

Goldberg's description reveals that even in very discrete transactions relations are present besides the exchange itself; besides the 'sale with a time lag'. For example, if *no* duties exist prior to the contract formation, then theft by the stronger party is more likely to occur than is exchange[4]. Nor can the parties 'determine their respective duties to each other for the duration of the agreement' unless some relation exists between them, e.g. a system of law, to keep each from doing as he pleases during the period, irrespective of the agreement. Nevertheless, transactions as described by Goldberg are very discrete indeed compared to the relational ways in which most exchange is conducted in the modern world, e.g. through employment and other exchange within a firm, through long term supply contracts, through consortia — the list is endless[5].

The focus of this chapter is on these more relational patterns. After an introduction to the interplay of neoclassical microeconomics, transaction costs and contractual relations it reviews briefly some of the important distinctions between discrete transactions and modern contractual relations. This is essentially description not analysis or, if one prefers, this section is definitional. There then follows an analysis of the problems such relations pose for neoclassical microeconomic analysis.

3.1 Neoclassical microeconomic model, transaction costs and relational contract

The term 'neoclassical microeconomic model' is limited in this chapter to the basic textbook model of the consumer and the firm. The consumer is assumed to be a totally self-interested utility maximizer[6]. This self-interest is expressed entirely through the exchange with other maximizers of particular subjects under examination. Thus the model always deals with interactions between *two* or more maximizing units[7]. The subjects of exchange must be sufficiently identifiable so that the user of the model can tell what the choice(s) concern(s). Normally this means that they must be relatively simple (or simplified in the mind of the exchangers or the modeller).. The subjects of exchange must also be quantifiable in some manner if the model is to reveal interesting information. Assumptions respecting the firm are similar, except that the utility the firm maximizes is profit, i.e. the difference between revenue and cost. This is the model and is, so far as I know, the only model upon which descriptions of economic efficiency in a technical sense[8] and hence predictions of what will constitute efficient behaviour, are based[9].

Since the famous article of Coase in 1960 increasing attention has been paid to the problem of transaction costs in the neoclassical model and a substantial body of scholarship now exists that focuses on it[10]. Arrow's definition of transaction costs, 'costs of running the economic system'[11], may be paraphrased for our purposes as 'costs of running the contractual relation'[12].

Because it is impossible to conduct exchange without transaction costs, and because they are variable, they are every bit as much a factor of production as capital and labour[13]. Any sensible application of the neoclassical model requires their inclusion whenever they are variable, affect other factors and are significant, which is generally likely to be the case. Nevertheless, as Oliver Williamson points out (1979, p.233) economists still quite commonly view transaction cost analysis with suspicion. There are undoubtedly many reasons for this, but I would suggest that one of them lies in the fact that analysis of transaction costs is often *not* neoclassical microeconomic analysis of transaction costs. Williamson's excellent article (1979) 'Transaction-Cost Economics: The Governance of Contractual Relations' and his chapter in this volume illustrate this.

A key element in neoclassical microeconomic analysis is exchange between maximizing units. In his discussion of transaction costs and their effect on choice of contract governance structures, Williamson treats the parties not as exchangers, but as if they were a *single maximizing unit*. For example: 'The interests of the principals in sustaining the relation are especially great for highly idiosyncratic transactions'.[14] This, according to Williamson, leads to the parties making arrangements for either trilateral governance, e.g. contractual enforcement in courts, or to unified governance, i.e. the firm[15]. This is not neoclassical microeconomic analysis, since there is no analysis of exchange or its terms. It is simply an argument that in cases of idiosyncratic transactions the maximizing unit of buyer-and-seller will find costs lower if it adopts a governance structure that sustains the relation than if it does not, just as the maximizing unit might find costs lower if it used coal, rather than oil, in production. The analysis tells us nothing of exchange, of allocation of risks or costs *between* buyer and seller, which is a key aspect of neoclassical analysis.

That Williamson is treating buyer and seller as a maximizing unit, and not making a neoclassical analysis of their individual choices of governance structures[16], may be obscured by the fact that the very subject of their (and his) concern is the prevention of their *subsequently* acting as separate maximizers, of limiting opportunism[17]. But his treatment of transaction costs and contractual governance in a non-neoclassical manner bears out a point made by Lowry[18] concerning relational exchange[19]. In relations there can be present a 'sense of productive increase from the relationship which can dwarf variations in expectation, or of long-term anticipations of mutual benefit that dwarf variations in shares received by the parties.' This 'sense' of the parties may virtually obliterate their separation as maximizers thereby making them effectively a single maximizer for many purposes including, for example, the selection of governance structures. This tendency obviously will be intensified by ignorance at the time of decisions about the consequences of future division of the economic pie. Thus boundedness of rationality[20] is an important factor in Williamson's ignoring of neoclassical analysis. At the time of decision about the governance structures to be adopted the parties will often have very limited information about the substantive effect of those structures on the future division of the pie to be produced by their efforts. For that reason their individual interests are best served by paying little attention to how the pie will later be divided and a great deal to its making[21].

The foregoing discussion implies that transaction cost analysis, whether non-neoclassical or neoclassical, is essential to any useful economic analysis of contractual relations, a conclusion I hope will be borne out by section 3.3 of this essay. It implies, however, no conclusion about whether the neoclassical model, modified by transaction cost analysis (even the non-neoclassical type), is sufficient for useful economic analysis of *all* contractual relations. Section 3.3 raises the question of whether the model, even so supplemented with non-neoclassical analysis, is always a sufficient tool.

3.2 Discrete transactions and modern contractual relations[22]

Discrete transactions differ from contractual relations in respect of many key characteristics. Among those most important to economic analysis are[23]:

(1) Commencement, duration and termination;
(2) Measurement and specificity;
(3) Planning;
(4) Sharing versus dividing benefits and burdens;
(5) Interdependence, future co-operation and solidarity;
(6) Personal relations and numbers of participants;
(7) Power.

Understanding of these characteristics may be aided by putting them in the context of a particular backdrop: how a smelting operation (*Smelter*) might secure the coal needed for its operations. Among the possibilities are:

(*A*) Spot purchase from a stranger of 500 tons of coal in a market of many sellers, *Seller's* agents delivering the coal by truck dumped at *Smelter's* yard, cash paid on delivery of each load.

(*B*) Same, except that *Seller* is the one from which *Smelter* usually buys its coal, terms are 30 days' credit, and *Seller* is tolerant of arrears for fairly lengthy periods.

(*C*) Once or twice a year, the *Seller* in illustration *B* buys as much as 5000 tons at a good price on speculation, but assuming that *Smelter* will probably be interested in stockpiling at a price lower than most of the market; so far *Smelter* has always bought, as it does this time.

(*D*) *Smelter* enters a firm forward contract with *Seller* for 500 tons of coal a week for eight weeks, at a fixed price.

(*E*) *Smelter* contracts with *Coal Mine* to buy all the coal it requires during one year; the specified price is subject to a quarterly escalator clause based on a designated market.

(*F*) Same, except that in addition to the escalator clause there is a provision: 'Should a party become dissatisfied with the price, the parties agree to negotiate about a new price and, in the absence of agreement, to refer the matter to *X* as arbitrator to determine a fair and equitable price.'

(*G*) Same, except that *Smelter* and *Coal Mine* have had similar annual contracts for ten years.

(*H*) Same, except that the latest contract, entered into this year, is for 20 years rather than one, requires *Coal Mine* periodically: to provide *Smelter* with extensive cost information; to allow *Smelter's* experts to monitor mining operations; and to receive from *Smelter* recommendations respecting new equipment, improved methods of management and the like. *Smelter* and *Coal Mine* also agree to build and operate a conveyor belt system from minehead to smelting plant, sharing the capital costs equally and operating the conveyor system jointly. As part of the deal *Smelter* gives *Coal Mine* a five-year loan to cover part of *Coal Mine's* costs of the conveyor system and, in order to satisfy other lenders, guarantees *Coal Mine's* half of a 20-year mortgage loan on the conveyor system.

(*I*) Same, except that the payment by *Smelter* to *Coal Mine* is in return for 20 per cent of *Coal Mine's* shares rather than a loan; *Smelter* is guaranteed two seats on *Coal Mine's* board of directors.

(*J*) Same, except that it is now 10 years later.

(*K*) Same as *I*, except that *Smelter's* percentage of shares is 51 per cent, and it obtains a majority on the board. *Coal Mine's* old management is retained and it is allowed to operate as a largely independent division of *Smelter*.

(*L*) Instead of the foregoing, *Smelter* merges with *Coal Mine* by mutual agreement. *Smelter-Coal* retains the same management and work force in the various divisions of the business, and hires a new engineering manager to supervise the building and operation of a conveyor system between minehead and smelter.

(*M*) Same, except that the merger occurs when *Smelter* acquires the controlling shares of a deceased *Coal Mine* stockholder, all *Coal Mine* management is promptly fired and tight centralized control of all operations is established.

(*N*) Same, except that it is now 40 years later.

With illustrations *L—N* we have moved to the penultimate relational pattern in modern contracts: the large firm itself[24].

3.2.1 Commencement, duration and termination

Discrete transactions start sharply, are short-lived and end sharply, either by clear performance of clear breach[25]. Illustration *A* is the clearest example of this. By illustration *B*, a spot purchase on 30 days' credit, these characteristics have begun (but only that) to erode. In *B* continuing relations between

Smelter and *Seller* blur the sharpness of both beginning and ending, a point emphasized by the occasional arrears. Duration is thus not just 30 days, but longer at both ends because of past and anticipated deals.

In contrast to illustration *A*, or even illustration *B*, illustrations *J* and *N*, for example, show well how large scale erosion of these discrete characteristics occurs in relations. In *J* (10 years into a 20 year requirements contract, joint conveyor, acquisition of 20 per cent of *Coal Mine* shares) the commencement itself of the relation was necessarily extended because it is not possible to plan and agree to such relations overnight. Moreover, the annual contracts preceding the present 20 year contract are sensibly viewed as part of the commencement of the present contract, because they undoubtedly provided much of the information, confidence, etc., leading to it. The expired duration of the contract is 10 years, with at least 10 years to go. So far as can be told, the relation has an indefinite future, with no sharp date of termination in prospect and renewal or other forms of continuance likely. Illustration *N*, where the merged corporation is now 40 years old, illustrates the relational aspects of these factors even more, so much so that commencement, duration and termination have now merged, for any practical purpose, into an operating present coupled with planning for the indefinite future[26].

In the illustrations lying between the most discrete and the most relational, much shading of commencement, extension of duration and blurring of termination occurs. Illustration *G* (tenth annual requirements contract, with price escalation and price arbitration clauses) demonstrates all three points. Requirements contracts of this kind are too complicated and require too much joint planning prior to any formalized commencement to start sharply, even though in the eyes of the law one may sometimes easily find such a sharp time of 'formation of the contract'. Moreover, whatever the bare legal situation may be, certainly the present annual contract did not in other senses 'commence' on the date it was signed, but had antecedent commencement in all the prior relations of nine years. Turning to duration, even in legal theory this relation is for a year, a far cry from the very short duration of the spot purchase in illustration *A*. In fact its duration is more than ten years. 'More than ten' because termination of the relation is not in sight, even though either party may have a legal right to terminate at the end of the current contract. Thus termination is also not sharp. This is not to say that it may not become sharp, e.g. if *Smelter* advises *Coal Mine* of a final decision to secure its coal elsewhere when the present one year contract expires. Should this happen the relation merely moves a great distance in the direction of a discrete transaction in so far as the future is concerned[27].

3.2.2 Measurement and specificity

Discreteness calls for measurement and specificity, as demonstrated by illustrations *A* and *B*, the spot market purchases. Price and quantity must be precisely defined along with the specific product, coal (undoubtedly of specified type, size, quality, etc.). In contractual relations two things happen respecting this factor. First, something that must eventually become very specific, e.g. the amount of coal actually delivered in the 38th week of a requirements contract, may have been very *non*specific at the start of the relation, i.e. 'requirements'. (This aspect will be treated in the next section, on planning.) Secondly, in modern contractual relations, while much either starts out or finishes measured and specified[28], much does not. For example, many kinds of labour beggar any effort at precise specification or measurement *at any time*, e.g. any managerial job, teaching, etc. So too, much of what individuals receive or pay in contractual relations — social and other psychic satisfactions and costs, such as prestige, power, discomfort, companionship, to name a few — remain nonspecific and nonmeasureable not only when initially planned, if they are, but later when actually acquired or incurred. Nor are such immeasureables limited to individuals. Institutions too have immeasureable gains and losses — reflected in the immense difficulty of measuring the goodwill or going-concern value of any firm.

Introduction of the conveyor system at illustration *H et seq*. permits easy demonstration of the foregoing points. The conveyor system and its capital costs may or may not have been specific and carefully measured at the time of the agreement. But whether they were or not, at some point, by the time the conveyor was finally in place and bills all paid, a certain amount of precision and measurement will reign. But it will not be universal — many of the overhead costs of the two companies, e.g. the time of their upper echelon management, will never be allocable to this activity without so much guesswork as to make any allocation almost meaningless. Moreover, even though some past costs may be specific, future costs for any given time will always be largely immeasureable until actually incurred. Similarly, whatever social and psychic satisfactions and costs are involved for the various participants in these joint activities they will be neither measureable nor specific but nevertheless very real. Moreover, their allocation may vary greatly and have marked effects on the relation. Turning, for example, to the later illustrations, there is a marked difference in distribution of such benefits and costs among *K* (*Smelter* 51 per cent control, old *Coal Mine* management retained), *L* (formal merger, otherwise retaining old management patterns) and *M* (merger after takeover, firing old management, centralized control).

3.2.3 Planning[29]

Planning in the discrete transaction focuses on the substance of the exchange, e.g. on the subject of sale, quantity, price, payment terms, as in illustrations *A* and *B*. But in relational contract, the planning of processes for conducting exchanges and other aspects of performance in the future, as well as conducting further planning, assume equal or even greater importance. Illustration *F* provides a simple example in the form of an agreement to negotiate price and use an arbitrator if negotiation fails[30]. In illustration *M* (merger after *Smelter* acquires majority control of *Coal Mine*) much of the initial planning, e.g. the new corporate charter, articles of incorporation, by-laws, etc., is of processes for conducting further planning, although some important substantive planning, e.g. arranging financing and distribution of shares, also occurs. (However, it should be noted that the very concept of share is a concept of process as well as substance.) As the relation proceeds, of course, substantive planning occurs regularly within such frameworks (and others, such as collective bargaining).

As the spot market illustration suggests, the specificity and measurement characteristic of discrete contracts result in very complete and certain planning[31]. On the other hand, when the subject is long-term requirements (one year, formally, in *E*, *F* and *G*, and 20 in *H*—*K*), flexibility must be introduced. If planning is equated with certainty or even with carefully calculated risk planning, this flexibility reduces completeness of planning. While planning of processes, e.g. the corporate governing structure, may be relatively complete for long periods, planning of the substance of exchanges, e.g. salaries, is necessarily relatively complete for only short periods. The very planning of processes in lieu of the substance of exchanges is a confession of incompleteness respecting planning of the latter.

Participation in planning also differs between discrete transactions and contractual relations. In *A*, the first spot-market illustration, market forces resulted in the planning and creation of a certain product, mined coal, as well as a price for it and *Smelter* simply took the results of the planning as given. But even in *A*, *some* mutuality of planning was essential simply to assure that *Smelter's* gates would be open and money to pay would be on the premises. This becomes more obvious in *B*, where the 30-day credit was probably a negotiated provision. As the illustations progress in relational directions, more and more joint participation in planning is encountered, until the merger illustrations, in which all future planning is merged within one complex planning entity[32]. As will be seen in the discussion of power, some of the planning will be bilateral, i.e. negotiated, and some will be unilateral, i.e. by command within a hierarchy of some kind.

Finally, there is a difference in bindingness of planning for discrete transactions and planning in contractual relations. The former is intended to be completely binding on both parties[33]. A high level of bindingness may occur in contractual relations, e.g. the union wage scale for the period of a short collective bargaining agreement. However, because of the need for flexibility in contractual relations, even substantive agreed planning is often recognized as being subject to change, either by negotiation and agreement or by exercise of unilateral power[34]. Moreover, much planning in relations is not bilateral planning requiring further agreement for it to be undone but unilateral planning, e.g. directions by the Vice President for Production. This is in theory revocable by the commander without consent of those commanded. Thus, unilateral revocation, however constrained it may be in fact, is expected to and does take place in contractual relations. In illustration *H* if the conveyor system becomes uneconomic, *Smelter* and *Coal Mine* may agree to scrap it, a bilateral revocation of planning. But in illustrations *K—N* this might be done unilaterally by *Smelter* (or *Smelter-Coal* respectively) over the objections of minority shareholders of *Coal Mine*, employees, unions, etc.[35]

3.2.4 Sharing versus dividing benefits and burdens

Illustration *A*, the first spot-market transaction, sharply divides benefits and burdens, assigning each kind explicitly to one party, e.g. market risks of owning coal pass to buyer when the contract is made and physical risks transfer when it is delivered, the trucking is entirely the responsibility of the seller, etc. This is still true in illustration *B* where credit is extended. But *B* is already a bit down the road towards a sharing of benefits and burdens, since *Seller's* quid pro quo for transferring the coal, the price, is now less absolutely assured, and *Seller* shares with *Smelter* some of the risks of *Smelter's* financial condition, as is demonstrated by the occurrence of arrears. Illustration *C*, where *Seller* buys on speculation with a reasonable expectation that *Smelter* will buy at a mutually advantageous price, reflects a different kind of blurring of sharp divisions of benefits and burdens. For example, if the market suddenly drops *Smelter* might nevertheless buy from *Seller* at a relatively high price because the informal arrangement is of value to it and it wants *Seller* to keep trying in the future.

The requirements contracts, illustration *E et seq.*, show a further mutualization of interests. Should the demand for *Smelter's* produce decrease, resulting in lower production and hence smaller coal requirements, some of the costs will be borne by it and some by *Seller*. Similarly, higher *Smelter* production and sales will usually benefit both parties. The large sharing element in the joint building and operation of the conveyor system in illustration *H* is enhanced further in illustration *I*, where *Smelter* also acquires a direct interest in *Coal Mine's* profits through share ownership. The final illustrations, of mergers, find division of burdens and benefits replaced entirely with sharing between the pre-existing 'entities'. However, it will be noted that division, like measurement and specificity, remains on a large scale within the new entity, e.g. salaries, wages and dividends. Nevertheless, division does not eliminate sharing of burdens and benefits within the entity; modern contractual relations are characterized by both. All connected with *Smelter-Coal* in illustrations *L—N*, for example, will be affected by success or failure of the conveyor system. Variations in the proportion and kinds of sharing and division between particular participants and classes of participants affect the degree but not the existence of sharing.

3.2.5 Interdependence, future co-operation and solidarity

The interdependence of the discrete transaction is so short-lived as to be easily overlooked. This is especially so in any analysis assuming the existence of markets; a participant in a market exchange is not dependent on the other participant to the exchange but is only dependent on the market, i.e. a large number of possible participants willing to supply the goods or services he wants. Thus in illustration *A*, for only a brief period between the placing of the order and performance of the deal on both sides are *Smelter* and *Seller* interdependent. (Even here the presentiation concepts likely to dominate thinking about such a transaction tend to obscure that interdependence.)

The interdependence between exchangers becomes more obvious in more relational patterns. In illustration *D*, a firm forward contract for a fixed quantity at a fixed price, for example, the parties have created an eight week period during which *Smelter* is dependent on *Seller* for coal, and *Seller* is dependent on *Smelter* to pay for coal as promised.

Increased interdependence in contractual relations tends to be accompanied by a need for increased future co-operation and increased complexity of such co-operation. For example, in illustration *A*, the only co-operation required of *Seller* is its performance: loading the coal on to trucks, driving them to *Smelter's* yard and dumping them. And the only co-operation required of *Smelter* is opening the gates, directing traffic and payment. A requirements contract with an escalation clause however (illustration *E*), requires a good bit more, e.g. notice of quantities, delivery times, passing of information about price changes, to say nothing of dealing with the snags inevitably developing in a long-term contract. Moreover, as we move into more relational spheres the co-operation becomes more complex and interwoven between the parties. The co-operation required in illustration *A* is mainly that of producing and accepting an independent performance at the appropriate time(s). But the co-operation required in illustration *H*, which involves a jointly built and operated conveyor system, will be far more complex and the activities of the parties will be far more interwoven.

One aspect of the foregoing is the need in relational contract to co-operate in future planning, planning that will involve exercises of choice. For example, the joint conveyor system will require great amounts of day-to-day joint planning, even after it is built: work schedules, accounting programmes and maintenance programmes, to mention a few. That *Smelter* and*Coal Mine* are likely to create a jointly owned organization to do this for them in a unitary, administrative manner simply emphasizes this point. Indeed, all the illustrations from *I et seq.*, through to the mergers demonstrate increasing intensification of the amount and complexity of co-operation necessary to secure the benefits of interdependence and reduce its risks (and other costs).

The reference to the risks of interdependence raises the issue of solidarity. Interdependence often has a high utility, because otherwise utility maximizers would not incur large costs putting themselves into that state. Moreover, interdependence often generates forces tending to keep it going and to make it a reliable basis for conducting economic activities. For example, the mutual interest in the joint conveyor system in illustration *H* will have a strong effect in keeping *Smelter* and *Coal Mine* securely interdependent in the future.

But present interdependence alone cannot always be counted on to continue without some kind of external reinforcement. Such reinforcement may be found in illustration *A*, for example, in the external forces (among them legal) precluding *Smelter* from hijacking coal trucks and *Seller* from snatching the purchase price without delivering the coal. These will normally keep the parties securely interdependent for the required time, i.e. until the coal is delivered and paid for. Similar external reinforcements, e.g. legal property rights and contract law, continue to play an important role in contractual relations as well. But in addition, internal obligations also develop in relations. For example, in illustration *C*, *Smelter*, having benefited a number of times from *Seller's* speculative purchases, may feel an obligation to share the downside losses out of recognition that *Seller* is trusting it to do so, even though almost surely it has no legal obligation[36].

The word solidarity (or trust) is not inappropriate to describe the web of interdependence, externally reinforced as well as self-supporting, and expected future co-operation discussed above. The most important aspect of solidarity for the purposes of this chapter is the extent to which it produces similarity of selfish interests, whereby that which increases (decreases) the utility of one participant increases (decreases) the utility of the other. This may be demonstrated by introducing 30 days' credit into illustration *A* (spot market, *Smelter* and *Seller* strangers). To the extent that legal remedies for debt are effective, *Smelter's* self-interest in paying *Seller* is identical to *Seller's* self-interest in being paid. (Altruism would be a strange word to apply here, but the upshot may be the same.) Seldom, if ever, is this merger complete but it is omnipresent, immensely significant and, in a vast range of circumstances, complete for most practical purposes[37].

Illustration *A* (with credit added) demonstrates how similarity of interests may be produced by external forces such as sovereign law. This aspect of solidarity may and does arise, however, internally in relations, as the earlier discussion of sharing of benefits and burdens suggests.

3.2.6 Personal relations and numbers

The essence of personal relations in the discrete transaction is what sociologists call nonprimary relations. These involve only a very small part of the personality, are very limited in scope and are nonunique, i.e. it does not matter *who* the other party to the relation is. The contracting and deliveries in the spot market illustrations (*A* and *B*) demonstrate how relatively free of primary relations at least part of a complex economic activity can be[38].

It is unnecessary to go to illustrations as relational as mergers to find primary relations in which 'the participants interact as unique and total individuals' responding to 'many aspects of' each other's 'character and background' (Broom and Selznick, 1977, pp. 126–128). It is unlikely, for example, that *Smelter* and *Coal Mine* would be entering extensive requirements contracts, illustration *E et seq.*, especially repeatedly, without extensive primary relations developing between some sales and purchasing personnel, delivery and receiving employees, attorneys, accountants and probably others. And certainly from illustration *H* (joint conveyor system) on to the more extensively relational patterns, countless primary relations are inevitable in accomplishing the basic task of securing coal from minehead to *Smelter*. Modern internal corporate life may only seldom develop primary relations as close as those in family life but they can be very close and very extensive.

Large numbers are not essential to primary relations — witness marriage and the nuclear family — indeed to some extent large numbers inhibit extreme closeness in primary relations. But large numbers nevertheless have an important role in enhancing relational aspects of contracts because they tend to preclude the *non*primary relations upon which the discrete transaction depends. In theory at least it is not large numbers *per se* in the economy that cause this but large numbers *within* contractual relations not discretely separated. For example, an 18th century cottage industry achieved more discreteness, both among workers and between workers and entrepreneur, than did a 19th century mill. Each worker, isolated in his cottage[39], might perform all the tasks related to weaving and deal only briefly each week with the factor, who brings the yarn, picks up the cloth and pays for it. In the mill, the same number of people, now weavers, mechanics and assistants, operating under the supervision of the mill manager, inevitably become involved in a single, very complex relation, in which primary relations will abound. Increased division of labour, complex machinery, and other factors have led to an organization in which this occurs. Illustration *H et seq.* demonstrate a similar phenomenon at work in modern contractual relations.

Thus, the large contractual relations, which constitute the great majority of subjects of microeconomic analysis, involve large numbers of persons engaged in extensive primary relations at various levels who are organized under a wide variety of bureaucratic structures.

3.2.7 Power: bilateral and unilateral

The only power[40] in the paradigmatic discrete transaction—the present exchange of existing goods — is generated by property rights. These give each party the power to withhold its goods from the other. To achieve what it wants, namely the enhancement of its utility by exchange, that party must secure the consent of the other party. Such power, usefully labelled *bilateral*, is found also throughout contractual relations wherever agreement is required for their conduct.

When exchange is projected into the future, i.e. everything does not occur simultaneously with the deal, a different kind of power is normally created: unilateral power. For example, the extension of credit in illustration *B*, results in *Seller* having power to impose its desires on *Smelter*. If *Smelter* does not pay, *Seller* can use legal process to try to collect the debt, whether *Smelter* likes it or not[41]. Thus, to the extent that such remedies are effective, *Seller* has command or unilateral power, and the parties are in a hierarchial position.

Unilateral power may often be held by both parties, even parties to a quite discrete transaction. In illustration *D* (firm forward contract) *each* party has unilateral legal power exercisable if the other breaches the contract. Patterns of power can easily change, however. In illustration *D*, if the contract allows 30 days' credit for each delivery, *Seller*, once it has made all deliveries, is the *sole* holder of unilateral power.

The unilateral power thus far discussed arises through the exercise of choice. Its content is shaped by the form of that choice, e.g. to purchase 500 tons of coal a week. In a discrete transaction however, the exclusive source of the creation of the power itself lies outside the parties, in this case in the positive law enforcing contractual promises[42]. The exercise of consent simply draws on power made available by the sovereign. Similar patterns occur, but do not stand alone, in contractual relations, e.g. a collective bargaining agreement in America, where it is enforceable at law.

Contractual relations introduce complicating new dimensions to power, bilateral as well as unilateral. Not only does bilateral power continue to exist and to be exercised *after* some originating deal, if there is one, but it becomes a major continuing factor in any continuing contractual relation[43].

Illustration *I*, (joint conveyor system, 20-year requirements contract, *Smelter* as minority stockholder) shows this particularly vividly. *Smelter's* rights to monitor *Coal Mine's* operations, to make recommendations about equipment, management, etc., and to have directors on *Coal Mine's* board are meaningless except as components in negotiational and agreement processes. So too with respect to co-operation in the building of the conveyor and even more so in its operation over at least 20 years.

In addition, in relations unilateral power is not only far more ubiquitous and complex than in discrete transactions but it can be 'turned on' in ways other than by the exercise of choice by the participants. An example is a statutorily imposed obligation not to discriminate on racial grounds in promoting employees, which creates unilateral power in potential or actual discriminatees. Moreover, the source of power itself, as well as its turning on, may come from among the parties not solely from outside them, as in the case of the discrete transaction, where their exercise of choice simply draws on external power, e.g. positive law. For example, the power of a manager to direct particular work activities derives not from external positive law but from the employment relation itself. This becomes especially evident where collective bargaining is present, particularly in a country like Britain where such agreements are unenforceable at law. But the ubiquitousness of this kind of power is derived less from formal sources than from the fact that, like any human relations, contractual relations create unilateral power based on dependencies of various kinds. Among these are those resulting from sunk costs, costs that can be recouped solely through the relation, e.g. the earning years an employee has lost during employment for which he can secure full compensation only if he remains long enough for the company pension to vest.

A further complication concerning power in relations is its common lack of specificity, if not in theory, then in fact. The power of *Smelter* in illustration *E* to vary its requirements for coal is only vaguely delimited even in law[44] and even less delimited in practice. In the merger illustrations, the diffusion of power occurring in fact, in theory or in both, *within* the firm, inevitably creates a lack of specificity respecting power.

Another complication is the interplay in contractual relations between unilateral power and bilateral power. The exercise of bilateral power in the discrete transaction is free of unilateral power beyond that resulting from each party's property rights over the subject matter of the exchange. In contractual relations, however, one or more participants can often bring other unilateral power to bear on negotiations and agreement. For example, in collective bargaining negotiations an important factor may be the unilateral power of management to close an unprofitable plant or of a union to engage in a secondary boycott of the company's product.

Finally contractual relations constantly generate changing power balances. In a discrete transaction, with its single exercise of bilateral power, the power status quo derives from outside the transaction. Thus, in illustration *A*, the extent of *Seller's* power to extract a price for the coal from *Smelter* will depend on *Smelter's* alternatives in an active market occurring in the existing status quo of property rights. The discrete transaction itself generates no force affecting this power[45]. In illustration *L* however (joint conveyor system, requirements contract, complex financial and ownership linkings, after ten years of operation), the relation itself will have become a major determinant of both unilateral and bilateral power positions at any given moment. This will be true not only of the now much interlinked 'entities' —

Smelter and *Coal Mine* — but also of individuals and of organizational sub-units. Thus, contractual relations continually generate their own status quo which affects both bilateral and unilateral power.

3.3 Neoclassical microeconomic analysis of contractual relations

Two characteristics of the neoclassical model cause difficulty in the economic analysis of contractual relations. One is its essentially static character and the other is its assumption of zero relations between the transacting parties whose behaviour is analysed. Both characteristics require brief explanation before examination of the difficulties they cause.

Static character. The static character of the neoclassical model derives from its foundation in the exercise of choice, any particular exercise necessarily (in theory) being an instantaneous event[46]. Of course, exercises of choice may come in rapid succession but logical use of the model requires either an assumption that during the period analysed all exercises of choice will remain mutually consistent[47], or a specific accounting for inconsistencies. In either case the theory is based entirely on presentiation (bringing the future into the present) in which each choice is collapsed into a single instant exercise. If each succeeding exercise of choice is assumed to be entirely consistent with preceding ones, the entire sequence is in essence one exercise of choice made at the beginning. The entire sequence is thus presentiated (the future brought into the present). The model remains static. If, on the other hand, inconsistencies occur and are not improperly ignored in application of the model, then each inconsistent exercise is a new, but fully presentiated, exercise. Using the model then becomes a series of applications to a series of different circumstances, not an expansion of the model into a nonstatic model. Neither route escapes the limitation of the concept of exercise of choice to an instantaneous, discrete event. The neoclassical model remains a unitime model, no matter how much of the future it purports to presentiate, no matter how many times it is applied serially.

Zero relations. Whenever analysis omits any specific consideration of the relations between two parties, one of two logical possibilities exists. One is an assumption of zero relations between the parties or that relations between the parties will have zero effect on the analysis. The other is an assumption that the relations between the parties will be adequately reflected in the factors that are considered, e.g. price. The defects of such assumptions when the model is applied to contractual relations will be explored shortly.

Since transaction costs are the 'cost of running the contractual relation' recognition of their importance brings with it recognition of at least some of the relations between participants in exchanges as factors in the analysis. There is, of course, no assurance that any given transaction cost analysis will, or even can, encompass *all* the relations between the participants[48]. Thus any discussion of the zero-relation assumption requires bifurcation; it must address use of the model both with and without transaction cost treatment of relation. In the discussions following, both possibilities will be considered where appropriate.

Before turning to the specific problems that relational characteristics pose for neoclassical microeconomic analysis, a point made at the beginning of this chapter should be stressed. *All* transactions worth economic analysis, even the most discrete, take place in the context of *some* social setting which creates relations between the parties. Not even the theoretical discrete transaction of neoclassical analysis can avoid an assumption that some relation prevents the parties from stealing instead of exchanging and making promissory words binding[49]. It is important to remember this because distortions resulting from the omission of these relations affect the analysis of any transaction, heavily discrete or otherwise[50]. The most important point to be made here is that relational factors are not peculiar to certain kinds of contractual relations and nonexistent in discrete transactions[51]. Rather, they are present throughout the entire contractual spectrum, although more extensive and complex in some kinds of relations than in others. Thus the points made in this chapter pertain to all contracts even though less acutely to more discrete contracts.

It is worth recalling here that it is the 'textbook model' of the consumer and firm that is treated in the following paragraphs. What follows is not intended as a comment on how existing economic analyses of contractual relations have or have not surmounted the hurdles outlined[52]. Rather it is intended as a description of the hurdles and a comment on the relative difficulties of overcoming them through use of 'textbook theory' microeconomic analysis, even supplemented by transaction cost analysis of a non-neoclassical nature.

3.3.1 Commencement, duration and termination

Extended commencement of a relation fails to fit the instant-choice paradigm of the neoclassical model. The commencement of the relation in illustration *H*, for example, (20-year requirements contract, jointly operated conveyor system, etc.) involves a complex *succession* of exercises of choice and agreement. None of these encompasses the whole relation. The final formal agreement does so in theory (and to some extent, in legal effect) but in fact most of the exercise of choice and agreement precedes its execution, occurring as the mutual planning progresses. The exercise choice is thus an incremental process in which parties gather increasing information and gradually agree to more and more as they go along. Indeed, the very process of exercising choice in such circumstances, e.g. through engineering studies, may entail major parts of the total costs of the whole project as finally agreed[53]. This process can easily lead to decisions that would be irrational if analysed in terms of a single instant choice, irrespective of the moment when it is assumed to have occurred. The very process of mutually exercising choice (assumed in the paradigm as an instantaneous event) involves costs, including sunk costs. Thus the commencement itself of the relation can, *at best*, be sensibly analysed only by a *series* of applications of the standard model as increasing information is acquired[54].

Extended duration also affects the application of the neoclassical model, mainly because of the time it provides for other relational factors to operate. For example, in illustration *J*, where the requirements contract is half-way through its twenty-year life and the parties have been operating the conveyor system jointly for ten years, the passage of time has undoubtedly resulted in the building of many primary relations among *Smelter* and *Coal Mine* employees. Nevertheless, long-term contractual relations, such as those between corporate bondholders and corporations, may lack other relational characteristics to such an extent that neoclassical analysis encounters relatively few relational pitfalls[55]. Thus it is not duration *per se* that matters, but what extended duration permits to happen. For this reason, it is best to examine the effect of extended duration through consideration of the other relational characteristics.

The absence of termination in contractual relations or its projection far ahead, especially at presently indefinite dates, also causes difficulty for an instant-choice analytical model. An element of uncertainty is introduced that must be taken into account: an element that seldom lends itself to accurate calculation in terms of risk. For example, in illustration *G*, *Smelter* and *Seller* have had annual requirements contracts for 10 years and presently expect to have more in the future. This rather vague expectation may easily lead one or both to make decisions that would be irrational if viewed in terms of a termination at the end of the present contract[56] or even in terms of a specified risk of termination.

Indefiniteness of termination also has a durational effect even when actual duration turns out to be short. For example, a franchise terminable on short notice by either party but expected by both to last indefinitely, will generate many more relational characteristics (even though it would be cut off early if things go wrong) than similar relations expected from the beginning to be of short duration. The very existence of such indefiniteness will from the beginning cause the parties to act in ways that might appear irrational if analysed in discrete terms of a predetermined fixed time for termination.

3.3.2 Measurement and specificity

For most purposes the effectiveness of the neoclassical model as a tool of useful social analysis is directly proportional to the information available to the parties when choice is exercised. In illustration *A*, one has little difficulty with the conclusion that, in all probability, both *Smelter* and *Seller* end up better off by reason of the spot purchase than if it had not occurred. This conclusion is based on an assumption that both had at their fingertips all important information needed and that only a rare occurrence, if that — e.g. a bad break in the market — would make either consider the transaction to have been a managerial error[57]. In relational contracts, however, the increase in number of the elements difficult to specify and measure when choice is exercised increases the boundedness of rationality. As noted earlier, requirements contracts and price escalator clauses are, for example, bald recognitions of the boundedness of rationality and of the need to supply a *process* for governing future exchanges without knowing what the substance of those exchanges will be. Neoclassical microeconomic analysts are accustomed to dealing with such problems through risk analysis. But it should be recognised that as contracts become more relational, e.g. illustration *I* (20-year requirements contract, joint conveyor system, *Smelter* guaranteeing *Seller's* loan, and *Smelter* acquiring shares and seats on *Seller's* board), such analysis becomes increasingly tenuous. In analysing such relations guesswork and intuitive judgment must necessarily replace a great deal of rational calculation, even with respect to factors that will at some point become quite specific and measured, such as many of the wage costs for operating the conveyor ten years hence. Most important, however, is the postponement of the exercise of choice to make substantive exchanges in favour of the building of processes and structures, including trust, for conducting exchange in the future. Neoclassical analysis is, at best, ill at ease with all of these 'soft' phenomena.

Further difficulty is caused for neoclassical analysis by factors such as prestige, power and productivity of managerial and other difficult-to-measure labour, that can *never* be quantified. A perfectly rational decision to go ahead with the conveyor system, which includes hiring highly qualified engineer *X*, may look bad retrospectively as a series of little strokes over the years reduces his powers of success but not by enough to fire him. Moreover, the introduction of complex satisfactions (and costs) into the contractual relation deprives the model of its predictive capacity to whatever extent it is unable (or otherwise fails) to take them into account. For example, *Smelter* might choose the route of illustration *M* (merger, firing *Coal Mine's* management, tight centralized control) rather than that of illustration *I* (just described) because of the lust for power of the president of *Smelter*. This might be at the cost of nonmaximization of other *Smelter* utilities, both specific and measurable and nonspecific and nonmeasurable. Failure of the model to take this kind of factor into account deprives it of predictive accuracy.

The foregoing phenomena are not limited to conflict-of-interest issues. It may be, for example, in deciding whether to fire *Coal Mine* management in illustration *M*, that top *Smelter* management is influenced by the need to find prestigious positions for some of *Smelter's* best junior executives, who might otherwise leave the company to *its* detriment.

The most important significance of the foregoing paragraphs in terms of the issues raised here is not in relation *per se* to the long debate about the maximizing behaviour of firms. What is more important is recognition that nonmeasurable and nonspecific satisfactions (and costs), whether involving conflict-of-interest or not, are factors in all complex contractual relations, not just those that have coalesced sufficiently closely to be called a firm. In a great many contractual relations, such as employment, they are of major significance. Any economic analysis failing to take them into account runs serious risks of inaccuracy.

3.3.3 Planning

Planning in contractual relations raises problems for neoclassical analysis because of the static character of the analysis mentioned earlier. As already noted, much relational planning is the planning of *processes* for accomplishing substantive planning and exchange in the future. The choices exercised in planning these processes may, of course, be subjected to a neoclassical type of analysis. But the substantive exchanges later produced by using the processes are no longer necessarily the product of the kind of exercises of choice postulated by the neoclassical model. Rather they will be the products of choice confined by the pre-existing governing structures and processes. For example, in illustration *F*, if one of the parties becomes dissatisfied with the price and the matter goes to arbitration, the arbitrator will decide the price. (The party most satisfied with the arbitrator's decision will have successfully invoked unilateral power respecting the exchange, rather than the bilateral power the neoclassical model postulates.) The model cannot have a major role in analysing such decisions[58]. Since it cannot have a central role in analysing future *substantive* exchanges at the beginning either, in such cases there is never a time when it can do more than fiddle around the edges in analysing substantive exchange patterns.

Nor does the neoclassical model necessarily work better where contract planning is so flexible as to leave future exchanges apparently wide open to free future agreement. For example, at the end of the 20 year requirements contract in illustration *H*, the parties are free to negotiate a new deal with no legal obligations such as arbitration to hem them in. But since each is a joint owner of the still functional conveyor system, for all practical purposes a bilateral monopoly is likely to exist, *Smelter* being by far the best customer for *Seller*, and *Seller* by far the best supplier for *Smelter*. As noted earlier the neoclassical model has little or nothing to tell us about the behaviour of bilateral monopolists (Cook and Emerson, 1978). Yet this, or something like it, is very common in contractual relations, e.g. in collective bargaining (*see* Williamson, 1979, and this volume, chapter two).

A final point to be made about planning is its bindingness. The presentiated character of the neoclassical paradigm presupposes that choice once exercised *is* exercised, that is, that it is irrevocable[59]. This is clearly reflected in its legal analogue, classical contract law (*see* Macneil, 1974b). In relations, however, a great deal of planning, including planning that reflects mutual exercises of choice, is intended to be far less than 100 per cent binding on the parties, i.e. it is tentative to some degree, and known to be at the time of the agreement. For example, in illustration *K* where *Smelter* acquires a controlling interest in *Coal Mine*, even a fairly explicit understanding that the old management would be retained and given much autonomy might very well be understood to be subject to override or serious modification by *Smelter*. Such planning is thus not an exercise of choice within the paradigm of the neoclassical microeconomic model. (How far it varies depends upon how tentative it is understood to be.) Treating it as such is very likely to result in distorted economic analysis.

3.3.4 Sharing versus dividing benefits and burdens

The paradigm of the neoclassical model presupposes sharp division of benefits and burdens between the parties, with one party's benefit equalling the other party's burden and vice versa. This does not preclude application of the model to sharing, as many economic studies, e.g. of sharecropping, demonstrate. But it does require that the sharing aspect be taken into account. For example, in illustration *C*, *Seller's* selling the coal purchased on speculation at less than could be secured from other potential repurchasers would appear irrational in the absence of recognition that *Smelter* had 'purchased' that low price by impliedly agreeing to share the downside risks of the market. Similarly in that illustration, if the market dropped unexpectedly a purchase by *Smelter* at a price above the market price would appear irrational in the absence of recognition that such purchase is part of a sharing relation viewed as mutually beneficial. Similarly in requirements contracts, illustration *E et seq.*, the price cannot be accurately analysed without taking into account the sharing of good and bad risks in fluctuations of *Smelter's* requirements. In the more relational illustrations from *F—N* the need to take into account the effects of sharing becomes ever more important[60].

Thus, to have a claim to accuracy, neoclassical microeconomic analysis of any contractual relation must take into account the extent to which sharing, rather than sharp division of benefits and burdens, is the prevailing pattern.

3.3.5 Interdependence, future co-operation and solidarity

Although much might be written about the effect of these characteristics on neoclassical analysis of contractual relations, I wish to deal with only one aspect: costs. Satisfying needs for interdependence, future co-operation and solidarity (or trust) in contractual relations imposes heavy costs on participants. Illustration *C* may be used to show this as well as some of the difficulties that result for neoclassical analysis.

Suppose in illustration *C* (*Smelter* purchases 5000 tons 'at a good price on speculation, but assuming that *Smelter* will probably be interested in stock-piling') that the market price has dropped, to $34 a ton. In order to break even *Seller* must receive $35 per ton from *Smelter*. *Smelter* pays the $35, although it had no legal obligation to do so and coal was readily available at $34 elsewhere. We may reasonably infer that *Smelter* has paid $34 a ton for the coal, and $5000 ($1 a ton) for the maintenance of interdependence, etc., with *Seller*. So far the situation poses no great problem for neoclassical analysis.

But suppose that the market in question is riddled with this sort of relation between buyers and sellers. Now there is no standard outside the relation between *Smelter* and *Seller* enabling us to measure how much *Smelter* is paying for the coal and how much it is investing in interdependence, etc. If *Smelter* pays $35 a ton when the rest of the market is paying around $34 we may infer that it is buying more interdependence, etc., than other buyers. But we have no idea how much of the other buyers' price is for coal and how much is for interdependence.

When we move from the sale of commodities in markets to patterns such as those in the merger illustrations, the interdependence factor becomes so important and the dearth of external, market-type information so extensive that neoclassical analysis of behaviour becomes virtually impossible. This is particularly so as far as trust is concerned[61]. There is, for example, much evidence that one of the most important of human techniques for developing trust is to make gifts[62], using that term broadly enough to include all instances of giving more or demanding less than required to accomplish a particular exchange. In the case of the latter the 'gift' may be viewed as proof that the giver is willing *not* to maximize utility from each exchange as it occurs, a representation that he takes into account the interests of the other. This poses great problems for neoclassical analysis in the absence of external standards, which cannot be derived by positivist analysis, but only by empirical examination. The difficulties are *not* resolved by recognition that in every exchange each party is trying to maximize on two fronts; first, whatever is the focal point of this exchange, e.g. coal and dollars, and secondly, relational security, e.g. trust. Even such recognition, much as it is needed in understanding contractual relations, leads to a dead-end for neoclassical analysis. As long as the relational mechanism is sacrifice of gain from *this* exchange to achieve relational security, it operates in the exact opposite direction from 'normal', discrete maximization. In the absence of some technique of measuring *one* of these by some external standard, it is impossible to tell from the behaviour itself how much each was being maximized. In illustration *C*, discussed above, where all comparative market data is riddled with dual maximization of coal-at-lowest-price goals and relational-security goals, for example, it is impossible to tell whether *Smelter* was paying $2 for the latter and $33 for the former, or $5 for the latter and $30 for the former, etc.

Almost any contractual relation is replete with this sort of difficulty at all stages, but the difficulty becomes more evident when things go wrong. If there is anything that is plain in the economic world it is that seldom do participants in contractual relations go for the jugular when trouble arises (*see* Beal and Dugdale, 1975; Macaulay, 1963a; 1963b). The high transaction costs of fighting are undoubtedly one explanation, but even discounting for that factor, a huge residue remains that can only be explained by the willingness of the parties to sacrifice immediate exchange-gains to increase relational security (*see* Williamson, 1979, p. 244).

3.3.6 Personal relations and numbers

As stated earlier, the great majority of contractual relations subjected to microeconomic analysis involve large numbers of persons engaged in extensive primary relations at various levels and organized under a wide variety of bureaucratic structures.

Since each of the persons involved is, in neoclassical theory, a maximizer of utility, the base point of examination, to be consistent with the theory, must be *each* individual within the relation. The need to avoid the unmanageability of such analysis has led to such concepts as the firm, which can be treated singly. To do this, however, requires *inter alia* ignoring two cogent factors. One is the presence of primary personal relations *within* the contractual relation, with their immense effect on the complexity of what constitutes individual maximization in any given situation. The other is the necessity for complex bureaucratic structures to organize efforts of large numbers. These also have an enormous effect on human behaviour, including, of course, an impact on primary personal relations and direct and indirect effect on what constitutes individual maximization in any given situation.

This is not the place to revisit the many arguments about the firm as a maximizer. All that is necessary is to point out that the same kinds of issues arise in *any* contractual relation. Moreover, they arise in countless situations where the assumptions of centralized control that permit the concept of a single maximizing firm simply do not apply. In illustration *H* (20 year requirements contract, jointly operated conveyor system, etc.), for example, consider the complex and ever changing primary relations and bureaucratic structures at the interface between *Smelter* and *Coal Mine*.

These constitute a partially independent contractual relation eluding both the autonomous centralized tightness of the neoclassical firm and the instantaneous, zero-relation exchanging processes of the discrete transaction. Any economic analysis with a pretence to accuracy must take into account both the primary relations and the bureaucratic structures involved in this vital, omnipresent interface[63].

3.3.7 Power: bilateral and unilateral

Accurate economic analysis of relations requires taking power[64] into account in a number of ways omitted in the neoclassical discrete transaction paradigm. That paradigm starts from a base in which each party has whatever power is derived from possessing property rights in the goods and services subject to possible exchange. I call this bilateral power, as each party can prevent an exchange by refusing to agree to one.

(1) The existence of bilateral power is a continuing state in relations, choice is not exercised once and for all but repeatedly. Thus to be accurate a single neoclassical analysis must collapse all the possible (and conflicting) ways *future* choice may be exercised into its concept of instantaneous choice at the beginning. This is a very speculative endeavour even in as simple a contractual relation as illustration *E* (one year requirements contract). Engaging in such unitime analysis of more complex and lengthy contractual relations passes all levels of reason and sense. At best, only by a series of repeated applications of the unitime model is any approximation of reality possible.

(2) Ubiquitous, complex and continuing unilateral power in all participants in contractual relations conflicts with paradigmatic neoclassical assumptions that the only power in exchange is that presentiating the effect of exercises of choice. (Unilateral power is that not requiring consent of another at the time it is exercised, e.g. the power to sue successfully for damages for breach of contract, or the power in *Smelter* to decide what its production, and hence its requirements of coal, will be.)

(3) The fact that unilateral power may be switched on other than by consent and that it may be generated within the relation, e.g. in industrial employment relations by the power of a union to discipline a member, necessarily causes difficulties for an analytical model based solely on *consent*-triggered external power[65]. (An example is the legal power to enforce a contract once it is formed by an agreement.) Who, what, when, how and why all require examination if predictive accuracy is to be achieved, as does the question of the effect of the power. Again, the complexity that results requires, at a minimum,

repeated applications of any unitime model, together with an account of the differences in input that occur between those applications.

(4) The nonspecific, diffuse character of much power in continuing contractual relations makes extremely difficult the application of a model that operates most effectively with binary, on–off power, e.g. the right to sell or keep quantifiable goods. How, for example, is the power of the *United Mine Workers* to be taken into account in an economic analysis of illustration *H* (20 year requirements contract, joint ownership and operation of the conveyor system, etc.)? Suppose that two years after the contract is entered, the *UMW* gradually starts opposing certain important practices relating to transfer of coal from the mine face to the conveyor. *UMW*'s power respecting this matter is difficult to predict or measure at any given time, will fluctuate a great deal and is subject to trade-off with others than *Coal Mine* and *Smelter*, e.g. the government coal safety bureaucracy. Nevertheless it may vitally affect the relations between *Smelter* and *Coal Mine* and must be a factor in any accurate microeconomic analysis.

(5) Closely related to the foregoing are difficulties posed by the interplay of unilateral power in contractual relations. As noted above, in the discrete transaction paradigm of neoclassical economics the only unilateral power bearing on the exercise of bilateral power is the property status quo. The model does not easily take into account the existence of diverse kinds of unilateral power bearing on continuing and therefore future exercises of bilateral power.

(6) Relations generate constant change in power conditions, from both internal and external sources. Once again this creates immense difficulties for a unitime model and once again its users can pretend to accuracy only by making repeated applications.

(7) Account must be taken of the propensity of humans to seek power as a goal in its own right, i.e. of the widespread utility of power *per se*. In analysing a discrete transaction, power motivations may be collapsed along with all other kinds of motivations into a single desire to maximize the subjects of the particular exchange, e.g. the least dollars for the most coal, and vice-versa for the seller. But accurate relational analysis does not permit single-minded focus on such specific subject matters as coal and money. In relations the enhancement or maximization of power may often have a utility to decision-makers that will affect the terms of particular exchanges in confusing ways, just as was the case with respect to sharing burdens and gains in order to enhance solidarity[66]. Analysis ignoring this additional 'commodity' is likely to be inaccurate.

To summarize the foregoing, a unitime model, even if applied repeatedly to successive circumstances, cannot cope with the complexities of power within any extended complex contractual relation[67].

3.4 Conclusion

The existence of relations in all real-life transactions raises theoretical problems for the neoclassical microeconomic model founded on the discrete transaction. Even putting aside the theoretical difficulties, however, a range of practical problems precludes effective simple application of the model to contractual relations of any complexity. At the very least this includes a large percentage of real-life contractual relations. Only repeated application of such a unitime model can purport to be accurate and then only if careful account is taken of changes *between* each application. The alternative is to tear out relatively small pieces of the relations and treat them as if they were discrete. But that is not analysis *of the relation* and can make few claims to useful positive (or normative) analysis in terms of the overall relation. The process of repeated unitime analysis, coupled with accounting for change between the unitimes, necessarily becomes so complex and so full of unfounded assumptions as to raise serious questions of accuracy whenever any extensive contractual relation is involved. The addition of transaction cost analysis is a recognition of these limitations, and addition of non-neoclassical transaction cost analysis, such as that of Williamson (1979), expands the area of effectiveness of the model markedly. However, there are serious limits even with these additions. When the limits are reached, those who seek accuracy are then thrown back on other far more complex models with far richer classificatory apparatuses than that offered by the neoclassical microeconomic model.

Notes to chapter three

1 This article was written in considerable part while I was enjoying the physical and collegial hospitality as an Honorary Fellow of the Faculty of Law, University of Edinburgh, during a sabbatic leave from Cornell Law School, and supported in part by a Guggenheim Fellowship. Bless them all!

2 To presentiate: 'to make or render present in place or time; to cause to be perceived or realized as present'.

3 Lowry, letter to author, 3 January 1980. The quotation in the text can be better understood in its context:

> . . . they [certain economists] are insisting on looking at contract as a transaction equivalent to a sale which is explainable by exchange-price theory in the neoclassical mode. From that perspective, what legal scholars call contract is nothing more than a sale with a time lag, a sale of futures, or, as Morris Cohen once put it, a system for distributing risk. In other words, these economists are tending to understand contract solely as a gambling arrangement with a long time lag, so that there is always a loser who wants to *shirk*, *cheat*, or in some way evade his obligation of paying the piper when he finds that he is losing. This is a purely commercial perspective couched in terms derived from trade when values are already created and their fruits are being distributed. There is no sense of productive increase from the relationship which can dwarf variations in expectation, or of long-term anticipations of mutual benefit that dwarf variations in shares received by the parties. These economics people, working from the more rigid neoclassical perspective, seem to insist on trying to evaluate the ongoing

relationships as measurable only in terms of crystallized, quantifiable perspectives at the time of the initial transaction. This approach is more or less necessary if the format of price theory is going to be used. Only by insisting that short-term, subjective greed is the primary measure of personal commitment and that commitments are quantified in terms of the value judgments at the time of the initial transaction, can the subsequent dealings and reactions be analyzed in a consistent, quantitative way, projecting greed reactions through the ongoing dealings.

4 A point wittily made by Lowry (1976); cf. Hobbes (1914) pp. 70—71.

5 Even exchanges appearing to be very discrete, such as purchases and sales on commodity exchanges, are deeply integrated with relations as is evidenced by the complex rules of commodity exchange, governmental regulation, etc.

6 The self-interest may, of course, in theory include desires to aid the welfare of others. But the effect of this possible social impact is severely limited in the model by the fact that the only way to express such socially oriented self-interest is through the terms of exchange of the particular subject being examined, e.g. choosing to settle for less in an exchange than if altruism was not present.

The consumer is also assumed to be rational, i.e. to act consistently with certain basic mathematical principles. He would not, for example, prefer *C* to *A*, if at exactly the same time he would prefer *A* to *B*, and *B* to *C*. While this assumption may appear to be essential to the working of the model, it is not, see e.g. Posner (1977), p. 4. Its lack of importance derives from the fact, explored later, that the model is an instant-time model. All that can be known in its application is that a consumer is postulated to choose something, e.g., *A* for *C*. Whether this is irrational because he would have preferred *A* to *B*, and *B* to *C*, is mere conjecture. No basis exists for inferences about irrational desires that may or may not have been bouncing around in his head. Nor are they needed for the model to 'work'. But, if a consumer is found to make inconsistent selections in rapid succession, the model still supplies no technique for ascertaining whether the consumer started with irrational desires or simply changed his taste rapidly with the passage of time or, for example, had altruistic or other motives respecting another trader in one of the trades accounting for the apparent discrepancy.

7 *Part* of the model e.g. the demand curve, can be examined without paying attention to other parts, e.g. the supply curve, for limited purposes but use of the entire model requires linking the parts through exchange.

8 '. . . exploiting economic resources in such a way that "value" — human satisfactions *as measured by aggregate consumer willingness to pay* for goods and services—is maximized.' Posner (1977) p. 4.

9 Economists would not, of course, purport to describe efficiency in a given situation without assumptions of various kinds respecting transaction costs, externalities, presence of competition, stability of preference, etc. The last-named is necessary because of the instant-time character of the model, discussed later.

10 Williamson (1979) p. 233 lists some of the leading work.

11 Quoted in Williamson's essay, this volume, section 2.1.2.

12 The two definitions merge since, as I have suggested elsewhere (Macneil, 1980), the nation-states, indeed the entire world economy, are themselves massive contractual relations. But the micro-focus of this essay makes it unnecessary to press the relational analysis that far.

13 In spite of his commitment to transaction cost analysis Williamson does not commit himself to such a formal recognition. He differentiates between production expense and transaction costs rather than recognizing the latter as part of the former: 'economizing on production expense and economizing on transaction costs . . . the object is to economize on the *sum* of production and transaction costs.' (1979) at p. 245. Goldberg used this idea, but only in a hypothetical way: 'If the reader can stand a *somewhat strained interpretation*, the contractual procedures can be viewed as a third factor of production . . .' (1976), p. 51 (emphasis added). There is nothing strained about this since transaction costs

meet any defensible list of the essential characteristics of a factor of production.

14 Williamson (1979) p. 249. Idiosyncratic transactions are those where 'the *specific identity* of the parties has important cost-bearing consequences'. Ibid. at 240, see also this volume section 2.3.2 para. 4. An example would be an employment relation where employer has trained the employee for a particular task.

15 Williamson (1979) p. 253. As between the two Williamson argues that the greater the frequency of the transactions between the parties the more likely it is that the firm will be the more cost-effective structure.

16 He does not, of course, imply that these issues cannot be analysed in neoclassical terms, he simply does not do it himself, nor does he evidently think such analysis is in any way essential to the conclusions he reaches. Nor do I.

17 Williamson (1970) p. 234: 'Opportunism is a variety of self-interest seeking but extends simple self-interest seeking to include self-interest seeking with guile.' It is evident from Williamson's discussion in his essay in this volume (see section 2.3.1) that he views guile as an essential element of opportunism. I disagree. For the neoclassical model to be used at all, it is, of course, clearly necessary to distinguish opportunism from self-interest seeking *at the time of an initial agreement*. By definition, self-interest seeking, unlimited by external standards, is the essence of that model and its definition of efficiency. It is, however, unfortunate that Williamson focuses on guile as the distinguishing element because opportunism occurs without guile and guile is not the essence of the problem.

Suppose a corporation agrees to buy its requirements of a particular product from a seller for five years, knowing that seller is planning to amortize over the whole five years its cost of retooling to meet buyer's idiosyncratic specifications. Buyer fully intends to perform. Three years later managerial control of buyer passes into new hands and the new managers find that the product can be purchased for much less elsewhere. Buyer so advises the original seller and breaches its agreement. There is no guile here, either at the original point of agreement or at the time buyer acts in a self-interest seeking manner three years later. But the possibility of such subsequent self-interest seeking clearly was something that both parties would want to guard against with a governance structure. In ordinary parlance, one would have little difficulty in calling it opportunistic.

When stripped of guile, how is opportunism to be distinguished from the self-interest seeking of maximizing units that consistitutes the grist for the neoclassical microeconomic mill? The answer lies in the ordinary definition of the word: 'taking advantage of opportunities with little regard for principles or consequences'. At the time of the original agreement, governed (hypothetically) by the model, no principles or consequences exist counter to the maximizing of self-interest. At the time of the breach they do. But where did they come from?

The principles come from the relation between the parties, particularly from the seller's reliance on it and his interest in not having the buyer benefit in ways contrary to the agreement. (Seller relied, of course, by the retooling, and buyer received the first three years' product at a price not reflecting all the retooling costs.) It served the interests of the buyer and seller as a maximizing unit (or otherwise) to adopt *ab initio* a governance structure protecting the seller's reliance and restitution interests against opportunism, guileful or guileless. Klein, Crawford and Alchian (1979) are in accord in not focusing on guile and in dealing with the reliance and restitution interests as key factors, but under the economic label of appropriable quasi rents. For discussion of the restitution, reliance and expectation interests at law, see Fuller and Perdue (1936–1937). See also Atiyah (1979).

To understand opportunism and the governance structures that deter its occurrence requires its redefinition: 'Self-interest seeking contrary to the principles of the relation in which it occurs.' In the initial, i.e. neoclassical model, self-interest maximizations there are no such principles. In relations there are. We need not seek out here all the sources possibly giving rise to them; it is sufficient to identify one source: exercise by a utility-maximizing unit of a choice to be bound in some way in the future, i.e. in perhaps old-fashioned terms, exercising freedom of contract.

18 Lowry, letter, n. 3, above. In such circumstances there can be a 'constantly shifting base so that a general aura of mutuality is the binding force, with individuals willing to take the initiative in establishing good will by building relationships'. Cf. Williamson (1979) pp. 240–241: 'Other things being equal, idiosyncratic exchange relations which feature personal trust will survive greater stress and display greater adaptability'.

19 For a discussion see Goldberg (1980), who borrowed for his title this phrase introduced some years ago in Macneil (1974a).

20 Bounded rationality might be defined as rationality that knows its limits. See Williamson's essay in this volume, section 2.3.1, for an excellent summary of this important concept developed by Herbert Simon.

21 This must not be taken as suggesting a necessary absence of maximizing behaviour by each party respecting choice of governance structures believed to favour one party more than the other. It simply means that often nothing of the sort occurs or if it occurs involves only limited aspects of the structures.

22 Hereafter often called contractual relations, relational contract or simply relations.

23 Williamson comments on a considerably longer list in Macneil (1974a): 'Serious problems of recognition and application are posed by such a rich classificatory apparatus.' (Williamson, 1979, p. 3 and this volume section 2.2.) True, and one of the reasons the list is condensed here. But his comment, even in context, smacks slightly of wanting to fit the real world to the model, rather than the other way around. A 'rich classificatory apparatus' of *some* kind is essential if contractual relations are to be both understood *and* subjected to successful economic analysis.

24 In terms of the analysis here, *Smelter–Coal* is a bundle of contractual relations or, more accurately, a single extremely complex contractual relation. Since concern here is with the *insides* of relations, it is unnecessary to determine whether in relations with customers, other suppliers, banks, etc., it has become some kind of a profit or utility-maximizing persona or unity. (Employees, including management, as well as stockholders, are considered as being inside the relations. In real life so are the others mentioned above, although the intensity of relational characteristics obviously varies. Distinctions between internal and external are artificial in significant measure.)

On the economics of the firm see Coase (1937) and Klein, Crawford and Alchian (1979). The market–firm dichotomy is not one I accept. Rather economic organization seems to me to follow a spectrum from discrete to relational contract, with the many variations of the firm being relatively hierarchical arrangements towards the relational end of the spectrum.

The ultimate relational pattern of modern contracts in most respects is not the firm, small or large, but the nuclear family. Because it is so revealing of relational characteristics, it will occasionally be used along with the above illustrations as a basis for examining the key characteristics listed above.

25 In the perfectly working paradigm of the discrete transaction clear performance and clear breach are economically identical, since the law that enforces promises is presumed to provide without cost the exact equivalent of performance.

26 The exception is the participation of individuals in the relation; they will come and go. In illustration *J* a substantial number of the people initially involved will probably have died or retired by now. The differences between commencement, duration and termination of the relations, on the one hand, and membership in it, on the other, are explored in Macneil (1980; 1974a).

27 Cf. Macneil (1974a) at pp.786–797, which notes how careful counting, a discrete characteristic, increases as termination looms in relations.

28 This contrasts with many contractual relations in primitive societies. See Macneil (1980).

29 Macneil (1978b) deals with this subject extensively in the context of transactional–relational analysis; cf. Macneil (1975).

30 In fact the example is far from simple. Behind the arbitration clause lies a highly complex structure of process and procedure relating to arbitration. Often the parties incorporate some of this

specifically, e.g. by reference to rules of the American Arbitration Association, but whether explicitly incorporated or not, it is there, much of it in a well developed body of arbitration law.

31 It is possible to overemphasize this. Such legal principles as frustration, impossibility, mistake and a host of hurdles to recovering full damages for breach erode this certainty. Nevertheless, barring relatively rare trouble, the planning is certain and complete.

32 Planning the relation and planning admission of new members, e.g. employees, into an existing relation must be distinguished. See note 26, above. The latter may very well accept what is presented to them, just as do buyers in a market. But even they, once admitted to the relation, start playing planning roles. See Macneil (1980).

33 They can, of course, negotiate a new binding deal undoing the old binding one but that is precisely how such modification would be viewed in a discrete transactional setting and, not so incidentally, in the doctrine of consideration of classical contract law.

34 See discussion below *re* bilateral and unilateral power. Macneil (1978b) deals with these problems in detail.

35 The distinction between bilateral and unilateral, horizontal and vertical, negotiational and command is quite clearcut in theory; in fact the two merge: most commands are subject to potential or actual negotiation with subordinates and most negotiation involves elements of unilateral power on one side or both.

36 *Almost* surely, because the law does develop obligations out of behaviour of this kind, and it would take little more in some jurisdictions for the court to find an implied promise or even an express one from, for example, some vague remark of *Smelter's* purchasing officer. Lewis (1969) and Ullman-Margalit (1977) explore how repeated behaviour develops conventions. And conventions, of course, easily become legal contracts or, rather, avoid becoming legal contracts only with difficulty.

37 The importance in solidarity of factors such as friendship, altruism and other aspects of sociability should not minimized. But, since this essay is addressed primarily to utilitarian analysis, it focuses largely on the more obviously utilitarian aspects of interedependence and solidarity.

38 But only part. *Seller*, after all, has employment relations with the drivers who drive the trucks delivering the coal. The limitations on the usefulness of discrete transactions are suggested by the difficulty of discovering any complex economic activity in which they form anything except a small part of the *total* activity. This alone should make us ponder the wisdom of a broadly applied system of economic analysis founded on the discrete transaction paradigm.

39 Apart from his family, which organized the work very relationally where more than one member participated.

40 Power is used here to mean the ability to impose one's will on another irrespective of or by manipulating his wishes.

41 It is possible to analyse such power in bilateral terms. The party not wishing to perform may be viewed as having a choice of performing or suffering the legal consequences. Its exercising the latter choice may be viewed as a form of agreement with the party with the legal power. There is nothing inherently illogical or incorrect about this but it by no means eliminates the problems posed for neoclassical analysis by the existence of unilateral power. As will be seen, note 59, below, the presentiation assumptions of the neoclassical model preclude the introduction of such a second-chance choice subsequent to the original deal.

42 Choice, of course, turns on the power but it is no more the source of the power itself than the act of flipping an electric switch is the source of power for an electrical appliance. Like flipping the switch, exercise of choice is the act of drawing on power available from elsewhere, the electric generating plant or the law as the case may be.

43 Bilateral power continues to exist either to terminate or modify a discrete transacion after it is entered. But doing either is inconsistent with the presentiation concepts of discrete transactions, *unless* the termination or changed arrangements is viewed as a wholly new discrete transaction. See note 33, above. (The new one is inevitably less discrete than the first one because the participants are no longer strangers or, in real life terms, as much strangers as they were the first time.)

44 UCC s. 2-306(1). 'A term which measures the quantity by the . . . requirements of the buyer means such actual . . . requirements as may occur in good faith . . . .'

45 Viewed in micro terms; in macro terms a Marxist, certainly, and many non-Marxists would disagree.

46 See Goldberg's description (1976, pp. 49 and 51) of the paradigmatic contract of neoclassical economics: 'in a single joint exercise of their free choice'.

47 Cf. Becker (1976), p. 5, 'the combined assumption of maximizing behavior market equilibrium, *and stable preferences*, used relentlessly and unflinchingly, form the heart of the economic approach as I see it.' (Emphasis added.)

48 Especially among devotees of a model so strongly oriented to the notion that individual choice maximizers exist in a social vacuum.

49 A balance of physical power may suffice to prevent stealing and permit exchange of existing goods but it does nothing to make promises binding. Moreover, the kinds of balances of power permitting immediate exchanges between those who would steal (and kill) if the chance arose, is hardly an adequate basis for analysing economic activities in any extant social system. But even if it were it does not take care of the problem of making words into binding promises.

50 It may well be that much heavily discrete transactional behaviour can be soundly analysed in spite of the omission. But given the omnipresence of relations in human exchange, a sound tool to social analysis of general applicability might be expected to *start* with the assumption of relations rather than with the assumption of their nonexistence, as in the case of the neoclassical model (except for its hidden assumptions). The burden would then be on the user of the model who desires to omit the relational elements to convince others that in the particular instance omission of the relational factors does not affect the result in significant ways. This is more than a mere matter of heurism; the assumption of nonrelation between parties is an intensely ideological one.

The opposite assumption is in a sense less ideological, since it happens to be a far truer description of real life. Nevertheless any given insistence on the importance of relations (in general or specifically) may be just as ideological as an assumption of their nonexistence.

51 This is another way of saying that a truly discrete transaction is virtually unthinkable. Certainly it is entirely unthinkable if exchange is projected into the future.

52 There are many ways to 'surmount' the hurdles. Sometimes, for example, very careful transaction cost analysis within the neoclassical model will do the trick. Sometimes going outside the model to other economic tools, as does Williamson (see section 3.1) is necessary. It may or may not be readily apparent when the latter has occurred.

53 Another example is the practice in the construction of complex buildings of having architects, engineers, etc., *and* the building contractor all work together with the owner from the inception of site location, building design, etc.

54 Distortion may nevertheless occur even in the series because the neoclassical model imposes the necessity of taking a series of instant, fully-presentiated pictures in circumstances acted on by the parties as an uninterrupted continuum.

55 Corporate bond relations are by no means entirely free of such characteristics, however, with the role of trustee of the bonds always lurking in the background and becoming an active one in the event of trouble. The trustee is likely to have many relational ties with the corporation and has fiduciary relations with the bondholders even in the absence of trouble.

The absence of most relational characteristics also permits the existence of active markets in long-term contracts of this kind. It is no coincidence that a market should arise relating to an economic area where neoclassical analysis can be most easily applied, or vice versa. Trading of discrete transactional contracts is much easier (and surer) than the trading of complex relations, just as economic analysis is easier (and surer). Contrast, for example, the sale of a corporate bond with the 'sale' of a professional athlete's contract to another team.

56 The fear that franchisees commonly so act is undoubtedly a major factor behind legislation limiting the power of franchisors to terminate franchises, e.g. The Dealers Day in Court Act, 15 USC ss. 1221 *et seq*. Standard economic

analysis of such legislation can easily overlook this factor and thereby reach distorted conclusions about optimality.

57 Any businessman is likely to regret buying high or selling low. But ordinarily, since forward contracts are essential to continued sales and production expected to be profitable, businessmen commonly accept the normal bad as well as the normal good consequences of the boundedness of rationality respecting any given transaction.

58 It may have peripheral roles, such as analysis of decisions whether to push the matter to arbitration or to settle with what can be negotiated, etc. The arguments of game-theorists that their discipline is more in point than neoclassical economics take on added persuasiveness when the subject of negotiations is process rather than simple substantive exchange. Cf. Morganstern (1972).

59 One of the many difficulties with various economic analyses of contract damages is that the neoclassical model starts with an assumption that choice is exercised at the time of the *deal*. (This is an aspect of the static limitation mentioned earlier.) This means that each party is stuck with all the consequences of that exercise. If the exercise of choice is in the form of a promise, that means the promise *will be* performed. But discussions of the efficiency *v.* nonefficiency of various contract remedies necessarily presuppose a second look at whether the promise must be performed (or the economic equivalent: damages levied equal to performance).

Allowing of any remedy other than one actually accomplishing performance or supplying its economic equivalent *changes the choice originally made*. That choice thereby becomes retroactively *either* to perform the promise *or* to suffer a nonequivalent remedy. There may be perfectly good reasons for so treating the party's expressions of commitment, including, for example, a custom that this is what the promise means. But it is completely inconsistent with the logic of the model to say that the promise was an exercise of a choice *to perform*, and then to allow the promiser out with something less than equivalence of performance itself. Since I intend to deal with this problem in detail elsewhere, no citations are given here.

60 The most dramatic illustration of this is the nuclear family, rather than the firm.

61 For recognition of the importance of trust see Williamson (1979).

62 Sahlins (1974); Mauss (1967). The solidarity functions of exchange are analysed in Macneil (1980).

63 This is illustrated by Williamson's treatment of contract governance as a unitary maximizing phenomenon, yet between two maximizing parties, see discussion, section 3.1.

64 As noted earlier, note 40, power is used here to mean the ability to impose one's will on another irrespective of or by manipulating their wishes. The role of power in contractual relations is discussed extensively in Macneil (1980).

65 As Nutter said in his last article in which he rejected the idea that economics could be a universal social science: 'There is also the important role played by coercion. The economic approach is of virtually no use in analyzing behavior brought about through the use of force or the threat of its use, because the economic paradigm applies to voluntary choice, difficult as it may be to define accurately.' (1979), p.268.

66 To the extent that sacrifice is a social technique for building power, cf. Sahlins (1974), the analytical problems presented are not merely analogous but identical (at least in immediate terms).

67 Williamson (1979) suggests one possible approach to changes required in economic thinking to deal with this phenomenon.

References

ATIYAH, P. S. (1979), *The Rise and Fall of Freedom of Contract*, Oxford University Press.

BECKER, G.S. (1976), *The Economic Approach to Human Behavior*, University of Chicago Press.

BEALE, H. and DUGDALE, T. (1975), Contracts between businessmen: planning and the use of contractual remedies, *British Journal of Law and Society*, **2**, no. 1, 45–60.
BROOM, L. and SELZNICK, P. (1977), *Sociology*, 6th ed., New York: Harper and Row.
COASE, R. H. (1937), The nature of the firm, *Economica*, **4**, no. 16, 386–405.
COASE, R. H. (1960), The problem of social cost, *Journal of Law and Economics*, **3**, no. 1, 1–44.
COOK, K. S. and EMERSON, R. M. (1978), Power, equity, and commitment in exchange networks, *American Sociological Review*, **43**, 721–739.
FULLER, L. L. and PERDUE, W. R., Jr. (1936–1937), The reliance interest in contract damages, *Yale Law Journal*, **46**, 52–96, 373–420.
GOLDBERG, V. P. (1980), Relational exchange: economics and complex contracts, *American Behavioral Scientist*, **23**, no. 3, 337–352.
GOLDBERG, V. P. (1976), Toward an expanded economic theory of contract, *Journal Economic Issues*, **10**, no. 1, 45–61.
HOBBES, T. (1914), *Leviathan*, Everymans ed., London: J. M. Dent.
KLEIN, B., CRAWFORD, R. G. and ALCHIAN, A. A. (1978), Vertical integration, appropriable rents, and the competitive contracting process, *Journal of Law and Economics*, **21**, no. 2, 297–326.
LEWIS, D. K. (1976), *Convention: A Philosophical Study*, Cambridge, Mass.: Harvard University Press.
LOWRY, S. T. (1976), Bargain and contract theory in law and economics, *Journal of Economic Issues*, **10**, no. 1, 1–22.
MACAULAY, S. (1963a) Non-contractual relations in business: A preliminary study, *American Sociological Review*, **28**, No. 1, 55–69.
MACAULAY, S. (1963b), The use and nonuse of contracts in the manufacturing industry, *Practical Lawyer*, **9**, no. 7, 13–40.
MACNEIL, I. R. (1974a), The many futures of contracts, *Southern California Law Review*, **47**, no. 3, 691–816.
MACNEIL, I. R. (1974b), Restatement (second) of contracts and presentiation, *Virginia Law Review*, **60**, no. 4, 589–610.
MACNEIL, I. R. (1975), A primer of contract planning, *Southern California Law Review*, **48**, no. 3, 627–704.
MACNEIL, I. R. (1978a), *Contracts: Exchange Transactions and Relations*, 2nd ed., Mineola, NY: Foundation Press.
MACNEIL, I. R. (1978b), Contracts: adjustment of long-term economic relations under classical, neoclassical, and relational contract law, *Northwestern University Law Review*, **72**, no. 6, 854–905.
MACNEIL, I. R. (1980), *The New Social Contract: An Inquiry Into Modern Contractual Relations*, New Haven, Conn.: Yale University Press.
MAUSS, M. (1967), *The Gift: Forms and Functions of Exchange in Archaic Societies*, Cunnison transl., New York: Norton.
MORGENSTERN, O. (1972), Thirteen critical points in contemporary economic theory: an interpretation, *Journal of Economic Literature*, **10**, 1163–1189.
NUTTER, W. G. (1979), On economism, *Journal of Law and Economics*, **22**, no. 2, 263–268.
POSNER, R. A. (1977), *Economic Analysis of Law*, 2nd ed., Chicago, Ill.: Little, Brown.
SAHLINS, M. (1974), *Stone Age Economics*, London: Tavistock.
ULLMAN-MARGALIT, E. (1977), *The Emergence of Norms*, Oxford University Press.
WILLIAMSON, O. E. (1979), Transaction-cost economics: the governance of contractual relations, *Journal of Law and Economics*, **22**, no. 2, 233–261.

CHAPTER FOUR

Judicial control of standard form contracts

M. J. Trebilcock and D. N. Dewees

4.1 Introduction

Standard form contracts have suffered a bad press from both judicial and academic members of the legal fraternity over recent years. At least in a consumer setting, the hostility to standard form contracts seems predicated on two principal propositions. First, it is said that the use of standard form contracts is a manifestation of monopoly. Secondly, it is pointed out that the use of standard form contracts is typically characterized by imperfect information for some of the parties to them. In both cases the legal implication is much the same: the courts should be extremely cautious about enforcing such contracts. This essay attempts to evaluate both the monopoly and informational arguments for limiting the enforceability of standard form contracts.

The monopoly argument is made perhaps in its most strident form by Kessler (1943, pp. 632, 640):

> Standard contracts are typically used by enterprises with strong bargaining power. The weaker party, in need of the goods or services, is frequently not in a position to shop around for better terms, either because the author of the standard form contract had a monopoly (natural or artificial) or because all competitors use the same clauses. . . . With the decline of the free enterprise system due to the innate trend of competitive capitalism towards monopoly, the meaning of contract has changed radically . . . . Standard contracts in particular could thus become effective instruments in the hands of powerful industrial and commercial overlords enabling them to impose a new feudal order of their own making upon a vast host of vassals.

In *Macaulay v Schroeder Publishing Co Ltd*[1] Lord Diplock echoed a similar view. His Lordship said that standard forms of contract are of two kinds. The first, of early origin, are widely used in commercial transactions, are the result of extensive prior negotiations by the parties, and are adopted because 'they facilitate the conduct of trade'[2]. Examples cited were bills of lading, charter parties, insurance policies, and contracts of sale in the commodity markets. Here, his Lordship said, there is a strong presumption that the terms of these contracts are fair and reasonable because they are used by parties 'whose bargaining power is fairly matched'[3].

As to the second class of standard form contracts (essentially consumer-type transations) such a presumption was said not to apply. These were said to be of comparatively modern origin and are '*the result of the concentration of particular kinds of business in relatively few hands*'[4]. Said to exemplify this category were the ticket cases. The identifying characteristics of contracts falling into this category were described as follows[5]:

> The terms of this standard form contract have not been the subject of negotiation between the parties to it, or approved by any organization representing the interests of the weaker party. They have been dictated by that party whose bargaining power, *either exercised alone or in conjunction with others providing similar goods and services*, enables him to say: 'If you want these goods or services at all, these are the only terms on which they are obtainable. Take it or leave it.' To be in a position to adopt this attitude toward a party desirous of entering into a contract to obtain goods or services provides a classic instance of superior bargaining power.

Slawson (1971), in a widely noted article, develops the informational argument against standard form contract:

> Private law which is made by contract in the traditional sense is democratic because a traditional contract must be the agreement of both parties. Unless a contract is coerced, therefore, the 'government' it creates is by its nature 'government by and with the consent of the governed'. But the overwhelming proportion of standard forms are not democratic because they are not, under any reasonable test, the agreement of the consumer or business recipient to whom they are delivered. Indeed, in the usual case, the consumer never even reads the form, or reads it only after he has become bound by its terms. Even the fastidious few who take the time to read the standard form may be helpless to vary it. The form may be part of an offer which the consumer has no reasonable alternative but to accept. . . . The effect of mass production and mass merchandising is to make all consumer forms standard, and the combined effect of economics and the present law is to make all standard forms unfair . . . . The conclusion to which all this leads is that practically no standard forms, at least as they are customarily used in consumer transactions, are contracts. They cannot reasonably be regarded as the manifested consent of their recipient because an issuer could not reasonably expect that a recipient would read and understand them (ibid., pp. 530, 531, 544).

A similar view is expressed by Lord Reid in *Suisse Atlantique*[6]:

> The consumer has no time to read [standard form clauses], and if he did read them, he would probably not understand them. And if he understands and objects to any of them, he would probably be told he could take it or leave it[7].

Notwithstanding these criticisms of standard form contracts, the critics also sometimes acknowledge that they are not solely engines of abuse. For example, Karl Llewellyn (1931, p. 731), who viewed standard form contracts as often amounting 'to the exercise of unofficial government of some by others, via private law', acknowledged the following virtues:

> They save trouble in bargaining. They save time in bargaining. They infinitely simplify the task of internal administation of a business unit, of keeping tabs on transactions, of knowing where one is at, of arranging orderly expectation, orderly fulfilment, orderly planning. They ease administration by concentrating the need for discretion and decision in such personnel as can be trusted to be discreet. This reduces human wear and tear, it cheapens administration, it serves the ultimate consumer. Standardizing contracts is in this a counterpart of standardizing goods and production processes, as well as a device for the adjustment of law to need (Llewellyn, 1939, p. 701).

Kessler (1943, p.632) also acknowledged that 'in so far as the reduction of costs of production and distribution thus achieved is reflected in reduced prices, society as a whole ultimately benefits from the use of standard contracts. And there can be no doubt that this has been the case to a considerable extent.' Slawson (1971, p. 530) similarly accepts that 'the predominance of standard forms is the best evidence of their necessity. They are characteristic of a mass production society and an integral part of it. They provide information and enforce order. . . . These services are essential, and if they are to be provided at reasonable cost, they must be standardized and mass produced like other goods and services in an industrial economy.'

In addition to his comments in *Macaulay v Schroeder Publishing Co Ltd* on the role of standard form contracts in commercial markets[8], Lord Diplock in *Federal Commerce v Tradax Export*[9] elaborated on the advantages of standard form contracts, at least in commercial transactions[10]:

> No market such as freight, insurance or commodity market, in which dealings involve the parties entering into legal relations of some complexity with one another, can operate efficiently without the use of standard forms of contract and standard clauses to be used in them. Apart from enabling negotiations to be conducted quickly, standard clauses serve two purposes. First, they enable those making use of the market to compare one offer with another to see which is better; and this, as I have

pointed out, involves considering not only the figures for freight, demurrage and despatch money, but those clauses of the charterparty that deal with the allocation of misfortune risks between charterer and shipowner, particularly those risks which may result in delay. The second purpose served by standard clauses is that they become the subject of exegesis by the courts so that the way in which they will apply to the adventure contemplated by the charterparty will be understood in the same sense by both the parties when they are negotiating its terms and carrying them out.

These various advantages of standard form contracts all essentially reduce to savings in transaction costs, in economic terms. In fashioning a legal strategy, whether judicial, legislative or administrative, for policing the enforceability of standard form contracts, the relative weights to be attached to the three dominant characteristics imputed to them, i.e. monopoly, information asymmetries and reductions in transaction costs, must be established. That standard form contracts are able to realize reductions in transaction costs seems uncontroversial, even amongst critics of such contracts, and we therefore focus our attention on the first two characteristics, which, as we will see, are much more problematic. How we resolve these issues is not a trivial matter for the law of contracts; Slawson (1971, p. 259) asserts, probably correctly, that:

> Standard form contracts probably account for more than ninety-nine percent of all the contracts now made. Most persons have difficulty remembering the last time they contracted other than by standard form; except for casual oral arrangments, they probably never have. But if they are active, they contract by standard form several times a day. Parking lot and theater tickets, package receipts, department store charge slips, and gas station credit card purchase slips are all standard form contracts.

The importance of anchoring any doctrinal restrictions on the enforceability of standard form contracts firmly in well-founded rationales is illustrated by the history of the doctrine of fundamental breach. The doctrine had its origins in judicial attacks on disclaimer clauses in consumer standard form contracts which excluded all liability for product defects. As the doctrine has since evolved, it is at once both too narrow and too wide. It is too narrow in that there appears to be no reason at all why judicial intervention on the ground of transactional unfairness should be confined to 'fine print' disclaimer clauses which exclude or limit liability with respect to product defects. All kinds of other 'fine print' clauses in contracts, such as consumer credit or insurance contracts, seem to raise exactly the same kinds of problems as disclaimer clauses. Moreover, to focus a rule of invalidity exclusively on disclaimer clauses in contracts is to invite the substitution of other 'harsh' clauses in the same contracts. For example, despite a long line of 'ticket' cases invalidating disclaimer or limitation of liability clauses, in *Bata v City Parking Canada Ltd*[11], the Ontario Supreme Court held that a parking lot ticket which emphasized that charges were for 'parking space only' turned the contract from a bailment into a licence and excluded the normal duties of a bailee. Previous decisions had held that fundamental breach of these duties could not be protected by a disclaimer clause[12]. Secondly, the doctrine is clearly too wide in the sense that it allows business parties of significant substance and sophistication to avoid contractual obligations entered into, as far as one can tell, with full appreciation of their implications. For example, in *Canso Chemicals Ltd v Canadian Westinghouse Co Ltd*[13] a company operating a new $8 million chemical plant had purchased a piece of electrical machinery (a rectifier) for the plant costing $266 380. The contract contained a clause excluding liability of the seller for defects in the machinery in respect of any special or consequential damages or damages for loss of use. The machinery was operating at less than full capacity for a period while defects in it were remedied by the seller. The buyer sued the seller for loss of profits incurred during this period. The majority of the court allowed recovery holding that the defects were sufficiently serious as to amount to a fundamental breach of contract, to which the limitation of liability clause was inapplicable. The dissenting judge pointed out[14] that it was incongruous to be applying this doctrine to a transaction between two 'very large companies, with wide experience in selling and buying equipment and other products. This is not the typical case of conditions in fine print on the back of a ticket or bill of lading where ". . . the customer has not time to read them, and if he did read them, he would probably not understand them. And if he did understand and object to any of them, he would generally be told he could take it or leave it"[15]. It is rather a case "where parties are bargaining on terms of equality and a stringent exemption clause is accepted for a quid pro quo or other good reason"[16].'

Similarly, in *Harbutt's Plasticine v Wayne Tank and Pump Co Ltd*[17] where a substantial manufacturing concern was able to escape the effects of a limitation of liability clause in a machinery supply and installation contract into which it had apparently entered with its eyes open, and to upset the insurance arrangements that had been made by the defendant on the basis of the quite reasonable understanding that it was protected by its exculpatory clause[18]. Why? There may have been very good reasons, in terms of policy, for so holding but these were not articulated by the court. Certainly, *Canso Chemicals* and *Harbutt's Plasticine* seem a long way removed from the type of transactions involved in the early fundamental breach cases, such as *Karsales v Wallis*[19] where a used car which the consumer had bought from a dealer was left at the consumer's premises at night a mere shell, with the cylinder head broken, all valves burnt out, two pistons broken and incapable of self-propulsion. Intuitively, the court's rejection of the seller's attempts to take refuge behind a disclaimer clause in a standard form contract seems defensible. However, failure by the courts to specify the basis of such an intuition has led to the erection of a legal doctrine that has become aimless and incoherent in its application. Fortunately, the recent decision of the House of Lords in *Photo Production Ltd v Securicor Transport Ltd*[20], rejecting the doctrine in a commercial setting, holding that commercial parties should be free to allocate risks in any way they see fit, and overruling *Harbutt's Plasticine*, appears to recognize this danger. This recognition is further reflected in the enactment of the UK Unfair Contract Terms Act 1977[21], which invalidates some types of terms outright, while subjecting others to a test of 'reasonableness' informed, in some cases, by enumerated statutory criteria. This forthright approach to unfair contract terms reduces the need for courts to engage in the 'contortions' criticized by the House of Lords in *Photo Production Ltd*. However, the open textured nature of the discretion with which the courts are invested in various contexts under the Act means that courts remain a central control agent in many standard-form contract settings. The importance of soundly-based judicial constraints on the enforceability of standard form contracts therefore remains undiminished.

4.2 Standard form contracts and monopoly

4.2.1 Problems of diagnosis

The difficulties that courts are liable to encounter in evaluating the validity of a claim that the use of a standard form contract is evidence of monopoly power and thus a ground for non-enforceability, perhaps under the rapidly developing doctrines of unconscionability and inequality of bargaining power or under the statutory discretion conferred on them by the Unfair Contract Terms Act 1977, is well illustrated by the decision of the House of Lords in *Macaulay v Schroeder Publishing Co Ltd*[22]. The central facts in the case were these. An unknown 21-year-old popular-songwriter (hereinafter the plaintiff) entered into a contract in 1966 with a firm of music publishers (hereinafter the defendants). Under this contract (in standard form) the plaintiff assigned the copyright to all his songwriting output for the term of the contract to the defendants in return for agreed royalties (generally 50 per cent of the net royalties received by the defendants) in the event of songs being published. The term was for five years, renewable automatically for a further five years if the plaintiff's royalties during the first term exceeded £5000. The defendants could terminate the agreement at any time on one month's notice, and were entitled to assign it and any copyright held under it, without the consent of the plaintiff. The plaintiff had no right to terminate and could only assign the agreement with the consent of the defendants. The plaintiff received a payment of £50 against future royalties on the signing of the agreement. A unanimous court (Lords Reid, Diplock, Simon and Kilbrandon and Viscount Dilhorne) held that the contract, in so far as it was unperformed, was unenforceable, affirming a unanimous decision of the Court of Appeal (Russell and Cairns LJJ and Goulding J) that the contract was contrary to public policy[23]. In each case the exclusive character of the contract was held to impose unreasonable restraints on the ability of the plaintiff to market his services.

Lord Diplock after expressing the views quoted above on standard form contracts went on to point out that the fact that the defendants' bargaining power *vis-à-vis* the plaintiff was strong enough to enable them to adopt this take-it-or-leave-it attitude raised no presumption that they had used it to drive an unconscionable bargain but that special vigilance on the part of the court was called for to see that they had not. The fact that the court struck down the contract means, of course, that in the court's view the defendants' superior bargaining power had in fact been abused in the terms they had exacted from the plaintiff.

It is submitted that the assumptions underlying Lord Diplock's analysis of the use of standard form contracts are fallacious. First, the proposition that the use of consumer standard-form contracts is the result of the concentration of market power is generally without factual foundation. The reason why such contracts are used is exactly the same as for their use in a commercial context, that is to 'facilitate the conduct of trade' or, in economic terms, to reduce transaction costs. If an agreement had to be negotiated and drafted from scratch every time a relatively standard transaction was entered into, the costs of transacting for all parties involved would escalate dramatically. Moreover, it is a matter of common observation that standard forms are used (for this reason) in countless contexts where no significant degree of market concentration exists. Dry-cleaners have standard form dry-cleaning agreements, hotels standard registration forms, credit grantors standard financing agreements, insurance companies standard life, fire and automobile insurance policies, real estate agents standard sale and purchase agreements, landlords standard leases, restaurants set menu and price lists, and, for that matter, department and grocery stores set product ranges and price terms. The fact that in these cases a supplier's products are offered on a take-it-or-leave-it basis is evidence not of market power but of a recognition that neither producer nor consumer interests are served by incurring the costs involved in negotiating separately every transaction. Moreover, even the presence of dickering between parties, standing alone, is ambiguous as between the presence or absence of competition. Dickering may, for example, be merely a reflection of attempts by a monopolist to price discriminate among customers by ascertaining and exploiting different demand elasticities. The use of standard forms is a totally spurious proxy for the existence of market power. The real measure of market power is not whether a supplier presents his terms on a take-it-or-leave-it basis but whether the consumer, if he decides to 'leave it', has available to him a workably competitive range of alternative sources of supply. Whether this is or is not so simply cannot be derived intuitively from the fact that a particular supplier is offering non-negotiable standard-form terms. It is a matter for independent inquiry. If the market is workably competitive, any supplier offering uncompetitive standard-form terms will have to reformulate his total package of price and non-price terms to prevent consumers (at least consumers at the margin, who are the decisive consideration in such a market) from switching their business to other competitors. This point is acknowledged by Slawson (1971, p. 553):

> It is not an absence of an opportunity to dicker, but a narrowing of choice which coerces, and a sufficient range of choice to make a contract non-adhesive is present if an individual has the ability to choose among a variety of materially different standard forms, although he may be powerless to change any of them by 'dickering'.

Again, whether there is 'a sufficient range of choice' available is a matter for independent inquiry.

It is, of course, true that general use of common standard-form contracts throughout an industry may, on occasion, be evidence of cartelization. But here one must be discriminating. If a reasonable choice of different packages of price and non-price terms is available in the market, albeit all through the medium of different standard-form contracts, then obviously the allegation of a 'fix' will not stand up. Even where all contracts are the same, in perfectly competitive markets where the product is homogenous, commonality of terms is what one would expect to find (for example, the wheat market). Every supplier simply 'takes' his price and probably other terms from the market and is powerless to vary them. In a perfectly competitive market, with many sellers and many buyers each supplying or demanding too insignificant a share of total market output to influence terms, all participants, sellers and buyers, are necessarily confronted with a take-it-or-leave-it proposition. Thus uniformity of terms, standing alone, is ambiguous as between the presence or absence of competition.

It is clear that the music publishing industry does not conform to all the criteria of a perfectly competitive market, given that the products (that is, the service packages) offered by different suppliers to composers are presumably widely differentiated. Because each package may possess a degree of uniqueness, each supplier may have a small measure of ability to adjust price and output combinations in relation to his differentiated product[24]. But, provided that a substantial measure of substitutability is possible between one supplier's product and those of others, the market is a workably competitive as most real-world markets are likely to be. Moreover, as experience in the anti-trust context has demonstrated, an industry whose products are widely differentiated will almost never be able to sustain a stable cartel, as the possibilities for cheating on agreed price and output restrictions are extensive and largely unpoliceable. This difficulty in the way of effective cartelization is, of course, compounded if the industry comprises many firms and entry barriers are low; both of these conditions are features of the music publishing industry, as we shall see.

The suggestion by Lord Diplock that consumer standard-form contracts are explicable only on the basis that they are dictated by a party whose bargaining power, either exercised alone (monopolization) or in conjunction with others (cartelization), enables him to adopt the position that these are the only terms on which the product is obtainable, simply does not stand up as a matter of *a priori* analysis. This is not to suggest that monopolization or cartelization may not in fact have been present in *Macaulay*. But not a shred of relevant evidence was adduced on this issue.

In contrast, in the landmark US case on manufacturers' products liability, *Henningsen v Bloomfield Motors Inc*[25], where the New Jersey Supreme Court struck down as unconscionable certain restrictive provisions in Chrysler's new car warranty, the court relied heavily on the fact that the 'Big Three' automobile manufacturers controlled 93.5 per cent of passenger-car production in 1958 and that the warranty was a uniform warranty promulgated by the Automobile Manufacturers Association comprising all the major automobile manufacturers, including Chrysler. Thus the existence of substantial and demonstrated market power and proof of explicit cartelization in relation to warranty terms provided a defensible basis for judicial intervention. The court said: 'The gross inequality of bargaining position occupied by the consumer in the automobile industry is thus apparent. There is no competition among car makers in the area of the express warranty. Where can the car buyer go to negotiate for better protection?'[26] The court in *Macaulay* was in a position to say none of these things. Indeed, had it chosen to examine data on the structure and performance of the music industry (which it did not), it is unlikely that it could have defended contractual invalidation on a monopolization or cartelization rationale. Before looking at this data, one or two preliminary observations are in order.

First, even if market concentration exists, there will be the intractable problem, highlighted in many anti-trust cases, of determining whether, and to what extent, it has produced anti-competitive effects. Relative long-run industry profit rates are sometimes considered an alternative or additional, indicator of non-competitive behaviour, and may be equally relevant in a case such as *Macaulay*. However, for a variety of reasons, neither the market-concentration test, the profit-rate test nor related tests can be readily applied in practice to yield reliable predictions of non-competitive behaviour (Scherer, 1980, p. 56 *et seq.*). Whether in ordinary civil litigation between private parties there will normally be sufficient economic incentive for parties to invest in the complex task of producing reliable economic evidence on the issue of abuse of market power raises further problems[27].

Secondly, the corporate structure of the defendants in *Macaulay* made it presumptively implausible that they had monopoly power or were playing a dominant firm role in the industry. The defendants were a wholly owned subsidiary of a US parent company, whose sole shareholders and directors were a husband and wife. They were also the sole directors of the defendant subsidiary[28].

With respect to aggregate data on the United Kingdom music industry, unfortunately the British Census of Production does not disaggregate the numbers of firms or concentration data for either the music-publishing industry or the record-manufacturing industry. However, to cite suggestive figures, *Billboard's* 1975–76 International Buyer's Guide lists 428 United Kingdom music publishers (after consolidating affiliates). While the defendants in *Macaulay* appear to have been only in the music-publishing business, significant integration between music publishing and record manufacturing has occurred, so that figures on record manufacturers are also worth citing. *Billboard* lists 276 United Kingdom record and tape manufacturers/distributors/importers (after consolidating affiliates and multiple labels) and 54 independent record producers. These numbers appear to suggest a dynamic and highly competitive music industry, probably comprising more competing firms than several of the industries cited in Lord Diplock's first category.

Because experience has shown that industry type tends to generate similar industry structures across industrialized economies, patterns in the United States music industry are worth brief mention (Caves, 1977, pp. 18–19; Scherer, 1980, pp. 50–51). In 1965, an executive of a United States music publishing house in a description of the industry, said that there are 'thousands' of music-publishing firms in the United States, one of the reasons being that they can be started up with very little capital: many attorneys know that often the only space required is a file drawer in their office and a telephone answering service. The industry was described as highly volatile, with a large annual turnover of firms (Brettler, in Taubman, 1965, p. 8). *Billboard's* 1975–76 International Buyer's Guide lists 1466 United States music publishers (after consolidating affiliates), 1027 record manufacturers (after consolidating affiliates and multiple labels) and 404 independent record producers.

4.2.2 Problems of prescription

The intent of the doctrine of inequality of bargaining power, at least as applied in *Macaulay* to standard form contracts, is clearly to redistribute the incidence of costs between contracting parties, for example, to make it less costly for songwriters to secure publishers' services and more costly for publishers to provide them or, in other words, to adjust the relative values exchanged.

The effects of the doctrine can most easily be considered by taking two polar market models: a perfectly competitive market and a monopolized market[29]. By assumption, in a perfectly competitive market both for the final product and for intermediate inputs, no excess profits are being made (that is, no profits beyond a reasonable return on capital), so that any reduction in industry profits will also induce a reduction in output and thus in intermediate inputs (for example, the work of unknown songwriters). The response of firms in such a market to a cost-increasing rule (for example, all contracts terminate on non-publication) will be to offset this cost increase with an appropriate reduction in the prices they are willing to pay for songwriters' services as a factor input in the production of music or records. In the music publishing industry, the most obvious way of reducing the price paid for songwriters' services is for firms to cut their royalty rates. Alternatively, or in addition, because of the reduced prospect now of returns on successful composers' efforts (because of greater ease of contractual termination) publishers in their turn will presumably find it no longer rational to make the same investment in promoting unknown songwriters. Probably they will 'carry' high risks for shorter periods before setting them adrift. If this is what unknown songwriters were really demanding, why had not some publishers in the market already found it in their interests to meet that demand? If, going further than regulating termination provisions, royalty rates were also frozen at their previous level by an additional rule, firms would then reduce their demand for this class of writer, perhaps partly substituting the services of more established songwriters by paying them more to produce more, or the services of 'unknown' songwriters from other jurisdictions. Indeed, at the limit, music publishers may demand that composers compensate them directly for their promotional efforts on a composer's behalf, thus inducing a composer (rather than a publisher), in effect, to make an investment in human capital by securing at his own expense the services of an agent (a common arrangement in other contexts). In other words, any attempt to regulate the full wage (that is, the nominal wage plus other, non-explicit, 'wage' terms of the contract which regulate returns to the recipient) payable to unknown songwriters will operate like a minimum wage law, perhaps benefiting some writers whose services continue to be retained and prejudicing others whose services are displaced by substitution away from them and towards other factors of production[30]. The lesson of economics, in this context, is that legal liability rules are unlikely to be able to affect the broad balance of advantage between buyers and sellers.

If the market for the final products of songwriters' service is monopolized, the analysis changes little. A single music publisher, acting as a monopolist in the sale of a songwriter's output, is also likely to respond to a cost-increasing rule (for example, termination on non-publication) by reducing royalties or 'carry' periods. He has limited ability (depending on the price elasticity of demand and supply for his product)[31] to pass on increased costs to consumers of the final product, and thus has an incentive to minimize costs in a similar way to firms in a competitive industry. Even assuming supra-competitive profits, further rules which proscribe reductions in royalty rates or other contract variations (that is, increase the full wage to songwriters) will generate similar economic incentives to those facing firms in a competitive industry to make substitutions of other factors. Even the relatively enlightened decision in *Henningsen*[32] fails to address the likely response of automobile manufacturers (assuming monopoly power) to imposed warranty terms of greater stringency than those previously prevailing and whether consumers end up any further ahead in the light of that response.

Only in the situation where a music publisher is acting as a monopsonist (that is, sole buyer) of songwriters' factor-inputs in the production of the final products being marketed by the publisher could rules imposing an increase in the full wage payable to songwriters avoid displacement effects[33]. The problems of identifying such a factor market and of determining the magnitude of an imposed wage increase which is possible without creating displacement effects are, however, acute[34].

In short, to attempt comprehensive wage rate regulation and control over employment of factors by judicial fiat in an industry like the music publishing industry, with many firms and substantial product differentiation, would make the acknowledged problems of public utility regulation look easy. Anything less comprehensive is like squeezing putty.

4.3 Standard form contracts and information asymmetries

4.3.1 Problems of diagnosis

Clearly, for the transaction cost savings attributed to standard form contracts to be realized, almost by definition there can be little or no bargaining by parties to individual transactions about the terms proposed in a supplier's standard form contracts, at least outside the broad parameters of price, subject matter and quantity. We have already noted that the absence of dickering about terms is unremarkable in itself if the consumer has a sufficient range of choice of contractual offerings available to him in the market. However, while dickering in individual transactions may not be indispensable to equality of bargaining power between consumer and supplier, the argument can plausibly be made that at least a consumer needs to be able to read and understand the alternative contractual offerings available to him in order to realize the advantages of choice. A criticism of standard form contracts, as we have seen, has been that typically the consumer neither reads nor understands the contents of most standard form contracts that he/she enters into. For the purposes of the ensuing discussion, it will be assumed that this claim is frequently true. Does it follow that a supplier has an unconstrained ability to impose uncompensated risks or obligations unilaterally on an uninformed consumer?

We would argue that even where a consumer has not read or understood the terms of a standard form contract, it will not necessarily follow that a supplier is an unconstrained term-setter. One of the most important determinants of whether contract terms in such circumstances might be considered fair, in the sense of having been effectively disciplined by market forces, is the role of the marginal consumer (*see* Schwartz and Wilde, 1979). In the standard form context, his presence may influence the general market behaviour of a supplier at two separate junctures: at the time of contract formation and at the time of performance.

With respect to the determination of the initial terms of a contract, the issue will be whether, at the margin of the market, there are enough consumers who are sensitive to the content of these terms to bring effective pressure to bear on suppliers, e.g. by threatening to switch business, to modify them in an acceptable way. Thus, it is conceivable that if only 10 per cent of the buyers of a particular class of goods or services studied all terms scrupulously before contracting and were influenced in their choice of contractual offerings by their evaluation of the so-called fine print clauses, this might create effective competitive pressures on each supplier in the relevant market to adjust the terms of all his contracts so as to minimize the risk of losing the potential business.

Perhaps more important than the impact of marginal consumers on the initial formulation of standard form contracts terms is their impact on the subsequent enforcement of these terms. A consumer's expectations as to reasonable performance by a supplier will, in many cases, be shaped not by the terms contained in the formal contract (which we are assuming he has not read or understood) but by a complex set of other factors, including previous general or specific market experience, advertising claims etc. A supplier, in deciding whether to avail himself of terms in a contract which excuse performance but which deviate from consumer expectations so derived, may have to reckon with a potential consumer reaction that treats this as tantamount to contractual non-performance. This may take the form of threats to initiate legal proceedings, threats to withdraw future business, or threats to undermine the supplier's credibility with other potential customers. Again, if enough consumers at the margin of a supplier's clientele would be likely to react in these ways that a supplier's profits or even survival is threatened, the supplier may have to determine performance generally by reference to the expectations of these marginal consumers.

Two major qualifications must be noted on the effectiveness of the discipline which marginal consumers may bring to a market. Both of these involve subtleties that render them elusive on an operational level. First, in any given market, a supplier may judge the value of the marginal consumers' business to be less than the gains to be realized by exploiting the infra-marginal consumer (i.e. the consumer who is either ill-informed about the initial contract terms or ineffective in challenging unsatisfactory subsequent performance, or both). In this event, the supplier may choose to forego altogether the business of the marginal consumers and adjust the terms accordingly for his remaining customers (*see* Schwartz and Wilde, 1979). Secondly, and more plausibly, the supplier may attempt to discriminate between his marginal and infra-marginal consumers, either in the initial contract terms or in subsequent contractual performance, or in both. While the question of whether discrimination is occurring in a market on a non-cost justified basis has proved to be one of the most notoriously difficult issues in the whole of anti-trust law (*see* for example, Posner, 1976, p. 188 *et seq.*), it is submitted that this issue lies at the heart of many concerns over the enforceability of standard form contracts and should influence accordingly the legal responses to those concerns.

Thus, in the light of these considerations, the question we are left with in any particular transactional setting is: when is the influence of marginal consumers in that context sufficient protection to consumers who do not read, understand or challenge the quality of performance under standard form contracts into which they have entered?

In answering this question some simple models of the behaviour of markets for goods or services where standard form contracts are used may be helpful. We will consider only the case of a reasonably competitive market, since the monopolistic case has been discussed above. We will first assume that each seller treats all of his customers equally, not discriminating among them in any way, and examine the factors which lead to a competitive or non-competitive combination of price and contract terms, evaluating the allocative and distributional effects of the results. Secondly, we will assume that each seller can discriminate among his customers according to the quality of the information they possess about alternative contractual offerings and to their willingness to pay. Here again we will examine the nature of the equilibrium that results in the market in the presence of information impairment and evaluate the allocative and distributional effects of this market condition.

Non-discriminating sellers

In this model, each seller offers his goods to all of his customers at the same price (P) and the same contract terms (T). Let X equal the percentage of consumers in this market that is perfectly informed about P and T for each seller. If all customers are perfectly informed, so $X = 1$, and all have identical tastes, then all sellers will offer the same combination of P and T which we can represent as P' and T'. A seller who asks a higher price or offers less desirable terms would be deserted by all customers in favour of the competitors. Thus competition under these conditions will force out the seller who fails to offer fully competitive terms.

If some uninformed consumers appear in the market, so that X is less than one, then we must have a mechanism for allocating these uninformed consumers among various sellers. If they are completely uninformed, we may assume that they select a seller by a random process. If they are partially informed, they may purchase at combinations of P and T that are somewhat but not greatly less satisfactory than the competitive equilibrium. As X declines, the number of buyers willing to pay P greater than P' or accept T less than T' will increase until at some point the seller can survive by selling only to this uninformed group of buyers. How far must X fall before some sellers offering non-competitive P and T combinations can survive? This depends upon the minimum efficient scale for a seller, the mechanism of allocating uninformed customers and the magnitude of the gap between the competitive P' and T' and the P and T that uninformed customers will accept.

Schwartz and Wilde (1979) make some assumptions about market power and show that where X is greater than one-third the market is likely to behave in a competitive fashion while if X is less than one-third it may not. This result however is critically dependent on a number of assumptions. If the minimum efficient scale for a seller is small, the non-competitive seller can survive in the face of a larger X. If uninformed buyers are distributed uniformly among all sellers, non-competitive sellers will survive in the face of a larger X than would be necessary for their survival if even the uninformedtend to be driven away from non-competitive sellers. If for example all uninformed consumers know that they are uninformed and as a result shop only at major department stores that have a reputation for providing roughly competitive P and T, then only knowledgeable consumers will buy from independent sellers, and a non-competitive independent could not survive.

Schwartz and Wilde (1979) review several search models which recognize the cost of consumers searching for a better price and assume that they stop this search when it is no longer profitable for them, or that they search over a fixed number of sellers, or that they pursue some mixed strategy. These models yield either a single price, a cluster of prices around the competitive price or a continuum of prices from the competitive to the monopoly level. Schwartz and Wilde suggest that one can assess the competitiveness of a market by examining the distribution of prices that results. They conclude that a continuous distribution of prices over a substantial range suggests a market that is not competitive.

The literature that Schwartz and Wilde review assumes that the good is homogeneous and that the price varies. Our problem however allows both the price and the contract terms to vary which yields a problem similar to that of a heterogeneous good. The relevant literature divides such goods into search, experience and credence goods. A search good is one with charcteristics that can be indentified upon examination, which in our case would include contracts the meaning of which is clear upon a quick perusal. An experience good is one the quality of which cannot be determined by examination but can be determined with use. This would include standard form contracts which are impenetrable or incomprehensible to the layman, but where repeated use of the contract will quickly reveal the nature and consequence of the terms contained therein. A credence good is one the quality of which cannot be determined either before or after purchase. This would correspond to a contract the terms of which are never understood by the buyer. An example might be some elements of an estate plan which come into force only after the contracting party has died. The implication of these categories is that it is easiest to be informed and thus X will be highest for search goods and for experience goods purchased frequently, and hardest to be informed, so X will be lowest, for credence goods or experience goods purchased infrequently. To ensure a competitive result, informed shoppers must understand the terms of the contracts by one of the methods above.

What if all customers differ not only in the amount of information they possess but also in their taste for product characteristics and for contract terms? If there is a sufficient number of informed consumers such that they essentially dictate the P and T offerings that survive in the market, then uninformed consumers will consume the same mix of P and T as the informed consumers. If the tastes of informed consumers are a representative sample of the tastes of all consumers, then the mix of P and T being offered will be appropriate for all consumers, although individual uninformed consumers may purchase at a P and T different from that which they would have chosen if they were fully informed. If on the other hand the informed consumers are not typical, then the uninformed consumers will be offered an inappropriate mix of P and T. Not only will individual uninformed consumers receive something other than their preferred P and T, but the entire range of P and T may differ from that which the uninformed would have chosen if they had been informed. For example, if informed consumers are more risk-averse than uninformed consumers, the uninformed may find themselves paying for more protection from risk than they wish to buy. Spence (1975) shows that in a monopoly if the informed consumers are not typical of all consumers then the price and quality offered by the monopolist will tend not to be the ideal price-quality combination. A similar problem arises in our context.

In addition, if customers have heterogeneous tastes, some will refuse to purchase at a P and T combination that others would accept. If the market does not behave competitively, so that some sellers offer uncompetitive P and T combinations, then some uninformed customers will not purchase at all if the sellers that they visit offer P and T combinations worse than their reservation combination. This result is clearly inefficient.

If X is too small to yield a competitive result, what is the nature of the equilibrium that results? Akerlof (1970) shows that with informed sellers and uninformed buyers a market may completely fail to exist. In his example, no sales of used cars may result when buyers are prepared to pay for a car of average quality yet sellers always offer used cars of below average quality. The implication is that it is possible for contract terms to be offered on such unfavourable terms that the good or service in question is not purchased at all. This result is clearly inefficient and both buyers and sellers are worse off than if the market operated.

Rothschild and Stiglitz (1976) show that where customers differ in the costs which they impose on sellers, as may happen with insurance contracts, firms may offer limited combinations of *P* and *T* in order to force high risk customers to reveal themselves by paying a high price to receive generous coverage. In short, some combinations of *P* and *T* will not be offered because high risk individuals could choose them and impose costs on the insurer who does not know which are the high risk individuals. This makes low risk individuals worse off or causes the market to fail completely. Once again, this information imperfection leads to an inefficient result. In addition, there is a distributional consequence in that low risk individuals may be worse off than if the information imperfection were removed while high risk individuals are no better off.

Goldberg (1974) shows that in the case of standard form insurance policies an inability to assess the terms of those policies may lead to a combination of low price and harsh contract terms. He demonstrates that this result is inefficient as compared to the higher price and more generous contract terms that would occur with perfect information.

All of the above cases lead to allocative inefficiency and losses by some classes of customers. The losses by customers need not however lead to offsetting excess profits by sellers. If there is easy entry into the sales business, then a normal rate of return in that business may be expected. Any above-normal rate of return may lead to entry that would drive the rate of return down. There may however be some cross-subsidies among different customer classes, and inefficient overall contract terms. These cross-subsidies may survive competitive entry because sellers or buyers do not have adequate information to avoid the subsidy.

Suppose there is a consumer externality, in that a consumer can complain about the *P* and *T* combination he received from a seller and influence others not to buy from the seller. In a market without discrimination among customers, perfectly informed would-be buyers will not be affected by such information but uninformed and partly informed would-be buyers may be affected. A large volume of accurate complaints by vocal customers may bring the market toward an efficient result. At a minimum, it will tend to force sellers to offer the *P* and *T* combination desired by these vocal customers, who may or may not themselves be typical of all consumers. If the complaints are inaccurate in that the *P* and *T* combination was in fact satisfactory or was better than described by the complaining customer, such complaining customers will push the market equilibrium to satisfy their demands, and thus in general away from efficient solutions. In short, the possibility of a customer externality gives to the customers causing such an externality a disproportionate influence on the market that may or may not be efficient depending upon the characteristics of those customers.

What should courts look for in non-discriminating markets to determine whether a possible information problem has led to non-competitive results? Clearly, if one can observe directly the proportion of informed consumers this will be valuable, with a higher proportion of informed consumers raising a presumption of more competitive results. In the absence of direct observations on consumer information, information about the dispersion of prices for a homogeneous good may be useful in assessing the competitiveness of the market. If the good is heterogeneous, in that T can vary, information about the dispersion of P and T is of little help in assessing the competitiveness of the market since such dispersion may simply reflect heterogeneous consumer tastes for T. However a dispersion of P at a given level of T does suggest a non-competitive result. Other things being equal, a competitive result is less likely to occur for a heterogeneous good, because the information that might be collected is more complex than if the good is homogeneous. If informed consumers can be identified, then the market will behave more competitively if they are typical of all consumers than if they are atypical. If the minimum efficient scale of the seller is large, he is less likely to survive while offering non-competitive price and contract terms than if the minimum efficient scale is very small. All of the above of course assumes that the basic structure of the market is a competitive one. A non-competitive market structure offers opportunities for selling at non-competitive P and T combinations regardless of the existence of the information problem.

Discriminating sellers

Suppose that sellers can discriminate among their customers by offering different P and T combinations to informed and uninformed customers. Presumably customers who are perfectly informed about the P and T offerings of all sellers will purchase at the competitive P and T combination, whether those purchases are marginal to the market or not, that is, whether or not those customers derive some consumer surplus from their purchase. Even if some informed consumers are willing to pay considerably more than P' or accept considerably less than T', there is no need for them to do so since while they are infra-marginal to the market, they are marginal to any particular firm and can take their trade from one firm to another until they find one offering the competitive combination.

Imperfectly informed consumers will be offered P greater than P' or T less than T' if the seller can identify them as imperfectly informed and if they are not marginal consumers to the market at P' and T'. If an uninformed consumer is not prepared to pay more than P' for the good on any contract terms, he cannot be charged more than P'. Since he is uninformed however he may purchase under terms worse than T' at price P'.

Sellers might identify uninformed and non-marginal consumers by pre-sale discussions or by some characteristic of the customer that correlates with poor information, such as being a tourist or a newcomer to town. Alternatively, a seller may offer a poor combination of *P* and *T* to all shoppers but improve his offer if the initial offer is rejected. In many parts of the world, such a bargaining process is common for most purchases, although it is uncommon for many goods in North America.

When sellers can identify uninformed consumers and can discriminate against them, a non-competitive market may result even when *X* is large and the uninformed portion of the market is small. Even if 95 per cent of all customers are well informed, the seller may be able to raise *P* or lower *T* when he can identify that he is dealing with one of the uninformed five per cent. This is not possible with self-service stores offering price-labelled goods. It is more likely where there is customer assistance by sales personnel, where the good is heterogeneous so there is no fixed price, or where the price is large so that negotiation is possible. Infrequent purchase will also be harmful to the competitive functioning of a market since this will tend to increase the proportion of uninformed consumers. The purchase of new and used cars tends to satisfy these criteria, as do various forms of insurance.

What are the allocative effects of sellers discriminating in this fashion? First, consider discrimination only in the price charged. One might assume that a seller who simply raises prices along a demand curve will not discourage purchases and therefore will cause no inefficiency in a competitive market. However the above-normal rate of return generated by this price discrimination will lead to the additional entry of firms until selling costs are raised such that the rate of return drops to a normal level despite the price discrimination. The end result is consumers paying higher than competitive prices because of price discrimination, a normal rate of return to sellers and inefficiently high selling costs. There is no effect on the marginal informed consumer because he can insist on shopping at firms that offer a competitive price. Secondly, consider discrimination in the form of reducing contract terms *T* for uninformed buyers. Where the discrimination takes the form of reducing the quality of contract terms rather than raising the price, the infra-marginal uninformed buyer is again not discouraged from purchase but he will be dissatisfied with the contract terms after purchase. Once again, there may be a welfare loss from this discrimination even in the case of infra-marginal consumers. Over time, if uninformed consumers know the average *T* offered, but not the *T* that they are buying, discrimination against uninformed buyers will lower the average *T* and thus lower the willingness to pay of these buyers. As in Akerlof's used car case (1970), this may lead to inefficient market operation or to the market completely failing to operate.

Now consider the case where some aspect of contract performance occurs substantially after the contract is formed. For example, when a new car is purchased one first purchases the vehicle and may later receive some service performance under the warranty. Let us assume that the buyer receives the necessary service, and the question is whether he pays for it or whether the cost is borne by the seller. In a world of perfect information, buyers would know at the time of purchase not only the explicit terms of the warranty but also the implicit terms: how each dealer would respond to demands for free warranty service of various types; and they would take that performance into account in their purchase decision. In a world of imperfect information, some or all buyers will not know how the seller will perform on the warranty until they make their demands for warranty service. In transactions such as the latter (which we call 'separable' transactions) bargaining over certain explicit terms (e.g. price) occurs at the time of contract formation while bargaining over certain other implicit terms (e.g. warranty service) occurs at the time of subsequent tender of performance.

Here, we can again segment consumers into a perfectly informed proportion X and a remainder who are uninformed. If the perfectly informed proportion understand from the outset what treatment they will be given at the time of service, they will presumably make an integral decision at the time of purchase and will receive competitive terms. Uninformed consumers will purchase without regard to the contract performance and will then discover when they demand warranty service whether their dealer will charge for it. Let us assume that the competitive terms of sale include the warranty service in the sale price P'.

While perfectly informed consumers will only buy from sellers who in fact provide the warranty service free of charge whether or not the explicit contract provides for this, uninformed consumers may buy from sellers who will charge for the service when they can get away with it. Assuming that the service has to be performed for the vehicle to operate properly, no customer is marginal at the time the service is required. Thus uninformed buyers who purchased from discriminating sellers will all be forced to pay for this service if this is what the explicit terms of their contract provide. Since by definition this behaviour does not affect the purchase decision, nor whether the service is performed, it might appear that there is no allocative effect of this discrimination. As in previous cases however, the extra profits yielded by discriminating against uninformed consumers cause entry into the auto sales business until the cost of selling is raised (perhaps because each seller is inefficiently small) and the rate of return brought back to normal. Once again, there is in the long run a misallocation of resources resulting in inefficiently high selling costs. As before, discrimination may take place even when the proportion of informed consumers is very high, so long as the costs of indentifying uninformed consumers are not high.

In the separable transaction, all buyers are given the same explicit terms (warranty) when the contract is formed. How does the seller decide whether to discriminate against a customer when the warranty service is performed? Presumably this depends on the marginal costs of, and marginal revenue from, such discrimination. Even where the customer is captive and thus not marginal, the seller may worry about the loss of goodwill associated with trying to cheat a customer who recognizes that he is being cheated and protests. If the only way to identify an uninformed consumer is to offer him a poor deal and be prepared to negotiate, sellers who pursue this strategy may find that some informed consumers may refuse to deal with them, because of their distaste for the bargaining process. Thus the very process of discrimination can generate some costs that limit its application.

The possibility of externalities among consumers may again be considered here. Take the case of the consumer who when told that he must pay for service threatens to tell all his friends or write to a newspaper complaint column alleging that the seller is a thief and a scoundrel. Since many consumers would not take this step, this is consistent only with the model of heterogeneous consumer tastes. Since such threats are futile when all customers are treated similarly, this is consistent only with the case in which sellers can differentiate between customers. This externality is a possible cost of attempted discrimination.

One question that arises in the case of the customer externality is whether a customer may be given inefficiently generous contract terms. The answer is clearly yes. Suppose for example that the competitive result is that the dealer pays for service under the warranty for repair *Y* while customers have to pay for repair *Z*. A complaining customer who demanded that both *Y* and *Z* be performed at no cost to him might in fact succeed in his demand if the seller was afraid that the harm to his goodwill from this customer complaining to his friends and to newspaper columns would be greater than the marginal costs of performing repair *Z*. Even if the customer's claims are unjustified in that the dealer has lived up to his contractual obligations, with a large uninformed public prepared to believe the customer's claim, the dealer may be 'blackmailed' into inefficient performance. The customer may as a consequence demand service that is worth less to him than the social cost of performing it if he is certain that he can avoid payment for this service. Thus the customer externality can generate not only distributional effects, but also potentially inefficient resource allocation effects. The dealer will have to cross-subsidize the excess service he gives to complaining customers by providing insufficient service to other customers who do not complain. The problem is that once we allow for some customers who may demand excessive service and who can impose an externality, we can no longer be certain whether the market will provide too much or too little service under a given set of contract terms, or offer contract terms that are too generous or too harsh. This is particularly sobering since the set of assumptions discussed in this case are not implausible for a number of consumer situtions.

4.3.2 Problems of prescription

In cases where a court might conclude that marginal consumers have not adequately disciplined a supplier's contractual behaviour, what judicial interventions might be usefully contemplated? A modest proposal would be for the doctrine of unconscionability to penalize contractual documents which in their wording or organization are apt to mislead consumers. It is clear that a number of warranties or guarantees are deceptive forms of advertising. For example, warranties that in the bold print offer 'life-time' guarantees of, for example, mufflers or carpets, when 'life-time' in the fine print is defined as meaning as long as the product happens to last, are clearly deceptive. Similarly in the case of 'guarantees' that take more rights away from the consumer than he would have had at law without any guarantee at all. A useful adjunct to such a rule might be judicial abolition or confinement of the parol evidence rule in a consumer standard-form setting, in order to protect consumers for the reasonable reliance on information conveyed to them in advertisements or at point-of-sale but not incorporated in the ensuing formal contract. This adjunct would create additional incentives to suppliers to ensure the accuracy of this information[35].

A more expansive formulation of a rule against unfair surprise might impose conspicuousness, intelligibility and specific assent requirements with respect to clauses creating substantial divergences from the reasonable expectations of the consumer as reflected in the terms available to other consumers at the margin of the market. Such a rule would of course avoid outright prohibitions of such clauses but instead would attach conditional prohibitions which could be avoided by compliance with the required standard of conspicuousness, etc. Thus, such a rule would avoid imposing preferences on the parties while at the same time improving, hopefully, the quality of information in the market or at least the thickness of the margin of sophisticated consumers whose actions tend to 'make' the market.

The courts would need to apply this second formulation of the rule against unfair surprise with a great deal of caution. First, they would need to avoid the problems associated with assuming unjustified discrimination between two classes of consumers without really investigating why different contractual offerings for each of the two groups might in fact be justified. Either cost differences or heterogeneous tastes may explain different terms. For example, the House of Lords in *Macaulay* seemed to attach significance to the fact that established songwriters were able to secure better contracts from the defendant music publisher than the plaintiff, as an unknown songwriter, had been able to do. It is by no means clear how this reflected adversely on the fairness of the transaction between the plaintiff and the publisher in *Macaulay* — one would expect good songwriters to get better contracts than bad ones (or at least unknown ones). Secondly, the courts in applying such a rule would face difficulties in a market where a margin of sophisticated consumers cannot be easily identified and therefore the market benchmarks against which the issue of substantial divergence might be determined cannot be easily identified. Such markets seem likely to be rare but may exist in cases such as certain classes of door-to-door sales. Thirdly, it will often be difficult for the courts to hold everything else about a contract constant when comparing a challenged clause with provisions in other contractual offerings in the market. Fourthly, rules designed merely to improve the information contained in a contract cannot focus too exclusively on particular types of clauses, given the substitution effects that such rules are likely to generate.

In addition to these reservations, one may question how effective an information-oriented response is likely to be to information problems with standard form contracts. Even if one were to assume that some of the more common categories of standard form contracts, for example, hire-purchase contracts and insurance contracts, were all printed in large type and written in English that anybody with the minimum of education and modest intelligence could read, one suspects many consumers would continue not to read most of these kinds of contracts in any detail before signing them. When one asks why, many consumers probably rely in part on the constraints (real or illusory) imposed by other consumers at the margin (i.e. they let the market shop for them). In addition, the reading of complicated forms in detail denies the principal virtue of standard form contracts — reduced transaction costs. More importantly, consumers are probably recognizing that the information problem they often face is not that of working out what particular clauses mean in the sense of how they allocate certain risks, but is instead the problem of applying information to their personal circumstances. For example, in the case of an insurance policy which allocates risks in different ways between a consumer and his insurance company, he may understand perfectly how the policy allocates those risks, but what he may have difficulty in assessing is how likely it is that certain risks may materialize and, if they do, what kinds of costs are likely to be entailed. Thus, how likely is it, as a matter of probability, that his house will catch on fire, and if it does how much damage is likely to be done? If there are exemptions for earthquake, Acts of God, fires caused in certain ways, certain classes of property, etc., his problem lies in assessing whether his personal circumstances at any given time during the currency of the policy wil fall within one of thosc clauses and what costs will be entailed for him if they do. This is not information that can be conveyed by the policy, or at least not easily, and as between the insurance company and the consumer, this may be information to which the consumer has superior access (no matter how difficult), relative to the insurance company (which may in part explain why coverage for certain kinds of risks is excluded) (*see* Priest, 1981). Moreover, even if all clauses in all insurance policies were clearly written, the consumer would face a formidable task in comparing alternative offerings, which involves calculating a net worth for the various policies given different patterns of coverage and exemption. Again, it is difficult to see how improving the clarity or conspicuousness of what are at present fine print clauses can address this problem. In other words, it is one thing to acquire relevant information; it may be quite another thing to process it effectively.

In limiting cases, a more substantial form of judicial intervention may be justified than that contemplated by rules against unfair surprise, which are directed at the contents and format of the initial contract. Recalling the importance of examining not only the contents of standard-form contracts but the performance in fact rendered thereunder, it may be that an infra-marginal consumer should be able to upset a transaction where he can show a very substantial divergence between the value of the performance he has received from a supplier and the value of the performance typically realized by marginal (sophisticated), but otherwise similar, consumers in the same market. In other words, unjustified forms of performance discrimination, where very substantial and clearly proven, may properly raise a strong presumption of unfairness even though there may be no discrimination in the initial contract terms. The performance typically realized by marginal consumers supplies the source of the 'shadow terms' governing the dealings of infra-marginal consumers. Two caveats would need particularly to be observed with such a rule. First, 'discrimination' based on cost differences or heterogeneous consumer tastes is clearly benign. Secondly, being an infra-marginal consumer cannot be an entirely costless activity, because of information deficiencies. If it were, moral hazard problems would arise that might lead to the disintegration of any margin of informed consumers[36]. The requirement of a *substantial* divergence between the performance realized by infra-marginal consumers and that realized by marginal consumers may leave sufficient incentives for the former group to undertake an efficient level of self-protective measures.

4.4 Comparative institutional competence

An important issue raised by the foregoing analysis of problems of diagnosing forms of market failure symptomized by standard form contracts, and problems of prescribing legal responses to those failures (where they exist), is the comparative competence of courts, amongst our various legal institutions, to control standard form contract abuses.

As to the first objection to standard form contracts that was considered — monopoly — it is submitted that the difficulties exemplified in the decision in *Macaulay v Schroeder Publishing Co Ltd* suggest extreme caution on the part of courts in withholding enforcement of standard form contracts on the grounds of inequality of bargaining power (or unconscionability or lack of reasonableness) involving alleged abuse of monopoly power. First, because of inadequacies in evidence and expertise, inferences of monopoly are frequently likely to be drawn incorrectly by the courts. There is simply no systematic relationship between the use of standard forms and market structure. Secondly, even where such inferences are correctly drawn, the courts do not have at their disposal in ordinary contract litigation the remedial instruments required to foreclose second-order substitution effects. A compelling case would seem to exist for relying principally on anti-trust policy or public utility regulation to respond to any market structure problems of which standard form contracts may be symptomatic.

As to the second objection to standard form contracts that was considered — information asymmetries — the role of the marginal consumer is critical in two respects: first, as a source of generalized competitive discipline of an informationally impaired market and, secondly, where this discipline is ineffective (because of the thinness of the margin or discrimination between marginal and infra-marginal consumers), as a source of 'shadow' terms that the courts might look to in fashioning protection for the infra-marginal consumer. When intervening in standard form contract enforcement because of information failures, we have suggested that the courts would be wise to adhere closely to market benchmarks derived from a careful scrutiny of the realized expectations of marginal consumers in the relevant market. Even here, of course, the courts should proceed with care. Differences in the treatment of different groups of consumers may simply reflect differences in costs or preferences. Moreover, the courts cannot be so ready to intervene that being an infra-marginal consumer becomes costless. Such a policy may induce the disintegration of effective margins of consumers in a market and in the long-run exacerbate rather than mitigate problems in that market. Where no margin of sophisticated consumers can be reliably identified in a market and information problems are pervasive, judicial intervention on an *ad hoc* basis is likely to be an inadequate response. As in the case of monopoly, a market so badly disrupted probably calls for a legislative or regulatory response where some base-line terms can be imposed *ex ante* on parties and market forces confined to those parameters of transactions where information imperfections are less severe (*see* Schwartz and Wilde, 1979; Belobaba, 1980; Hasson, 1978).

The analysis in this chapter suggests a rather narrow role for the courts in policing standard form contract abuses. We have argued that these abuses are less pervasive than are commonly asserted and that where they occur the courts have a limited capacity for redressing them. Only in reasonably well-functioning markets where failures are relatively exceptional would reliance on the courts as the primary control agent seem justified. In markets afflicted with serious structural or informational problems, case-by-case sniping, especially given the barriers to suit that are often faced by consumers with small-scale claims, seems unlikely to be as effective a legal response as broader-gauge legislative or regulatory intervention.

We should conclude this discussion of the possible market failures caused or represented by standard form contracts with a caveat about the implication of finding such failure. We have identified a number of cases that may lead to contract terms being offered that differ from those that would be offered in a perfectly operating market. We have described such results as inefficient. One should not, however, automatically conclude that a particular government intervention, or *any* possible intervention, is necessarily welfare-improving. All corrective policies involve some costs for administration and may impose some additional costs in the marketplace. These costs must be weighed against the benefits of the policies. Only a case-by-case analysis can determine whether the benefits of a policy exceed its costs. It is possible that many situations involving problems may not justify intervention because feasible corrective policies are even more costly than the original problem. One must not blindly assume that the cure is preferable to the disease.

Notes to chapter four

1 [1976] 1 WLR 1308, HL
2 Ibid. at 1316
3 Ibid.
4 Ibid. (our emphasis)
5 Ibid. (our emphasis)
6 [1967] 1 AC 361, HL
7 Ibid. at 406
8 See note 1 above.
9 [1977] 2 All ER 849, HL
10 Ibid. at 852
11 (1973) 43 DLR (3d) 190 (Ont. SC)
12 See also *Heffron v Imperial Parking Co* (1974) 3 OR (2d) 722, CA
13 (1974) 54 DLR (3d) 517 (N.S.CA)
14 Ibid. at 523
15 *Suisse Atlantique*, [1967] 1 AC 361 at 406, HL *per* Lord Reid
16 Ibid.
17 [1970] 2 WLR 269, CA.
18 See Swan and Reiter (1978), pp. 6–105 and 6–106; but see *Linton Construction Ltd v CNR Co* (1974), 49 DLR (3d) 548 where the Supreme Court of Canada, in upholding a clause limiting liability for delay and misdelivery of a telegram, stressed the fact that insurance was available to the sender.
19 [1956] 1 WLR 836, CA.
20 [1980] 2 WLR 283, HL.
21 1977, c. 50.
22 See note 1 above.
23 [1974] 1 All ER 171, CA.
24 Often referred to by economists as a monopolistic competition. For the original development of this concept, see Chamberlin (1933). For an elementary discussion of the theory, see, e.g. Mansfield (1975) p. 301 *et seq*.
25 (1960) 161 A (2d) 69 (N.J.SC)
26 Ibid. at 87; but see section 4.2.2 at note 32.
27 In the US, where the private anti-trust suit has become a major instrument in the enforcement of the anti-trust statutes, a combination of treble damage recovery provisions, liberal class action rules and contingent fee arrangements supply this incentive. In the UK, in litigation like that *Macaulay* none of these features is present.
28 See Russell LJ in *Macaulay*, above, note 23 at 172.
29 For a general discussion of the market effects of various consumer protection laws, see Cayne and Trebilcock (1973).
30 For an analysis of the effect of a minimum wage on competitive factor markets, see Alchian and Allen (1969) pp. 508; Leftwich (1970 pp. 274–275. For an analysis of the effect of a common cost increase of a factor of production on supply and demand conditions for the final product in a competitive market, see Alchian and Allen (1969) pp. 366–369; both intermediate and final market conditions are relevant to an assessment of such an increase; see Leftwich (1970) chapter 16; Mansfield (1975) chapter 13.
31 By way of analogy with the effects of a sales tax on supply and demand conditions for the final product, see Mansfield (1975) p. 280; Samuelson

(1973) pp. 387, 388; Sichel and Eckstein (1974) pp. 362–364.

32 See note 25 above.

33 For a discussion of the effect of a minimum wage law on a monopsonized factor market see, e.g. Leftwich (1970) pp. 295, 296; Rees (1973) p. 75 *et seq.*; Lipsey, Sparks and Steiner (1973) pp. 346–348.

34 Ibid.

35 See s 4(7) of the Ontario Business Practices Act SO 1974, c. 131, abolishing the parol evidence rule in many consumer contexts.

36 For a discussion of this issue, see Kronman (1978).

References

AKERLOF, G. (1970), The market for lemons: qualitative uncertainty and the market mechanism, *Quarterly Journal of Economics*, **84**, no. 3, 488–500.

ALCHIAN, A. and ALLEN, W. (1969), *Exchange and Production Theory in Use*, Belmont, Calif.: Wadsworth.

BELOBABA, E. P. (1980), The resolution of common law doctrinal problems through legislative and administrative intervention, in *Studies in Contract Law*, (Reiter, B. J. and Swan, J. eds.), Toronto: Butterworths.

CAVES, R. (1977), *American Industry: Structure, Conduct and Performance*, 4th ed., Englewood Cliffs, NJ: Prentice Hall.

CAYNE, D. and TREBILCOCK, M. J. (1973), Market consideration in the formulation of consumer protection policy, *University of Toronto Law Journal*, **23**, no. 4, 396–430.

CHAMBERLIN, E. H. (1933), *The Theory of Monopolistic Competition*, Cambridge, Mass.: Harvard University Press.

GOLDBERG, V. P. (1974), Institutional change and the quasi-invisible hand, *Journal of Law and Economics*, **17**, no. 2, 461–492.

HASSON, R. (1978), The unconscionability business — a comment on Tilden Rent-a-Car Co. v Clendenning, *Canadian Business Law Journal*, **3**, no. 2, 193–198.

KESSLER, F. (1943), Contracts of adhesion — some thoughts about freedom of contract, *Columbia Law Review*, **43**, no. 5, 629–642.

KRONMAN, A. T. (1978), Mistake, disclosure, information and the law of contracts, *Journal of Legal Studies*, **7**, no. 1, 1–34.

LEFTWICH, R. H. (1970), *Introduction to Microeconomics*, New York: Holt, Rinehart and Winston.

LIPSEY, R. C., SPARKS, G. R. and STEINER, P. O. (1973), *Economics*, New York: Harper Row.

LLEWELLYN, K. N. (1931), What price contract — an essay in perspective, *Yale Law Journal*, **40**, 704–751.

LLEWELLYN, K. N. (1939), Book review: the standardization of commercial contracts in English and continental law, *Harvard Law Review*, **52**, no. 5, 700–705.

MANSFIELD, E. (1975), *Microeconomics*, 2nd ed., New York: Norton.

POSNER, R. A. (1976), *Antitrust Law*, University of Chicago Press.

PRIEST, G. (1981), *A Theory of the Consumer Product Warranty, Yale Law Journal*, forthcoming.

REES, A. (1973), *The Economics of Work and Pay*, New York: Harper Row.

ROTHSCHILD, M. and STIGLITZ, J. E. (1976), Equilibrium in competitive insurance markets: an essay on the economics of imperfect internation, *Quarterly Journal of Economics*, **90**, no. 4, 629–650.

SAMUELSON, P. A. (1973), *Economics*, 9th ed., New York: McGraw-Hill.

SCHERER, F. M. (1980), *Industrial Market Structure and Economic Performance*, Chicago: Rand McNally.

SCHWARTZ, A. and WILDE, L. L. (1979), Intervening in markets on the basis of imperfect information: a legal and economic analysis, *University of Pennsylvania Law Review*, **127**, no. 3, 630–682.

SICHEL, W. and ECKSTEIN, P. (1974), *Basic Economic Concepts*, Chicago: Rand McNally.

SLAWSON, W. D. (1975), Standard form contracts and democratic control of lawmaking power, *Harvard Law Review*, **84**, no. 1, 529–566.

SPENCE, A. M. (1975), Monopoly, quality and regulation, *Bell Journal of Economics*, **6**, no. 2, 417–429.

SWAN, J. and REITER, B. J. (1978) (eds.) *Contracts*, Toronto: Butterworths.

TAUBMAN, J. (1965) (ed.) *The Business and the Law of Music*, New York: Federal Legal Publications.

PART TWO
Tort

Tort has been the subject of extensive and varied economic investigation. A feature of the more recent literature has been its sole emphasis on allocative efficiency, to the neglect of justice and compensation issues. In Veljanovski's chapter the normative content of the efficiency criterion is discussed in the context of the choice between negligence and strict liability. Although the essay does not develop a theory of rights, it does demonstrate the inseparable relationship between the essentially normative question of who should be assigned initial rights to compensation and the choice of 'efficient' liability rules. In contrast to Veljanovski's market-based analysis of tort, Burrows questions the relevance and consistency of such an approach in the case of nuisance and environmental pollution. In particular, Calabresi and Melamed's analysis of nuisance liability rules is critically examined and found to be deficient in several crucial respects. The moral of the story is that the evaluation and implementation of centralized instruments of control is unavoidable.

The final chapter by Bishop is a prescriptive application of economics using recent developments in the economics of information. The essay provides a critical analysis of the existing law relating to negligent misrepresentation, and outlines criteria for the limitation of liability[1].

Notes to part two

1. For some other applications of the economics of information see Kronman (1978), Posner (1979) and Schwartz and Wilde (1979).

References

KRONMAN, A.T. (1978), Mistake, disclosure, information and the law of contracts. *Journal of Legal Studies,* **7**, no. 1, 1–34

POSNER, R.A. (1979), Privacy, secrecy, and reputation, *Buffalo Law Review,* **28**, no. 1, 1–55

SCHWARTZ, A. and WILDE, L.L. (1979), Intervening in markets on the basis of imperfect information: a legal and economic analysis, *Pennsylvania Law Review,* **127**, no. 3, 630–682

CHAPTER FIVE

The economic theory of tort liability—toward a corrective justice approach

Cento G. Veljanovski

5.1 Introduction

Although the quest to establish an integrating principle of tort law has been described as a 'pursuit of futility'[1], many legal scholars have nonetheless sought to do so[2]. A number of comprehensive theories now exist that, with varying degrees of success, provide a rational conceptual basis for liability for accidental losses in society (e.g. Fletcher, 1972; Posner, 1972; Calabresi, 1970; Epstein, 1973; Klemme, 1976). Many of these theories draw heavily, if not exclusively, on economics. The appeal of economics to legal scholars engaged in this endeavour derives partly from the evident importance of economic considerations in appraising schemes for the allocation and compensation of accident losses and partly from the widespread belief that economics is value-free and furnishes firm conclusions and prescriptions when the law is evaluated against the benchmark of economic efficiency[3]. Although relatively unused in England[4], the efficiency-based analysis of tort has become an increasing feature of the North American literature[5]. However, it has not been without its critics (e.g. Leff, 1974; Polinsky, 1974; Baker, 1975; Liebhafsky, 1976), nor are its central tenets and assumptions universally accepted[6].

A principal reason for the scepticism displayed toward economic theories of law is their reification of economic efficiency and consequent failure to consider issues of justice, equity and wealth distribution which its proponents frequently concede are of equal, if not fundamental importance. This essay is a preliminary step in the direction of remedying the imbalance that has occurred in the literature, without rejecting the efficiency approach itself[7]. Instead efficiency will be recast in a more general framework in which it shares equal 'billing' with notions of justice, some of which provide the implicit normative basis for the existing literature.

The basic thesis advanced in this chapter is that *if* the object of tort is to correct market inefficiencies then economic efficiency does not constitute an adequate theory of liability unless it is combined with a normative theory of rights or entitlements. Once this is recognized then, as will be shown, the answer to the question whether accident victims should be compensated by those who injure them and under what conditions depends fundamentally on the value judgment as to whose rights should be protected by law. Justice is thus seen not as a goal which necessarily competes with economic efficiency but an essential ingredient of an economic theory of tort liability.

This chapter is organized as follows. In section 5.2 the legal and economic objectives of tort are discussed together with an introduction to the main concepts that form the basis of recent contributions to the economic theory of liability, in particular the economic reformulation of negligence. This is followed in section 5.3 by an outline of the basic elements of the proposed corrective justice framework that has as its objective the integration of economic efficiency and justice notions. The framework is then used to provide a comparative analysis of the distributive and corrective justice norms underlying negligence liability and strict liability. Finally in section 5.4 several other topics that have been of concern to tort theorists are briefly examined to reveal the interrelationship between efficiency and justice.

5.2 The legal and economic objectives of tort liability

The law of torts is concerned with redressing civil wrongs. In this chapter we deal primarily with one branch of tort; the liability for accident losses — negligence (fault liability) and its alternatives — for which the legal remedy is pecuniary compensation[8]. Broadly then, tort liability can be defined as a body of rules that selectively shifts the victim's loss on to the defendant when there has been a compensable violation of the victim's rights.

5.2.1 Legal objectives of tort

It is frequently stated, following Holmes (1881), that tort law (and society) has no interest in shifting the loss from the victim of an accident to others unless this serves some social objective. The legal and social objectives ascribed to tort's loss-shifting arrangements have been varied, ranging from vindication, preserving the peace by 'buying off' the victim's desire to retaliate, ethical retribution, compensation and deterrence[9]. Among legal scholars there is no general consensus as to the dominant objective of tort liability. For example the recent English Royal Commission on Civil Liability and Compensation for Personal Injury offered the following analysis of fault liability: 'There is elementary justice in the principle ... that he who by his own fault injures his neighbour should make reparation' because it 'expiates the wrongdoer's feeling of guilt' and 'appeases the victim's feeling on indignation'[10]. However, more common are less moralistic interpretations that reflect the nature and structure of tort's doctrines and remedies: that damages aim at compensating the victim, and the selectivity of compensation based on fault. The fact that the remedy is 'full' compensation has suggested to many that the goal of tort is compensation whereas for others the discriminatory provision of tort compensation based on fault implies that its dominant goal is to deter wrongdoing. Indeed it has been a feature of the literature, both economic and non-economic, to focus exclusively on one or other of these goals.

Overwhelmingly, the legal literature focuses on the reparative aspects of the tort action. Fault liability is assessed in terms of its ability to provide accident victims with timely and adequate compensation, and its economic dimensions are generally restricted to that of administrative efficiency. Economic arguments have also been used to support the widening of defendant liability, begun by workmen's compensation, that has been witnessed this century under labels such as superior risk bearer, loss distribution and enterprise liability (*see* Blum and Kalvan, 1965, pp. 54–65; Keeton and O'Connell, 1965, ch. 5; Klemme, 1976). Often these applications of economics have been rather dubious[11] and moreover the theories have sought to be prescriptive rather than descriptive of the actual law and its development.

The deterrence rationale for tort views tort, to quote Glanville Williams (1951, p. 144), as 'a judicial parable designed to control the future conduct of the community.' Tort liability aims to prevent wrongdoing or, more specifically, to reduce the number and severity of accidents. For example, Salmond states unequivocally that 'pecuniary compensation is not the aim of tort' it 'exists for the purpose of preventing men from hurting one another' (Heuston, 1977, p. 13). The deterrence theory of tort liability is not widely subscribed to by legal scholars. Its rejection is based largely on the unfounded empirical assumption that the fear of damages does not encourage greater care and that accident prevention can best be encouraged by other means[12]. This position is stated by James (1948, pp. 549–550):

> There is however an altogether different approach to tort law. Human failures in a machine age cause large and fairly regular — though probably reducible — toll of life, limb and property. As a class the victims of these accidents can ill afford the loss they entail. The problem of decreasing this toll can best be solved through the pressures of safety regulations with penal and licensing sanctions, and of self-interest in avoiding the host of non-legal disadvantages that flow from accidents. But when this is all done, human losses remain. It is the principal job of tort today to deal with these losses.

In contrast to the waning of deterrence theories among lawyers and the courts[13], the economic approach sees deterrence as the central goal of tort liability. The law of torts is seen as an incentive system designed to bring about pressures that will encourage efficiency in accident prevention. This approach differs from the older literature on the deterrence function of tort by giving the notion of deterrence and fault liability specific economic interpretations.

5.2.2 Economic principles of tort liability

The 'new' economics of tort liability goes beyond broad statements of economic efficiency to fairly detailed examinations of the economic content and rationale of legal doctrines and remedies. Although this application of economics has generated a diverse and sometimes conflicting literature, there are nonetheless several key concepts that are common. In view of the technical nature of most of the more important contributions to the economics of tort, the basic principles of the economic approach and their application to tort law will be reviewed (e.g. Brown, 1973; Diamond, 1974).

Economic efficiency

In general economic efficiency requires the minimization of three costs: the losses due to accidents, the costs of preventing accidents and the costs of administering a system of accident law[14]. This is not the widest possible definition of efficiency nor is it necessarily the most appropriate one for the evaluation of accident law. Economic efficiency is a concept that is contextual — its definition depends on the objectives to be attained, the nature of costs and benefits considered relevant and the binding resource constraints.

In this essay the narrowest definition of efficiency will be used. An accident is viewed as a cost-imposing event for which, in principle, all the consequences are capable of being expressed in monetary terms. Accidents inflict losses on victims and third parties; preventing accidents consumes resources: the efficient or cost-justified level of accidents balances these two offsetting costs such that their sum is at a minimum. Thus the efficiency goal of accident law, to use Calabresi's well known phrase, is to 'reduce the sum of the costs of accidents and the cost of reducing accidents'[15].

Implicit in this definition of efficiency are several assumptions and notions. The first is the assumption that there exists an inverse relationship between safety expenditure and the frequency and severity of accidents. Accidents can be reduced by committing more resources to safety and the economic problem is essentially one of locating the optimal trade-off between the safety costs and the accident-related losses. Secondly, individuals are assumed to behave *as if* they are rational cost-minimizers and to respond to an increase in costs by substituting lower (net) cost alternatives. Thus, if the costs of accidents go up, say, because common law damages have increased, the cost-bearer is assumed to increase his level of care if this results in net cost saving. Thirdly, economic efficiency is an *ex ante* notion. Individuals are assumed to be *expected* cost-minimizers and devote resources to reduce the *risk* of injury. Safety decisions are therefore made in a state of highly imperfect information that is nonetheless expressible in (objective) probability terms. Although such *ex ante* analysis often yields results and conclusions similar to the traditional *ex post* approach of legal scholarship, this will not always be the case. Consider the valuation of damages. The *ex ante* nature of the economic approach implies the use of *ex ante* damage valuations, which may on occasion diverge markedly from traditional legal measures. In personal injury and death cases the appropriate economic damage measure is derived from the willingness to pay of the group at risk to reduce the accident rate sufficiently to save one statistical (unknown) life and not the sum that would compensate the actual victim[16]. In the extreme case of death, where the victim cannot be compensated, there still exists calculable economic damages derived from a potential victim's trade off between money and risk. Recent empirical evidence suggests that damages calculated in this way are several orders of magnitude greater than damages awarded by the courts which are based on the loss to survivors[17]. The *ex ante* basis of the economic approach also leads to a differing view of the legal system. Law and legal procedure are evaluated from the perspective of an incentive system rather than that of a dispute resolution mechanism[18].

In the remainder of this chapter, and in common with other economic models of liability rules, the efficient accident rate will be defined solely in terms of direct accident and safety costs, thus ignoring the administrative costs of the legal system[19]. This is done solely for the purpose of focusing the discussion more sharply on the doctrinal issues and does not imply that liability rules that are 'efficient' using this definition will also be efficient using a broader and empirically more relevant definition. It thus ignores, for example, the frequent criticism of tort that administratively it is excessively costly. A more comprehensive efficiency analysis would incorporate these administrative costs and balance them against the benefits of the tort system. But again, such an exercise would require a statement of the objectives of the tort action in order to define the appropriate benefits to be used in the appraisal. If victim compensation is seen as the primary goal then the administrative costs would be compared with the compensation received; if deterrence is the goal then the relevant comparison would be with tort-induced reductions in the accident rate. This elasticity of the notion of economic efficiency again emphasizes its contextual nature.

While the exclusion of administrative costs from the efficiency calculus obviously renders the discussion largely irrelevant to practical policy, this chapter is not aimed at providing an overall assessment of the actual efficiency of the tort system. Rather it is an application of economics to legal theory, specifically to provide a theory of tort doctrines.

In order to distinguish the concept of efficiency used here from wider and alternative definitions, it will be referred to as deterrence efficiency.

The Coase Theorem and accident bargains

A fundamental economic principle of liability, due to Coase (1960), is that where informed and costless bargaining is possible between injurer and victim the cost-justified level of accidents will result without the need for judicial intervention. The gains from trade inherent in an inefficient level of safety will encourage the parties to voluntarily negotiate a mutually advantageous accident bargain that minimizes their joint costs/losses. The expected losses inflicted by accidents provides the victim with an incentive to negotiate with injurers to reduce his expected losses. As long as the willingness to pay of those injured exceeds the costs incurred by the injurer in reducing the risk of injury, a bargain will be struck. Through a series of such incremental accident bargains the social costs of accidents will be reduced and the existence of net cost savings will encourage bargaining until the cost-justified level of accidents has been reached.

Moreover, the ability of accident bargains to achieve deterrence efficiency is not affected by the law. If the injurer is made legally liable for the victim's losses he will bargain with the victim for the 'entitlement' to impose accident risks in return for (*ex ante*) compensation. Again such accident bargains will continue until deterrence efficiency has been attained.

In its original statement this proposition, which has become known as the Coase Theorem, asserted that the cost-justified accident rate remained invariant with respect to the initial assignment of liability. In general, this will not be the case. Liability rules have distributive consequences that may affect the terms of individual accident bargains such that when the victim must be paid to bear the risk of injury the accident rate will be lower, though still cost-justified (*see* Burrows, 1970). Even if the distributive effects of the law do not affect specific accident bargains they will affect the general pattern of demand and hence the efficient allocation of resources in the economy.

There are two other important notions derived from the Coase Theorem. The first is what can be termed *joint care/causation*[20]. That is, all accidents are, from an economic perspective, jointly caused and therefore jointly avoidable. Coase's discussion drew attention to the fact that resource allocation conflicts are inherently reciprocal — regardless of who actively inflicts harm it can be avoided by removing either the victim or the injurer. The practical import of the notion of joint care is that deterrence efficiency requires that both parties to an accident face cost-justified pressures for accident prevention. Thus liability rules designed to achieve deterrence efficiency must be structured so that both the injurer and the victim have an incentive to avoid accidents.

The second notion is that the efficiency justification for tort liability arises from the infeasibility or imperfection of accident bargains due to transaction costs. Transaction costs are the costs that impede market solutions; they are the costs of search, negotiation, and contract specification, policing and enforcement. Thus if it were not for transaction costs contractual bargains would provide market deterrence that would be adequate for economic efficiency. Transaction costs can be divided into two overlapping categories — physical transaction costs and information transaction costs; their significances correspond broadly with non-market and market cases respectively. The physical transaction costs associated with actually locating, negotiating with, and consummating bargains between cost-bearers and imposers will frequently be prohibitive, thereby precluding a bargaining solution. The classic examples are environmental pollution and road accidents. In other situations accident bargains are feasible and actually do take place, but their terms inadequately reflect social cost savings because one or both of the parties are ill-informed. For example, in perfect labour markets workers will only voluntarily subject themselves to the risk of injury if they receive additional wages that compensate them for their expected losses. However, if workers are ill-informed or cannot deal with risk calculations, the premium they demand will not reflect their expected losses and the market solution will fail to be efficient. Thus in both cases — accidents between strangers and those between people who are contractually related but ill-informed — market forces will fail to provide the cost-justified levels of accidents. That is, all or part of the accident losses will be *external* to the injurer's decision calculus and he will fail to undertake the cost-justified level of accident prevention.

Efficiency rationale of tort liability

The economic efficiency basis for tort liability is often referred to as market failure. As we have seen, in practice accident bargains do not take place either because transaction costs are prohibitive (road accidents) or because bargaining is uninformed (industrial accidents) so that the market deterrence of accidents is absent or weak. In these cases of market failure the number of accidents will be inefficiently high; this is a *necessary* economic condition for corrective intervention in order to reduce the accidents to the cost-justified level.

Tort liability is one instrument capable of internalizing accident losses thereby promoting deterrence efficiency. The economic approach views tort law as a set of loss (cost) allocation rules that shift (internalize) accident losses selectively with the implied objective of deterrence efficiency.

5.2.3 The economic reformulation of negligence

A distinctive feature of the economic tort literature has been its attempt to provide an economic definition of negligence. This was first suggested by Richard Posner in a provocative paper entitled *A Theory of Negligence*, in which he argued that negligence as actually applied by American courts in the mid-nineteenth century was an 'economic test' (Posner, 1972; pp. 32–33; 1977, pp. 122–123). Whatever the plausibility or accuracy of this view there does nonetheless exist an economic definition of negligence that will achieve deterrence efficiency (*see* Brown, 1973; Note, 1976).

Negligence or fault liability determines the defendant's liability for the victim's losses by comparing his conduct to that of a reasonable man, which is an objective judicial standard. A defendant will usually be held liable — at fault — if his conduct falls short of that which the court regards as reasonable. The economic reformulation of the reasonable man standard builds on Justice Learned Hand's comparatively recent statement in the American case of *Carroll Towing*[21]. According to Hand, the defendant's liability is determined by the courts according to the following 'quantitative' formula — the defendant is negligent if the likelihood of injury multiplied by the 'gravity' of the injury exceeds the 'burden of adequate precautions'. Read in economic terms the *Hand Test* appears to state that the defendant will bear the victim's loss if the costs to him of preventing the accident are less than the expected loss (the loss multiplied by the probability of injury). Expressed somewhat differently the defendant will only be liable if, on the basis of a rational cost calculation, he would have avoided the accident[22]. The *Hand Test* thus only shifts the loss when there is a net cost saving; when the defendant will be induced by the imposition of damages to avoid future losses. The economic interpretation of the *Hand Test* elegantly combines deterrence and efficiency considerations by making the economic avoidability of accidents the social justification for loss shifting.

Read literally the *Hand Test* would not result in deterrence efficiency. An economically correct version would compare not total costs, but the *marginal* costs of accidents and accident prevention to determine the defendant's liability (*see* Brown, 1973, pp. 331–335). This *Incremental Hand Test*, which some have suggested the courts do in fact use, would provide incentives for deterrence efficiency in the following manner (ibid., pp. 334–335). The *Incremental Hand Test*, properly administered, only makes the defendant liable for those losses that he could have avoided at a marginal cost less than marginal expected damages. A rational and knowledgeable defendant who was made liable for such damages would avoid them because prevention is the cheaper alternative. Thus basing liability on the efficiency criterion encourages the defendant to avoid all accidents deemed negligent by the courts. In the frictionless legal system envisaged as a result of the incentives conveyed by the economic negligence test, no accident which it is efficient to avoid would occur and hence no defendant would ever be found negligent. Moreover, on strict deterrence efficiency grounds there would be no justification for making the defendant liable for all losses because he will not be encouraged to take greater prevention measures. For those accidents that it is not efficient to prevent, and hence are not negligently caused, the defendant will find paying damages cheaper. Thus the selectivity of compensation in the tort system is also given a social justification — imposing on the defendant the losses due to cost-justified accidents does not enhance deterrence efficiency but neither does it militate against it.

Negligence also copes with the joint care issue. The threat of liability is sufficient incentive for the defendant to act in a cost-justified manner and as a consequence the plaintiff (victim) bears his own loss for the remaining accidents that are cost-justified. Thus victims are encouraged to minimize their losses and they therefore undertake cost-justified self protection (*see* Brown, 1973). It has been suggested by some that the (*Incremental*) *Hand*

Test by itself does not provide sufficient incentive for victim care, thus necessitating a similar test to be applied to his conduct through the absolute defence of contributory negligence (e.g. Posner, 1977, pp. 123–124; Schwartz, 1976). The reasoning supporting this argument is in fact incorrect and the result of a confusion between *ex post* and *ex ante* considerations. The *Hand Test* is sufficient to induce the victim to take cost-justified self-protection because he always bears the losses under a perfect tort system. There is thus no need for the defence of contributory negligence[23].

5.3 A corrective justice framework

The preceding discussion summarizes the central tenets of the efficiency-based analysis of tort. This literature conveys the impression that economics is value free and that it 'provides a policy basis for the rule of negligence liability' (Schwartz, 1978, p. 701). While it is true that under the assumptions made negligence achieves deterrence efficiency, there exist a number of alternative liability rules that are equally efficient but, in addition, compensate accident victims for cost-justified losses. Thus the choice of negligence as opposed to these other rules reflects, as will be shown, a normative preference for one form of distributive justice. It is the purpose of this and the ensuing sections to make these distributive and corrective justice considerations explicit and to emphasize the normative content of the efficiency norm.

5.3.1 The framework

The proposed corrective justice approach attempts to unify efficiency and normative considerations in the economic theory of tort liability. The framework draws its principal elements from welfare economics and the appealing legal reformulation of Calabresi and Melamed (1972). In addition to the concept of deterrence efficiency two concepts of justice will be used; distributive justice and corrective justice. Distributive justice is concerned with the fair distribution of wealth and income in society. Corrective justice relates to the protection of individual rights or entitlements. It can be defined more specifically, following Epstein (1979, p. 50), as 'rendering to each person whatever redress is required because of the violation of his rights by others'.

The intimate connection between efficiency and justice can be shown by building on Calabresi and Melamed's analysis of legal rules. The authors characterize the choice facing a legal system as a two-phase one involving first a decision regarding individual rights, which can be called the entitlement decision, and secondly the corrective justice question of how to protect individual entitlements.

Entitlement choice — distributive justice

Whenever there is a conflict of interests between two or more individuals the 'law' must make a choice as to which of the parties is to prevail — that is, who is to be given the entitlement. In theory the entitlement choice is not an efficiency one but is largely normative. The Coase Theorem informs us that efficiency does not provide any guidelines for the choice of entitlements other than the requirement that they be negotiable where perfect accident bargains are feasible. Any set of initial entitlements will result in efficiency. Instead the entitlement decision is best viewed as one of distributive justice[24]. As Calabresi and Melamed state (1972, p. 1098) 'the placement of entitlements has a fundamental effect on a society's distribution of wealth.' Moreover it has an impact on what the efficient allocation of resource is. In economic theory the value of goods and services is determined in exchange and depends on both individual preferences and wealth. Entitlements, because they influence the distribution of wealth, will change the pattern of demand and hence the economic value of goods and services in the economy. As a consequence, for each different initial assignment of entitlements there will be a different efficient allocation of resources. This relationship, the inseparability of efficiency, economic value and wealth distribution, again emphasizes the non-efficiency nature of the entitlement decision.

The efficiency appraisal of law therefore presupposes an initial assignment of entitlements that reflects some conception of distributive justice. Acceptance of any set of accident bargains as a basis for the efficiency appraisal of law implicitly connotes acceptance of their distributive justice, since one can point to an infinite range of other hypothetical bargains with the identical technical property of economic efficiency, but with different distributive effects. It must never be forgotten that market outcomes are in the first place legally sanctioned outcomes, and that the terms on which exchange occur are a product of the assignment of legal rights among traders.

Entitlement protection — corrective justice

Entitlements are not self-protecting and may be disputed, violated or destroyed. They thus need to be protected by the law if the initial assignment of entitlements is to have any meaning. Calabresi and Melamed identify three modes of entitlement protection that differ as to the nature and degree of what can be termed 'entitlement tradeability'. Entitlements can be protected by :

(1) *Property Rule* The entitlement can be traded upon payment to the holder of his asking price in a voluntary transaction prior to the transfer to the purchaser. A property rule thus provides absolute protection of the entitlement holder's rights, and permits only *ex ante* trading of entitlements through consensual market transactions.

(2) *Liability Rule* The entitlement can be involuntarily taken or destroyed upon payment of objective damages (price) determined by some third party. That is, the entitlement can be transferred in a non-market transaction provided the recipient pays damages after the transaction. Such entitlements can be said to be *ex post* tradeable. Liability rules are a way of facilitating entitlement transfers in situations where accident bargains are precluded by transaction costs. As Calabresi states 'liability rules are intensely practical. They enable actions to take place when contractual behaviour, before harm, would not be feasible. Damages after harm replace such unfeasible agreements.' (Calabresi, 1978, p. 529).

(3) *Inalienability Rule* The initial entitlement is assigned and its transfer is not permitted.

Legal examples of these three modes of protecting entitlement are easy to provide. Entitlements protected by property rules are those for which injunctive type remedies are available (injunctions in nuisance, specific performance in contract) and those for which damages are the remedy are protected by liability rules. The Inalienability Rule tends to be the province of the criminal law, for example, the illegality of slavery.

5.3.2 Corrective justice analysis of tort

Negligence versus strict liability

Tort liability rules are an instrument of corrective justice and the choice of tort liability rule is implied by distributive justice considerations. Tort liability protects the initial assignment of entitlements by offering to the entitlement holder damages for the destruction or violation of his rights. The entitlements he holds by virtue of the distributive justice of the system, in turn imply a pattern of corrective justice particularly relating to whether accident victims should or should not be compensated for all their losses.

In order to elaborate on this proposition consider two polar entitlement assignments in the context of accidents between strangers and where bargaining is frictionless. Assume that the entitlement is assigned to the injurer such that he may impose on the victim unintentional losses without the need to compensate him. In this situation the victim will be required to pay the injurer if he wishes him to take greater precautions. Costless bargaining would ensure that the cost-justified level of harm is imposed. Distributionally a regime of injurer entitlements sees compensation flowing from victims to injurers in the process of purchasing the formers entitlement to impose risks. The distributive justice implied by this assignment of entitlements at least has injurers compensated for their prevention cost, and victims bearing their own (cost-justified) injury losses. If instead the victim is given the entitlement to be free from the risk of injury unless compensated to bear the risk, then compensation will flow from injurer to victim in the trading process. The injurer will be willing to pay the victim compensation to bear additional accident risks as long as compensation is cheaper than prevention. Thus, the only difference between these two entitlement assignments is distributional — when injurers are favoured, victims go uncompensated for cost-justified losses, whereas they receive full compensation when they hold the entitlement.

When the market fails and accident bargains do not take place, liability rules are needed to simulate the hypothetical outcome of these accident bargains. This requires liability rules that encourage the cost-justified level of safety and satisfy the corrective justice constraint that individual rights derived from the initial assignments of entitlements be protected.

Negligence is a corrective justice regime premised on an initial assignment of entitlements to injurers. As we have seen, when the injurer has the entitlement compensation flows from victims to injurers to achieve deterrence efficiency. Negligence replicates this distributional outcome, in as much as accident victims are not compensated for cost-justified injuries. However, compared with the ideal accident bargain, victims do better because the cost-justified level of care is encouraged by negligence liability without the need for the victim to pay the injurers for the reduction in risk. Barring this difference, negligence approximates the market outcome when entitlements favour injurers. Under both situations victims bear their own losses and look to third parties for insurance.

The corrective justice of victim entitlements, on the other hand, is based on a system of strict liability. Under both the hypothetical contractual solution and strict liability, the injurer compensates the victim for all losses and decides for himself when prevention is cheaper than compensation. But again the distributional effects of strict liability only approximate those of victim entitlement-based accident bargains. As will be shown, the injurer comes out relatively better off (*see* the second part of section 5.3.2, below).

Thus efficiency provides support for both negligence and strict liability and it does so because of the intimate and inseparable relationship between the ideal contractual solutions that resolve conflict situations, and distributive and corrective justice. An efficiency theory of tort liability provides indeterminate guidelines for the choice of liability rules, although efficiency considerations will feature in the definition of the cost-justified level of care (and hence standard of care) and the structure of doctrines, when the administration of the tort system is costly[25]. The crucial point, however, is that victim compensation is *not*, as is often argued, incompatible with efficiency or a mere detail but really the fundamental issue[26].

Graphical representation

This section illustrates in more detail the distributional differences between negligence, strict liability and their corresponding accident bargain equivalents.

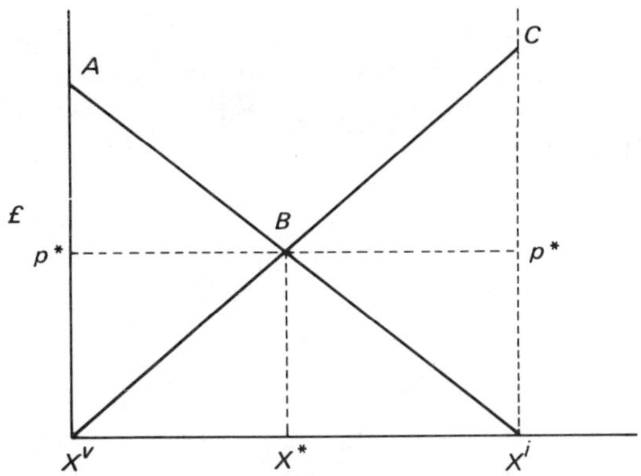

Figure 5.1 *The gains from efficiency*

In *Figure 5.1* the standard economic representation of accidental injuries is portrayed (*see* Turvey, 1963; Polinsky, 1979). The upward sloping line (X^vC) represents the marginal external damages inflicted by the hazardous activity, whereas the downward sloping line, read from left to right, gives the marginal cost to the injurer of preventing accidental losses. The intersection of the two schedules gives the cost-justified level of care, X^*, which has the property of minimizing the joint costs of the two parties. The points labelled X^i and X^v give the initial starting points for bargaining when the injurer and the victim are given the initial entitlement respectively. Thus, at X^i the injurer takes no precautions, as shown by zero safety costs, and at x^v he either takes the precautions necessary to remove all the risk or goes out of business. According to the Coase Theorem regardless of the point from which bargaining begins the parties will choose X^*, the efficient level of injurer care[27]. The distribution of the gains from efficiency, however, depends on who has the entitlement in bargaining situations or, when the market fails, which liability rule is in operation. Assume for simplicity, that payments for additional care are based on a marginal cost pricing rule. That is, for each unit increase/decrease in care the party required to make the payment offers p^*. Strictly this will not be the case because in the bilateral bargaining situation under consideration the exact distribution of efficiency gains is indeterminate; only the limits are known.

Envisage now the distributional consequences of bargaining when the injurer is assigned the entitlement. The final distributional outcomes as derived from *Figure 5.1*, are summarized in *Table 5.1*. The victim pays the injurer $X^ip^*BX^*$ as part of the bargain to reduce the accident rate. Both parties gain from this transaction as indicated by the plus signs attached to the net redistributive effects, as listed in *Table 5.1* (upper left-hand box.) When transaction costs are prohibitive, negligence will encourage the cost-justified level of care by imposing on the injurer the victim's loss for inefficient carelessness. The damage schedule facing the injurer is zero for cost-justified levels of care and kinks upward to the marginal damage schedule thereafter i.e. X^vX^*BC. A cost minimizing injurer would thus choose X^* to avoid his common law liability under negligence.

However, negligence only approximates the distributional terms of the accident bargain it seeks to replicate. The victim comes out better under the negligence rule than if bargaining were possible because there is no longer an 'entitlement payment' involved. As a result of the simulation of deterrence efficiency achieved by negligence there is no longer a mutual gain — the injurer incurs a net loss ($-X^iBX^*$) and the victim receives all the gain due to the enhancement of deterrence efficiency ($+ X^iCBX^*$).

Table 5.1 *Summary of the distributive effects of market and liability solutions*

Entitlement holder (bargaining starting point)		Net distributive effects relative to X^i or X^v	
		Accident bargain	Liability solution
Injurer (X^i)	Entitlement payment	$+ X^ip^*BX^*$	Negligence
	Net gain/loss		
	victim	$+ p^*CB$	$+ X^iCBX^*$
	injurer	$+ X^ip^*B$	$- X^iBX^*$
			(losses uncompensated)
Victim (X^v)	Entitlement payment	$+ X^vp^*BX^*$	Strict liability
	Net gain/loss		
	victim	$+ X^vBp^*$	0
	injurer	$+ p^*AB$	$+ X^vBA$
			(losses compensated)

Similarly, under strict liability the injurer does better than he would if bargaining were possible. With the victim given the entitlement bargaining would begin from X^v and given the assumptions of the model, the injurer would pay the victim an entitlement payment of $X^vp^*BX^*$ to impose the risk of an accident. Again both parties gain from this transaction; the injurer in terms of avoided safety costs and the victim by the entitlement payment that exceeds his losses (*see* lower left-hand box, *Table 5.1*). When bargaining is not possible, strict liability is the appropriate rule. Under strict liability the victim receives only compensation for his losses and therefore loses the additional entitlement payment that he would have received had bargaining been feasible i.e. $+ X^vp^*B$. This is received under strict liability by the injurer, who obtains all the *net* efficiency gain from the movement towards deterrence efficiency.

This simple model illustrates that the element of coercion inherent in liability rules results in the party who is *not* assigned the initial entitlement doing better under a liability rule than had bargaining been feasible. Moreover, under negligence victims do relatively better than do injurers, because they appropriate all the efficiency gain whereas the latter only appropriate the *net* gain.

The interesting implication of the above analysis is that strict and negligence liability do not satisfy the corrective justice requirement that entitlements be (fully) protected. Under each rule the initial entitlement holder is *not* compensated at all (negligence) or possibly as well (strict liability) as he would be had a contractual solution been feasible. Under negligence the injurer does not receive compensation for his additional safety precautions and under strict liability the victim's compensation may be less than had bargaining taken place. This can be further emphasized by pointing to liability rules that would achieve full distributional symmetry. The protection of injurer entitlement would require an appropriately calculated subsidy to injurers to increase their level of care and a corresponding tax on victims[28]. Thus, not negligence but what Calabresi and Melamed (1972, p. 1116) have identified as a rule of 'partial eminent domain coupled with a benefit tax' would fully protect injurer entitlements. Unlike negligence, full corrective justice is possible through strict liability. In order to replicate the distributional outcome of a victim-entitlement based market, damages need only be overcompensatory, i.e. incorporate a 'bonus' payment in excess of actual damage. Indeed, this may frequently occur through the award of pain and suffering damages[29].

Liability in contract

The distributional effects so far discussed are only applicable to accidents between strangers. Where the accident bargain is associated with a transaction for some other good or service then the redistributive effects identified above will not take place[30].

Consider the case of industrial accidents where the accident bargain occurs as part of the labour transaction. In an ideal setting, regardless of the initial assignment of entitlements, the employer always fully compensates the worker for his losses. If the law is silent as to liability for losses, the worker will demand a wage premium that reflects his expected injury costs[31] and when the employer is made liable, compensation will be received instead as damages or employer-financed accident insurance. The existence of a contractual wage that reflects the implicit terms of the accident bargain adjusts to offset the reallocation of liability, so that in real terms the law has no (*ex ante*) distributive effects. The effects of the law are only nominal, changing the compensation received from the employer from a wage premium to explicit accident compenation and lower wages.

The analysis of product accident or defect situations is very similar but differs in one minor respect — the loss is not observable in the price of the product when the manufacturer is not liable. Under *caveat emptor* (injurer entitlement) the buyer will incorporate the expected loss into his purchase decision and discount his willingness to pay for the good by this amount. The 'full' price of the good is therefore the buying price plus expected damages. If the law changes to *caveat venditor* (victim entitlement) the expected loss that was implicit in the purchase decision is now registered in the market as an observed higher price for the commodity. The change in entitlements again has no effect on product quality or the real income of manufacturers and consumers.

The reason for the *ex ante* distributional neutrality of entitlement assignments in these contractual cases is the existence of a concurrent contractual price that adjusts to offset the burden of changing entitlements and liability rules.

The efficiency of liability rules in contractual cases is not as straightforward as that between strangers if imperfect information is accepted as the source of market failure. Unless liability rules correct perceptions, the rules will not be able to achieve full deterrence efficiency and will need to be complemented by other corrective devices, e.g. 'tort fines'[32]. But from a corrective justice perspective, liability should be placed on the better-informed side of the market (usually the employer/manufacturer) so that the victim's entitlement is protected. If this is not done, the employer/manufacturer will under-compensate entitlement holders and thereby gain.

5.4 Some applications

5.4.1 From absolute to fault liability—the judicial subsidy thesis

It is generally asserted that with the advent of the industrial revolution in North America tort liability underwent a transformation from absolute (injurer) liability to fault, and that this represented a policy on the part of the judiciary, either conscious or otherwise, to subsidize infant industry[33]. This *judicial subsidy view* of tort focuses on the redistributive effects implied by the change and correctly identifies the preference that it gave to hazardous industries, particularly railways[34]. A number of comments can be made on this thesis.

First, the strict liability of the common law was based on causation and is to be distinguished from more recent variants (e.g. Calabresi and Hirschoff, 1972) — '*A* hit *B*' was sufficient to establish *A*'s liability for *B*'s loss. In a non-industrial society such a liability rule can be given an efficiency rationale. In a society where insurance markets are non-existent and the criminal law relatively undeveloped, an uncompensated injury or death may encourage members of the victim's family to engage in retaliatory self-help remedies: extracting an eye for an eye by inflicting a loss on the injurer or his family. This would obviously escalate the real resource costs to society and strict liability (compensation) was a way of buying off (appeasing) the victim's need for costly retaliation[35]. With industrialization the frequency and extent of accidents increased and with it the gradual acceptance that they were an acceptable 'cost' of living in an industrial society. This presumably reduced the tendency of victims and their family to retaliate and hence the rationale for strict liability.

Secondly, it is clear that the change to negligence marked a fundamental reassignment of entitlements in favour of injurers. As Green (1958, p. 13) aptly remarks, 'The concern of centuries for the injured party was transferred to the offending party for whom the common law had theretofore shown slight consideration.' The change distributionally favoured injurers, relative to their treatment under strict liability, by relieving them of the burden of compensation for cost-justified accidents. Thus the judicial subsidy thesis is valid even though the change does not necessarily imply an under investment in safety by individual firms although, in the long run, the aggregate number of accidents will be higher under negligence than strict liability. This is because the higher profits under negligence will attract more firms into hazardous industries[36].

The corrective justice approach puts this transition and current developments in accident law into perspective. The change to negligence marked, first, a reassignment of distributive entitlements wherein, secondly, efficiency considerations could influence the structure of doctrines and remedies. The approach thus reconciles the two conflicting interpretations of negligence — negligence both favours industry and achieves shortrun deterrence efficiency. Furthermore, the corrective justice approach stresses the vacuousness of pure efficiency interpretations of accident law evolution. A theory currently in vogue is that the common law has evolved to promote deterrence efficiency, specifically in its choice of negligence liability[37]. But as we have seen this implies first and foremost a choice of distributive entitlements and the need for a complementary theory of how and why the entitlement choice is made. The movement from strict to fault and, during this century, to no-fault liability all reflect fundamental changes in the distributive justice underlying accident law. It is only after such a transition has occurred that efficiency considerations will begin to assert themselves in the evolution of efficient rules and procedures[38]. In other words, a satisfactory theory of legal development must be both wealth and efficiency based.

5.4.2 Joint care and common law defences

So far we have tended to ignore the issue of joint care both as it affects accident bargains and efficient liability rules. In practice tort law rarely makes one party fully liable for the other's losses, but provides the defendant with a number of defences that will defeat the plaintiff's action. These defences are invariably based on the actions or intentions of the victim, which either indicate that he 'caused' the accident or consented to the imposition of the risk of injury.

Joint care presents no problem for accident bargains. Under injurer entitlement the victim will take self-protection or pay the injurer to increase his care, on the basis of who can prevent accidents more cheaply. Likewise, when the victim is entitled to compensation the injurer will pay him either to bear the risk or to prevent it, in the proportion that each represents the least cost alternative. Thus the accident bargain, in effect, consists of two payments — the entitlement payment and reimbursement for cost-justified self protection.

Replication of the accident bargains in joint care situations requires that the victim's incentive for self-protection be preserved. This is done by a number of defences that defeat the victim's action where he has contributed to his loss by exercising insufficient care. As has already been argued for negligence, the absolute defence of contributory negligence is not needed. A properly administered negligence system would provide the appropriate incentive for the victim to take efficient self-protective measures. Strict liability, however, requires some type of defence because it gives rise to a moral hazard problem. If a victim is compensated for his actual losses regardless of his actions, the incentive for self-protection will be dramatically reduced.

As many have observed, one solution to the provision of optimal incentives for self-protection is an absolute defence of contributory negligence in a system of strict liability (e.g. Posner, 1973; 1977, pp. 123–124). That is, to totally deny the victim compensation when he has exercised inefficient care. This strict liability/contributory negligence rule is, in fact, the *reverse* of the negligence rule[39]. It illustrates the general proposition that in joint care situations deterrence efficiency can be achieved if for one party the standard of care (liability) is defined in terms of the efficient level of precautions.

However, the economic case in favour of contributory negligence has been greatly overstated in the literature (especially by Posner, op. cit.). As I have argued, it is not necessary under negligence, nor is it required under strict liability. The key to the latter contention lies in the way the accident bargain resolves the joint care problem, while at the same time providing the victim with 'full' compensation. The accident bargain encourages the victim to take efficient self-protection by reimbursing his safety costs plus some of the efficiency gain. The liability rule analogue of this solution is some version of what in America is called comparative negligence or what in England is contributory negligence, with damages apportioned according to the degree of the plaintiff's fault. Thus corrective justice requires strict liability plus a defence of comparative negligence, not the absolute defence of contributory negligence.

This contention might be criticized because it can be shown formally that any apportionment of damages will reduce the victim's incentive to take care[40]. But this criticism results from the wrong way of looking at the problem. Strict liability only leads to moral hazard problems if the victim receives compensation for actual damages regardless of his actions. If instead his compensation is fixed at the level that would have occurred had he taken efficient care (that is, it is in the nature of a lump-sum payment) the victim's incentive for efficient self-protection will not be impaired. In practice, the calculation of damages on this basis will result in less than full compensation when the plaintiff has been contributorily negligent, i.e. comparatively negligent[41].

The contention can be further illustrated by considering how the law handles liability for breach of contract. The usual remedy for breach of contract appears to be strict liability — the breaching party compensates the other for his *net* losses. The prominence of strict liability in contract law has been described by Posner (1977, p. 142) as a 'puzzle' and rationalized on the grounds that contract breaches are less preventable than accidents — 'contract cases are less likely to involve an interactive mishap that both parties could prevent'. That is, joint care, and indeed care, which is central to the economic analysis of law, is asserted by Posner not to be relevant for contract cases. But surely the goal of contract law is to prevent both inefficient contracts from being formed and inefficient breaches from occurring. Posner's analysis, however, results from a misinterpretation of the liability rule in contract law, which is in fact a version of comparative negligence. The breaching party is not liable for the full loss but the loss that would have occurred had the non-breaching party taken cost-justified (reasonable) loss avoidance measures. This is known as the doctrine of mitigation and the damages given to the victim of a breach of contract are his cost-justified loss plus the cost of reasonable measures to minimize post-breach losses. This *mitigated damage measure* is similar to that which under a regime of victim entitlement would result from accident bargains.

5.4.3 Efficiency theory of entitlement and justice

From time to time it has been suggested that efficiency supplies a comprehensive theory of entitlements and justice. Several variants of this proposition have been proposed, but we shall only be concerned with those that have an immediate and direct bearing on tort law.

Recently Posner (1979, p. 125) has argued that efficiency provides the 'foundations for a theory of justice, both distributive and corrective,' and of rights[42]. Moreover, it is contended that most of the common law displays such economic normativism and that negligence 'is a moral system founded on economic principles' (ibid. p. 132). From the proposition that efficient law is just law, Posner derives a theory of rights that he suggests does not need to posit a just distribution of wealth. His efficiency theory of rights implies, inter alia, that rights should be exclusive, negotiable and that 'individual rights' (to life, liberty and labour) should be initially assigned to their 'natural owners'; that when transaction costs are present the assignment of rights should be to those that value them the highest; and a fault liability regime (ibid. p. 127).

The above discussion should, however, alert the reader to the over-extended nature of these claims. Efficiency supplies some guidelines to the form of rights — that they should be exclusive and negotiable, but not to their initial assignment in an ideal world (ibid. p. 125). As Posner admits, in an ideal world it is a matter of indifference, but he argues that the theory supplies determinate answers when transaction costs are positive. Entitlements should be assigned to their highest value users, i.e. to simulate the hypothetical (zero-transaction cost) market outcome. But as we have seen, economic value and perfect market outcomes are determined by, and differ according to, the initial assignment of entitlements. Posner's argument is circular, and incorrectly asserts that there is no need to posit *some* normative theory of distributive justice.

In relation to tort, the theory has some inconsistencies in its preference for negligence. First, negligence is not an exclusive right but a contingent right. The injured party is only compensated if the defendant acts inefficiently. Secondly, as Posner correctly states, corrective justice considerations require 'compensation to anyone injured by an infringement of the rights he holds by virtue of the distributive justice principles of the system.' (ibid. p. 127). As I have shown above, negligence is premised on a set of entitlements favouring injurers, which is a normative consideration. The failure of Posner to articulate this normative distributive preference of the common law makes this particular use of efficiency misleading. Secondly, negligence does not, as we have seen, fully protect injurer entitlements. Moreover, Posner's contention that efficiency requires that individual rights to life be assigned to their natural owners would seem clearly to support strict liability, not negligence.

Thus it is clear that tort questions, whether analysed in efficiency or other terms, require an anterior determination of the entitlement issue not derivable from efficiency or wealth maximization principles[43].

5.5 Conclusion

In this chapter I have sketched the rudiments of a corrective justice approach to tort liability that incorporates considerations of efficiency and justice, both distributive and corrective. While the positive economic theory of law can analyse existing laws in terms of efficiency, it needs to be stressed, particularly in view of statements to the contrary, that the particular choice of efficient law inherently involves value judgements, and is normative. Negligence may or may not be efficient in practice, but it is nonetheless based on an assignment of entitlements that favours those imposing harm on others. Under the same set of assumptions that shows that negligence achieves deterrence efficiency, strict liability can also be shown to be efficient. The fundamental and possibly most interesting questions concern why the common law opted for negligence and not strict liability and what forces govern the choice and evolution of accident law.

In this chapter the crucial role of justice notions in the efficiency theory of liability has been stressed. Economists are prone to ignore justice and wealth distribution considerations because they are not amenable to rigorous theorizing and generally characterize justice as being concerned solely with the distribution of wealth in society[44]. There is clearly a need for a more thorough consideration by both lawyers and economists of the role that various justice concepts do and can play in tort theory[45].

Notes to chapter five

1 James (1959) p. 315. James is generally of the pessimistic view that '[T]he truth is there is no single integrating principle of tort liability save one so broad it answers nothing' ibid. p. 320.

2 For surveys and critical reviews of this functional literature see Posner (1973), Steiner (1976), Atiyah (1977) Ch. 24, McCellan (1977), Eglard (1980) and White (1980) Ch. 6.

3 For surveys of this literature, see Posner (1975; 1979). Indeed one economist has argued that economists should take more note of legal scholarship (Ward, 1972); cf. O'Connell (1973).

4 This is partly due to differences in legal education between England and North America. In the latter, law is a post-graduate degree and hence most students will have a social science background that provides the basis for a more inter-disciplinary approach to legal scholarship. Thus observes one commentator: 'English [legal] academics tend to tidy up cases and annotate them.....American academics are social engineers.'; Roberts (1965) p. 201.

5 See general readings in Rabin (1976) and annotated bibliography in Veljanovski (1979).

6 Another reason explaining the failure of economics to be more acceptable to English legal academics is its overt market bias which is perceived to be normative. To quote the English tort scholar Atiyah (1977): 'Most of the growing literature on this subject is American in origin, and much of it is based on assumptions about private enterprise economics which are not widely or so strongly held in this country [England].' Ibid. p. 535, continuing, '[I]t is important not to underestimate the value of economic considerations..... But the economic way is not the only way.' Ibid. p. 554.

7 This is part of a larger work to be published by Butterworths (Toronto) under the auspices of the Law and Economics Program of the Faculty of Law, University of Toronto.

8 This excludes nuisance, for which injunctions are the primary remedy, although the framework developed later is equally applicable to nuisance.

9 See Williams (1951) for an interesting discussion of the goals of tort.

10 Pearson (1948) para. 267.

11 Kessler has observed a 'theory of enterprise liability has emerged, frequently based on vague and unanalyzed notions of public policy and economics.' Kessler (1964) p. 262.

12 This is a constant theme of Atiyah's writing, e.g. Atiyah (1977). However, see Stoljar (1974) for a cogent defence of the deterrence function of negligence.

13 The purpose of tort has been stated by the English courts to be compensatory in *Rookes v Barnard* [1964] AC 1129 (reaffirmed in *Broome v Cassell* [1972] AC 1027). Whereas one of the prominent law and economics scholars states 'the economic function of liability is evident: it is to bring about the level of accidents and

safety that the market would bring about if transactions were feasible — the efficient level.' Posner (1972) p. 37.

14 The term 'cost' as used in the text is defined widely to include both pecuniary costs/losses and the monetary equivalent of disutilities (e.g. pain and suffering), i.e. psychic costs.

15 Calabresi (1970) p. 26. Strictly speaking, Calabresi's statement is slightly incorrect. It should be read *expected* accident costs to reflect the *ex ante* nature of the efficiency analyses (see text below) and the probabilistic nature of accident costs.

16 See Mishan (1971) for an excellent discussion of the economic approach to damage valuation for deterrence purposes.

17 See Smith (1979) and Blomquist (1981) for surveys of the empirical estimates of the economic value of life.

18 Scott (1975) provides an interesting discussion of these two competing models and their implications.

19 In Calabresi's terminology the paper will only be concerned with primary cost minimization. See Calabresi (1970). pp. 26–31.

20 This should not be confused with the joint tortfeasor case. For a criticism of Coase's analysis of causation see Epstein (1973) p. 164 *et seq.*

21 *United States v Carroll Towing Co*, 159 F (2d) 169 (2d.Cir.1947). However Schwartz has observed 'the *Carroll Towing* opinion, celebrated as it is by academics, has had little real world influence standing on its own; ....*Carroll Towing* has never been cited by a single state court.' Schwartz (1979) p. 702 n. 20.

22 Although Posner's efficiency interpretation of the *Hand Test* does not rely on explicit judicial economizing it is clear that Hand did not have in mind a quantitative or monetary comparison. In an earlier case Hand states in regard of the formula '[A]ll these are practically not susceptible of any quantitative estimate, and the second two are generally not so, even theoretically.' *Conway v O'Brien*, 111 F(2d) 611 at 612 (2d Cir 1940).

23 For formal proof, see Brown (1973) pp. 341–343.

24 This is not to say that the entitlement decision is exclusively one of distributive justice. In principle any norm could be used to assign initial entitlements, such as, for example, causation. On the latter, see Epstein (1972).

25 Posner, whose writings constantly emphasize the deterrence efficiency properties of negligence, recognizes the indeterminacy of an efficiency theory of liability, but refuses to develop the normative implications inherent in his support for negligence. See Posner (1973) p. 221.

26 Posner (1977) p. 143. Cf. Posner (1979) p. 127. As Baker aptly comments: 'In addition to its efficiency effect, the legal decision is inevitably distributive — someone is awarded the right (or the money for its violation) and someone else is not..... In this sense, the economic analysis of the legal dispute *cannot* take the distribution as given, since the dispute is over what the distribution is.' Baker (1975) p. 7.

27 The issue of joint care is ignored here in order to focus on the distributional consequences of negligence and strict liability. Joint care is discussed in section 5.4.2.

28 This is akin to a Knightian double-tax/subsidy scheme; see Macaulay (1972).

29 Damages for pain and suffering have often been considered over-compensatory, either to defray legal costs or as a bargaining ploy. See Calabresi (1970) p. 225 and Pearson (1978) paras. 382–388. Blum and Kalven (1967) argue that corrective justice is not only concerned with deterring wrongdoing, but with satisfying the victim's feeling of indignation and they see damages for pain and suffering as 'recognition of dignatory aspects of accident injuries'. Ibid. p. 270.

30 For more rigorous treatments see Demsetz (1972) and Hamada (1976).

31 Empirical evidence exists that such 'accident bargains' do in fact occur in labour markets; see Smith (1979).

32 Indeed it is doubtful that any tax-type instrument could achieve full deterrence efficiency. For in addition to cost-justified levels of safety we also have consumers buying the wrong products and workers making uninformed job choices, and loss allocation rules will not lead to the optimal reassignment of individuals among goods and jobs. For an interesting analysis, see Spence (1977).

33 Gregory (1957), Green (1958) and more recently Horowitz (1977). Calabresi makes a similar claim: 'I do not suggest, of course, that nineteenth century judges made the transfer to fault liability on the basis of a rather complicated theory. But

their statements that non-fault liability would deprive our land of the benefits and promises of industrial expansion may represent a rough and ready, non-economist's way of recognising the fact that industry was simply not ready to bear all the costs, and that the country would in the long run be better off if it did not.' Calabresi (1965) p. 516.

34 The intentional version of this thesis, that judges consciously made this distributional choice, has been questioned by Pound (1940). But see Levy (1957) ch. 10 and Atiyah (1979). A similar intentional explanation has been advanced by Posner to rationalize the courts' apparent concern for deterrence efficiency; Posner (1972).

35 For a 'resource conservation' interpretation of this so-called force theory of liability, see Klemme (1976).

36 Posner criticizes this view by adopting a very specific definition of subsidy: 'since [negligence] does not connote..... an under-investment in safety, its adoption cannot be equated with subsidization in any useful sense of that term;' Posner (1972) p. 30. However, there is still a 'subsidy' to hazardous industries relative to strict liability and this increases the aggregate number of accidents. For formal proofs see Veljanovski (1979), Shavell (1980) and Polinsky (1980).

37 Beginning with Rubin (1977).

38 I am suggesting that a distributional-based theory of common law evolution may be needed such as, but not identical to, 'capture' theories that have been used to 'explain' the growth and form of public law. See generally, Stigler (1971) and Posner (1974).

39 Calabresi and Hirschoff (1972) pp. 1056–1059 were the first to recognize the deterrence symmetry of this rule. They refer to it as the Reverse Learned Hand Test.

40 See Brown (1973) pp. 346–347. Brown's conclusion that comparative negligence is inefficient results from his characterization of the standard and his assumption that when both parties act efficiently damages are halved, because they were equally 'negligent'.

41 For discussion of the appropriate damage measures under strict liability, see Holterman (1976), Browning (1977), and Wittman D., *Pigovian Taxes, Liability Rules and Regulation of Inputs*, Santa Cruz: University of California (no date).

42 For example, 'a system of rights or entitlements can be deduced from the goal of wealth maximisation itself.', Posner (1979) p. 135 'a just distribution of wealth need not be posited.' Ibid. p. 131.

43 Posner flatly rejects this in a recent interchange with Epstein. See Posner (1979) pp. 465–471. Also Epstein (1979a), (1979b) and (1980). Although the framework in this chapter differs from Epstein's by not outlining the elements of corrective justice, it is in basic accordance with the Epsteins main contention regarding the need for a normative theory of justice. As Epstein states in a recent paper linking his causal paradigm to a theory of rights (1979, pp. 76–77): 'In a world of zero transaction costs there is only one distribution of original rights that satisfies in full the demands of both corrective justice and wealth maximization: it is the assignment of rights specified by a theory of corrective justice. Such an assignment of rights has a unique advantage in terms of moral theory, and it suffers no offsetting efficiency disability....Since complete satisfaction of the justice requirement comes at no economic cost, the economic theory must give way.'

44 As Calabresi and Hirschoff (1972, p. 1080) comment 'Justice notions attach to other societal preferences which can only with difficulty be explained in terms of efficiency or wealth distributional preferences designed to make some groups richer....These other justice notions, which we are unable to describe in general terms, are crucial to the choice of liability rules.'

45 For example in contrast to the approach in this chapter Calabresi has regarded justice not as a goal of accident law but as a constraint — 'justice is a totally different order of goal than accident cost reduction. Indeed...it is not a goal but rather a constraint that can impose a veto on (accident law) systems.' Calabresi (1970) p. 25. Also see his discussion ibid. pp. 24–26. I regard it as puzzling that Calabresi should not allow justice to be traded for accident cost minimization in his normative theory of law. Surely there must be a better way of dealing with justice than to give it veto power over efficient liability regimes. Furthermore if trade-offs are allowed between justice and efficiency then the difference between justice and efficiency as 'goals' is more

apparent than real. It can be shown mathematically that if a constraint is substituted into an objective function the solution is identical to that when it is treated as constraint in the optimization process.

References

ATIYAH, P.S. (1977), *Accidents, Compensation and the Law*, 2nd. ed. London: Weidenfeld.
ATIYAH, P.S. (1979), *The Rise and Fall of Freedom of Contract*, Oxford: Clarendon Press.
BAKER, C.E. (1975), The ideology of economic analysis of law, *Philosophy and Public Affairs*, **5**, no. 1, 3–48.
BLOMQUIST, G. (1981), The value of human life: an empirical perspective, *Economic Inquiry*, **19**, no. 1, 157–164.
BLUM, W.J. and KALVEN, H. Jr. (1965), *Public Law Perspectives on a Private Law Problem — Auto Compensation Plans*, Boston: Little-Brown.
BLUM, W.J. and KALVEN, H. Jr. (1967), The empty cabinet of Dr. Calabresi, *University of Chicago Law Review*, **34**, no. 2, 239–273.
BROWN, J.P. (1973), Toward an economic theory of liability, *Journal of Legal Studies*, **2**, no. 2, 323–349.
BROWNING, E.K. (1977), External diseconomies, compensation, and the measure of damages, *Southern Economic Journal*, **43**, no. 3, 1279–1287.
BORROWS, P. (1970), On external costs and the visible arm of the law, *Oxford Economic Papers*, **22**, no. 1, 39–56.
CALABRESI, G. (1967), Some thoughts on risk distribution and the law of torts, *Yale Law Journal*, **70**, no. 4, 499–553.
CALABRESI, G. (1970), *The Costs of Accidents — A Legal and Economic Analysis*, New Haven: Yale University Press.
CALABRESI, G. (1978), Torts — the law of the mixed society, *Texas Law Review*, **56**, no. 3, 519–536.
CALABRESI, G. and HIRSCHOFF, J.T. (1972), Toward a test for strict liability in torts, *Yale Law Journal*, **81**, no. 6, 1054–1085.
CALABRESI, G. and MALAMED, A.D. (1972), Property rules, liability rules, and inalienability; one view of the cathedral, *Harvard Law Review*, **85**, no. 2, 1089–1128.
COASE, R.H. (1960), The problem of social cost, *Journal of Law and Economics*, **3**, no. 1, 1–44.
DEMSETZ, H. (1972), Wealth ownership and the ownership of rights, *Journal of Legal Studies*, **1**, no. 2, 223–232.
DIAMOND, P.A. (1974), Single activity accidents, *Journal of Legal Studies*, **3**, no. 1, 107–164.
EGLARD, I. (1980), The system builders: a critical appraisal of modern American tort theory, *Journal of Legal Studies*, **9**, no. 1, 27–69
EPSTEIN, R.A. (1973), A theory of strict liability, *Journal of Legal Studies*, **2**, no. 1, 151–221.
EPSTEIN, R.A. (1979a), Nuisance law: corrective justice and its utilitarian constraints, *Journal of Legal Studies*, **8**, no. 1, 49–102.
EPSTEIN, R.A. (1979b), Causation and corrective justice: a reply to two critics, *Journal of Legal Studies*, **8**, no. 3, 477–504.
EPSTEIN, R.A. (1980). *A Theory of Strict Liability — Toward a Reformulation of Tort Law*, San Francisco: CATO Institute.
FLETCHER, G.P. (1972), Fairness and utility in tort theory, *Harvard Law Review*, **85**, no. 3, 537–573.
GREEN, L. (1958), *Traffic Victim: Tort Law and Insurance*, Evanston: Northwestern University Press.
GREGORY, C.O. (1957). Trespass to negligence to absolute liability, *Virginia Law Review*, **37**, no. 3, 359–397.
HAMADA, K. (1976), Liability rules and income distribution in product liability, *American Economic Review*, **66**, no. 1, 228–234.
HEUSTON, R.F.V. (1977), *Salmond on the Law of Torts*, 17th ed., London: Sweet and Maxwell.
HOLMES, O.W. Jr. (1881), The Common Law, London: MacMillan.
HOLTERMAN, S. (1976), Alternative tax systems to correct for externalities, and the efficiency of paying compensation, *Economica*, **43**, no. 169, 1–16.
HOROWITZ, M.J. (1977), *The Transformation of American law, 1780–1860*, Cambridge, Mass.: Harvard University Press.

JAMES, F. Jr. (1948), Accident liability reconsidered: the impact of liability insurance, *Yale Law Journal*, **57**, no. 4, 549–570.

JAMES, F. Jr. (1959), Tort law in mid-stream: its challenge to the judicial process, *Buffalo Law Review*, **8**, 315–344.

KEETON, R.E. and O'CONNELL, J. (1965), *Basic Protection For the Traffic Victim*, Boston: Little, Brown and Co.

KESSLER, F.A. (1964), The protection of the consumer under modern sales law, part I, *Yale Law Journal*, **74**, no. 2, 262–285.

KLEMME, H.C. (1976), The enterprise liability theory of torts, *University of Colorado Law Review*, **47**, no. 2, 153–232.

LEFF, A.A. (1974), Economic analysis of law: some realism about nominalism, *Virginia Law Review*, **60**, no. 3, 451–482.

LEVY, L.W. (1957), *The Law of the Commonwealth and Chief Justice Shaw*, Cambridge, Mass.: Harvard University Press.

LIEBHAFSKY, H.H. (1976), Price theory as jurisprudence: law and economics Chicago style, *Journal of Economic Issues*, **10**, no. 1, 23–43.

MACAULAY, H. (1972), Environmental quality, the market and public finance, in *Modern Fiscal Issues*, (R.M. Bird and J.G. Head, eds.) University of Toronto Press.

McCELLAN, F.M. (1977), Clarification of tort policy: a comparison of the common law, Calabresian and Laswell McDougal approaches to the resolution of tort claims, *Wayne Law Review*, **23**, no. 3, 995–1056.

MISHAN, E.J. (1971), Evaluation of life and limb: a theoretical approach, *Journal of Political Economy*, **79**, 687–705.

NOTE, (1976), Origin of the modern standard of due care in negligence, *Washington University Law Quarterly*, no. 3, 447–479.

O'CONNELL, J. (1973), Tort lawyers and the economists: who can learn more from whom?, *University of Illinois Law Forum*, no. 3, 604–610.

PEARSON, LORD, (1978), *Royal Commission on Civil Liability and Compensation For Personal Injury*, London: Her Majesty's Stationery Office.

POLINSKY, A.M. (1979), Controlling externalities and protecting entitlements: property right, liability rule, and tax-subsidy approached, *Journal of Legal Studies*, **8**, no. 1, 1–49.

POLINSKY, A.M. (1974), Economic analysis as a potentially defective product: a buyer's guide to Posner's economic analysis of law, *Harvard Law Review*, **27**, no. 8, 1655–1681.

POLINSKY, A.M. (1980), Strict liability vs. negligence in a market setting, *American Economic Review (Papers and Proceedings)*, **70**, no. 2, 363–367.

POSNER, R.A. (1972), A theory of negligence, *Journal of Legal Studies*, **1**, no. 1, 29–96.

POSNER, R.A. (1973), Strict liability: a comment, *Journal of Legal Studies*, **2**, no. 1, 205–221.

POSNER, R.A. (1974), Theories of economic regulation, *Bell Journal of Economics and Managerial Science*, **5**, no. 2, 335–358.

POSNER, R.A. (1975), The economic approach to law, *Texas Law Review*, **53**, no. 1, 757–782

POSNER, R.A. (1977), *Economic Analysis of Law*, 2nd ed., Boston: Little Brown.

POSNER, R.A. (1979b), Epstein's tort theory: a critique, *Journal of Legal Studies*, **8**, no. 3, 457–476.

POSNER, R.A. (1979a), Utilitarianism, economics, and legal theory, *Journal of Legal Studies*, **8**, no. 1, 103–140.

POSNER, R.A. (1979), Some uses and abuses of economics in law, *University of Chicago Law Review*, **46**, no. 2, 281–306.

POUND, R. (1940), The economic interpretation and the law of torts, *Harvard Law Review*, **53**, no. 3, 365–385.

POUND, R. (1951), *Justice According to Law*, New Haven: Yale University Press.

RABIN, R.L. (ed.) (1976), *Perspectives on Tort Law*, Boston: Little Brown.

ROBERTS, E.F. (1965), Negligence: Blackstone to Shaw to ? — an intellectual escapade in a tory vein, *Cornell Law Quarterly*, **50**, no. 2, 191–216.

RUBIN, P.H. (1977), Why is the common law efficient?, *Journal of Legal Studies*, **6**, no. 1, 51–64.

SCHWARTZ, G.T. (1978), Contributory and comparative negligence: a reappraisal, *Yale Law Journal*, **87**, no. 4, 697–727.

SCOTT, K.E. (1975), Two models of the civil process, *Stanford Law Review*, **27**, no. 3, 937–950.

SHAVELL, S. (1980), Strict liability versus negligence, *Journal of Legal Studies*, **90**, no. 1, 1–25.

SMITH, R.S. (1979), Compensating wage differentials and public policy: a review, *Industrial and Labour Relations Review*, **32**, no. 3, 331–352.

SPENCE, M. (1977), Consumer misperception, product failure and product liability, *Review of Economic Studies*, **44**, no. 3, 561–572.

STEINER, J.M. (1976), Economic morality and the law of torts, *University of Toronto Law Journal*, **26**, no. 3, 227–252.

STIGLER, G.S. (1971), The theory of economic regulation, *Bell Journal of Economics and Management Science*, **3**, no. 1, 3–21.

STOLJAR, S. (1974), Accidents, costs and legal responsibility, *Modern Law Review*, **36**, no. 3, 233–244.

TURVEY, R. (1963), On divergencies between social cost and private cost, *Economica*, **30**, 309–313.

VELJANOVSKI, C.G. (1979), Economic myths about common law realities — economic efficiency and the law of torts, *Working Paper No. 5*, Oxford: Centre for Socio-Legal Studies.

VELJANOVSKI, C.G. (1979), *Bibliography in Law and Economics — Legal Liability and Negligence*, Oxford: Centre for Socio-Legal Studies.

WARD, B. (1972), *What's Wrong With Economics*?, New York: Basic Books.

WHITE, G.E. (1980), *Tort Law in America — An Intellectual History*, Oxford: Oxford University Press.

WILLIAMS, G. (1951), The aims of the law of torts, *Current Legal Problems*, **4**, 137–176.

CHAPTER SIX

Nuisance, legal rules and decentralized decisions: a different view of the cathedral crypt[1]

Paul Burrows

6.1 Introduction

A number of studies by lawyers have presented economic analyses of the use of the law, in particular tort law, to control pollution[2]. While they represent a welcome foray of lawyers into the analysis of pollution control, these studies nevertheless display some important weaknesses. The two weaknesses with which we shall be concerned here are, first, the fact that their approach is unbalanced by a concentration on the objective of efficiency in pollution control to the exclusion of matters of justice, as a basis for the evaluation of alternative legal instruments[3]. Secondly, even within the narrow confines of their efficiency analysis they investigate the problems of the selection of legal rules by using assumptions about the operability of markets (and about the significance of transactions costs in particular) that are recognized by most observers to be irrelevant to much of the pollution in the real world.

The focus of the subsequent discussion is an attempt to demonstrate the futility of establishing any criteria, for the selection of legal rules, that relate *only* to the ability of markets to generate efficient solutions to the pollution problem when the courts are in the enviable position of possessing (on the basis of *prima facie* evidence alone) perfect information about the consequences of abating pollution. The exercise which follows is essentially a negative one, to provide a case for the reorientation of law and economics research on pollution control. The argument is presented in the belief that the previous studies provide an obstacle to, rather than a vehicle for, the deepening of our understanding of pollution control problems[4].

6.2 Justice and efficiency defined

The definition of efficiency that will be adopted is quite conventional, and similar to that which is implicit in the previous work on the law and economics of pollution control. A legal rule will be described as efficient if it brings about all of the units of pollution abatement for which the benefits to society exceed the costs, and brings about no units of abatement for which the costs exceed the benefits. Abatement at this level will lead to the socially efficient level of pollution.

There is nothing in economic theory that can be used to justify the pursuit of an efficiency objective, since the choice of objectives relates to the fundamental values of society, which economics does not treat. *A fortiori* economic theory offers no justification for the recommendation of legal rules on the basis of their efficiency characteristics to the exclusion of considerations of justice. If analysts do make such recommendations then either they are claiming widespread acceptance of a pure efficiency approach, or their reasoning is faulty[5]. Since it is imaginable that society is not concerned solely with efficiency in the selection of the legal rules by which it is bound, it appears to be fruitful to consider the implications, for rule selection, of the simultaneous pursuit of efficiency and justice.

How should the justice objective be formulated? The short cut that will be adopted here is to analyse the legal rules *as if* the objective is to protect people from uncompensated damage by the activities of others[6]. By adopting this strategy we evade the important issues involved in justifying a particular interpretation of the notion of justice in order to concentrate on the neglected analysis of the consequences, for the selection of legal rules, of the simultaneous pursuit of efficiency and just protection from uncompensated harm.

6.3 Tertiary costs, information and general deterrence

It is possible to undertake the logical exercise of economic theorizing on the basis of any mutually consistent set of assumptions. However, since the aim of such theorizing in this area of study is to move towards guidelines for legal decisions, it is necessary to explore the implications of tertiary (transactions) costs that are sufficiently heavy to rule out net gains from private bargains that aim to alter the initial configuration of property rights[7]. The existence of heavy transactions costs is scarcely in dispute. Calabresi and Melamed (1972, p. 1119) say they are 'normal' in the pollution area. Michelman (1971, p. 670) says that tertiary costs may often be 'high — perhaps prohibitive'. A similar view pervades much of the economics literature on pollution control[8]. Calabresi and Melamed (ibid., *et seq.*) assume in their analysis of legal rules that their efficiency analysis can be extended to cover this normal case. An essential point in what follows is that this is not in fact the case.

The emphasis that will be placed upon heavy tertiary costs should not be interpreted as a belief that such costs represent the only, or even the most serious, obstacle to efficient private bargains. Many other obstacles are likely to be serious in practice, such as free-rider problems in large group (ie. public bad) cases, and the probability that difficulties will be involved in establishing a bargaining procedure that will yield efficient outcomes even when the group is small and perfect information is available to the parties involved[9]. The existence of obstacles of this kind places the onus of proof on those who would argue the feasibility of the 'market' methods of controlling pollution.

The important point in the current context is that the expected failure of bargaining solutions has serious consequences for the results of the efficiency analysis that has been used as a basis for judging alternative legal rules. Yet the study of the law and pollution control has been haunted for twenty years by the ghost of market solutions, and most lawyer-economists engaged in this activity have persisted in searching for the elusive ghost.

It is now necessary to be more specific concerning the role of legal rules as perceived by those who employ a market-based analytical framework. General deterrence is the establishment of negotiable property rights to provide a transactional framework within which bargains can take place between polluters and victims concerning the efficient levels of the polluting activities. It is distinguished from specific deterrence, which involves collective decisions on efficient (or otherwise appropriate) levels of the polluting activities[10]. In its extreme form specific deterrence involves prohibitive rules outlawing, say, pollution above a particular level. The essential difference between general and specific deterrence, it is argued, is that with general deterrence 'the decision about whether production justifies itself in view of accident costs — or the search for means by which production can be beneficially altered so that it will justify itself in view of these costs — is left...to the market.'[11] This is a rather vague market test, but it appears that the market is expected to generate two pieces of information that, we shall find, it is very important to keep distinct:

(1) Whether, if the least cost method of abatement is used, it would be socially efficient to partially or totally abate the interference. This requires a comparison of the marginal and total pollution damage costs with the marginal and total pollution abatement costs.
(2) Which is the least cost method of abatement.

The first of these pieces of information tells us the socially efficient *degree* of abatement; this is based on the second piece of information, which concerns both the method of abating that involves the least resources and the identity of the party that has this least cost method at his disposal.

We shall return to the question of information in section 6.4, but it is worth observing at this point that the distinction between general and specific deterrence is not the same as a private–collective distinction. It appears, for example, that collective decisions in court on the extent and value of damage costs associated with a particular quantity of pollution (i.e. a pure damages remedy) retain the characteristics of general deterrence, because the parties involved are left free to choose the future level of pollution and by implication the amount of compensation paid[12]. Similarly, negotiable injunctions fall into the general deterrence category since they may provide a framework for transactions, whereas statutory pollution standards are clearly specific deterrence. The classification is not always clear however: the use of an effluent charge to induce a fixed standard of effluent quality for firms as a group, is specific in the sense that the standard set for the group is centrally determined, but general to the extent that the charge allows individual firms to choose their own level of pollution. In retrospect it seems that the general/specific classification could be misleading, and we shall tend to refer to particular types of legal rule or remedy rather than to general classes of approach to pollution control[13].

6.4 Criteria for selecting legal rules

Let us come now to the central issue of the selection of legal rules and, by implication, the question of the usefulness of the market as an information-generating device. Calabresi and Melamed (1972, p. 1116 *et seq.*), following and developing the analysis of Michelman (1971, p. 670 *et seq.*), postulate four possible rules determining liability and the means by which the implied entitlements are to be protected:

(1) *Pollutee (victim) property* The pollutee's nuisance may be enjoined, using an injunction for enforcement, so that the victim has a right to freedom from interference or, if he prefers, to equivalent compensation while he allows the interference to continue.
(2) *Polluter liability* The polluter is liable for damages but the victim does not have the option of enjoining the polluting activity.
(3) *Polluter property* The polluter has the right to continue polluting at will unless he prefers to abate in exchange for the payment of equivalent compensation by the victim[14].
(4) *Pollutee (victim) liability* The polluter has the right to pollute unless the victim prefers to enjoin the polluting activity in exchange for equivalent compensation paid to the polluter.

Faced with the prospect of having to choose between these rules, Michelman (1971, p. 669), Calabresi and Melamed (1972, pp, 1096–7) have suggested the adoption of the least-cost-avoider and the best-briber criteria. These have been proposed as *sequential* criteria, the first being the preferred criterion, the second being a second-best choice when the absence of information prevents the first from being applied. Briefly, the argument has been developed as follows. Efficiency requires that pollution be abated by the party that can abate most cheaply, and that abatement should continue until the marginal damage associated with the last unit of pollution just equals the marginal cost of abatement. Consequently the damage cost should be imposed on the party best able to compare it with the marginal cost of the cheapest abatement technique, that is on the least-cost-avoider. If, however, there is uncertainty as to who the least-cost-avoider is, the court should impose the damage cost on the party who can most cheaply act to alter the initial entitlement if it proves to have been placed on a high-cost-avoider. The best-briber criterion aims initially to minimize transactions costs rather than abatement costs, with the hope that abatement costs will then be minimized through transactions.

A preliminary point to note by way of comment on these criteria is that there is considerable difficulty in interpreting the statement that the first criterion should be used in the absence of uncertainty and the second when uncertainty exists. The uncertainty referred to here is the absence of immediate, zero cost information (*prima facie* evidence) to the court on the costs of alternative abatement techniques. Unfortunately the world does not divide neatly into 'certain' and 'uncertain' situations in the sense of zero cost information and costly information. It will rarely, if ever, be the case that the least-cost-avoider is immediately obvious, simply because typically there will be a choice between several methods of abatement (e.g. altering the activity level of the polluter and possibly ending the activity, or altering the production technology of the polluter in one of a variety of ways, or altering the location of the polluter, or altering the level of activity, method of producing or consuming, or location of the victim). In reality the court is faced with various parties whose abatement costs could be evaluated given time and resources. Are we to conclude from the two criteria that generally the least-cost-avoider criterion is to be avoided if an attempt to discover the relevant abatement costs would involve the court in even £1 of court costs? Clearly the central question, *if* the two criteria are used, is how much investment in centralized evaluation is justified in order to avoid resorting to the best-briber criterion, given that it will also require court resources to discover the best-briber (if there is one). The very choice of the appropriate efficiency criterion therefore involves the court in the type of pollution-abatement evaluation that the criteria were allegedly designed to avoid.

Even at this conceptual level it is difficult to imagine the courts applying the Calabresian criteria without being involved, to a significant degree, in a centralized pollution evaluation. However, more serious problems arise when we consider in detail how the two criteria might be applied, bearing in mind the two types of information that the market is required to generate (*see* section 6.3). In essence, we aim to demonstrate that the criteria are irrelevant if tertiary costs are low and ambiguous if they are high (or if other obstacles to bargains exist).

6.4.1 Low tertiary costs[15]

In the unlikely event of bargaining and litigation costs being both small and symmetrical, in the sense of being independent of the decision on entitlements, the Calabresian criteria are *not needed* for efficiency. Whichever one of the four rules is selected the bargaining process will generate a move to the socially efficient pollution level. If the initial liability happens to be placed upon the highest-cost-avoider, then subsequent transactions will induce an efficient amount of abatement by the least-cost-avoider, in exchange for a compensation payment (by the highest-cost-avoider) equal to the abatement cost incurred. This is the main point of the Coase Theorem: the efficiency of resource allocation is not determined by the placement of liability in this idealized world (Coase, 1960). In addition this theorem applies whether the entitlement consists of a liability rule or of a negotiable property rule. On the other hand, the direction of the flow of compensation, and consequently the wealth of the polluters and victims, is influenced by the decision on entitlements.

The implication of this discussion is that the least-cost-avoider criterion is redundant in idealized bargaining. Naturally there is no need to resort to the best-briber criterion, and anyway all of the parties involved are best-bribers when tertiary costs are low and symmetrical. In fact there is no need for *any* efficiency criterion. The efficient, decentralized decision process will ensure that the least-cost-avoider does the abating, and that he does so to an efficient level. The courts do not need access to the two types of information that were previously identified. They can rely upon the polluters and victims to utilize the appropriate information in deciding whether to modify the initial entitlements and, if so, in what way and to what extent. Consequently the courts could feel free to settle liability according to notions of justice, whether they be just protection or distributive justice, or both. They could also make the choice between liability and property rules entirely according to their idea of the appropriate form of the protection. If they choose a property rule they are offering the party who receives the entitlement the option of physical protection, which he may forego in exchange for compensation if he wishes to. If they prefer a liability rule this option is not given; compensation *in lieu* is judged to be sufficiently desirable for the party with the entitlement not to be permitted to refuse it.

6.4.2 High tertiary costs

Foresaking now the enchanted world of perfect markets, the problems raised by high tertiary costs will be analysed in two parts:

Symmetric costs

In this case tertiary costs are too high to allow decentralized transactions whichever of the four legal rules is selected[16]. It is crucial to retain the distinction between the two types of information required of the market, for it is the failure to do so that leads Calabresi and Melamed into a confused and misleading analysis of this important case. Michelman (1971, p. 673) also fails to draw out the implications of high tertiary costs for the

Calabresian criteria beyond asserting that they 'seem to raise serious questions about the utility of highly decentralist versions of nuisance litigation as a "cost-internalizing" approach . . . .' We shall seek to establish the specific proposition that *where tertiary costs are high and symmetrical the least-cost-avoider criterion is ambiguous and the best-briber criterion is irrelevant.*

In the cases of the property rules (1) and (3) (section 6.4) high tertiary costs have the effect of converting initial entitlements into final pollution outcomes. If, for example, a court imposes an injunction prohibiting the *whole* of the interference created by a polluter, then a zero entitlement to pollute is the final outcome, since no release from the injunction that allows an intermediate pollution outcome can be negotiated. Similarly, a partial injunction on interference above a certain level effectively imposes that level as a maximum, since no release that allows a higher pollution level can be negotiated with victims. By contrast, if liability rules are used, then in principle there is more flexibility. Under polluter liability (3), for example, the polluter can choose a non-zero pollution level if he is prepared to pay equivalent compensation.

Let us now consider whether the Calabresian criteria for rule selection are able to facilitate decentralized decisions that would generate the two types of information previously identified. Leaving aside for the moment the justice of the different rules, we have the following results. First, given that transactions (bribes) are not feasible under any entitlement the best-briber will not be available as a last resort. Second, it can be demonstrated that the least-cost-avoider criterion is not categorical in its recommendations. *Table 6.1* represents a two-way classifiction of the possible states of the world that distinguishes two types of uncertainty; uncertainty about the identity of the least-cost-avoider (information type (2) in section 6.3) and uncertainty about the efficient level of pollution (information type (1)). All of the boxes in row *(a)* represent situations where the polluter is known to be the least-cost avoider on the basis of *prima facie* evidence. The boxes *(a1)*, *(a2)* and *(a3)* represent respectively the situations where no pollution, all pollution and only some pollution is known to be efficient, when the *polluter* undertakes any abatement, whereas box *(a4)* is the case where the efficient level of pollution is unknown on the basis of *prima facie* evidence[17]. A similar interpretation is given to row *(b)* except that now the *victim* is known to be the least-cost-avoider so that, for example, *(b1)* is the situation where zero pollution is efficient when the victim undertakes the abatement. The final row *(c)* represents uncertainty about the identity of the least-cost-avoider, and contains only one meaningful box. If the identity of the least-cost-avoider is unknown then the level of the lowest possible cost of abatement must be unknown, so that the efficient level of pollution cannot be known, and the boxes *(c1)*, *(c2)* and *(c3)* are consequently inapplicable. The remaining box *(c4)* is, however, probably the one which most frequently confronts courts in dealing with pollution problems in the real world. In this

Table 6.1 *The ambiguity of the least-cost-avoider criterion: the selection of rules that can yield efficient outcomes*

	Efficient level of pollution known from *prima facie* evidence			Efficient level of pollution unknown from *prima facie* evidence (4)
	No pollution is efficient *(1)*	All pollution is efficient *(2)*	Only some pollution is efficient *(3)*	
Polluter is known to be least-cost avoider *(a)*	Victim property (1) with total injunction *or* Polluter liability (2)	Polluter property (3) *or* Victim liability (4) *or* Polluter liability (2)	Victim property (1) with partial injunction *or* Polluter liability (2)	Any of the four rules *could* be right; only Polluter liability (2) is a safe choice
Victim known to be least-cost avoider *(b)*	Polluter property (3) *or* Victim liability (4)	Polluter property (3) *or* Victim liability (4) *or* Polluter liability (2)	Polluter property (3) *or* Victim liability (4)	Rules (2), (3) or (4) *could* be right; either polluter property (3) or victim liability (4) is a safe choice
Least-cost avoider unknown from *prima facie* evidence *(c)*	Not applicable (see text)	Not applicable (see text)	Not applicable (see text)	Any of the four rules could be right; none is known to be

situation there is no conclusive *prima facie* evidence either on the identity of the least-cost-avoider or on the efficient level of pollution.

The problem of selecting a legal rule in each of the situations can now be described in order to substantiate our proposition that the least-cost-avoider criterion does not tell us which rule to prefer on efficiency grounds. In box *(a1)* the damage resulting from pollution is so high, relative to the abatement costs that would be incurred by the polluter if he abated, that *total* abatement back to zero pollution is efficient. In the absence of transactions between the parties, total abatement by the least-cost-avoider requires the liability to be placed on the polluter. However, this total abatement could be achieved either by imposing a (total) injunction on the whole of the polluting activity (i.e. a ban on all polluting, under rule (1)), or by requiring full payment of damages by the polluter, rule (2) (in which case the polluter will choose to abate totally). The Calabresi criterion leaves us indifferent between these two rules[18]. Similarly, in box *(b1)* the efficiency objective is to induce total abatement by the victim and this could be achieved by giving the polluter an entitlement to pollute backed either by property rule (3) or by the liability rule (4).

This analysis of the case in which total abatement is efficient can easily be extended to cover the intermediate case in which it is efficient to abate some but not all of the pollution, boxes *(a3)* and *(b3)*. The same rules which provided the appropriate incentive to abate in cases *(a1)* and *(b1)* do so also in *(a3)* and *(b3)*, with one modification. The modification is that if the victim property rule (1) is adopted in case *(a3)*, then efficiency requires that the (partial) injunction be set such as to outlaw only the units of pollution that lie above the socially efficient level. One general implication of the total abatement (column *1*) and partial abatement (column *3*) cases is that the least-cost-avoider criterion is not sufficient for the choice of a specific legal rule even when the courts have perfect information of both kinds. The criterion is, however, sufficient for *efficiency* in these cases, and the choice between the efficient legal rules (e.g. victim property and polluter liability in box *(a1)*) can be left to non-efficiency considerations.

By way of contrast consider the other extreme situation, boxes *(a2)* and *(b2)* in which *no* abatement is efficient whoever is the least-cost-avoider. Here all but the victim property rule (1) will lead to the efficient outcome. Rule (1) will constrain the polluter to abate even when *any* abatement is inefficient, but the other rules will not do so. Polluter property (3) clearly leaves the polluter free to pollute, and even if the victim were the least-cost-avoider his comparison of damage costs and abatement costs would reveal that no abatement is worthwhile. Victim liability (2) provides compensation to the victim for the nuisance caused, but the polluter will find it worthwhile to pay the full compensation implied by zero abatement. The important implication of the zero-abatement cases is that the use of the least-cost-avoider criterion is *neither necessary nor sufficient* for efficiency. It is not necessary because in both *(a2)* and *(b2)* either polluter liability or victim liability will be efficient, and it is not sufficient because establishing a property rule (1) against the polluter will be inefficient even if the polluter *is* the least-cost-avoider.

The unhelpful nature of the Calabresian criteria for the selection of legal rules is further exposed when we consider both the uncertain situations *(a4)* and *(b4)* in which only the efficient level of pollution is unknown, and the uncertain world *par excellence* *(c4)*, where the identity of the least-cost-avoider is not known either. Consider the cases *(a4)*, *(b4)* and *(c4)* in turn.

Essentially box *(a4)* reflects uncertainty as to whether the real world is really represented by *(a1)*, *(a2)* or *(a3)*. In other words the polluter is known to be the least-cost-avoider, but the efficient level of pollution is not known by the court. It is apparent from the previous analysis that unless we know which of the boxes *(a1)*, *(a2)* or *(a3)* applies, none of the four rules can be rejected as inefficient, since each of them is appropriate in at least one of the three cases. We can *safely* predict an efficient outcome only from polluter liability (2), which is efficient in each case. If the polluter is known to be the least-cost-avoider, therefore, the polluter liability rule offers a safe market test of the efficient pollution level, whereas an entitlement to the victim backed by property rule (1) does not. Of course, if litigation costs were high even the polluter liability rule would not necessarily offer a safe efficiency test. These conclusions are not produced by Calabresi and Melamed's own analysis (1972, pp. 1118–1119) because they jumped from a world in which tertiary costs are low directly to one in which the least-cost-avoider is unknown.

Box *(b4)*, in which the victim is known to be the least-cost-avoider, but the efficient level of pollution is not known, is similar to *(a4)* except that the ambiguity is greater. Any of the rules (2), (3) and (4) *might* lead to an efficient outcome, and either a polluter property rule (3) or victim liability (4) is a safe choice. In general, if the efficient level of pollution is not known, but the identity of the least-cost-avoider *is* known, then imposing the cost on the least-cost-avoider is safe. But, depending on who the least-cost-avoider is, enforcing the entitlement with a property rule may or may not be safe, so the least-cost-avoider criterion is not sufficient to guarantee the selection of an efficient rule.

As a guide to rule selection the Calabresian criteria are finally destroyed in the real world case *(c4)*. Calabresi and Melamed (1972, p. 1119) argue that 'we are likely to turn to liability rules whenever we are uncertain whether the polluter or the pollutees can most cheaply avoid the pollution.'[19] If the court awards the pollutee damages against the polluter, they continue, 'economic efficiency will have had its due; if [the polluter] cannot make a go of it, the nuisance was not worth its costs.' (ibid. p. 1120). The advantage of the liability rule, apparently, is that it enables us 'to test the value of the pollution'. Now this sequence of argument contains a confusion between the two different types of information that we have identified. The implication of Calabresi and Melamed's logic is that when we do not know who is the least-cost-avoider we should use a liability rule to test for the efficient level of pollution![20] They do not recognize the problem that a liability rule will only lead to an efficient outcome *if* liability is placed on the least-cost-avoider. If his identity is not known then, with transactions ruled out by high costs, there is no way of finding it out through decentralized decisions. The advocacy of liability rules must therefore hinge not on their generation of the information concerning the identity of the least-cost-avoider, but rather on their generation of the information on the efficiency of different pollution levels. But unless we know, or can guess correctly, the identity of the least-cost-avoider there is *no* rule that can guarantee the selection of the level of pollution that is preferred by the least-cost-avoider when he bears the cost. In other words there is no rule that can guarantee the attainment of the efficient levels of pollution and pollution abatement through decentralized decisions. Any of the four rules *might* be efficient but none is *known* to be; the Calabresian criteria do not tell us how to make the choice without resorting to a full centralized court evaluation of the damage and abatement costs associated with the pollution.

To conclude the discussion of the world with symmetric transactions costs let us broaden our view to consider some implications of the pursuit of justice. If provision for the just protection of victims is to be an integral part of the legal approach to pollution control, then the selection of legal rules in one sense becomes more determinate yet simultaneously becomes more complicated. Considering the three situations in column *(4)* of the table, the number of rules that will be efficient *while also being just* is limited to polluter liability (2) in box *(a4)*, none in *(b4)*, and victim property (1) and polluter liability (2) in *(c4)*. The emptiness of box *(b4)* reflects the fact that none of the four rules can provide just protection of victims while giving the victims, but *not* the polluter, an incentive to undertake the abatement that is efficient. The use of either polluter property (3) or victim liability (4), while it is a safe choice from an efficiency point of view in this case, is unjust. On the other hand, imposing the pollution damage cost on the polluter leads to high-cost abatement. Efficiency and justice are necessarily in contention when the victim is the least-cost abater, and the *assumption* required by the Calabresian recommendation of victim liability in this case, is that legal rules should pursue efficiency alone. Even if this were acceptable when the victim is known to be the least-cost abater, when both types of uncertainty prevail, box *(c4)*, the efficiency gain from sacrificing justice becomes uncertain too. Those who would resist the sacrifice of justice for an efficiency gain which is certain, would *a fortiori* oppose the imposition of liability on the victim in this case. Once more our analysis points to the frailties of the Calabresian criteria as a guide to rule selection.

Asymmetric costs

It can be argued that if it were the case that tertiary costs were high for some polluters or victims and low for others, then decentralized decisions might be made feasible by giving the entitlement to the high-cost-transactor (worst briber), thereby forcing the best briber to initiate transactions to alter the initial entitlement. As far as efficiency is concerned it does not matter (so the argument goes) whether or not the best briber is also the least-cost-avoider because, assuming that some abatement is efficient, the best briber could bribe the least-cost-avoider to abate. Thus Calabresi and Melamed (1972, p. 1119) argue, in connection with property rules, that if the polluter is the best briber then economic efficiency will be achieved by using victim property (1), but not by using polluter property (3), as a starting point for the polluter to buy the right to pollute. Similarly, with liability rules the cost of collective valuation may not be symmetrical under rules (2) and (4) and 'the choice between liability entitlements [might] be based on the asymmetry of the costs of collective determination'.[21]

There are several grounds on which this suggested use of the cost asymmetry as a guideline for rule selection can be criticized. In the first place it is of dubious logical validity. If the cost asymmetry is so strong that bargains would yield net gains if they are initiated by the best briber, then the best briber would perceive a potential gain and set about bargaining *whether or not* he held the entitlement. In theory, therefore, the achievement of socially efficient bargains should not depend on the law even when a strong asymmetry exists. Consequently Calabresi and Melamed's argument must rely on the presumption that best bribers will in fact indulge in their best bribes *only* if they do not have the legal entitlement. Perhaps if pollution victims (who are best bribers) are happy with the entitlement to be free of pollution damage, then they will not be bothered if they forego a potential gain from offering to release the polluter from an injunction in exchange for substantial compensation. In other words, Calabresi and Melamed's argument requires an element of inertia to be associated with the acquisition of the entitlement.

Secondly, even if such inertia is allowed the analysis based on a cost asymmetry is problematic, because it proves to be very difficult to demonstrate sufficiently general propositions about the likely magnitude of tertiary costs under different entitlements, to support the use, on efficiency grounds, of a best-briber criterion (*see* Mishan, 1967; Burrows, 1970). Several points can be made that cast serious further doubt on the applicability of the criterion.

In the first place, even with inertia it is not sufficient simply to establish the existence of an asymmetry. If the best-briber criterion is to offer a method of selecting entitlements that will provide a starting point for decentralized decision, it is necessary to demonstrate that the asymmetry is so substantial that transactions are feasible under one entitlement but not under another. There does not seem to be any way of achieving this demonstration without resorting to the (notoriously difficult) measurement of bargaining and litigation costs. It is possible, however, to establish a presumption of *symmetry* on the grounds that the theoretical reasons for expecting an asymmetry are weak, and to this possibility we now turn.

Consider the reasons that have been offered for expecting tertiary costs to be asymmetric. In the context of property rules it is usually the existence of large numbers of victims that is alleged to imply an asymmetry, bargaining costs being greater, it is supposed, if the entitlement is given to the many victims than if it is given to the few polluters[22]. Now while it is certainly true that the costs of bargaining will be higher when larger numbers of victims and/or polluters are involved it is not self-evident that the choice of *entitlement* will affect the size of the costs. If the onus is placed upon the group of victims the costs include those of identifying other members of the group, of reaching an agreement on a unified policy (including the offer to be made and the share to be paid by each individual) and of contacting and bargaining with the polluter. In addition there will be the difficulty of victims who refuse to contribute a share of the offer in the expectation that they will enjoy free the benefits of reduced pollution resulting from the bargain. If, on the other hand, the polluter loses the entitlement decision and must initiate bargaining in order to lift an injunction on his activity, the costs include the identification of the members of the offended group and of contacting and bargaining with the group, together with the costs incurred by the group in reaching an agreement on its acceptance of offers made by the polluter as well as on the shares to accrue to each victim. In addition there is the problem of hold-out by the victims as a group, or by individuals within the group. No clear expectation emerges as to the likely relative magnitudes of bargaining costs under the two property rules, and certainly there is no reason to expect transactions to be possible from one entitlement but not from the other.

As far as litigation costs under the two liability rules are concerned, the only reason that seems to have been given for expecting an asymmetry is the following argument by Calabresi and Melamed. The problem is one of ascertaining whether the appropriate compensation is easier to value and to administer if the polluter is paying the victims under rule (2) than if the victims are paying the polluter under rule (4). Calabresi and Melamed say that damages paid to victims may be hard to value and the costs of contacting all victims and getting them into court may be prohibitive, whereas 'objective damage' (that is the polluter's abatement cost) paid by the victims to a polluter may be easy to assess[23]. It is true that the valuation of abatement costs may often be easier than the valuation of damage costs, but it is unlikely to be easier to persuade victims to come into court to *pay* 'objective damage' than to *receive* subjective damage. On the contrary, a large group of victims who are expected to pay a polluter to abate would presumably litigate endlessly to avoid the burden if it were substantial. Nothing can therefore be said *in general* about the relative magnitudes of total litigation costs under the two liability rules.

An attempt has been made to play, without much enthusiasm, the game of investigating the applicability of the best-briber criterion. Once the desire to ensure the just protection of pollution victims is accepted, the case for penalizing the best-bribers, even if they could be identified, appears even more shaky. If the victims happened to be the worst bribers, then a just solution would also be efficient. But it has been argued that a configuration of tertiary costs that would allow bargains to take place under polluter liability or victim property but not under the other rules, is unlikely to be common. Therefore the best-briber criterion offers little guidance for the legal control of pollution even if one accepts the fundamental but questionable assumption that the best briber will initiate bargains if, and only if, he does not hold the legal entitlement.

6.5 Conclusion

The conclusion is that there is no reason to expect a single minded, efficiency-orientated choice of legal rules to generate the efficient pollution outcomes through the decentralized decisions of polluters and victims.

If progress is to be made in the direction of efficiency and justice in the pollution context, we must look to more centralized policies of pollution evaluation and control[24]. The statutory control instruments are not necessarily incompatible with a *compensation* role for tort law damages actions. What is more, private actions may offer both an extra means of enforcing the statute law, through actions for breach of duty by the enforcement officers, and a way of providing the flexibility needed for the control of small scale, local interferences that are too diverse to legislate against (for example, nuisance from bonfires and barking dogs). But the emphasis here is on a residual role for private law.

Markets and tort laws have existed for centuries. By comparison, a systematic statutory approach to pollution control is a recent innovation. If the markets, allied with private law rights and actions, were potentially so effective a method of controlling pollution, one may wonder why the pollution problems are now so serious. The answer is that markets do not handle the significant pollution problems, and it would be better if the legal analysts did not behave as if they do or can. The ghost of market solutions can be laid to rest in the cathedral crypt, while the artist paints a view of the cathedral that gives a better perspective.

Notes to chapter six

1 This title relates to the imagery of Calabresi and Melamed (1972, fn. 2) in a way that should become apparent by the end of the paper. I am grateful to Cento Veljanovski for suggestions that have strengthened the argument in several places.

2 The ones that are most relevant to this paper are Calabresi and Melamed (1972) and Michelman (1971), but see also Posner (1973).

3 A similar criticism can be made of many contributions by economists in this area. Of the lawyers, Michelman (1971) is apparently uneasy with the omission of justice (see p. 673, fn. 47), whereas Calabresi and Melamed (1972) appear to believe that little can be said on 'other justice' issues in the absence of transcendental meditation (p. 1102).

4 Polinsky (1979) provides evidence for the influence of these studies when he refers to Calabresi and Melamed's 'important article' (p. 1, fn. 2). The above comments should not be interpreted as a belief that no analysis has previously been offered of the methods of *centralized* pollution control. On the contrary Michelman (1971), p. 674 *et seq.* explored these methods; Polinsky (1979) discussed tax solutions, as have many economists (for a survey of the main points of this literature see Burrows (1979)). The conviction remains, however, that the studies of pollution control that are based on decentralized decisions through markets are more influential among lawyers than they are among economists!

5 A third possibility is that efficiency and justice are thought to be the same thing (Posner, 1975), and that this view is claimed to have widespread support. The subsequent discussion will assume a rejection of this view.

6 It would not be difficult to modify the analysis to allow for the fact that society may expect people to bear *some* non-zero level of harm without compensation (cf. Polinsky, 1979). What is required for our analysis is that, in general, justice implies a lower level of uncompensated harm that does efficiency.

7 'Tertiary costs' is the term used by Calabresi (1971) for transactions costs including bargaining, litigation and enforcement costs. The term 'property right' is taken to mean general entitlement whether this comprises a liability rule or a property rule (on which see section 6.4).

8 See for example Baumol and Oates (1975) who do not even bother to discuss private bargaining solutions.

9 Dick (1976) surveys these problems as does Burrows (1979), ch. 3.

10 See, for example, Michelman (1971), pp. 652–3. The distinction between general and specific deterrence originated in Calabresi (1971).

11 Michelman (1971), p. 653. In the present context read 'pollution damage costs' for 'accident costs'.

12 It is apparent that a very particular type of damages liability is being assumed here, namely one in which, *ex ante*, the party knows the price of polluting (or being free from pollution) in the future. The term 'damage' is being used as a synonym for pollution costs; the term 'damages' means a compensation remedy.

13 Michelman seems similarly dissatisfied with the terms, (1971) section IV, and Calabresi, writing with Melamed (1972), does not use them.

14 That is, formally no nuisance is found, although the legal layman may find 'no nuisance' and 'polluting at will' an odd juxtaposition of terms.

15 The case of low tertiary costs will be used to represent the idealized market situation in which not only are these costs unimportant, but also the other obstacles to market operations are absent.

16 This does not imply, of course, that the *type* of tertiary costs is independent of the rule chosen. Whether, for example, it is out-of-court bargaining costs or litigation costs in damages suits that are 'high' depends on the choice between property and liability rules.

17 The conventional theory of efficient pollution suggests that no pollution is efficient when marginal damage costs exceed marginal abatement costs over the whole pollution range; all pollution is efficient when the reverse is true; and only some is efficient when marginal abatement costs exceed marginal damage costs at the lower pollution levels but are less than marginal damage costs at the higher pollution levels. In this last case an intermediate pollution level is efficient. See Burrows (1979), fn. 15, pp. 172–3.

18 A choice could, of course, be based on the expected litigation costs under the two rules, but this has nothing to do with the Calabresian criteria.

19 In practice in English law the courts only turn to liability rules when the damage is small. See Ogus and Richardson (1977).

20 Michelman (1971), p. 669, in interpreting the Calabresian criteria, avoids this error, by stating that if we do not know who is the least-cost-avoider, liability should be loaded on the best briber. This does not, however, solve the problem where transactions are ruled out by high symmetric tertiary costs.

21 Calabresi and Melamed (1972), pp. 1120–1121. Michelman does not pursue the question of symmetry though he does make the general statement that 'only on the assumption that liability is restricted to money damages, and will not encompass injunctions, is it at all clear that factories can bribe more cheaply than homeowners can,' (1971), p. 670.

22 This assumption is to be found in Mishan (1967), section IV, and a similar assumption is used by Calabresi and Melamed (1972), p. 1119.

23 (1972), pp. 1120–1121. We ignore their comment about assessing the *benefits* of pollution abatement since this is irrelevant to rule (4), the 'objective damage' payment being based solely on the abatement cost incurred by the polluter.

24 See Baumol and Oates (1975) and Burrows (1979) chapter 4. Throughout this paper we have followed the previous analysts in defining an efficient pollution level solely in terms of a comparison of the marginal abatement and marginal damage costs. A broader definition would state that a pollution reduction resulting from a bargain is efficient only if it generates net benefits (i.e. the difference between damage and abatement costs) in excess of the tertiary costs involved. High tertiary costs then make bargains inefficient. Centralized control instruments could be efficient in this sense only if they generated net benefits in excess of the administration and enforcement costs.

References

BAUMOL, W.J. and OATES, W.E. (1975), *The Theory of Environmental Policy*, Englewood Cliffs, NJ: Prentice-Hall.

BURROWS, P. (1970), On external costs and the visible arm of the law, *Oxford Economic Papers*, **22**, no. 1, 39–56.

BURROWS, P. (1979), *The Economic Theory of Pollution Control*, Oxford: Martin Robertson; Cambridge, Mass: MIT Press.
CALABRESI, G. (1971), *The Costs of Accidents: A Legal and Economic Analysis*, New Haven: Yale University Press.
CALABRESI, G. and MELAMED, A.D. (1972), Property rules, liability rules and inalienability: one view of the cathedral, *Harvard Law Review*, **85**, no. 6, 1089–1128.
COASE, R. (1960), The problem of social cost, *Journal of Law and Economics*, **3**, no. 1, 1–44.
DICK, D.T. (1976), The voluntary approach to externality problems: a survey of the critics, *Journal of Environmental Economics and Management*, **2**, no. 3, 185–195.
MICHELMAN, F.I. (1971), Pollution as a tort: a non-accidental perspective on Calabresi's costs, *Yale Law Journal*, **50**, no. 3, 647–686.
MISHAN, E.J. (1967), Pareto Optimality and the law, *Oxford Economic Papers*, **19**, no. 3, 247–287.
OGUS, A.I. and RICHARDSON, G.M. (1977), Economics and the environment: a study of private nuisance, *Cambridge Law Journal*, **36**, no. 2, 284–325.
POLINSKY, A.M. (1979), Controlling externalities and protecting entitlements: property right, liability rule, and tax-subsidy approaches, *Journal of Legal Studies*, **8**, no. 1, 1–49.
POSNER, R. (1973), *Economic Analysis of Law*, Boston: Little, Brown and Co.
POSNER, R. (1975), The economic approach to law, *Texas Law Review*, **53**, no. 4, 757–782.

CHAPTER SEVEN

Negligent misrepresentation: an economic reformulation

William Bishop

7.1 Introduction

The common law has long looked more indulgently upon words than upon acts. For decades the courts denied liability for negligent statements altogether, and even now the scope of liability for words is more restricted than that for acts. Before 1964 *Derry v Peek*[1] was thought to have settled the issue, deciding that, fraud apart, no liability lay in tort for an erroneous statement. In that year *Hedley Byrne v Heller*[2] established such liability for the first time; but in that case the House of Lords restricted liability to cases in which there was some 'nexus' or 'special relationship' or even a 'relationship equivalent to contract'. Different treatment of acts and statements has occasioned much comment, both favourable and unfavourable. Many scholars agree with Professor (now Mr. Justice) Linden's comment (1977, p. 389) on developments in this branch of the law:

> There is every reason to believe that [the law's] ultimate destination will be liability to all reasonably forseeable users of such information.

In this chapter the existing justifications of the special rule for statements will be examined briefly and shown to be unpersuasive. Then the present common law rules will be analysed using the tools of contemporary microeconomics, and shown to have a justification in the criterion of economic efficiency. The theory will reveal that some very different economic considerations underly different contexts in which statements are made. Economic considerations will suggest that courts should discriminate more finally that they now do and will suggest an economic test for the exclusion of liability for some classes of misrepresentation. The theory will suggest that Linden J's prophecy is unlikely to be fulfilled.

The principal subject of this paper will be negligent statements causing financial loss. Cases in which physical loss was in question will be referred to principally for the purpose of explaining the relevant theoretical considerations.

7.2 Conventional debate

Legal scholars have canvassed a variety of justifications for restricting the scope of liability for negligent statements. A full treatment of this literature would make this chapter too long, but the two main themes will be examined. The speech of Lord Reid in *Hedley Byrne v Heller* provides a suitable starting place. Lord Reid said[3]:

> The most obvious difference between negligent words and negligent acts is this. Quite careful people often express definite opinions on social or informal occasions even when they see that others are likely to be influenced by them; and they often do that without taking that care which they would take if asked for their opinion professionally or in a business connection.

Fleming (1977, p. 164) has endorsed these words. However, Lord Reid's observation provides no justification at all for the rule. If habitually quite careful people set spring guns in their rose bushes no one would argue that the courts should deny recovery to the victim. A major function of tort law is to induce people to take the appropriate care. What is required is some reason why statements are different.

Lord Reid's next comment, which raised the second common justification for special representation rules, is more interesting and hints at the economic model to be developed below. He said[4]:

> Another obvious difference is that a negligently made article will only cause one accident, and so it is not very difficult to find the necessary degree of proximity or neighbourhood between the negligent manufacturer and the person injured. But words can be broadcast with or without the consent or the foresight of the speaker or writer. It would be one thing to say that the speaker owes a duty to a limited class, but it would be going very far to say that he owes a duty to every ultimate 'consumer' who acts on those words to his detriment. It would be no use to say that a speaker or writer owes a duty but can disclaim responsibility if he wants to. He, like the manufacturer, could make it part of a contract that he is not to be liable for his negligence: but that contract would not protect him in a question with a third party, at least if the third party was unaware of it.

Again Lord Reid's comment is echoed by Fleming (1977, pp.164–165). But again the observation is unconvincing, though suggestive. The issue is not liability to the ultimate consumer but liability to the foreseeable consumer. That the ultimate consumer is by definition foreseeable in cases of products liability does not mean that all ultimate users are foreseeable where words are concerned[5]. Nevertheless, if a negligent statement can be reasonably foreseen as likely to cause loss, and if care by defendant would be less costly to him than the cost of damage to the plaintiff, then should not the law encourage that care? This is the obvious application of the general negligence standard of care, whether that be understood in the usual, perhaps vague, way or in the more systematic 'economic' way as encapsulated in the Learned Hand Test (Fleming, 1977, p. 168). Cardozo J summarized this second line of thinking with his usual force and clarity when he declined to hold a firm of accountants liable for negligent statements about a company's finances. He said that this would create liability 'in an indeterminate amount, for an indeterminate time, to an indeterminate class.'[6] It was this fear that prompted Lord Denning in his dissenting judgement in *Candler v Crane Christmas*[7], where he favoured negligence liability for statements to exclude certain classes of activity. He said[8]:

> Again, a scientist or expert (including a marine hydrographer) is not liable to his readers for careless statements in his published works. He publishes his work simply for the purpose of giving information, and not with any particular transaction in mind at all. But when a scientist or expert makes an investigation and report for the very purpose of a particular transaction, then, in my opinion, he is under a duty of care in respect of that transaction.

Fleming (1977, p. 168) has perceived that the argument, as put, is unpersuasive. He notes Denning LJ's 'curious doubts concerning the hypothetical hydrographer', and observes that 'Asquith LJ's alarm at the prospect of the vast liability that would be entailed if he were liable for loss of a giant liner seems based on the startling premise that the greater the damage the more reason for excuse.' Fleming's view is that the example of the marine hydrographer is a case of physical loss and that this makes all the difference. But this is not convincing. Financial losses are costs too, and there is no fundamental difference between financial and physical costs. True the risk of losing life or limb will command a high price in a perfect market (the substitute market of the courtroom may underestimate the price in the Commonwealth (*see* Rea, 1979) and possibly overestimates it in some cases in the USA[9]), but all goods are ultimately commensurable. If the reader really doubts this let him ask himself whether he would ban Sunday motoring if he could — it would save some lives and cost much enjoyment to others. Our own behaviour shows us that even the risk of death has a price notwithstanding much rhetoric to the contrary. So Fleming's quoted argument, which is the obvious argument from both standard negligence language and from economics, applies, it seems, to all cases of financial loss. It leads us, as does the first argument above, to the conclusion that Linden reached: there should be liability to all reasonably foreseeable users of such information. The conventional debate yields no justification for the common law rule, which restricts liability for negligent statements to a plaintiff class that is defined more narrowly than is the class to whom duties are owed in respect of negligent acts.

The Learned Hand test for negligence was mentioned above. This famous formula, which will be important in the analysis to follow, was laid down in *United States v Carroll Towing*[10]. Judge Hand said that the defendant is liable to the plaintiff in tort for negligence if the cost to the plaintiff of the damage multiplied by the probability of its occurring exceeds burden (i.e. the cost) of precautions to the defendant. If these costs are assessed in respect of the marginal act of avoidance then it can be interpreted as a rule that directs potential defendants to take avoidance action when the marginal social cost of avoidance is less than the marginal social cost of the accident avoided[11]. This is the familiar formula of microeconomics for realizing the efficient allocation of scarce resources among competing ends. Here it will be assumed that the common law negligence standard is in practice equivalent to the Learned Hand calculus, even though not all common law courts cite, or even are aware of, Judge Hand's formula.

7.3 Information production and appropriability

Statements or representations are a form of information. If we are to integrate them into a coherent economic theory of tort liability then we must understand the peculiarities of information when considered as an economic good. For a long time economists assumed away any problems arising from imperfect information. Generations of students, including the writer, were told that one necessary and innocuous assumption of standard supply and demand analysis was that all buyers and all sellers have perfect information about price, quality, competing products and the future. For the most part the theory worked well enough for the purposes at hand. But many phenomena are excluded by the assumption of perfect information. Beginning in the early 1960s, and gathering force at the end of that decade, a new economic theory emerged to deal with information imperfections (*see* Stigler, 1961; Arrow, 1971; Akerlof, 1970). So fruitful were these efforts that some economists have even spoken of the 1970s as 'the decade of information theory'. These theories have many applications to law, although, as always with rather abstract theoretical ideas, the applications are far from obvious. These theories are crucial to understanding the highly imperfect, implicit markets that constitute the subject matter of legal studies[12].

One peculiarity of information, considered as an economic good, is that the person who produces it may not, and usually will not, be able to appropriate all the social benefit that flows from its production[13]. The meaning and the significance of this are best considered by means of an example. Suppose someone discovers air currents in the upper atmosphere that can be predicted easily. This information will be valuable to anyone flying an aircraft, as this knowledge will enable him to chart his flight path so as to minimize fuel costs. It is unlikely that the discoverer will be able to become rich through his discovery even though the discovery saves many millions of pounds worth of resources that would otherwise be wasted. First, he may not be able to convince the purchaser of its value without giving him the very information he is trying to sell. Secondly, even if he sells the information to one airline, then that airline can easily pass the information on to others, perhaps at some financial gain to itself. If it seeks to guard the information it will have closely to control its employees, see that they never change jobs and so on. In general, information, once produced, can be reproduced to others at small cost. Even though the social benefit of the information is large the private benefit to the producer is small. Legal systems often make considerable efforts to reward information producers through patent and copyright laws and the like. But these techniques are costly and are usually available only where the information is used to sell a product in the market — only then are policing costs relatively low.

Consider an attempt by the legal system to reward those who produce information by requiring all users of information to pay fees to the producer each time the information is used. Such a law would generate costs of several kinds to society; in particular, private enforcement costs, public enforcement costs and error costs. The private enforcement costs are easy to see. The individual information producer must establish his property right. He will wish to monitor use and transmission of his information and to sue to collect his fees. These activities will consume real social resources, that is they will generate real costs to society. The public enforcement costs are the costs of police, courts etc., which also require society's real resources, in this case paid for by the taxpayers. The error costs are the third and most important item. The task of distinguishing those cases where valuable information has been produced for which someone should be rewarded is, even in theory, a difficult one. An attempt to enforce such rights in a practical world would be at best a 'hit and miss' process. Mistakes will be costly to society. For example suppose a firm is awarded a right to a fee where others would have got the information anyway, or where they do not value the information as highly as the fee prescribed. In either case the price charged will be a burden to the alleged 'users' that they should not have to bear and which will, to that extent, discourage consumption or productive use of the information in question. Such costs are likely to be very large[14].

The typical market in economic theory is the market for goods. The producer of a good sells it to the user, appropriating to himself all, or substantially all, of the benefit of the good that his efforts brought into existence[15], so that private benefit equals social benefit. If the producer must pay all of the social cost of producing the good, then he will produce it only so long as the marginal social cost of so doing equals the marginal social benefit.

One objective of tort law is to ensure that the producer faces the full social cost of production. When these diverge from private cost they are called external costs of production. Nuisance and negligence law typically are concerned to internalize these external costs to the producer. When this is done production will be optimal in quantity and price, in the sense that all those goods, and ony those goods, will be produced whose marginal social benefit equals their marginal social costs of production[16].

The contrast with the information market is sharp. Here the market will fail to achieve the social optimum. This happens not because of an external cost but because of an external benefit; the market failure is not on the supply side but on the demand side. The information producer may be faced with the full social cost, but because he cannot cover those costs through sale of the product to those who benefit he does not produce as much of the good as is socially optimal; indeed he may produce none at all[17].

The application of this analysis to liability for negligent misrepresentation is the following. Such a liability rule is an attempt to make the information producer confront the total social cost of his action. But if he cannot reap the total social benefit he will not produce enough, if any, information. If there were no liability rule and if the private costs of information production were small, then the optimal amount might be produced — though the quality of the information would often be lower than ideal[18]. But if the costs are augmented through liability there is, as we shall show, a risk of inducing producers to curtail production, leaving us worse off than before.

A numerical example may help. Assume that the marine hydrographer referred to by Lord Denning could produce a map the information in which is worth £100 million. The cost of charting the seas is £1 million. Maps can be sold for a total of £2 million. The cost of eliminating all errors is £4 million. Clearly to get the best social advantage resources should be spent up to £5 million (£1m + £4m) to produce high quality information of (say) £200 million value. However, in the absence of liability rules the map maker will spend only £1 million and produce a less accurate map worth £100 million.

Now consider an attempted legal intervention to remedy this market failure. Negligence liability for accidents is placed on the hydrographer and his map-making firm. A fully accurate map is more valuable because there are fewer shipwrecks. The shipwrecks that now occur must be paid for by the hydrographer. The damages might total up to $100 million. Even if they are only a fraction of that sum the hydrographer will conclude that he cannot make a profit, or even break even, in this business and will cease map-making. But this means that an economic activity valued at £100 million and costing only £1 million does not occur. It is this type of problem that has worried courts and has given us special rules for negligent statements.

The rules which have emerged are interesting because they can be understood as achieving what economists call a 'second best' solution to the problem of non-appropriability of the benefits of information (*see* Lipsey and Lancaster, 1957). The leading Canadian case on negligent statements will serve as a particularly clear example. In *Haig v Bamford*[19] the recurring issue of the liability of accountants was considered. The defendants had negligently prepared a financial statement for a company knowing that the statement would be used by potential investors in that company. This was a private company and was probihited by law from extending an invitation to the public to subscribe for shares or debentures. For that reason the number of potential investors would necessarily be limited. The Supreme Court of Canada held the accountants liable. They held that since, on the facts before them, the number of investors in a private company was limited by law, these investors were a determinate group, and the case fell within Cardozo J's dictum of 'accounts prepared for the guidance of a specific class of persons'[20]. This meant also that there was a relationship strong enough to come within the 'special relationship' required for liability under the decision of the House of Lords in *Hedley Byrne v Heller* (*see* section 7.1).

Dickson J giving the judgment of the court was keenly aware of the value of accountants services to others than those who employed them. He said[21]:

> The increasing growth and changing role of corporations in modern society has been attended by a new perception of the societal role of the profession of accounting. The day when the accountant served only the owner-manager of a company and was answerable to him alone has passed. The complexities of modern industry combined with the effects of specialization, the impact of taxation, urbanization, the separation of ownership from management, the rise of professional corporate managers and a host of other factors have led to marked changes in the role and responsibilities of the accountant and in the reliance which the public must place upon his work. The financial statements of the corporations upon which he reports can affect the economic interests of the general public as well as of shareholders and potential sharcholders.
>
> With the added prestige and value of his services has come, as the leaders of the profession have recognized, a concomitant and commensurately increased responsibility to the public. It seems unrealistic to be oblivious to these developments.

To understand this decision consider first an ideal world of perfect markets for accounting services, a world in which accountants are liable for losses caused by negligently produced information but also a world in which accountants could collect fees from all persons who benefit from the information they produce. In such a world the optimum amount of information will be produced. An accounting firm will spend on misinformation avoidance only if it thereby avoids loss to victims of at least £1. At some point it will be cheaper for victims to incur the loss than for the firm to spend more on avoidance — that point might or might not be at or close to the point of zero misinformation. A completely error-free information service might cost more than its value to consumers. In such a case some misinformation would be efficient. This is the usual negligence calculation under the Learned Hand Test.

But the real market for accounting services is not like this. The actual market demand will be substantially less than the full demand in an ideal world. This is because many persons who do not pay for the information will benefit from it owing to the non-appropriability problem. Also the supply of accounting services offered will be different. In general where accountants are not liable for negligently caused loss they will be able to offer services at a lower price than they would have to charge if they had to pay such judgment costs (or insurance premiums).

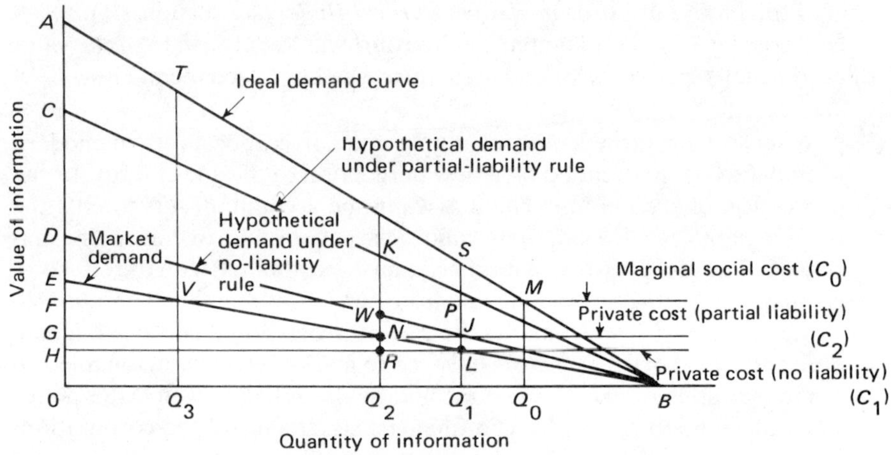

Figure 7.1 *Welfare economics of the decision in* Haig v Bamford

Figure 7.1 illustrates the welfare economics of the decision in *Haig v Bamford*. *AB* is the hypothetical ideal demand for information, and C_0 is the cost of such information if there is no appropriability problem and if accountants are liable for all negligently caused injury. For simplicity marginal cost is assumed equal to average cost. Then Q_0 units of accounting services would be produced. This is a social optimum because it realizes the maximum consumers' surplus, *AMF*.

EB is the *market* demand for accountants' services and C_1 is the cost of those services where there is *no* liability for negligent misrepresentation. Since we assume perfect competition in this market the cost is also the price. In these conditions Q_1 units of accounting services will be produced[22].

However, these services will not be identical to the Q_0 units produced under optimal conditions. They will be of lower quality and therefore fully informed consumers would value them less highly. *DB* represents the hypothetical full demand for these lower quality services — that is, the hypothetical demand assuming all benefits of information are paid for by users. Under these conditions *DJLH* represents the consumers' surplus with no misrepresentation liability. This is smaller than *AMF*, the consumers' surplus under ideal conditions (i.e. where there is no non-appropriability problem and a Learned Hand negligence rule is in force). Society would be better off spending *FPLH* more on misinformation avoidance and getting *ASJD* extra units of consumers' value (larger than *FPLH*) for a net gain. But the market does not provide the right incentives.

Suppose the court in *Haig v Bamford*[19] (or for a similar example, *Candler v Crane, Christmas*[7]) had simply imposed full negligence liability for statements of the sort that is imposed for acts under *Donoghue v Stevenson*[23]. That would add substantially to the costs of those firms that supply accounting services — without adding to those firms' revenues. Since the cost will be higher, a higher price will be demanded by those firms, and less accounting services will be purchased[24]. But the quality of what is produced will be higher. If the quantity discouraged is larger and the extra value of the better quality is small, then imposing liability may leave society worse off than it was under the admittedly imperfect world of no liability. It seems to be a uniform intuition amoung courts in the common law world that such extensive liability, in the absence of cheaply enforceable information property rights, would indeed be a cure worse than the disease.

In *Figure 7.1* the common lawyers' intuitions are given geometric interpretation. A negligence rule raises firms' costs to C_0. Market demand is assumed to be unchanged[25]. Only Q_3 units will be produced, far below optimum, with at most *ATVF* units of consumers' surplus — smaller even than *DJLH*.

But the court in *Haig v Bamford*[19] declined to choose between the two extremes of non-liability (costs set at C_1) or full *Donoghue v Stevenson*[23] liability (costs set at C_0) for accountants. Instead they imposed liability on accountants for *some* of the damage caused by their misinformation. Liability is owed only to those within a special relationship. This adds to accountants' costs, but probably much less than would liability to all persons who suffer loss. This is represented in *Figure 7.1* by C_2. Since the cost is higher, prices will rise and so less accounting services will be produced. In *Figure 7.1* the amount of accounting services demanded falls from Q_1 to Q_2. This causes a welfare loss of *WJLR*, the consumers' surplus on the units that now disappear. But there is a corresponding gain: the prospect of liability will act as an incentive to accountants to produce better information. This better information, though still not ideal, has increased value, represented by hypothetical demand curve *CB*. Whether society is on balance better off than with non-liability depends on the relative magnitudes of the gains and losses. Courts evidently perceive a limited liability as generating a net gain. They perceive the accounting services market as one in which a little incentive has a favourable effect, but in which a large incentive will be counter-productive — largely because of the problem of non-appropriable benefits in information production.

This case is shown in *Figure 7.1.* Since *CKWD* (the welfare gained by having higher quality information) is larger than *WJLR* (the welfare lost on those units of information not consumed when production falls from Q_1 to Q_2) the effect is a net improvement in welfare. Total welfare *(CKNG)* is larger than that produced under either the no-liability rule *(DJLH)* or under the full-liability rule *(ATVF)*, although still not so large as under full liability without a non-appropriability problem *(AMF)*.

This analysis raises the obvious question: why not impose full liability and require all users to compensate the information producer? The answer to the question is equally obvious: the enforcement and error costs of so doing would be so large that when subtracted from *AMF* the final gain would be smaller than the *CKNG* achieved by *Haig v Bamford*[19]. In other words, though *AMF* is ideal it is unattainable in practice and *CKNG* is therefore the second-best alternative.

Whether the courts' perceptions of the facts are accurate or not is a complex question and one that can be answered conclusively only by a detailed investigation requiring experimentation with different rules. That is an expensive and difficult process. The writer thinks it likely that the courts' intuitions are correct, and capture the essential features of the many cases of negligent misrepresentation with which they must deal. If so, the emerging rules of restricted negligence liability for negligent misrepresentation can be viewed as a subtle and sensitive attempt to grapple with a very complicated 'market failure' by means of a liability rule that is efficient in the sense in which economists use that term[26].

7.4 Two party negligent misrepresentation: transaction costs and quality signalling

Most commentators have analysed negligent misrepresentation with an implicit assumption that one legal rule or test is appropriate, or at least relevant, for all cases falling under that description. But when considered from the point of view of economic analysis it becomes clear that the crucial considerations are very different in different cases.

In *Holman v Delta Timber*[27] the plaintiff, a building contractor, received a tender from the defendant, a timber merchant, quoting a supply price for specified timber. It was the lowest of three bids and on the basis of costing calculations using that price the plaintiff entered into a construction contract. Later the defendant discovered a calculation error and revoked his offer. The plaintiff was obliged to seek timber elsewhere at an additional cost of $3274.06 (New Zealand dollars). The plaintiff sued for this sum, claiming that the tender amounted to negligent misrepresentation.

The nature of the information produced here is very different from that in *Haig v Bamford*[19] or that of the hypothetical marine hydrographer. It is very specific information and probably of no value to anyone except the plaintiff. So there is no reason to suppose that the market would fail to give the correct incentive if liability were imposed. Much more important here is the fact that the parties are in negotiations with one another. In such a case the cost of transactions is low. It seems unlikely that any liability rule matters a great deal. First, consider the case where the law imposes liability. If liability is potentially more costly to the merchant than its value to the builder, then the merchant will disclaim liability. If it is more valuable to the builder he will specify that tenders must guarantee price without revocation — or he will telephone the merchant to confirm the tender and make a contract conditional on his being awarded the construction contract. Next consider the converse case where there is no liability imposed by law. If liability is more costly to the merchant than its value to the builder, the builder will be unwilling to pay the price that the merchant demands for a guarantee, when the builder telephones to ask for one. If liability is more valuable to the builder than its cost to the merchant the merchant will accept the builder's price for the contract of guarantee. Of course all prices here may take the form of higher or lower contract prices for the tendered good. This is an example of the Coase Theorem (Coase, 1960). The liability rule adopted by the court will not in general affect the efficiency of the final relationship between parties who can bargain at low cost.

Nevertheless it would be wrong to conclude that the decision on this question does not matter *at all*. Negotiating a contract or a discharge of liability in tort is not costless. It takes time on both sides. Transactions costs are low but they are not zero. The best from an efficiency point of view that the court can do is to select the rule under which fewest changes are sought by merchants and builders. This rule will minimize the cost of transactions provided all switches are of equal cost, that is, provided moving from merchant tort liability to non-liability or vice versa costs the merchant the same sum as it costs the contractor to move from contractor liability to non-liability or vice versa. If they have different costs then the court should choose the rule that minimizes the expected total cost of transaction.

In *Holman v Delta Timber*[27] the Supreme Court of New Zealand decided that the merchant was under no liability for his carelessly calculated tender. It is difficult to quarrel seriously with that decision, especially as it is claimed above that it cannot matter very much. This is one of those cases in which any rule will do so long as it is clear.

This analysis of *Holman v Delta Timber*, which suggests that though there is a statement it should be considered as an ordinary negligence case, is substantially applicable to any two-party case in which no serious argument can be mounted on grounds of non-appropriability, and resultant under-incentive to produce valuable information. The two best known Commonwealth cases are *Esso Petroleum v Mardon*[28] in the English Court of appeal and *Nunes Diamonds v Dominion Electric Protection Co*[29] in the Supreme Court of Canada.

In *Esso v Mardon* Esso negligently made an erroneous statement in precontractual negotiations. In consequence the plaintiff entered into a contract with Esso and suffered loss thereby. The Court of Appeal held that Esso were liable and that the fact of a subsequent contract did not prevent tort liability arising. Lord Denning[30] was (inter alia) prepared to treat the statement as a warranty, as were his brethren[31]. This is the way in which American law has long dealt with careless pre-contractual statements (*see* Prosser, 1971, pp. 704–721). Lord Denning construed the statement not as a warranty that sales would be 300 000 gallons annually, but as a warranty that Esso had taken care in preparing that estimate. Again the question is: which prima facie assignment of liability will minimize the cost of transactions. Here the answer is a little clearer than in *Holman v Delta Timber*[27]. Almost certainly the cost of care to Esso was less than the cost of error to Mardon so that a rule making Esso liable is likely to minimize transaction costs. Furthermore parties probably expect care in costs of this kind.

Where parties normally trade under standard expectations the assignment of liability to the party who is expected to perform up to that normal level of care will serve an additional economic purpose. It induces a party who is not performing at that standard *to signal this fact to the other party*, through disclaimer. The information about the other party's standard of performance is valuable information. This is a cheap way of providing it in the marketplace and its cost of production to Esso (i.e. the transactional cost of disclaiming) is almost certainly lower than its value to Mardon. If parties normally expected tenders to be non-revocable then this would apply to *Holman v Delta Timber*[27] as well. (But there seems no reason to think that non-revocability is considered normal.) Further, the standard of care expected of a party by his potential contract partners in preparing estimates (*Esso v Mardon*[28]) or tenders (*Holman v Delta*[27]) will normally be higher as the value of the transaction increases. Esso's estimate was far more important to Mardon's transaction than Delta's estimate was to Holman.

In *Nunes Diamonds v Dominion Electric Protection Company*[29] a diamond merchant alleged that the burglar alarm company had negligently misrepresented facts that gave the impression that its alarm was safer than in fact it was. There was considerable uncertainty as to the facts and therefore as to causation. Dominion and Nunes Diamond had agreed by contract at the time of installation that Dominion was not to be insurer. The alleged negligent misrepresentation arose later and was the action of a junior, and obviously inexpert, employee of Dominion. The Supreme Court of Canada held Dominion not liable, saying that the contract governed and excluded tort liability. Spence J and Laskin J in dissent rejected the idea that contract could exclude tort liability for negligent misrepresentation. They also held that on the facts Dominion had been negligent.

There is an economic argument for the majority's view. Consider the incentives created by the rule the minority favoured. Dominion would be unable by contract to limit clearly its liability to Nunes. It would always risk being vicariously liable for some unlucky statement of an employee. It would find it profitable to instruct employees to give no information of any kind to customers, and even to forbid any unsupervised contact by employees with potential litigants.

So it seems that under the Learned Hand criteria Nunes should not be allowed to recover, as it can avoid the loss more easily than can Dominion. This is sometimes summarized by saying that Nunes is the least-cost avoider of, or least-cost insurer against, theft.

Nevertheless the minority too had a point. A simple rule of non-liability will leave Dominion with no incentive to take some modest precautions, not amounting to ultimate insurer, that are cheap to Dominion but valuable to Nunes. One example is the not very costly burden of informing its clients of new findings on the reliability of the burglar alarm systems it supplies. It is socially efficient that they take these more modest precautions. Efficiency here dictates some sharing of 'liability' between the parties. The difficulty with the minority view is that it would have substituted too much incentive where before there had been too little.

The essential problem lies in the shadowy role of contributory negligence in this tort. In normal negligence litigation a victim can be held to contribute to his own injury. In negligent misrepresentation the tort can be roughly defined as 'reasonable reliance by the plaintiff on the negligent misrepresentation of the defendant'. Reasonable reliance subtracts out contribution before the negligence sums are computed. In effect it functions in exactly the way that contributory negligence did before the enactment of apportionment statutes — it functions as an all-or-nothing bar. Before the various law reform statutes it was possible to observe courts attempting desperately to fit the fact into this all-or-nothing mould when many cases cried out for apportionment. Perhaps this was the dilemma of the Canadian Supreme Court in *Nunes Diamonds*[29]. Perhaps the loss that occurred could have been most cheaply prevented by both parties having some incentive, although there is good reason to think that Dominion's incentive should be much smaller. It might seem odd to hold Dominion negligent but Nunes contributing (because most reasonable men would have placed less reliance on Dominion's word, and taken additional precautions) to the extent of 90 per cent — nevertheless that may have been the most efficient solution. An alternative way of reaching such a solution is to hold Dominion in breach of a contract term to provide reasonable information — with rescission as a remedy — damages being barred by the express contractual term that Dominion was not to be insurer.

It should be noted that there is nothing in these analyses of *Holman, Esso* and *Nunes* to suggest that a statement is a crucial, or even important, fact meriting special rules.

7.5 Three party negligent misrepresentation

We have seen that some cases of negligent misrepresentation involve problems of non-appropriable benefits of production, and that other cases are semi-contractual in nature involving only questions of how to minimize the cost of transactions, or of how exactly to apply the normal negligence analysis. There exists a third category that is intermediate between these two.

In *Hedley Byrne v Heller*[2] an advertising agency wished to obtain information on the financial soundness of Easipower Ltd. The agency approached its bank the National Provincial, who asked Heller and Partners, merchant bankers, for the information on Easipower, who were their clients. Heller negligently said that Easipower was sound, but disclaimed liability. The House of Lords held that in the absence of a disclaimer Heller would have been liable.

There is *an* argument against liability here based on non-appropriability. The information about Easipower might well be useful to others than Hedley Byrne. But the argument is not nearly as strong as with maps and accounting services. The number of others interested was likely to be smaller, as the information was rather vague in character and specific to the needs of the plaintiff. It was not published in a semi-public document with the obvious possibility that many would read it and rely on it. Even so, an appropriability argument is relevant. Without the special relationship limitation many banks might decline to give any information at all. The special relationship allows them to give it and to disclaim liability effectively. Without it the bank might be unable to give the valuable information without incurring unacceptable costs to itself. The requirement of a 'special relationship' allows the bank to perform a cost-benefit analysis of information-giving, and to avoid liability if its customers are not willing to pay for the costs to the bank of compensating those who lose because of information error.

The nature of the bank's incentives is interesting. Why should a bank give information at all? The obvious reason is that it gets a benefit in return. National Provincial's customers expected it to obtain financial information for them. Heller's customers expected it to supply information so that they could obtain credit. Any bank which refused to give information would have dissatisfied customers who sought rival banks that would supply this service, and this is true both of the customer who receives information and the customer about whom it is given. Judges are well aware of this. In *Mutual Life v Evatt*[32] Lord Reid (dissenting) said[33]:

> ...the individual who gave the advice must have had general or special authority from the company to give it, or at least that the company must have held him out as authorised to give it. It is not suggested that this company was so limited by its memorandum and articles that it could not give such authority. We are unable to see how a company can authorise the giving of such advice otherwise than as a part of its business activities. So long as a company does not act ultra vires it is for the company to determine the scope of its business. It appears to be quite common practice for businesses to perform gratuitous services for their customers with the object of retaining or acquiring their goodwill. If they incur expense in doing so it has never so far as we are aware been suggested that such expense is not a business expense. And we think that where companies do perform such service both they and their customers would be surprised to learn that the company is under no obligation to take any care in the matter.

In *Hedley Byrne* Lord Devlin said[34]:

> The service that a bank performs in giving a reference is not done simply out of a desire to assist commerce. It would discourage the customers of the bank if their deals fell through because the bank had refused to testify to their credit when it was good.

It seems fairly clear that both banks were receiving a benefit and the customer, Hedley Byrne, was paying in this sense: that it paid for a package of services one of which was advice and information. It clearly benefited not only National Provincial but also Heller. If Heller adopted a practice of not giving information to other banks it would not receive any in return when needed. In a broad sense consideration was present here, consideration both as detriment to promiser and benefit to promisee. It existed because there was a trading relationship between Hedley Byrne and Heller in the same sense that there was a trading relationship between Mrs. Donoghue and the manufacturer Stevenson in *Donoghue v Stevenson*[24].

In both cases a good (ginger beer, information) is produced by one party (Stevenson, Heller) sold to another (to a vendor for cash, to National Provincial Bank in return for favours in the future) and resold to the plaintiff (Mrs. Donoghue or her companion paid cash, Hedley Byrne paid in that its contract for services with its bank included normal expectations of information exchange). Economically a price *was* paid, although no cash changed hands on the day Hedley Byrne telephoned the bank. To focus on an absence of consideration in the narrow sense is to miss the underlying economic reality. Indeed Heller also received a valuable benefit in the form of custom from Easipower, because implicit in that banker–client relationship was an expectation that information would be supplied to enable the client to obtain credit.

In his speech in *Hedley Byrne* Lord Devlin laid stress on the absence of consideration[34]. In reality consideration is not absent but only diffuse and easier to make a mistake about — although no easier to mistake than in the cases of unilateral contract. Perhaps the absence of privity gives us a better clue as to why we tend to analyse this case as tort and not contract. Economically there is no essential difference between tort and contract — both deal with market relationships and both seek to maximize the value of output in some market (*see* Posner, 1977, part 2). The difference lies in the fact that where the parties have in fact agreed we have good evidence of the value they placed on performance and on its cost. This subjective value is the true measure of value in economic theory. Where the parties have not agreed we do not have this evidence and we must ask: what would they have agreed if they had negotiated? This question is asked *faute de mieux*. We analyse a case as contract when it is possible to answer some questions (though never all of them) by asking for the real, proper, subjective valuations of the parties instead of the second best objective valuations imputed to them by courts. One function of the privity limitation in contract is to separate out those cases where it is useful to ask for evidence of some actual subjective valuations, as revealed in market behaviour, from those where this is not a useful exercise and where only the second-best 'reasonable man' valuations are available.

Professor Atiyah (1978, p. 207 *et seq.*) has recently argued that a contract is only evidence of what is reasonable — that objective valuations rather than subjective ones are important. This is not the assumption of economic theory and it seems to the writer to be exactly the converse of the truth. Subjective valuations of the parties are what matter; the pity is that we do not more often have reliable evidence of them.

Returning to the facts in *Hedley Byrne*, benefit flowed to Heller from two directions: Easipower's custom and return favours from National Provincial and other banks. In this sense, as Lord Devlin noted, Hedley Byrne Ltd paid for the advice they got. The 'special relationship' requirement can be understood as equivalent to the consideration requirement in contract. It seeks to separate out those who have 'paid' for the information from those who have not. Economically it is a method of pricing. Notice that this is not required in *Donoghue v Stevenson* because it is automatically present where goods are concerned; normally only one person can drink the beer but for every bottle someone must have paid the price — there is no non-appropriability problem — and so there is no possibility that costs will greatly exceed revenues, thus discouraging production. That is the efficiency aspect. It is also possible to phrase the effect as one of fairness: only those who have paid should be allowed to recover if they lose. We can say to the man who complains of loss: you were not required to use the information and you intentionally used it to benefit yourself. This is unlike an accident case in which the victim would have behaved in the way that he did even if the injurer had been entirely absent. There is a possible moral objection in the case of statements that does not appear in the case of accidents to someone taking a free ride on another's efforts. The writer prefers the economic explanation, but it does not conflict with this plausible fairness argument.

7.6 Public authorities

The fourth important class of negligent misrepresentations are those committed by public authorities. An economic theory of public authority liability will extend beyond statements, which will be only one example of a liability founded on other efficiency considerations. Only one of several aspects of public authority liability will be considered here.

An important class of government activity is concerned with reducing transactions costs in the market place. Governments often subsidize or monopolize certain activities because they perceive that the cost of so doing is smaller than the social benefit to consumers. The cost is met sometimes by fees for the service and sometimes by taxes, which may or may not be designed to fall on those who benefit from the public activity in question. There are many examples of this. The land registry was set up to minimize the costs of land transactions. Inspectors certify the quality of buildings to reduce or eliminate the high cost (partly waste) of private insurance against risk of defect. The examples could be multiplied. One famous example, not itself a representations case, but having a public purpose of transactions cost reduction, was *East Suffolk Catchment Board v Kent*[35]. There the Catchment Board negligently repaired a wall that had burst during a flood. They did it so negligently that what should have taken a few weeks took many months, with loss to a farmer. The House of Lords held that the Board could not be held liable for doing badly that which they were not legally required to do, but which they had undertaken gratuitously. The hollowness of this reasoning is apparent when we remember that a Catchment Board is a public authority designed to reduce the cost of farming (and perhaps other activities) in a certain river valley. To avoid the waste of each farmer walling his land or taking expensive crop insurance, the Board is set up so that each farmer can rely upon it to keep flood risk low and to remedy flooding swiftly when it occurs. If the Board fails to perform its tasks to the level expected, then future farmers can be expected to spend resources on individual protection or avoidance — *exactly the waste of resources the board was designed to eliminate.*

Examples like this can be multiplied. The negligent statement cases of *Dutton v Bognor Regis UDC*[36], *Ministry of Housing and Local Government v Sharp*[37], and *Hodgins v Hydro Electric Commission of Nepean*[38] are examples of this. Where public authority liability for an activity is concerned it is always in order to ask: would the expected cost to the treasury of imposing liability exceed the expected cost to society resulting from uncertainty among users of the public service, and subsequent expenditures by them to minimize the effects of that uncertainty? Only rarely will the public cost be high. The potential private waste will be harder to calculate, but it can be very high indeed. A presumption against any public authority immunity or restricted liability seems sensible on efficiency grounds. Note, however, that the fact that statements are involved is merely incidental and not central to the justification for imposing liability. To consider these cases as akin to *Hedley Byrne*[2] or *Haig v Bamford*[19] is to be obsessed by formal similarities to the detriment of sound analysis.

7.7 Conclusion

Economic analysis suggests the following approach to cases of negligent misrepresentation. Courts should in general apply ordinary rules of negligence. However where the misrepresentation in question results from the production of valuable information there is a prima facie case for more restricted liability. Liability should be restricted when:

(1) the information is of a type that is valuable to many potential users,
(2) the producer of the information cannot capture in his prices the benefits flowing to all users of the information,
(3) the imposition of liability to all persons harmed would raise potential costs significantly enough to discourage information production altogether.

When these three conditions are met the court should impose liability on the defendant in relation to a limited class only. This class should include all information users with whom the producer has a trading relationship, whether direct or indirect. The class can be extended beyond this, but such extension should be limited by the principle expressed in (3), that is it should not be extended so widely that potential defendants would be discouraged from engaging in the activity that generates the information.

One caveat is required. The losses in negligent misrepresentation cases are usually purely financial losses with no physical injury involved. Such losses have been assumed here to represent real costs to society. However in some cases this may not be so. A solution to the general problem of 'economic loss' may qualify the conclusions reached above. But the qualifications (if any) are likely to be matters of detail — the essential economic argument developed here will remain valid, regardless what conclusion is reached on the general economic loss problem[39].

Notes to chapter seven

I thank G. Assaf, D. Dewees, R. Prichard, S. Rea, M. Trebilcock, S. Waddams, J. Ziegel and the Law and Economics Program of the University of Toronto.

1 (1889) 14 App Cas 337.
2 [1964] AC 465.
3 Ibid. at 482–83
4 Ibid. at 483
5 Lord Reid's argument is even weaker when one observes that persons other than the ultimate consumer can be injured by defective products e.g. the pedestrian who is killed when defective car-brakes fail.
6 *Ultramares v Touche* (1931) 174 NE 441 at 444.
7 [951] 2 KB 164.
8 Ibid. at 183.
9 Where the civil jury is often accused of acting with erratic generosity towards victims and surviving relatives.
10 *United States v Carroll Towing Co* 159 F (2d) 169 (1947) and see Posner (1972).
11 The concept of marginality is important in economic thinking. An example will show the simplicity of the basic idea. Suppose two types of precaution could be taken. Precaution *A* would cost £5 and reduce expected accident cost by £20. (Expected cost is reduced probability times cost, or reduced cost times probability or a combination of both.) Precaution *B* would cost a further £8 and reduce expected accident cost by a further £4. Here only precaution *A* should be taken because, though the total cost of *A* and *B* (£13) is lower than total value of prevention (£24) nevertheless the marginal (or 'extra') prevention cost, *B* (£8) is greater than the marginal (or 'extra') value of prevention (£4). It is better to spend only £5 for a net gain of £15 (£20 minus £5) rather than spend £13 for a net gain of only £11 (£24 minus £13).
12 In the case of the law of tort, the market for accident prevention.
13 First noted by Arrow (1971). The existence of information-supply industries is consistent with this hypothesis so long as some of the benefit is appropriable by the producer.
14 See Posner (1977) p 430 *et seq*. for a similar argument in another context.
15 More precisely he appropriates from each unit of benefit produced enough of the benefit at least to cover the cost of producing the marginal unit. Some part of the benefit usually goes to the consumer as consumer's surplus.
16 Here the term 'externality' is used without prejudice to the important point made by Coase, that the tortious act is a cost to the activities both of tortfeasor and of victim. The problem of external cost control is complicated by several factors that are ignored here, such as the distributional element in the concept of optimality, market imperfections and problems of open-ended liability.
17 This assumes that transactions costs are high. If they were not high the Coase Theorem shows that optimality will be achieved despite the external benefit of information production since that theorem applies symmetrically to external costs and benefits.
18 Accuracy is here assumed to be costly, e.g. checking figures and verifying sources consumes resources. The producer will not incur enough of these costs unless he has sufficient incentive to do so. Often this incentive is not supplied by his immediate purpose or his immediate customer.
19 [1976] 3 WWR 331
20 *Ultramares v Touche* (1931) 174 NE 441 at 446.
21 Ibid. at 338.
22 Here the curves have been drawn to represent a clear simple case where $Q_1 < Q_0$. If C_0 is so low as to be near the horizontal axis then Q_1 could exceed Q_0. In this and in succeeding examples it is also assumed for simplicity that the consumer units lost when information production is curtailed below the ideal are those units with lowest consumers' surplus. A more sophisticated analysis would complicate the argument to no purpose.
23 [1932] AC 562.
24 Many firms are now required by law to publish audited accounts. These firms cannot avoid paying the price for accounting services even if imposition of misrepresentation liability raises it far above present levels. In these cases it seems there would be no problem of information underproduction. However, other inefficiencies could be induced. First consider firms near the borderline between those required by law to publish

audited accounts and those not so required. Costs of doing business will shift in favour of smaller firms without any underlying social cost differences, leading to production of some goods and services at higher real cost than would be the case without the liability rule. This is inefficient in that production consumes more of society's resources than necessary. Secondly accountants will seek to disclaim liability by proclaiming to as many users as possible a disclaimer of liability for their statements. These efforts will consume real resources — though they may be efficient — as long as marginal loss avoidance by information users is more costly to them than are the costs of disclaimer to accountants.

25 It would be more satisfactory to assume that higher quality information induces a shift in the market demand curve just as it does in the hypothetical full demand curve. However this would make the diagram very complex and would not affect the conclusion: that a net improvement is possible if a limited liability rule is imposed by the court.

26 A market failure occurs when some factor — for example monopoly or high transaction costs or non-appropriability of benefits of information – prevents simple incentives to private production from achieving an efficient use of society's resources.

27 [1972] NZLR 1081.

28 [1976] 2 All ER 5.

29 (1972) 26 DLR (3d) 699.

30 [1976] 2 All ER 5 at 13–14

31 Ibid. at 21 (per Ormrod LJ) and 26 (per Shaw LJ)

32 [1971] AC 793.

33 Ibid. at p. 811

34 [1964] AC 465

35 [1941] AC 74.

36 [1972] 1 QB 373.

37 [1970] 1 All ER 1009.

38 (1972) 28 DLR (3d) 174.

39 The writer proposes a general economic theory of economic loss in tort in a forthcoming paper.

References

AKERLOF, G. (1970). The market for lemons: qualitative uncertainty and the market mechanism, *Quarterly Journal of Economics*, **84**, no. 3, 488–500.

ARROW, K. (1971). *Essays in the Theory of Risk-Bearing*, Chicago: Markham.

ATIYAH, P.S. (1978). Contracts, promises and the law of obligations, *Law Quarterly Review*, **94**, 193–223.

COASE, R. H. (1960), The problem of social cost, *Journal of Law and Economics*, **3**, no. 1, 1–44.

FLEMING, J. (1977), *Law of Torts*, Sydney: Australian Law Book Co.

LINDEN, A. M. (1977) *Canadian Tort Law*, Toronto: Butterworths.

LIPSEY, R. G. and LANCASTER, K. (1957), The general theory of the second best, *Review of Economic Studies*, **24**, no 1, 11–32.

POSNER, R. A. (1972), A theory of negligence, *Journal of Legal Studies*, **1**, no. 1, 29–96.

POSNER, R. A. (1977), *Economic Analysis of Law*, 2nd ed. Boston: Little Brown.

PROSSER, W. *Law of Torts*, 4th ed. St. Paul, Minn.: West Publishing Co.

REA, S.A. (1979), *Lump Sum Damages versus Periodic Payments* unpublished paper on file at Law & Economics Program, University of Toronto

STIGLER, G. S. (1961), The economics of information, *Journal of Political Economy*, **69**, no. 5, part 2, 94–105.

PART THREE

The judicial process

The chapter by Bowles begins with an explanation of the relevance of economic analysis to the study of legal procedure, and then illustrates the use of such analysis by applying it to the paying-in system and the problem of court organization. The essential point made is that the behaviour of the various participants in legal procedures will depend on the structure of the procedures themselves. An evaluation of procedures must therefore rely, in part, on the development of behavioural theories able to predict the responses of the participants.

Ogus is concerned with legal rulemaking that takes the form of the establishment of precise quantitative rules. He concludes that economic considerations are important in rule formation, and that judges' notions of transactions costs and social costs influence their choice of the degree of specificity of rules.

In his essay Adelstein examines the system of induced guilty pleas. He views the study as an exercise in the comparative analysis of the evolution of systems of criminal 'price-exaction', which in this case centres on the development and exercise of prosecutors' discretion in the English and American legal systems.

Finally in this section, Bowles and Whelan consider the problem of the losses that are incurred by foreign plaintiffs when court awards are made in sterling at times when the currency is depreciating. The authors view the 1975 *Miliangos* decision as a watershed, but explain that the implementation of the new rules has given rise to difficulties that are as yet unresolved.

CHAPTER EIGHT

Economic aspects of legal procedure

Roger A. Bowles

8.1 Introduction

Legal proceedings utilize economic resources that could be used for other purposes. This simple assertion has a wide variety of implications for the design of legal institutions as well as for the sort of behaviour that may be expected from those engaged in the proceedings. It is the object of this chapter to explore a number of such issues. This analysis does not claim to provide the policy maker with instant answers, but it may contribute to an understanding of the economic aspects of legal procedure and may thus illuminate some of the problems that the policy-maker confronts.

There are three main parts to this work. The first is concerned with presenting some background remarks on the parts of economic analysis that are useful in the discussion of legal procedure and assumes that the reader has little or no knowledge of economics. The second part is concerned with an illustration of how a particular piece of legal procedure may be scrutinized with the help of economic analysis, the example being the paying-in system that operates in the context of personal injury cases in England. The third part is concerned with a further illustration of the application of economic analysis to legal procedure, namely, the problem of the organization of courts and in particular the questions raised by the jury system and the way in which decisions are made about which cases come to be heard in courts.

The basic argument upon which we rely throughout is that the behaviour of both those 'using' legal procedures and of those who operate the procedures will be sensitive to the structure of the procedures. This has the consequence that changes in the procedural structure will have systematic and thus essentially predictable effects upon the behaviour of those involved in the system. Economic analysis is able, it will be suggested, to cast light upon such behaviour with the result that better information may be derived both about how existing institutions operate and about the likely consequences of any procedural reform.

8.2 Analytical background

8.2.1 Resources, values and costs

We have stressed that legal procedures entail the use of economic resources. It will be argued that the volume of resources used by different sorts of procedure will influence the choice of procedure. An essential preliminary therefore is some discussion of what is meant by an economic resource, particularly since the economist generally works with a rather broader definition of the term than other scholars. In essence, an economic resource is any good or service that is potentially of value in some way. 'Value' in this context is normally measured by ascertaining the highest price that any prospective buyer will offer to pay in order to acquire the resource. An important counterpart to the notion of value is the concept of opportunity cost. The opportunity cost of a resource currently being used in some specific way is given by the value that the resource would have if it were freed from its current use and applied to the most valuable competing alternative use. For example, the opportunity cost to a worker of remaining voluntarily unemployed is given by the disposable income that he thereby foregoes, that is to say the amount by which his purchasing power would increase if he were to take the best paid job available.

The next step is to investigate the ways in which the central notion of opportunity cost (hereafter abbreviated to 'costs') may be applied to an analysis of legal procedure. The argument is that the services of *all* the individuals engaged in, and the facilities used in, legal proceedings will generally have positive costs. From this it is but a short step to argue that in choosing between different forms of legal procedure society may well wish to scrutinize the costs of each. It might, however, be pointed out at this stage that legal institutions seem sometimes to be based on the premise that the opportunity cost of many of the participants is zero or at best small. The time that jurors, witnesses or parties in a case spend on court-related activities for example seems to be often overlooked — and yet this time could be used in various productive ways and so has a cost. This is not of course to say that it is 'inefficient' or 'unwise' to use resources in the course of legal proceedings. 'Justice' is likely to require high resource inputs even if it is to be only imperfectly achieved. What is at issue here is, first, how may legal proceedings be devised so that a given amount of 'justice' can be produced at least cost and secondly how many resources is society willing to devote to raising the amount of 'justice' produced when these resources could be used for other socially-valuable purposes. If it were easy to identify the 'value' of justice and the lowest costs entailed by the achievement of any given level of justice, it would be a straightforward matter to deduce the right balance between the use of costly resources and the sacrifice of justice. Justice, like any other good, would be produced up to, but not beyond, the level at which the last unit of justice contributed as much additional benefit as it cost to produce. What then are the difficulties?

The difficulties fall into two main categories, the positive and the normative. The first category contains problems related to the prediction of how law and legal institutions will impinge upon citizens and of the responses that changes in law or legal institutions will precipitate. The second category contains problems relating to the evaluation of different states of affairs, requiring that moral judgments be made about the weight to be attached to the well-being of different citizens. Accepting the conventional view of economics as a positive, scientific discipline[1], we concern ourselves here only with problems of the first category. This approach has the consequence that the analysis cannot itself be used to make assertions about which sorts of legal procedures are 'best' in an overall sense. The aim rather is to make assertions of the kind 'if a change of this kind were to be made it would affect the following individuals in the following ways ....'

Perhaps the major positive problem in the area with which we are concerned is that a great proportion of instances entail considerable uncertainty. The existence of sets of rules that govern legal proceedings may itself be interpreted as a response to uncertainty and to the high costs of administering justice. Small societies, particularly if undeveloped, may rely upon a system in which legal procedure is not a matter of there being a very long list of explicit rules but rather there being a series of implicit rules or customs that govern the treatment of the party or parties involved. In large advanced societies customs may come to be a less effective way of organizing or applying the law. The greater the anonymity of individual parties in proceedings and the more complex the law itself and the criteria applied to decide cases, the greater is likely to be the pressure for some relatively formal set of procedures. Expressed slightly differently, one may argue that as the costs of informal methods rise in relation to the costs associated with more 'bureaucratic' procedures, so there is a tendency for informality to give way to formality[2].

When the set of legal procedures is being designed initially, or is being reformed, it can be argued that the designers are likely to wish to minimize the overall costs incurred by the new system and to assure themselves that the new state of affairs will be superior in some respects to the previous one. If the designers follow the kind of advice that economists would be likely to give them, they will take account not just of the level of public expenditure to be anticipated under the new procedures but also of the costs that would be incurred by all parties including those who may be expected not actually to utilize the procedures themselves.

That is to say that in addition to isolating the opportunity costs that may exist but are not literally expressed as a market transaction, it is necessary to look at the costs that may be incurred (or avoided) by parties not directly involved in the proceedings. To use a rather extreme illustration of why these so-called 'externalities' may be relevant, suppose that the size of the majority of a jury required before a verdict of 'guilty' could be reached were to be reduced. One might argue that the volume of crime committed would fall, for even if the record of convictions against (true) criminals were poor, crime would now be prospectively more hazardous and thus a relatively less attractive activity than before. Note of course also that such a change would increase the probability of convicting those who are actually innocent and this is likely, other things being equal, to be regarded as undesirable. Indeed, one might infer from existing practice that such losses would greatly outweigh the possible deterrent effect of easier convictions.

Related to the idea that legal proceedings may have some unexpected repercussions on others is the observation that the costs that are generated by legal procedures for prospective users may themselves have an influence upon the number of people relying upon different forms of procedure. Thus whilst one may use the rather general argument that the set of legal procedures will take an informal or formal pattern depending upon the relative costs of each, so too one may argue that the introduction of formal procedures need not necessarily militate against continued reliance to some extent upon informal approaches. Probably the best-known effects of this kind arise in the context of contract. In both North America and the UK it has been observed that traders in many markets rely upon customary trade practices rather than upon the formalized system of contract law (Beale and Dugdale, 1975; Macauley, 1963). It is possible, however, to envisage changes in the structure of contract law that would change the degree of reliance upon legal remedies. Traders find it expensive to use formal modes of negotiating and enforcing contracts, and provided that they are in stable circumstances where they frequently buy and sell from the same people, they may find it cheaper to rely upon the more informal approach. When analysing the 'costs' of a particular set of legal rules, it is well to keep in mind that a great deal of activity is going on below the surface and that changes in the rules may thus set in motion much greater adjustments than originally anticipated.

It is important to observe that the choice of procedural rules will influence the uncertainty to which the parties are subject. The distribution of this uncertainty between the parties may itself have important effects, as indeed will be illustrated below in the case of the UK's system of personal injury compensation. As a prelude to discussing the implications of uncertainty for the choice of procedural rules it is most useful to make some general remarks about the economic theory of behaviour under uncertainty.

8.2.2 Behaviour under uncertainty

Under conditions of certainty, where all costs are known to all individuals in advance, life is straightforward: everyone chooses the course of action that is most beneficial to them. Consumers are assumed to maximize utility, where utility depends positively on the levels of the goods and services consumed, whereas firms are generally assumed to be maximizing profits. In the event of uncertainty, however, the concepts of certain cost and value are no longer sufficient: something has to be said about how individuals respond to being unsure about what costs they will incur or what gains they will make. The additional analytical apparatus needed for this purpose is fortunately readily available.

The analysis of behaviour under uncertainty is based upon the proposition that individuals can make coherent and consistent choices between alternative courses of action, where the outcomes associated with one or more of these courses of action contains some element of uncertainty or risk. Choices of this kind can generally be characterized as being amongst alternatives each of which has a number of possible outcomes, each outcome being expressed in terms of a financial gain or loss with a probability assigned to it. To give a simple example, an individual might be invited to join a lottery in which he pays $1 for a ticket and is told that 499 other tickets have been sold (his being the last one), and that the one and only prize is $601. Without for the moment worrying about why anyone might be prepared to run lotteries on such terms, we may ask ourselves whether the individual to whom the offer was made will accept it or not.

If the individual believes that only 499 other tickets have been sold and that the draw to find the winning ticket will be 'fair', then we may presume that he assigns a probability of 1 in 500 to winning. It is important to emphasize that in this analysis we are dealing with subjective probabilities, i.e. with the guesses or estimates made by the individual about the likelihood of different outcomes. The individual thus faces the choice between:

(1) Refuse the offer and thus maintain existing wealth, W_0.
(2) Accept the offer, pay the $1 entry fee and *either*:
  (*a*) Increase wealth to $[(W_0 - 1) + 601]$ with probability 1/500, i.e. WIN.
  (*b*) Have reduced wealth of $(W_0 - 1)$ with probability 499/500, i.e. LOSE.

The objective or 'actuarial' gain (A) from buying the lottery ticket in question is positive and may be defined as:

$$A = 600 \times 1/500 + (-1) \times 499/500 \tag{1}$$

Giving an expected gain of approximately 20 cents.

More generally, actuarial gain A may be denoted as the sum of gains, where each gain (x_i) is weighted by the probability (π_i) with which it occurs, taking care to note that these 'gains' may be negative, i.e. may be losses. Thus we have:

$$A = x_1 \pi_1 + x_2 \pi_2 + \ldots + x_i \pi_i + \ldots + x_n \pi_n \tag{2}$$

$$= \sum_{i=1}^{n} x_i \pi_i$$

where there are *n* possible outcomes. Whereas the gains can be positive or negative, the probabilities must all lie between zero and one and must in total add up to one, for otherwise we do not have a completely exhaustive list of possible outcomes.

From this definition of the actuarial value of any uncertain prospect may be derived some indispensable terms. An individual who is described as *risk averse* will turn down some prospects that offer a positive actuarial gain, in addition to steadfastly declining any prospects with zero or negative gains. It may be possible, therefore, to find some individuals who are sufficiently risk averse as to reject offers to gamble on the terms specified in the example. *Risk preferers* on the other hand will always accept prospects for which A exceeds zero (denoted $A>0$) and will be interested in some cases of apparently 'unfair' prospects that entail $A<0$. It is widely assumed in discussion of the design of legal institutions that most people are risk averse, that is that they will consistently refuse 'unfair' prospects. The existence of a gambling industry, however, presupposes either that the group of people who do gamble either consistently overestimate their likely winnings and/or enjoy the process of losing money, or that these people genuinely are risk preferers. Note that firms 'supplying' the gambling industry cannot, in the longer run, be risk preferers since they will go bankrupt if they consistently offer buyers the prospect of positive gains ($A>0$). *Risk neutral* individuals are those people who will take fair gambles and avoid unfair gambles and thus be indifferent about taking or avoiding gambles that are 'just fair' ($A=0$). It is argued by some authors that many firms and in particular, insurance companies, fall into this category as will be explained below. For the moment it is important only that we have established a framework within which *any* uncertain prospect or set of prospects may be analysed.

The final stage in setting out the analytical background involves a further discussion of the notion of 'cost'. An almost universal distinction is made between *private* and *social* cost. The former refers to those costs of an activity borne by the individual engaging in the activity whereas the latter refers to the sum of private costs and of those costs of the activity incurred by third parties. The existence of any divergence between the two is generally taken to indicate prima facie evidence of resource misallocation. If for example a firm in the course of production emits smoke that does extensive damage the costs of which it does not have to meet, social costs may greatly exceed private costs. In such circumstances the firm is effectively being enabled to buy too much pollution and create costs that in overall terms are not justified by the savings that the firm thereby makes.

It should be noted that in the case of both private and social cost there may be a wide variety of elements that might not immediately be thought of as 'costs'. To take a rather extreme example, the motorist who injures a pedestrian but suffers no harm to his car and has the claim for damages made by the pedestrian met by his insurance company, may nevertheless incur costs. These costs may include time lost from work, psychological damage resulting from the experience of the accident, time spent giving evidence about the accident in court, higher insurance premiums in future and so on. Anything that makes the individual worse off or deprives him of other opportunities in this way may be treated as a cost and will be something that the individual would pay some positive sum to avoid. The likelihood that some of these effects may be rather difficult to measure is not sufficient grounds for exempting them from the category of costs. Further distinctions between different sorts of costs can be drawn. Posner (1973) for example in his discussion of legal procedure and judicial administration distinguishes 'error costs', which are the 'social costs generated when a judicial system fails to carry out the allocative or other social functions assigned to it' and 'direct costs' arising from the use of the time of lawyers, judges and litigants. Calabresi (1970) in his work on accidents identified different types of costs. First there are the costs of accidents themselves — direct sorts of costs that depend upon the number of accidents taking place and their severity. Secondly, taking the volume of accidents as given there are different ways of organizing the compensation that is to be paid to victims — and these different ways entail different amounts of costs. Thirdly, once the mechanism for allocating compensation has been chosen, costs may depend upon exactly how this mechanism is operated.

8.3 Procedural issues

Legal procedures take a wide variety of forms, even within single legal jurisdictions. The object of this section is to outline how the analysis of the previous section may be used to illuminate three particular procedural issues, and will hopefully give the reader a feel for the approach that will allow him to apply the arguments to other procedural problems. The choice of issues to be examined here has been deliberately limited to those areas that have been discussed in the rapidly growing literature concerned with the application of economic analysis to law.

8.3.1 The payment-in system

The making of payments into court in tort cases in the UK is a device that is designed to reduce the delay and uncertainty experienced by plaintiffs seeking to recover damages. At any stage before the case is actually heard in court, the defendant can pay a sum of money into court. The plaintiff has the choice of accepting this sum in settlement of his case or of proceeding. In the latter case, should the court eventually make an award that lies below the sum paid in, the plaintiff will have to pay the costs of the defendant (and his own costs) from the date of payment-in to the date of final judgment. While the aim of this system is to encourage defendants to make reasonable offers to settle before the possibly large volume of resources entailed in a court hearing are committed, it may be argued that this system is not necessarily attractive from the point of view of plaintiffs. The essence of the argument is that it allows defendants to exploit the likelihood that plaintiffs are risk averse.

In order to analyse this procedure we begin by assuming that the plaintiff makes estimates of the amount of damages that he thinks a court will award[3]. These estimates will take account of the likelihood that there will be

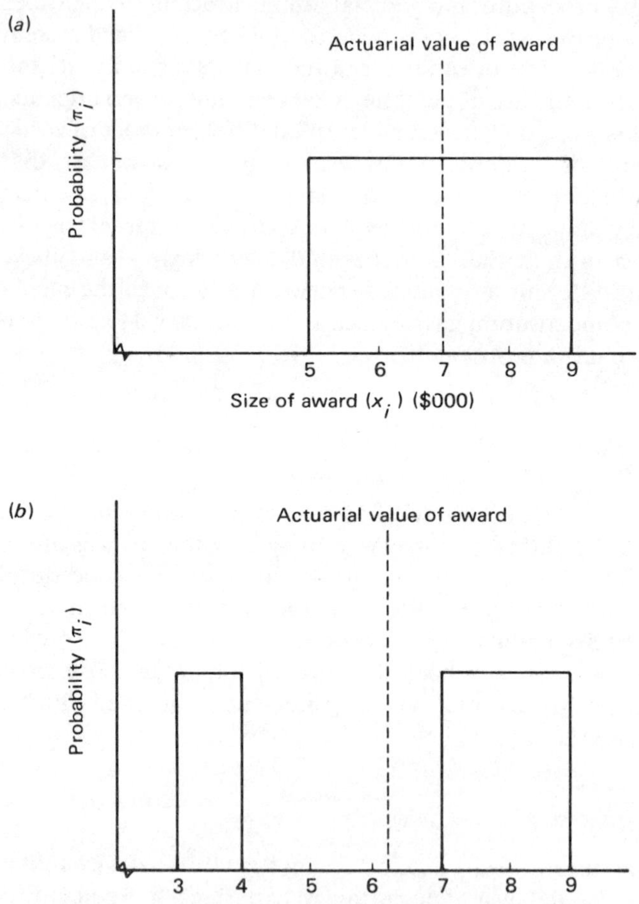

Figure 8.1 *(a) Initial probability distribution of damages. (b) Probability distribution of net damages under the payment-in system*

dispute about liability and about the appropriate quantum of damages. This information can be expressed in the form of a subjective probability distribution. For simplicity, let us assume that the plaintiff thinks it equally likely that he will be awarded $5000, $6000, $7000, $8000 and $9000 by the court as illustrated in *Figure 8.1(a)*. The individual may ignore his own costs since these also will be awarded against the defendant. From our earlier analysis we may argue that a risk-neutral individual would have no preference between facing the prospect of going to court in the circumstances outlined and receiving $7000 in lieu. The risk-averse plaintiff would settle for rather less than $7000 and possibly for not much in excess of $5000.

Let us suppose that the defendant pays a sum of $*D* into court, where $*D* lies between $5000 and $9000. The immediate effect of this on the plaintiff, given the rules of paying-in, is to induce a shift in the distribution of the award schedule. Taking the costs of each party from the date of payment-in onwards as $*C*, there is a leftward shift of $2*C* units of all awards that were originally of size *D* or less. Thus if for example $6500 should be paid in and it is expected that each party will subsequently incur legal expenses of $1000, the five possible amounts (all equally probable) with which the individual ends the day are now given as $3000, $4000, $7000, $8000 and $9000. The plaintiff considers the matter and observes from *Figure 8.1(b)* that the actuarial value of the likely damages in the event of his proceeding has declined from the initial level of $7000 to a new level of $6200. Further, he observes that not only has the mean or actuarial level of net damages fallen, but the variance (a measure of dispersion) has increased[4]. Both of these changes operate in the same direction: they both encourage the risk-averse plaintiff to accept a smaller sum in settlement of his claim. To put the point more forcibly, a given risk-averse plaintiff will now settle for a sum that is both below the actuarial value of net damages expected (after payment-in) from the court and is also below the sum for which he would have settled before the payment-in took place.

As far as what actually happens is concerned it is necessary to say something about the defendant's position. The first point to note is that the defendant may not know very much about the plaintiff and he will generally not know what probabilities the plaintiff (or the plaintiff's advisers) assign to the different possible outcomes in the event of the case going before the courts. Neither will the defendant have any precise picture of how risk-averse (or otherwise) the plaintiff might be. The argument advanced by Phillips and Hawkins (1976) and Phillips, Hawkins and Flemming (1975), however, is that while the defendant's capacity to exploit the plaintiff will be limited by such uncertainty, we may expect defendants in many instances to be considerably less risk-averse than plaintiffs. The reason for this assertion is essentially that the defendants in personal injury cases are frequently insurance companies, whereas the plaintiffs are generally individuals that are accident victims. Insurance companies, it is argued, deal with large numbers of risks and can rely on this to reduce the variation to which their net income is subject[5]. Risk neutrality or, at worst, a small degree of aversion to risk may thus be taken to characterize the attitude of such companies. This asymmetry in the attitudes towards risk of the parties enables the insurance company to consistently offer lower sums in out-of-court settlement negotiations than it would be prepared to if plaintiffs were less risk-averse.

It might in passing be noted that this means that if the insurance market is competitive, and thus premiums reflect the costs of meeting likely claims, then those who engage in the activity that is generating the injuries are effectively being forced to self-insure. Suppose that each motoring injury gave rise to losses to the plaintiff of $1000 on average but that the procedural rules (such as the paying-in system) and the size of awards made by the courts was such as to induce plaintiffs to settle for around $800 on the average. One could then argue that the accident victim would have to contribute $200 towards his own losses, while being able to take out insurance through conventional market channels for the remainder. Motorists as a whole may well prefer, as potential plaintiffs, to be able to avoid this problem of incomplete cover in return for actuarially-fair (or even unfair) premiums.

Despite, or possibly because of, the problems to which the payment-in system may give rise, one is prompted to ask whether such a system may not have compensating advantages. A clue to the answer is to be found in the fact that, according to Elliott and Street (1968) for example, if the plaintiff turns down the amount paid into court and is subsequently awarded a lower sum 'the court regards him as having lost the action at trial'. Plaintiffs who lose actions have, at least in civil cases, to meet the costs of the defendant, for only in this way it is argued can the scarce resources of court time be successfully rationed. Note, however, that this does not necessarily imply that the cases that are heard by the courts are those in which the evidence is strongly in favour of the plaintiff. In clear-cut cases where it is simple to predict accurately the likely findings of the court, matters will probably be resolved out of court, since in this way the parties can reduce the total amount of expenditure they 'waste' on legal services. If the defendant knows for example that the court will instruct him to pay the plaintiff $1000 there is little sense in his incurring legal expenses of $500 even if he knows that the plaintiff will not settle out of court for less than $1400. Should the parties take quite different views over the likely outcome of a court hearing however, or should the plaintiff be happier to take risks than the defendant, then it is likely that a negotiated settlement will not take place out of court and the case will have to be heard.

It is clear that a very high proportion of cases are actually settled out of court, and this led Phillips, Hawkins and Flemming (1975) to an interesting conclusion. They argue that if the judges award the 'correct' amount of damages in cases decided in court, a bonus should be added to the damages to offset the risks assumed by the plaintiff in taking his case so far. Such a bonus system could, if appropriately organized, have the effect of raising the level of settlements negotiated by plaintiffs *out of court* to the level that is agreed to reflect 'fair compensation'.

8.3.2 The jury system

The use of juries in legal decision-making is a widespread practice. In the UK they are largely, although not exclusively, employed in serious criminal cases. Much of the debate about juries has focused on the question of how juries reach their decisions: there remains great uncertainty about how verdicts are reached because of the virtual impossibility of getting access to the deliberations of jurors. For current purposes this issue is of rather less importance than the more basic decisions about the circumstances under which the courts will use juries in trials and the related decisions of how large juries are to be and how jurors are to be chosen.

The first point to make is that, as has generally been recognized, the use of a jury entails considerable cost because it requires that a number of people have to sit through the trial itself, hear all the evidence and then spend some time discussing their verdict. Some care is needed, however, with the notion of cost in this context. Following the argument used previously, it may be noted that the opportunity cost of a juror is given by the amount of production that he would have generated were he not spending time in court. To the extent that the payments made by the courts to jurors do not reflect the full losses that jurors (and thus society) incur, an analysis of expenditure on payments to jurors will understate the real costs involved.

A brief look at the system that currently prevails in the UK indicates that payments made by the courts to jurors seriously underestimate the costs involved. In the first place, employers are encouraged (by moral suasion rather than any material incentive) to continue paying the wages and salaries of workers called up for jury service. If the employer withholds all or part of the worker's wages, the worker can apply to the court for compensation for the amount of (after-tax) earnings lost. Such compensation is at present, however, limited to a maximum of £14 per day (approx $30). On a pro rata basis, this maximum corresponds to about £3500 p.a., the after-tax earnings of a single person with a salary of the order of £4500 p.a. This estimate is on the generous side, because it is being assumed that the worker will work 50 weeks a year. Clearly, if employers choose not to subsidize jury service, a great number of jurors will lose heavily since the *average* earnings of those subject to jury service is probably in excess of the maximum level of compensation. Jury service may thus be thought of as a progressive tax levelled selectively upon those chosen for jury service. Be that as it may, it seems that the systematic underestimation of the costs of jury trials is encouraged by the fact that the published figures on expenditure on the compensation of jurors are used as the basis for the calculation of costs. Thus we find Cornish (1971) for example, when discussing the choice between using juries and relying on one or more professional judges or a composite tribunal, that includes both judges and laymen, arguing as follows:

> ...the jury system is by no means cheap to run. Its true cost is much less easy to estimate than that of judicial salaries and pensions. It involves not only the direct payments to jurors themselves, but all the costs of administration, including such things as police protection for jurors when intimidation is feared. An accurate cost analysis of maintaining the jury system....would reveal that the expenditure involved is much greater than is often imagined.

Thus while we may agree with Cornish that *expenditure* on juries is often underestimated, we argue that the *costs* of juries may greatly exceed the true expenditure on them. To suggest that juries may be more costly than is widely supposed is not of course the same as arguing that the jury system be discontinued, for even if it could be shown that juries were more costly to run than were judges or panels of judges, it may well be that juries would be retained on the grounds that they produce decisions that society as a whole regards as more appropriate or 'better' than those produced by judges.

If this argument is to be sustained, however, something more has to be said about the 'quality' of decision-making under alternative systems. May one expect for example that people with different income-earning capacity will come to similar or dissimilar decisions? If the former is suspected then would it not be best to employ as jurors those whose talents are of least value in other uses? If it is suspected that decisions will be dissimilar then one may confront the question of whether it is worth incurring the high opportunity costs of using high-income jurors on the grounds that the resulting decisions will be of a sufficiently higher quality. Indeed, the rather scant economic literature in this area, notably Martin (1972), compares the problem of jury selection with that of using conscription to staff the armed forces. This line of argument suggests that the 'cheapest' (i.e. least cost in our rather technical sense) method of selecting juries is to make jury service voluntary and to fix the remuneration level of jurors so that the number offering themselves will be just sufficient to meet the number required. If such a procedure were followed the volunteers would presumably be the unemployed, those whose wages were relatively low and perhaps those who normally looked after children full-time if courts could provide low-cost crèches. In this way, the loss of production elsewhere in the economy could be minimized.

A likely objection to the use of voluntary juries is that it might have the effect of biasing the decisions reached in some way, although against this it may be noted that there are in any event biases of various kinds already built into the system. Returning for the moment to the maximum permissable level of compensation for jurors, to the extent that the court offices have discretion to excuse those called for jury service for a variety of reasons it is clear that high income earners may have a substantial incentive to seek to be excused. Equally, it seems that those employed by public authorities and large corporations are most likely not to suffer a loss of earnings because of the sympathetic attitude of their employers, and thus one may expect such workers (whose approach to decision-making may be systematically different from that of other groups of workers) to be 'over-represented' on juries. Arguments of this kind are, however, rather difficult to resolve because they require estimates to be made of how juries of different composition will respond to the same circumstances. It would be quite difficult to assemble the sort of information that would be needed in order to make reliable statistical inferences about the differences, if any, to be expected from juries selected on different criteria: this has recently been argued in the UK context by Baldwin and McConville (1979). If we overlook this difficulty for the moment, it is possible to pose a rather general formulation of the problem encountered in the design of a jury system. This formulation follows to some extent the work of Klevorick (1977), although many of the main features had been noted by earlier writers such as Posner (1973).

If we consider a particular case in which a party is accused of having committed some criminal act, an omniscient decision-maker will be able to establish with certainty the truth or otherwise of the allegation, abstracting from problems of intention and so forth. A jury selected to hear the evidence that is available will be able to form a view (given the decision rule in force) about the truth of the allegation. Since we may assume that there will probably not be absolutely overwhelming evidence one way or the other, the jury's view may be mistaken when compared with the 'truth'.

In order to examine such mistakes more rigorously it is convenient to introduce some simple terminology from the theory of statistical inference[6]. We begin by establishing a proposition or 'null hypothesis' that is to be tested, namely that the *defendant is innocent.* This proposition may be true or false. Should the proposition be true, but the jury concludes that it is false and convicts the defendant, a 'Type I' error has been made. Should the proposition be false, but the jury decides upon acquittal, a 'Type II' error has been made.

Errors of both kinds are costly. Wrongful conviction of the innocent, for example, entails losses to the person convicted that may be viewed as more serious than losses resulting from the conviction of genuine criminals, a view inferred from Stigler (1970). Wrongful acquittal on the other hand generates costs, among which may be a reduction in the deterrent value of sentences. Reductions in the probability of conviction on trial may be expected, other things being equal, to reduce the potential costs or hazards of embarking upon criminal activities, and may raise the volume of crime committed, Becker (1968), Anderson (1976).

As long as there is any possible doubt about the defendant's guilt, any conceivable institutional approach will be prone to making errors of either or both kinds. The overall cost of any particular approach will thus depend upon the frequency with which it makes errors of either kind, upon the relative costs of the different sorts of errors and upon the direct administrative costs[7]. Tullock (1971, ch. 5) argues that judicial systems will generally be preferable to jury systems if only because he thinks professional decision makers are much less likely to make mistakes than are amateurs. Klevorick (1977) is agnostic on this issue, confining himself largely to the issue of how changes in the size and composition of the jury may affect the different categories of cost. He makes the important point that the decision any single juror reaches will be influenced not just by his own perceptions of the evidence presented in court but also by the views taken by other jurors.

Evidence from the Baldwin and McConville (1979) study of UK juries suggests that Type II errors (wrongful acquittal) are thought to outnumber Type I errors. There are however a number of possible explanations of their finding. The 'mistakes' that they identify are those instances where professionals in court (principally lawyers) take a view that differs from the one formed by the jury, whereas one might argue that the professional view is itself far from infallible. Alternatively, it may be that juries take a stricter view of the criteria to be satisfied before convicting a defendant than do others in court or that they regard it as being much more important to avoid Type I errors than Type II errors. Any assessment of the relative merits of judicial and jury trials is plagued by the absence of reliable data about which defendants are genuinely innocent and by the need to make judgments about the costs attached to different sorts of errors. This argument should not however be taken to imply that any formal analysis is doomed to failure but rather to show that matters such as the design of the jury system may have an influence upon the volume of crime committed and more generally upon the level of well-being experienced by the community. The difficulties of establishing the strength and form of such influences cannot be ignored if informed policy-making is to proceed.

8.3.3 The public prosecutor's rationing problem

The third and final area of procedure to which some simple economics will be applied is the resource allocation problem faced by the public prosecutor. Despite ostensible differences in the structure of their systems, the UK and US face similar issues: there are limits on the number of cases that the courts can handle, on the amount of police time available for court-room purposes, on the amount that the prosecutor's office can spend on inputs of legal expertise and so on. The consequence of these constraints is that it is most unlikely that the prosecutor will be able to pursue all cases in which there is some chance of a conviction. If the prosecutor is thus forced to ration his resources in some way, it seems natural to enquire into the criteria that he applies in determining which cases to pursue and which cases to drop. This problem is very similar to the one facing a consumer who would like to buy large amounts of all sorts of goods and services but is hampered by limited income.

The public prosecutor, like other economic agents, may be thought of as having an objective that he pursues subject to various constraints. The suggestion of Landes (1971) is that the prosecutor is likely to try and maximize the volume of convictions, Z, that he expects to make, where 'volume' includes a measure of the size of the sentence in the event of conviction. The prosecutor is bound to work with expectations about both the probability of conviction and about the size of sentence, since he cannot be sure in advance how successful his pursuit of any given case will be. It is convenient for technical purposes to ignore variations in the length of sentence given in any particular instance and to focus purely on the probability π_i that the prosecutor assigns to getting a conviction in the i-th case. The contribution made by the i-th case to the prosecutor's success index will be given by the product of the probability of conviction and the length of sentence. That is to say that it is being assumed that the prosecutor will be indifferent between pursuing case A in which he thinks there is a 50:50 chance of conviction, conviction carrying a sentence of 15 years in jail and another case B in which he thinks he has a 3 in 4 chance of conviction where conviction carries a sentence of 10 years. The success of a prosecutor over some given period will thus be measured by the sum of expected sentences gained in the n cases pursued. The objective of the prosecutor may thus be thought of as being to select the n cases from the (*ex hypothesi*) greater number of cases available so as to maximize the volume of convictions, Z, i.e.

$$\text{Max } Z = \sum_{i-1}^{n} \pi_i S_i \tag{3}$$

where $\pi_i i$ is the probability of conviction in case i, and S_i is the sentence given on conviction in case i.

This however is only the first part of the story, since nothing has been said about how the prosecutor uses his resources. The probability π_i assigned to success in case i will almost certainly depend on the volume of resources devoted to it: gains may result from switching resources from one case to another once he has chosen the list of cases he is to pursue. It follows therefore that a genuinely optimal solution will entail the prosecutor knowing how sensitive the probability π_i is to changes in the volume of resources devoted to it. His decision will involve choosing both the most 'lucrative' set of cases to pursue, and the vigour with which each of them is to be pursued.

It can be shown from a formal treatment that at an optimum the prosecutor will have juggled with resource inputs until he reaches the allocation where the marginal contribution of the last dollar's worth of resources devoted to each case, in terms of the increase in expected sentence, is equal[8]. Not only is this result intuitively appealing (at least to economists!) but it also has some interesting implications for some of the issues that arise in this context.

Let us look at the implications for plea-bargaining. Despite frequent denials in the UK there is some evidence that plea-bargaining over sentence is used: see for example Baldwin and McConville (1977) and the discussion of Adelstein in chapter 10. In the United States, of course, it is quite legitimate and is widespread. Indeed from the model developed in this section it represents a very natural response by the prosecutor's office to the resource constraints that exist. In the event that court time is very limited and the amount of resources needed to raise the probability of conviction is significant, the prosecutor may find it expedient to offer lighter sentences to accused parties provided that they are prepared to plead guilty to lesser charges than those originally intended. In this way, relatively small resource inputs may be devoted to cases that offer prospects of reasonable sentences anyway. Provided that such offers may be voluntarily accepted or rejected by the accused one might argue that little harm is done, for the defendant's case is more speedily settled and may generally be expected to carry a lighter sentence than would otherwise be fixed (although the defendant may be disappointed by the quality of the 'justice' that he has received). Indeed we are now back to a set of circumstances that are very similar to those confronting the plaintiff in a personal injury damages suit; there are savings to be made if the parties can reach a settlement before going to court, and even if asymmetries in attitude to risk and the strength of bargaining position may enable public prosecutors, or defendants in personal injury cases, to appropriate the larger proportion of such savings, an out-of-court or pre-trial settlement will (in the limited sense of cost reduction) be mutually beneficial in most cases.

Whether public prosecutors in fact operate in ways that conform at all closely with the analysis presented here will depend on a variety of factors. The extent to which prosecutors are accountable is likely to be of importance: if they are themselves directly elected by the population at large then there may well be strong incentives for prosecutors to pursue strategies that maximize something like the volume of sentences generated. Against this it must be noted that the public's perception of whether prosecutors are doing a 'good job' may not be quite as rational as implied here: they may put greater weight on a high conviction rate in contested cases or on success in particularly heavily-publicized trials or on a variety of other indicators. In circumstances where prosecutors are less directly accountable there is great scope for speculation about how they might behave. The models of managerial discretion developed by Williamson (1964) suggest that they may try and divert some of the agency's budget to improving their own working conditions whereas more recent models of bureaucracy (Niskanen, 1971) suggest that pressure for expansion of the size of the prosecutor's office budget may be a prominent feature.

8.4 Concluding remarks

It has been the object of this chapter to suggest that economic analysis can shed light on some aspects of legal procedure. The object is not of course to claim that economics can by itself be regarded as a complete foundation for constructing a model of how legal procedure could or should be devised. Rather the object is to suggest that an area of the law such as procedure does throw up a wide variety of issues that economics has tackled in other spheres with some success. The notion of opportunity cost adds a dimension to the debate about legal institutions that has traditionally been rather lacking, particularly in the UK. It helps explain why people subject to legal rules and legal machinery behave as they do and how such behaviour, in conjunction with greater appreciation of the different sorts of costs generated by legal institutions, may give rise to sounder evaluation of the law. The postulate of cost minimization may help to rationalize existing legal institutions and also to help those taking decisions about institutional reform to become more fully aware of the consequences of pursuing different courses of action.

Notes to chapter eight

1 The classic statement of the positive–normative distinction is Friedman (1953). More recently a number of authors seem to have been moving towards the view that quite powerful inferences can be drawn from apparently positive analysis. Posner (1972, 1973) for example seems to argue that cost minimization, in which costs are comprehensively defined, is an objective that legal reform ought to pursue.

2 For deeper discussion of these arguments, see Hirsch (1974) and Posner (1980).

3 For a more detailed treatment of these sorts of issues see Friedman (1969) or Tullock (1975).

4 The variance in fact more than doubles, from £2 million to £5.36 million.

5 This is the so-called 'Law of Large Numbers'.

6 For further discussion, see any statistics test such as Yamane (1964).

7 In more technical terms, the problem can be expressed in the following way. Denoting aggregate costs as A_i for jury i, the optimal size and composition of a jury will be such as to satisfy:

$$\min_{i} A_i = f(\pi_{1i}, \pi_{2i}, C_i) \qquad (4)$$

where π_{1i} is the probability with which jury i makes Type I errors, π_{2i} is the probability with which jury i makes Type II errors and C_i are the direct opportunity costs of jury i.
Since all the components of equation (1) are governed by the size Q_i of jury i and its composition, indexed by a variable X,

the problem is to find a pair of values (Q^*_i, X^*_i) that will indeed generate the minimum referred to in equation (4). That is, we look for values such that:

$$\min_i \quad A_i = g(Q^*_i, X^*_i) \qquad (5)$$

8 If an amount r_i of the total resources available R are devoted to case i, and the relation between resource input to case i and the probability of conviction is written $\pi_i = \pi_i(r_i)$, the prosecutor's problem overall is to:

$$\max Z = \sum_{i=1}^{n} \pi_i(r_i) \cdot S_i + \lambda\left(R - \sum_{i=1}^{n} r_i\right) \qquad (6)$$

where λ is a Lagrange Multiplier.

Following Landes (1971) it may be simply demonstrated that the first order conditions require that:

$$S_i \cdot \partial\pi_i/\partial r_i = S_j \cdot \partial\pi_j/\partial r_j \qquad (7)$$

References

ANDERSON, R.W. (1976), *The Economics of Crime*, London: Macmillan.
BALDWIN, J. and McCONVILLE, M. (1977), *Negotiated Justice*, London: Martin Robertson.
BALDWIN, J. and McCONVILLE, M. (1979), *Jury Trials*, Oxford: Clarendon Press.
BEALE, H. and DUGDALE, A. (1975), Contracts between businessmen: planning and the use of contractual remedies, *British Journal of Law and Society*, **2**, no. 1, 45–60.
BECKER, G.S. (1968), Crime and punishment: an economic approach, *Journal of Political Economy*, **76**, no. 2, 169–217.
CALABRESI, G. (1970), *The Costs of Accidents: A Legal and Economic Analysis*, New Haven, Conn.: Yale University Press.
CORNISH, W.R. (1971), *The Jury*, Harmondsworth: Penguin.
ELLIOT, D.W. and STREET, H. (1968), *Road Accidents*, Harmondsworth: Penguin.
FELDSTEIN, M.S. and INMAN, R.P. (1976), *The Economics of Public Services*, London: Macmillan.
FRIEDMAN, A. (1969), An analysis of settlement, *Stanford Law Review*, **22**, no. 1, 67–100.
FRIEDMAN, M. (1953), The methodology of positive economics, in *Essays in Positive Economics*, University of Chicago Press.
HIRSCH, W.C. (1974), Reducing law's uncertainty and complexity, *UCLA Law Review*, **21**, no. 5, 1233–1256.
KLEVORICK, A.K. (1977), Jury composition: an economic approach, ch. 7 of Siegan (1977); an earlier technical version appeared in Feldstein and Inman (1976).
LANDES, W.M. (1971), An economic analysis of the courts, *Journal of Law and Economics*, **14**, no. 1, 61–107.
MACAULEY, S. (1963), Non-contractual relations in business: a preliminary study, *American Sociological Review*, **28**, no. 1, 55–69; reprinted by V. Aubert (1969), *Sociology of Law*, Harmondsworth: Penguin.
MARTIN, D.L. (1972), The economics of jury conscription, *Journal of Political Economy*, **80**, no. 4, 680–702.
NISKANEN, W.A. (1971), *Bureaucracy and representative government*, Chicago: Aldine-Atherton.
PHILLIPS, J. and HAWKINS, K. (1976), Some economic aspects of the settlement process: a study of personal injury claims, *Modern Law Review*, **39**, no. 5, 497–515.
PHILLIPS, J., HAWKINS, K. and FLEMMING, J. (1975), Compensation for personal injuries, *Economic Journal*, **85**, 129–134 and 'Reply' in same issue, 389–394.
POSNER, R.A. (1972), *Economic Analysis of Law*, Boston, Mass: Little, Brown Co.
POSNER, R.A. (1973), An economic approach to legal procedure and judicial administration, *Journal of Legal Studies*, **2**.
POSNER, R.A. (1980), A theory of primitive society, with special reference to primitive law, *Journal of Law and Economics*, **23** (1).
SIEGAN, G.H. (ed) (1977), *The Interaction of Economics and the Law*, Lexington, Mass: Lexington Books, D C Heath & Co.
STIGLER, G.J. (1970), Optimum enforcement of laws, *Journal of Political Economy*, **78**, 526–536.
TULLOCK, G. (1971), *The Logic of the Law*, New York: Basic Books.
TULLOCK, G. (1975), On the efficient

organisation of trials, *Kyklos*, **28** (2), 745–762.
WILLIAMSON, O.E. (1964), *The Economics of Discretionary Behaviour*, Englewood Cliffs: Prentice Hall.
YAMANE, T. (1964), *Statistics: An Introductory Analysis*, 2nd Ed., New York: Harper and Row.
ZANDER, M. (1976), *Cases and Materials on the English Legal System*, 2nd Ed., London: Weidenfeld and Nicolson.

CHAPTER NINE

Quantitative rules and judicial decision making

Anthony I. Ogus

In the body of law and economics literature, the problem of transactions costs is beginning to assume an appropriately prominent position as a crucial variable in the subject of analysis (*see* Calabresi and Melamed, 1972; Williamson, 1976). This development may be seen as a delayed reaction to a perhaps somewhat less obvious implication of the Coase (1960) theory of social cost. The statement that with zero transaction costs an efficient allocation of resources might be achieved however property rights are defined (Coase, 1960, p. 15) may be adapted to suggest that property right definitions are likely to vary according to the impact of transaction costs. In other words, in formulating the law, the legislature and judiciary should take account of the costs borne by those affected by the rule in acquiring information as to its content, using it as a directive for behaviour or as a basis for transacting with others, adjudicating on its meaning, or enforcing it through judicial or bureaucratic machinery. To the extent that judges respond in this way to the transaction cost problem, the practice may weaken Dworkin's thesis that, for constitutional reasons, they should not be predominantly concerned with economic efficiency objectives (what he described as 'policy' issues) in their decision making[1].

The influence of efficiency objectives on legal rulemaking has been the subject of a very illuminating study by Ehrlich and Posner (1974; *see also* Hirsch, 1974). In this essay it is proposed to build on their analysis by concentrating attention on a particular phenomenon — the formulation by judges of highly precise rules that we shall call 'quantitative' rules — with illustrations drawn from two areas of substantive law. We shall also attempt to relate these issues to some theories concerned with the evolution of judicial decision making.

9.1 Optimal precision of legal rules

In the formulation of rules there is clearly a wide spectrum between generality and specificity. At one extreme, the rule lays down a vague standard which expressly or impliedly confers considerable discretion on adjudicators or enforcers. The law of negligence, for example, bases liability for damages on the criterion of a failure to take reasonable care. While such generalizations are typical features of the judge-made common law, they exist also in legislative regulatory controls. Thus under the Control of Pollution Act 1974 proceedings may be taken against a person responsible for noise 'amounting to a nuisance' who is unable to prove 'that the best practicable means have been used for preventing, or for counteracting the effect of, the noise.'[2] At the other extreme, the rule may be couched in such precise terms as to suggest that the application of it to a given set of acts is purely a mechanical operation. Such 'hard-and-fast rules', 'rules of thumb' or, as we prefer to call them, 'quantitative rules' (Friedman, 1967; 1975, pp. 293–294; *see also* Raz, 1975, pp. 59–62) are to be found frequently in legislation (e.g. a will must be signed by *two* witnesses[3]) but emerge sometimes as part of judicial doctrine. Dating at least from the 17th century, there is a rule that for murder or manslaughter to give rise to criminal liability, the death of a victim must occur within a year and a day of the infliction of the injury[4]. This arbitrary condition was intended to overcome the difficulties of proving the causal link between the injury and death when there was a long interval between them.

It should be noted at the outset that the mechanical character of a quantitative rule can never be absolute. As Hart (1961, pp. 124–125) has observed, the fallibility of language means that rules will always contain an open-texture (*see also* Benditt, 1978, pp. 30–35; Jowell, 1975, pp. 134–135). The requirement under the Wills Act of attestation by two witnesses may require adjudication on what constitutes a 'signature'[5]; there is a question whether part of a day counts for the 'year and a day' rule (cf. Smith and Hogan, 1978, p. 270). In other words, the quantitative character of rules is a matter of degree not of kind (Dickinson, 1931). This should not lead us, however, into the minefield of rule-scepticism: we can still recognize that quantitative rules may confer on the law a high degree of (if not absolute) certainty.

What criteria should determine where along the spectrum between generality and precision a rule is to be placed by the legislature or the judiciary? In their study of rulemaking, Ehrlich and Posner (1974, pp. 262–267; *see also* Kennedy, 1976, pp. 135–135) identified certain costs and benefits that the precision of rules confers on a legal system, thus suggesting that there is, in theory at least, for any given problem a socially optimal degree of specificity. As regards the benefits of precision they list: increases in the marginal productivity of law-enforcers; reduction in the total amount of litigation and thus in the total costs of dispute resolution; the facilitation of out of court settlements and thus the reduction of negotiation costs; reduction in the length of trials; reduction in the costs of informing those directly affected or the public at large as to the content of the law; the facilitation of social control where regard need be had to a limited number of factual circumstances.

The costs of precision are perhaps less susceptible of succinct description but they include (Ehrlich and Posner, 1974, pp. 267–271, 277–280): the acquiring and evaluation of information necessary to formulate an individualized rule; the expenses involved in its promulgation (which in the case of politically controversial legislation may be quite high[6]); increase in the demand for legal expertise where the accumulation of individualized rules gives rise to great complexity; the increased need for amendment as inevitably individualized rules can adapt much less than generalized rules to economic and technological change. Perhaps most important of all is the cost arising from the 'imperfect fit' of precise rules. The more flexible a rule, the easier it is to accommodate decision making of 'hard cases', that is, to admit borderline cases that fall within the objectives of the rule, and to exclude those inconsistent with such objectives. The arbitrary character of quantitative rules necessarily gives rise to costs of over-inclusion (e.g. the social loss of deterring desirable activity) and of under-inclusion (e.g. the social loss of not deterring undesirable activity)[7]. While sub-rules and exceptions can be created to meet the problem, they will of course generate their own costs, as already described.

In evaluating these costs and benefits (if only on an intuitive basis) account must also be taken of the area of operation of the rules in question. Rules governing private disputes between individuals or commercial enterprises arising from property, contract, tort or family relationships are likely to be more general, at least if it is assumed that transaction costs do not impede negotiations between the parties. Here the costs of over- and under-inclusion are typically exceeded by the benefits of facility of application (Ehrlich and Posner, 1974, pp. 272–273). The crucial distinction for this purpose, though one relatively neglected in Anglo-American literature (cf. Kahn-Freund, Levy and Rudden, 1979, pp. 238–240), may be that between mandatory and non-mandatory rules (*ius cogens* and *ius dispositivum*). The notion that, subject to public policy constraints, parties may freely adapt or override private law standards suggests that in the absence of high transaction costs they operate only as a *general* framework within which more individualized behavioural patterns can be established according to the parties' volition. Where, however, transaction costs are high, thus hindering the refinement of the standard, one might expect greater precision in the rule. A useful example of the quantitative rule which may be rationalized on this basis is the so-called 'one-third' rule, on the basis of which alimony was assessed on the breakdown of a marriage (Cretney, 1979, pp. 310–314). The practice in the Ecclesiastical Courts was, in the absence of special circumstances, to order the husband to pay the wife such money as would bring her income up to one-third of their joint income[8]. While the rule was at one time discredited[9], it has nevertheless continued to be applied, if only as a starting-point in assessing an appropriate sum[10]. Its economic justification has been unambiguously stated by Morris (1971, p. 110): 'It meant that in thousands and thousands of cases ... orders would be agreed by negotiation between solicitors and so the expense involved in a fight ... at court could be avoided.'

The corollary of the above analysis is that *ius cogens* will tend to a greater degree of precision. The criminal law with its use of sanctions, including a potential loss of liberty, creates significant costs if it is over-inclusive (Ehrlich and Posner, 1974, p. 272; *but see* Kennedy, 1976, pp. 1695–1696); a fact reflected also, of course, in special rules of procedure and proof. Tax law with the major financial consequences of liability gives rise to similar considerations (cf. Monroe, 1979). Whether the practice of plea-bargaining (cf. Baldwin and McConville, 1977) or the granting of tax-waivers by the Inland Revenue[11] is sufficiently widespread to undermine the mandatory character of the law and thus to import into it a degree of 'negotiability' is a matter of some speculation; whether such practices are desirable is controversial; but to the extent that such phenomena are accepted as furthering social policy objectives, they may imply less precision in rulemaking than would otherwise be the case.

Those areas of public law that require bureaucratic machinery for administration and enforcement will be heavily weighted in favour of precise rules (Davis, 1979, ch. 3). Where a large number of cases have to be processed speedily the costs of over- or under-inclusion are likely to be exceeded by the costs of individual investigation (Friedman, 1967, p. 795; Raz, 1975, pp. 59–60). The point has been explicitly acknowledged in the recent debate on the reform of the discretionary elements in supplementary benefit law (DHSS, 1978). These were originally envisaged as extending only to 'exceptional' cases, but in the 1960s and 1970s were paid out on an increasingly routine basis for heating, dietary and clothing needs. A departmental review, published in 1978, recommended the replacement of the broad discretionary principle by a body of specific rules to cover 'the common and predictable needs of broad categories of claimants' (ibid., para. 1.14). Inevitably this proposal, as implemented in 1980[12], would 'involve some element of rough justice and some losers as well as gainers ... but ... the balance has tilted too far away from simplicity towards fine tuning which does not always achieve thc desired result.' (ibid., para. 1.15).

Other reasons have been proffered for precise rules in the bureaucratic sphere. In a political sense they can be seen as providing a shield for public officials (Jowell, 1975, pp. 20–21). The activities of these officials are more easily defended if they involve the mechanical application of rules; they are protected from the tensions and undue pressures involved in positive decision making, and the abuse of discretion is more easily avoided. Rules are more easily communicated to those affected and thus are less likely to lead to challenge, or so it is claimed (DHSS, 1978, para. 9.52).

It must not, however, be assumed that rule systems are always incorporated into formal legal instruments. It is not unusual for legislation, parliamentary or delegated, to confer a broad discretion, which is in fact exercised by an agency according to rules which are never published[13]. Not only do such practices conflict with some of the justifications for rules outlined above, but in strictly legal terms they are questionable. There has been a tendency of courts to hold that the routine application of rules cannot be regarded as a proper exercise of a broad discretion[14].

In locating the criteria for determining the choice between general and specific rules, we should not ignore some accounts of judicial decision making that have in the past been well received and which continue to attract some support. In his 'Theory of Judicial Decisions' Pound (1922; 1959, pp. 68–71) drew a distinction between cases involving contract and property rights which were to be decided by rules and cases concerned with 'human conduct' which could be dealt with more intuitively, often by the exercise of a discretion. The law of property and of commercial transactions involve a 'general' element that is susceptible to the mechanical application of rules: 'the rule ... works by repetition and precludes individuality in results, which would threaten the security of acquisitions and security of transactions .... Every promissory note is like every other. Every fee simple is like every other.' (Pound, 1959, pp. 70–71). In contrast, 'some situations call for the product of hands, not of machines, for they involve not repetition, where the general elements are significant, but unique events, in which the special circumstances are significant ... no two cases of negligence have been alike or ever will be alike.' (ibid.).

A somewhat milder version of this thesis has been accepted by some (but by no means all) of our judges. Thus Lord Denning has said that for the work of the Chancery Division (mainly concerned with dealings in land and the devolution of estates), 'certainty is, quite rightly, of paramount importance. It does not matter so much what the rule is, so long as it is certain.' (Denning, 1952, p. 8). But for the Queen's Bench Division, which is more concerned with the redress of grievances, 'justice is at least as important as certainty and probably more important.' (ibid., p. 9). The distinction has been employed in the areas of, for example, family and tort law to justify not only more general and therefore more flexible rules, but also a less strict adherence to the doctrine of *stare decisis* (Stevens, 1979; pp. 590–599).

Despite their intuitive appeal, these distinctions, at least as formulated, cannot be sustained. In the first place, the classification is itself superficial (Wasserstrom, 1961, pp. 102–105). Property or commercial cases may involve the need to redress grievances on a more individualized basis: it is not true that one property or commercial institution is just like another. How, for example, are we to regard cases in which deserted[15] or battered[16] wives claim some interest in the matrimonial home, or in which a contractual licensee seeks to have his possession of property protected against third party purchasers?[17] Secondly, even if the classification is to be admitted, its implications for the desirability of certainty and hence for the dichotomy between generality and specificity are less obvious than has been alleged.

The very great majority of claims for compensation based on the transgression of behavioural standards by others never reach the courts[18]: they are settled by the parties in the light of their prognostications as to what the court would decide[19]. That being the case, the benefits of certainty and therefore of greater specificity — the reduction of transaction costs — is as pertinent here as it is in relation to the more obvious instances of property and commercial disputes (Posner, 1977, pp. 441–443).

By focusing on the value of specific rules where they are used as guidelines for behaviour, in particular for transactions involving property and other rights, we may yet locate a distinction that builds on the intuitive appeal of that proposed by Pound but which is not subject to the objections outlined above. Scott (1975) has analysed two models of the civil process (*see also* Atiyah, 1978). The first, which he described as conflict resolution, is a method of achieving a peaceful settlement to private disputes. To achieve the primary goal of appeasing one party's sense of grievance or of forestalling vindicatory action by him, the court would tend to concentrate more on the complaint than on the defendant's conduct. The result may be a ruling that is in some sense arbitrary in that its rule-content is reduced and its value as a behavioural norm for others is low. Formally, the practice would typically be authorized by the conferring of a broad discretion on the decision maker. The alternative method incorporates the notion of behaviour modification. Atiyah (1978, pp. 3–4) refers to this as the 'hortatory function of law'. The primary aim is to formulate standards governing the conduct of all in the same or similar circumstances by imposing costs on those who contravene these standards. For this purpose, attention is normally concentrated on the defendant's behaviour rather than the plaintiff's complaint, and to minimize transactions costs the decisions must be consistent and predictable, hence the value of the specific rules.

9.2 Trends in judicial rulemaking

In the remainder of this chapter we shall attempt to relate the theoretical considerations described above to some aspects and trends in English judicial rulemaking. There is a twofold purpose in this exercise. First, it may shed some light on the controversial issue as to whether judges do, if only on an intuitive and unarticulated basis, take account of efficiency considerations[20]. The Dworkinian argument that judges should decide according to principle rather than policy — the latter notion expressly covers efficiency (Dworkin, 1977, p. 91) — is highly relevant here[21]. If, for example, it can be shown that judges without any authority, inspiration or guidance from the legislature, have formulated quantitative rules in relation to a large number of cases concerned with a particular problem in the knowledge that they are bound to lead to some arbitrary results, but also with the expectation that they will substantially facilitate the expedition of conflict resolution, we may have legitimate grounds for believing that there was an economic rationale for the decision. A reasonable inference is that, in their view, for the problem in question, the reduction in transaction costs outweigh the costs of over- and under-inclusion. Secondly, it may be instructive to consider whether there is any perceptible trend in judicial attitudes to the question: is there a 'natural' tendency to a greater specificity of rules? Friedman (1975, p. 293), for example, has argued that 'living rules of law will move toward objectivity as part of their life cycle ... they tend towards mechanical, quantitative forms. They have a theoretical resting point at which they are perfectly quantitative or mechanical.' Alternatively, as we shall argue, it may be suggested that judges indulge in some form of iterative process by which, through oscillation between greater generality and greater specificity, they may eventually arrive at an optimal precision of legal rules.

To generalize on patterns of judicial behaviour is inherently dangerous (Devlin, 1978): at any one time some individual judges may not conform with the majority opinion of their brethren. Thus today there is a manifest divergence between the attitude of Lord Denning MR, and that of his colleagues in the House of Lords (Denning, 1979, part VII). Yet for the limited purpose of our analysis we may be justified in having regard to shifts in the predominant judicial response to the task of rulemaking. We shall consider first general attitudes and then analyse tendencies in two specific areas of law.

As regards the primary distinction between the conflicts resolution and behaviour modification functions of judicial decision, with its implications for general and specific rules respectively, we can, over a period of several centuries, perceive significant shifts in judicial attitudes. The objective of individualized justice, in contrast to the mechanical application of fixed and certain rules, featured in the equitable doctrines formulated and administered in the Court of Chancery (Milsom, 1981, ch. 4; Allen, 1964, pp, 399–425). It is trite legal history that this aspect of English judicial practice suffered a marked decline in the 18th and 19th centuries (Atiyah, 1979, pp. 388–397). The doctrines that had admitted of great flexibility and discretion in their application were transformed into hard-and-fast rules, as precise and certain as the common law rules that they were originally designed to complement. 'The dialogue between certainty and justice, law and morals, had been acted out in real life; and the end of it was two systems of certainty, two systems of law.' (Milsom, 1981, p. 95). One of the important reasons for this development may be regarded as economic. Property rights would diminish in value if subject to the uncertain dictates of the Chancellor. There were social costs involved in the over-reaching of common law rules that might outweigh the benefits of individualized justice. The point had been appreciated even in the 16th century: 'where a common inconvenience will follow, if the common law be broken, there the Chancery shall not help.'[22]

Such perception was linked to growth of the behaviour modification function of judicial pronouncements. No doubt aware of the increasing extent to which judgments were regarded as laying down norms of conduct, particularly within the rapidly expanding commercial sphere — a process facilitated by the systemization of law reporting (Allen, 1964, pp. 221–232) —the courts devoted greater energy to rule and principle formulation and hence a greater degree of specificity: there was a manifest tendency to divert disputes away from factual issues into legal issues (Atiyah, 1979, pp. 390–392). It is, of course, no accident that the high point of this development occurred at a time when judges were caught up in the political economy movement and were consciously striving to create a framework of laws that would accommodate and support wealth-maximization goals, a process that would be facilitated by the greater certainty of the law (Atiyah, 1979, chs. 13–14).

It has generally been acknowledged that in the last two decades or so the trend has been reversed; there has been a perceptible shift in judicial attitudes from principle to pragmatism, what is sometimes unflatteringly referred to as 'ad hockery' (Atiyah, 1979, pp. 676–680). Judges have been less inclined to feel themselves tied down by precise rules, and prefer to shelter a decision on the facts behind a broader generalization[23]. Thus even the highly elaborate rules on offer and acceptance, which conventionally determine the formation of the contract, might, on one judicial view, be held inapplicable if they were to produce 'manifest inconvenience and absurdity'[24]. The *stare decisis* doctrine has been applied less rigidly (Cross, 1977, ch. 4); in particular, the House of Lords is no longer bound by its own decisions[25]. The rigid categorization of relationships that was thought necessary to found a claim in negligence has given way to more flexible principles[26]. Some judges have found ingenious ways whereby personal interests might prevail over clearly established property rights[27].

It would be wrong to exaggerate the strength of this movement: there is no question of returning to the broad discretionary practices of pre-industrial days. Rather it is evidence of a slight swing in the pendulum away from specific rules and certainty towards general principles and flexibility. It may be that the judges are becoming more conscious of the social and individual costs arising from the imperfect fit of specific rules and attributing smaller values to the increases in transaction costs that are associated with more general rules. It may also be — and we shall illustrate this argument below — that in their intuitive assessment of the relative costs and benefits of generality versus specificity, the judiciary tend to overestimate the costs and underestimate the benefits of the status quo. If this be the case, then they will engage in a continuous process of adjustment from generality to specificity and vice versa. Ideally, this oscillation will lead by an iterative process to an approximation of their perception of what is the socially optimal degree of precision.

9.2.1 Personal injury claims

The first special area of judicial rulemaking to be examined is particularly illuminating since the development from a general to a quantitative rule took place over a relatively short period (some twenty years) and because the transaction cost implications are reasonably clear. Personal injury claims for damages constitute a major legal activity in the United Kingdom: it has been estimated that about 250 000 are made every year (Pearson, 1978, vol. 1, para. 78). Those claims based on serious injuries, in which large sums are involved, are more hotly contested and give rise, proportionately, to greater amounts of administrative costs, particularly the time of lawyers, judges and insurance agents (ibid., vol. 2, para. 81). Subject to certain qualifications that need not concern us here[28], it may be accepted that aggregate social welfare is increased by the savings on administrative costs which are made when parties settle out of court instead of proceeding to litigation (Posner, 1973, pp. 400–402; Gould, 1973, pp 280–281). The Winn Committee on Personal Injuries Litigation recognized that 'the provision of facilities for the fostering of settlements is an objective which should be pursued by those who mould law and practice.' (Winn, 1968, para. 112). For a settlement to be reached the maximum that a defendant is prepared to offer must exceed the minimum that the plaintiff is prepared to accept. To achieve this, it is a necessary condition that both parties' estimates of what a court would award if the case were to go to trial must converge. It should therefore follow that increases both in the predictability of judicial awards and in the amount of information available to potential litigants on likely awards will increase the settlement rate, and reduce administrative costs (Posner, 1973, pp. 448–451).

One contentious issue in the serious case is typically the amount recoverable for non-pecuniary losses, generally referred to as damages for loss of amenity and pain and suffering (Ogus, 1973, pp. 194–215). The period 1950–1970 saw a major evolution in the law towards greater predictability and information. The process began when the participation of juries in personal injury trials, which clearly led to arbitrary and unpredictable awards, was actively discouraged and eventually suppressed altogether except where 'special circumstances' existed[29]. To enable judges, now alone responsible for the quantification process, to achieve greater consistency counsel were permitted to cite in argument awards in comparable cases[30]. This led to a demand among personal injury practitioners for more information on damage recoveries, which was met by the publication of collections of personal injury awards in cases that were not published in the ordinary law reports[31]. For the efficient use of such materials, however, two main obstacles remained. First, it was not the practice of judges to itemize awards under the various heads of loss; in particular, 'general damages' were not sub-divided as between non-pecuniary losses and future pecuniary losses[32]. After some judicial hesitation[33], this was remedied by requiring judges to distinguish between these two items[34]. Secondly, there was a disputed question as to whether the non-pecuniary element was to be based on a mainly objective assessment as to the degree of the plaintiff's injury or rather on a more subjective, and therefore more speculative, assessment of the plaintiff's loss of happiness resulting from his injuries. Two important decisions in the 1960s revealed a judicial preference for the former approach, with its clear implications of greater predictability[35].

The position was then reached in which the quantification of these non-pecuniary awards had become a question of law as well as a question of fact. There had emerged a judicial 'tariff' for the more frequently encountered physical conditions[36], and the Court of Appeal could correct serious divergencies from it[37]. While overt references to economic considerations are rare, it is nevertheless clear that reduction in the administrative costs of processing personal injury claims has been an important motivation in these developments. Thus, for example, in *Ward v James*, Lord Denning MR said: 'Parties should be able to predict with some measure of accuracy the sum which is likely to be awarded in a particular case, for by this means cases can be settled peaceably and not brought to court, a thing very much to the public good.'[38] On the other hand, particularly recently, there has been some perceptible, if only slight, shift away from wholehearted reliance on quantitative rules in this area. Judges have begun to warn that the 'conventional' figures drawn from other cases can provide only 'guidelines' that may be usefully adopted as 'starting points' in assessment, but which should be adapted to the particular facts of each claim[39]; that no two cases of personal injury are alike[40]. Others have stressed that the overriding objective of the damages remedy remains that of 'fair and reasonable compensation', and that too great an obsession with the correctness of amounts for particular heads of loss may lead to inappropriately high total awards[41]. Finally, and perhaps most significantly for our purposes, there have been some protests against the excessive citation of other decisions[42]. The implication is that the collection, investigation and comparison of a large number of precedents is sub-optimal because of the high transaction costs involved.

It may be suggested that the development of this area of the law of damages is consistent with the notion of an iterative process towards an optimal degree of specificity in the legal rules. Step by step, during a period of 20 years, the judges edged towards greater precision, with the aim of reducing transaction costs. During the last few years there has been some oscillation around the point reached, as they have become increasingly aware of the costs of imperfect fit and the fact that too great a reliance on quantitative rules might be counter-productive in terms of abating transaction costs.

9.2.2 The administration of welfare benefits

The second area of rulemaking to be considered is within the law of social security. The administration of welfare benefits requires a very large bureaucratic machinery and, in the light of the generalization made in section 9.1, we might expect a heavy concentration of precise rules. A rigorous investigation of the merits of every claim is clearly inconceivable (Jowell, 1975, p. 19); here the transaction costs associated with the tailoring of general rules to fit particular needs will normally exceed the social costs resulting from an imperfect fit. This is not to imply that the legislation governing the administration of benefits will inevitably formulate rules with great precision; rather that there will be a tendency by those administering the system of adjudicating claims to confine the discretion involved in general principles through precise rules. This clearly happened (albeit by informal means) in those areas of the old supplementary benefit law where broad discretions were conferred on officials[41]. We shall focus, however, on a similar process that has occurred in the law governing entitlement to contributory social security benefits, which was formerly known as national insurance law. Appellate decision making in this context is primarily the responsibility of the National Insurance Commissioners (*see* generally Micklethwait, 1976). Their rulings, especially those published by the HMSO, constitute an authoritative source of law and are binding on department officials (Ogus and Barendt, 1978, pp. lxiii–lxiv, 634–635). It may be objected that the Commissioners are not 'judges' in the fullest sense of that term, and that it is therefore inappropriate to treat their practices as examples of judicial decision making. The argument does not carry much weight. In a recent case, Lord Denning MR, explaining why the ordinary courts should be reluctant to depart from the case law established by the Commissioners, observed that they 'are judges, and their decisions are by statute final ... they give hundreds of decisions on points of law regarding the interpretation of the regulations. They know just how they work'[43].

A scrutiny of the Commissioners' decisions reveals a pattern of behaviour that consistently supports the model of judicial decision making advanced in this paper. On a number of important issues that call for resolution but on which the legislation is content to lay down a general discretionary principle, they have formulated a quantitative rule, sometimes of a very arbitrary nature. Faced with the problem of accommodating such rules to 'hard cases', that is cases in which the claimant's circumstances fall within the spirit of the legislative principle but fall outside the quantitative rule, they have subsequently tended to recoil from holding that the rules have an absolute mechanical character, and have reached a compromise by which the rule is to be regarded as generally applicable but not so as to exclude a different result where 'special circumstances' so require.

Under the rules governing entitlement to unemployment benefit, it is sometimes necessary to determine a claimant's 'normal' pattern of work before he became unemployed (Ogus and Barendt, 1978, pp. 94–97). In the years immediately following the introduction of these rules, no doubt with administrative convenience in mind, the Commissioner tended to regard as 'normal' only that which had happened in the period of 12 months prior to the claim[44]. This soon crystallized into a rule of law, so rigid in its application that regulations had to be introduced enabling the authorities to look beyond the 12-month period when, in prescribed circumstances (e.g. when employment had been irregular), it was not the appropriate test for 'normality'[45]. Such legislatively-created exceptions did not cover all 'hard cases' and in 1972 the Commissioner was forced to admit that the rule was only one method of determining on the facts what, at the time of the claim, was 'normal' for the claimant[46].

Sickness and invalidity benefit is payable to those who are 'incapable of work' (Ogus and Barendt, 1978, pp. 149–159) and 'work' here means 'work which the person can reasonably be expected to do'[47]. What is 'reasonable' for a person to do is clearly a matter of delicate judgment: in particular, is it sufficient for the claimant to show that he is incapable of work in his normal ocupation? If so, does the criterion remain the same for whatever period he has been off work? To limit the discretion, a quantitative rule was devised: for the first six months of indisposition a claimant need show only that he was incapable of following his usual occupation; once that period had elapsed he would have to show that he was unfit for other types of work (Fisher, 1973, appendix 7, para. 6–7). In a recent decision, a Commissioner expressed disquiet at too rigid an application of a rule that he admitted was introduced 'mainly for administrative reasons': 'reasonableness, rather than any specific measure of time, is the crucial matter.'[48]

For several purposes under the social security legislation, it is necessary to determine to what extent someone is financially dependent on another, generally a relative (Ogus and Barendt, 1978, pp. 383–398). Where the two persons concerned are members of the same household, which also comprises others, and the resources of that household are pooled, this becomes a most complicated matter. To obviate the need for a highly detailed and inevitably elusive enquiry into the financial arrangements of each household, the Commissioners have formulated an arithmetic method for calculating each household member's degree of dependence on each member contributing income to the family pool, based on a model of typical family behaviour[49]. The 'unit cost' of each family member is assessed by dividing the total family income by the number of individuals (counting two children as one adult). According to whether or not he is a contributor, each individual then has a surplus or a deficit of contribution over cost. The degree of dependency of an individual with a deficit on an individual with a surplus is then calculated by dividing the amount of total deficit proportionally between those providing the surplus. The model does not always conform with actual family situations. To combine the advantages of the rule with a degree of flexibility to cover 'hard cases', the Commissioners have reached a compromise position whereby they authorize departure from the method, but only where there is clear evidence that the model substantially conflicts with the actual circumstances of the given case[50].

9.3 Conclusions

There are other examples that could have been drawn from this area of law[51], but what has been described should be sufficient to indicate a pattern of behaviour in relation to rulemaking that, it is submitted, is of general significance. The following conclusions may be drawn from this study.

(1) Economic considerations play an important part in rule formulation.
(2) While precise estimates of (a) the transactions costs and (b) the social costs of imperfect fit arising from general and specific rules respectively, are difficult, some intuitive assessment of their impact enables judges to form a rough idea of the optimal degree of specificity in particular areas of law.
(3) The judges typically move towards the optimal position through an iterative process.

Notes to chapter nine

1 Dworkin (1977), pp. 82–88, 94–100. More specifically the grounds for his belief are: the non-democratic nature of judicial office, the retroactive effect of judicial decisions and a theory of rights that requires of judges (but not legislatures) a consistency with a pre-existing framework of principles. A suggestion that the thesis is weakened by transaction cost considerations was made in Ogus and Richardson (1977), pp. 322–323.
2 Control of Pollution Act 1974, s.58. On 'best practicable means', see Richardson and Ogus (1979), pp. 340–342.
3 Wills Act 1837, s.9.
4 3 Co Inst 52, affirmed in *R v Dyson* [1908] 2 KB 454.
5 In *Re Finn* (1936) 53 TLR 153 a thumb-mark was regarded as a 'signature'.
6 There is, of course, a crucial distinction between parliamentary and subordinate legislation, the scrutiny of which tends to be much less rigorous.
7 See, further, Jowell (1975), pp. 22–24 and the literature on strict liability v negligence as the basis of tort liability: e.g. Posner (1977), pp. 137–142; Products Liability Symposium (1970).
8 *Louis v Louis* (1866) LR 1 P & M 230.
9 E.g. *Kershaw v Kershaw* [1966] P 13.
10 See, especially, *Wachtel v Wachtel* [1973] Fam 72.
11 *Inland Revenue Commissioners v National Federation of Self- Employed and Small Businesses Ltd.* [1981] 2 All ER 93.
12 Social Security Act 1980, s.6.
13 The classic instance is the 'A Code', which contained rules for the exercise of discretion by officers of the Supplementary Benefits Commission, but which was never published as such. See on this Calvert (1978), pp. 398–400, and Fulbrook (1978), pp. 273–274. Another example is that of the Alkali Inspectorate: Frankel (1974), pp. 8–13.
14 E.g., *Sampson v Supplementary Benefits Commission* (1979) 123 Sol Jo 284, and see generally Galligan (1976).
15 Cf. *National Provincial Bank v Ainsworth* [1965] AC 1175.
16 Cf. *Davis v Johnson* [1979] AC 264.
17 Cf. *Binions v Evans* [1972] Ch 359.

18 The Pearson Royal Commission estimated that only about one per cent of personal injury claims reached the courts: Pearson (1978), vol. 1, para. 79.
19 See, generally, Posner (1973) and Phillips and Hawkins (1976).
20 Cf. Posner (1977), pp. 415–417; Dworkin (1977), pp. 96–100.
21 The thesis has given rise to a considerable amount of literature. See Dias (1979), pp. 254–256.
22 Anon (1612), Cary 12.
23 For an interesting recent example, see *Worsfold v Howe* [1980] 1 All ER 1028.
24 *Holwell Securities v Hughes* [1974] 1 WLR 155.
25 Practice Statement 1966 [1966] 3 All ER 77.
26 Cf. *Home Office v Dorset Yacht Co* [1970] AC 1004.
27 E.g. *Tanner v Tanner* [1975] 3 All ER 776.
28 The vindicatory benefit of litigation would be lost and, of course, not all claims involve financial remedies.
29 *Ward v James* [1966] 1 QB 273.
30 *Bird v Cocking* [1951] 2 TLR 1260; *Rushton v National Coal Board* [1953] 1 QB 495.
31 Summaries of awards in personal injuries were published in the monthly journal *Current Law* from 1952 and in 1954 appeared in the first edition of *Kemp and Kemp*, a practitioners' manual that collects and classifies both awards and judgments.
32 'General damages' comprised those losses that were not capable of precise quantification: Ogus (1973), pp. 3–4.
33 *Watson v Powles* [1968] 1 QB 596 and *Fletcher v Autocar and Transporters Ltd.* [1968] 2 QB 322.
34 *Jefford v Gee* [1970] 2 QB 130: subdivision was necessary because pecuniary and non-pecuniary damages attracted different amounts of interest.
35 *Wise v Kay* [1962] 1 QB 638; *West v Shephard* [1964] AC 326.
36 Cf. *Hennell v Ranaboldo* [1963] 1 WLR 1391. While recognizing the utility of current judicial practice both the Law Commission (1973), paras. 31–36, and the Pearson Royal Commission (1978), vol. I, paras. 377–380, found unattractive the suggestion of a legislative tariff.
37 There was a noticeable increase in the degree of control exercised by the Court of Appeal in the 1960s: McGregor (1972), pp. 977–978.
38 [1966] 1 QB 273, 300.
39 *Pakes v Rodge* (1973), Kemp and Kemp (1975), para. 8-501.
40 *Walker v John McLean* [1979] 2 All ER 965, 970; *Evans v Griffith* (1978), Kemp and Kemp (1975), para. 3-213; *Walsh v Houghton* (1978), Kemp and Kemp (1975), para. 7-715.
41 *Lim Poh Choo v Camden Health Authority* [1979] 1 All ER 332, 341; *Hughes v Goodall* (1977), Kemp and Kemp (1975), para. 7-714; cf. *Walker v John McLean* [1979] 2 All ER 965.
42 *Pratt v Tolson* (1972), Kemp and Kemp (1975), para. 10-671.
43 *R v National Insurance Commissioner, ex parte Stratton* [1979] QB 361, 368.
44 CU 518/49; R(U) 14/59.
45 S.I. 1959 No. 1278.
46 R(U) 1/72.
47 Social Security Act 1975, s.17(1)(a).
48 R(S) 2/78.
49 CSI 50/49; R(I) 1/57; R(I) 20/60. See generally Kahn-Freund (1953), pp. 164–173.
50 R(I) 46/52; R(U) 37/52; R(I) 20/60.
51 In relation to the effect on unemployment benefit of a trade dispute, the 'twelve-day rule' and the definition of a 'seasonal worker'; for the purposes of retirement pensions, the meaning of 'an earner ... to an inconsiderable extent' (the '12-hour rule'); for general purposes, the meaning of 'temporary absence' (the '6-months rules'). See Ogus and Barendt (1978), pp. 127, 133, 206, 392.

References

ALLEN, Sir C. (1964), *Law in the Making*, 7th edn., Oxford University Press.

ATIYAH, P.S. (1978), *From Principles to Pragmatism*, Oxford: Clarendon Press.

ATIYAH, P.S. (1979), *The Rise and Fall of Freedom of Contract*, Oxford: Clarendon Press.

BALDWIN, J. and McCONVILLE, M. (1979), *Jury Trials*, Oxford University Press.
BENDITT, T.M. (1978), *Law as Rule and Principle*, Hassocks, Sussex: Harvester Press.
CALABRESI, G. and MELAMED, A.D. (1972), Property rules, liability rules and inalienability: one view of the cathedral, *Harvard Law Review*, **85**, no. 6, 1089–1128.
CALVERT, H. (1978), *Social Security Law*, 2nd edn., London: Sweet and Maxwell.
COASE, R. (1960), The problem of social cost, *Jo Law and Economics*, **3**, no. 1, 1–44.
CRETNEY, S.M. (1979), *Principles of Family Law*, 3rd edn., London: Sweet and Maxwell.
CROSS, Sir R. (1979), *Precedent in English Law*, 3rd edn., Oxford: Clarendon Press.
DAVIS, K. (1969), *Discretionary Justice*, Urbana: University of Illinois Press
DENNING, Lord (1979), *The Discipline of Law*, London: Butterworths.
DENNING, Sir A. (1952), The need for a new equity, 5 CLP 7.
DHSS (1978), *Social Assistance: A review of the supplementary benefits scheme in Great Britain*. London: HMSO.
DEVLIN, Lord (1978), Judges, government and politics, *Modern law Review*, **41**, no. 2, 501–511.
DIAS, R.W.M. (1979), *A Bibliography of Jurisprudence*, 3rd edn., London: Butterworths.
DICKINSON, J. (1931), Legal rules, their application and elaboration, *University of Pennsylvania Law Review*, **79**, 1052–1096.
DWORKIN, R. (1977), *Taking Rights Seriously*, London: Duckworth.
EHRLICH, I. and POSNER, R. (1974), An economic analysis of legal rulemaking, *Journal of Legal Studies*, **3**, no. 1, 257–286.
FISHER, Sir H. (1973), *Report of the Committee on Abuse of Social Security Benefits*, Cmnd. 5228, London: HMSO.
FRANKEL, M. (1974), *The Alkali Inspectorate*, London: Social Audit.
FRIEDMAN, L.M. (1967), Legal rules and the process of social change, *Stanford Law Review*, **19**, 786–835.
FRIEDMAN, L.M. (1975), *The Legal System: A Social Science Perspective*, New York: Academic Press.
FULBROOK, J. (1978), *Administrative Justice and the Unemployed*, London: Mansell.
GALLIGAN, D.J. (1976), The nature and function of policies within discretionary power, *Public Law*, 332–357.
GOULD, J.P. (1973), The economics of legal conflicts, *Journal of Legal Studies*, **2**, no. 2, 279–300.
HART, H.L.A. (1961), *Concept of Law*, Oxford University Press.
HIRSCH, W. (1974), Reducing law's uncertainty and complexity, *UCLA Law Review*, **21**, no. 5, 1233–1256.
JOWELL, J. (1975), *Law and Bureaucracy: Administrative Discretion and the Limits of Legal Action*, Dunnellen Publishing Co.
KAHN-FREUND, O. (1953), Inconsistencies and injustices in the law of husband and wife, *Modern Law Review*, **16**, 34–49 and 148–173.
KAHN-FREUND, O., LEVY, C. and RUDDEN, B. (1979), *A Sourcebook of French Law*, 2nd edn., Oxford University Press.
KEMP, D.A. and KEMP, M.S. (1975), *The Quantum of Damages*, vol. 2, 4th edn., London: Sweet and Maxwell.
KENNEDY, D. (1976), Form and substance in private law adjudication, *Harvard Law Review*, **89**, 1685–1778.
LAW COMMISSION (1973), *Report (No. 56) on Personal Injury Litigation – Assessment of Damages*, London: HMSO.
McGREGOR, H. (1972), *Damages*, 13th edn., London: Sweet and Maxwell.
MICKELTHWAIT, R. (1976), *The National Insurance Commissioners*, London: Stevens and Son.
MILSOM, S.F.C. (1981), *Historical Foundations of the Common Law*, 2nd edn., London: Butterworths.
MONROE, H. (1979), Fiscal statutes: a drafting disaster, *British Tax Review*, no. 5, 265–273.
MORRIS, D. (1971), *The End of Marriage*, London: Cassell.
OGUS, A.I. (1973), *Law of Damages*, London: Butterworths.
OGUS, A.I. and BARENDT, E.M. (1978), *Law of Social Security*, London: Butterworths.
OGUS, A.I. and RICHARDSON, G.M. (1977), Economics and the environment: a study of private nuisance, *Cambridge Law Journal*, **36**, part 2, 284–325.
PEARSON, Lord (1978), *Report of the Royal Commission on Civil Liability and Compensation for Personal Injury*, Cmnd. 7054, London: HMSO.
PHILLIPS, J. and HAWKINS, K. (1976), Some economic aspects of the settlement process: a study of personal injury claims, *Modern Law Review*, **39**, no. 5, 497–515.
POSNER, R. (1973), An economic approach

to legal procedure and judicial administration, *Journal of Legal Studies*, **2**, no. 2, 391–458.
POSNER, R. (1977), *Economic Analysis of Law*, 2nd edn., Boston, Mass: Little Brown.
POUND, R. (1959), *An Introduction to the Philosophy of Law*, Yale University Press.
POUND, R. (1922), The theory of judicial decision, *Harvard Law Review*, **36**, 640, 802, 940.
RAZ, J. (1975), *Practical reason and Norms*, London: Hutchinson University Library.
RICHARDSON, G.M. and OGUS, A.I. (1979), The regulatory approach to environmental control, *Urban Law and Policy*, **2**, 337–357.
SCOTT, K.E. (1975), Two models of the civil process, *Stanford Law Review*, **27**, no. 3, 737–750.
SMITH, J.C. and HOGAN, B.W. (1978), *Criminal Law*, 4th edn., London: Butterworths.
STEVENS, R. (1979), *Law and Politics: the House of Lords as a Judicial Body, 1800–1976*, London: Weidenfeld and Nicolson.
SYMPOSIUM on products liability: economic analysis and the law (1970), *University of Chicago Law Review*, **38**, no. 1.
WASSERSTROM, R.A. (1961), *The Judicial Decision*, Stanford University Press.
WILLIAMSON, O.E. (1976), Franchise bidding for natural monopolies, *Bell Journal of Economics*, **7**, no. 1, 73–104.
WINN, Lord Justice (1968), *Report of the Committee on Personal Injuries Litigation*, Cmnd. 3691, London: HMSO.

CHAPTER TEN

The plea bargain in England and America: a comparative institutional view[1]

Richard P. Adelstein

10.1 Criminal price exaction and the development of procedure

From its earliest beginnings the common law has treated criminal punishment as a kind of restitution, a repayment by the offender of the damages caused by his unlawful behaviour[2]. Ours has long been a legal order of retributive punishment tempered by the norm of proportionality, one that seeks to adjust the punitive sanction to the 'gravity' of the offence and thus to exact an eye, but only that, for an eye. This element of proportionality is of central importance, for it suggests that the unconditional deterrence of all illegal activity is not in fact the fundamental organizing principle of Anglo-American criminal justice. Were the purpose of penal sanctions simply to deter all criminal behaviour, regardless of the harm it might do or the circumstances that might surround it, we would expect even trivial offences to be punished as severely as possible. Such a penalty structure would certainly discourage all but the most determined of wrongdoers, even where the social costs associated with their acts were very small, for cases in which the rewards or satisfactions derived by the offender from the act would exceed the great personal hardship imposed by punishments of this kind would be rare indeed.

The institution of proportional punishment, however, appears to contemplate a very different end. Where the personal cost the offender is forced to bear in the form of punishment is meant to reflect only the actual extent of harm his act has imposed upon the society at large, the law can be seen as tolerating (or encouraging) 'efficient offences' — those in which the material and psychic satisfactions of the act are reckoned by the offender to be greater than its full social costs as perceived by those who must bear them. To illustrate, imagine Jefferson sorely irritated, deliberating whether to punch his boss Hamilton in the nose. To simplify the exposition, let us assume that the total cost inflicted by such a blow upon Hamilton and those in society who would feel physically threatened or morally offended by it is £500, and that this sum would, with perfect certainty, be imposed upon Jefferson in the form of a fine should he commit the assault. The revenue from the fine would be transferred in full to Hamilton and the other, indirect victims of the crime. Jefferson is thus faced with the choice of committing the crime and bearing its £500 cost, or obeying the law and forgoing the satisfaction that the blow might bring. If Jefferson decides that the intangible rewards of breaking the law would be greater than the cost of the fine, he would 'trade' with his victims by punching Hamilton and paying the attendant price.

Moreover, one could assert that, when Jefferson's welfare is included in the analysis along with that of his victims, society as a whole is made better off by his decision to break the law. If Jefferson could have been prevented from perpetrating the assault, social welfare would have been increased by the equivalent of £500 (because the social costs generated by the punch would not have been incurred) but it would, at the same time, have been decreased by the equivalent of more than £500 (since, by hypothesis, the satisfaction Jefferson forgoes by obeying the law exceeds the disutility imposed by the fine). But when the 'trade' is completed, Hamilton and the indirect victims are fully compensated for the harm done to them, and are thus equally well off, and that part of society represented by Jefferson is better off than it would have been without the assault. Where punishments are determined in this way, the aim of the criminal process appears not to be unconditional deterrence, but rather (much like the law of tort and contract) the 'internalization' of the costs of criminal activity, forcing offenders to pay those costs in full rather than allowing their imposition upon others without recompense. The incidence of crime is thus controlled, but not eliminated; inefficient offences, like goods for which no buyer is willing to pay the full cost of production, are effectively deterred, but efficient offences continue to be committed and, in the sense outlined here, each such offence represents a net increment in social welfare.

In a series of earlier essays (Adelstein, 1978b; 1979a, b; 1981), I have developed the positive and normative aspects of this 'price exaction' model of the criminal process in some detail and applied it to the evolution of procedural rules governing negotiated guilty pleas and the imposition of capital sentences under American federal law. A central postulate of this analysis is that the characteristic feature of criminal acts is the element of 'moral cost' associated with them. The widely felt sense of outrage and moral opprobrium created by particular kinds of behaviour and their accompanying states of mind that distinguishes them from other acts that might also entail damage to property or physical or psychic injury to the person[3]. These moral costs are conceptually distinct both from the physical and financial sufferings endured by the direct victims of criminal acts and from the economic dislocations that result from the efforts of other individuals to protect themselves against similar victimization. They are primarily borne by individuals with no direct relationship to the offence itself or the parties involved in it, and result from personal feelings that the set of shared values from which the social fabric is woven and which preserve the peace have been unacceptably violated. A consequence of each individual's sense of right and wrong, they reflect the indignation created by acts that breach established and accepted moral codes of behaviour. Moreover, it is the offender's act itself and the *mens rea* that motivates it that impose these costs, and not necessarily the severity of the result or the actual harm done in economic and physical terms. Incompleted attempts and inchoate offences are thus treated as criminal acts and punished as such regardless of their ultimate outcome, and 'victimless' crimes may be understood as acts that generate *only* indirect moral cost rather than the combination of material and moral cost that results from offences in which there is an identifiable direct victim[4].

Given the existence of these costs, the institutions of criminal justice are faced with the extremely difficult tasks of assessing the full extent of social cost imposed by specific criminal acts, apprehending and convicting their perpetrators, and exacting a roughly equivalent 'punishment price' from them. But it is clear that the net social benefit that is, in principle, associated with efficient offences can be realized only if the substantial costs of actually completing the price exaction are smaller than the full social cost imposed by the original offence; nothing is gained if £100 in court costs must be expended to effect through price exaction the internalization of £50 in social damages. This economic link between the criminal law and the procedures through which it is enforced suggests that the criminal process must continually search out less costly means of exacting the punishment price if its ability to internalize the costs of criminal activity satisfactorily is to be preserved.

The initial vehicle for this adaptive response to the costliness of price exaction is the self-interested behaviour of the individuals directly involved in the compensatory transaction, the accused defendant and the prosecuting authority acting on behalf of those injured by the offence. Where material expenditure is concerned, it is these litigants who are best situated to assess the economic costs associated with the operation of the price exaction mechanism, and organizational forms within the criminal process have evolved that provide them with a continuing incentive toward procedural innovation in an effort to reduce these costs. Just as in the case of the criminal act itself, however, the process of completing the price exaction through the imposition of the punishment price generates real but nonmaterial costs, which are spread over a large class of cost bearers not immediately party to the price exaction procedure. But the organization of the prosecutorial function is such that these indirect costs cannot be fully accounted for within the structure of incentives and controls available to the litigants themselves. As a result, procedural forms developed in response to the material costs of price exaction may well impose nonmaterial social costs in excess of the economic savings involved. In both the English and American criminal processes the task of monitoring these innovations and the indirect social costs associated with them has devolved primarily upon the appellate courts, which retain the power to encourage or foreclose various approaches on the basis of judgments made generally at the behest of defendants who claim to have been unfairly treated. A great deal can thus be learned from the careful study of such judicial outcomes within the context of the price exaction model.

Our purpose here is to add a comparative dimension to the price exaction framework by applying it to the continuing evolution of a system of induced guilty pleas in the English criminal process and relating the insights thus gained to a parallel analysis of the more explicitly developed American 'plea bargain'. Though the two criminal processes themselves are characterized by historical but significant structural differences, the adaptive organizational responses that the pressures of very similar modern environments have drawn from them bear striking resemblance to one another in terms of both form and purpose. The power of the institutional analysis lies in its ability to illuminate the nature of this evolutionary process and the implicit value judgments expressed in its outcomes. In this way, I hope, it can contribute much to the emerging English discussion of the propriety and necessity of negotiated guilty pleas.

10.2 The negotiated plea in the price exaction framework

10.2.1 Incentives toward trial avoidance: economic cost considerations

The costliness of completing the compensatory transaction itself is a central consideration in the organization of both the civil and criminal processes, for the institutional rules that apportion these costs between the interested parties largely determine which and how many cases of unlawful cost imposition will in fact be mediated by the price exaction mechanism. An example drawn from the civil side will illustrate. Suppose Blackstone negligently breaks a fine inkwell, worth £100, owned by Coke. Blackstone ungallantly refuses to compensate Coke for the loss, and Coke envisions two possible avenues for recovering the inkwell's value. He could, at nominal immediate expense but with some possibility of discovery and apprehension, break into Blackstone's home and take £100 from his cash box. Alternatively, with considerable expenditure of time and money but, let us assume, perfect certainty of success, he could bring suit against Blackstone in the local court.

Now, if Coke's behaviour is 'rational' in the economic sense, he will seek to recover his £100 in the less costly way. Imagine for the moment that the criminal law does not exist and that Coke has no compunctions about burglary. Then, even if Coke is aware that his burglary would impose economic and moral costs upon the society at large, he has a clear incentive to ignore these external effects, commit the burglary, and thus avoid the costs of bringing suit. Without the criminal law, there is no sufficiently inexpensive way for these indirect cost bearers to hold Coke accountable for *their* losses. But, of course, a principal purpose of the criminal law is to force

Coke to account for just such indirect costs in planning his activities. By imposing a penalty sufficiently severe that, even when discounted by the probability of discovery and conviction, Coke's expected costs in a recovery by theft exceeded £100, the law could effectively foreclose that option and leave him only the alternative of bringing suit. If the costs of this latter course (which in the United States but not in Britain generally include his attorney's fees in full regardless of the outcome) also exceeded £100, we could safely expect Blackstone's original tort to go unchallenged. From another perspective, if we believe *a priori* that the bearer of these recovery costs *is* 'rational', the observation that his damages remain uncompensated would create an inference that Coke has reckoned the recovery costs as greater than the value of the inkwell.

Although the organizational arrangements involved are substantially more complex, and the information necessary for such precise determinations vastly more difficult to obtain, a similar set of decisions must be made in the criminal process. The process of price exaction is itself a costly enterprise, and the magnitude of this cost in individual cases or in entire classes of offences is a principal determinant of whether or not the criminal sanction will in fact be applied. Most obvious, of course, is the economic expenditure required to apprehend and convict offenders. Where these resource costs themselves exceed the full social cost imposed by a particular criminal act, there is, just as in our tort example, a clear rationale for leaving the law unenforced in that case, a point recognized long ago by Oliver Wendell Holmes (1963, pp. 76–77). Thus, for example, we observe the highly sporadic enforcement of traffic laws and petty misdemeanours, or shifts in patterns of enforcement as once 'serious' offences become, over time, more generally tolerated forms of behaviour, as in the case of the personal use of marijuana. Where feasible, moreover, we observe as well the evolution of institutional forms, such as the withholding of income taxes from wages, where the prosecution of individual offenders would be uneconomic in this sense but where the anticipated aggregate costs of illegal behaviour are very large.

Like the criminal offence itself, however, the imposition of the punishment price is a source of moral as well as economic cost. These moral costs are generated whenever citizens not directly involved with price exaction procedures perceive them to be 'unfair' or 'improper'. Again, the term 'moral cost' is not meant to imply normative judgment; it is simply a positive measure of disutility imposed by various kinds of behaviour. A prosecutor might well save money and gain convictions were he to extract confessions by beating defendants, but it seems clear that this tactic would impose a substantial moral cost, either because it would be perceived as generating false confessions and thus punishing the innocent (cf. Posner, 1973, pp. 410–415), or for broader reasons having to do with shared values expressed in constitutional guarantees or in a general sense of fairness.

Less dramatic but of more immediate interest is the relative extent of moral cost associated with alternative procedures of price exaction, such as conviction by guilty plea rather than by trial. While decisions to litigate, settle or forgo legal action altogether in the civil process turn almost exclusively on questions of economic cost, considerations of both economic *and* moral cost must direct the corresponding decisions on the criminal side. A full adversarial trial is an extremely expensive affair, and were the economic costs of price exaction the sole concern, a decision to allow punishment only upon conviction at trial would sharply raise this cost and with it the threshold below which prosecution becomes uneconomic. But if alternatives to trial generate moral costs in excess of the economic savings they entail, the trial itself becomes the mode of conviction that lowers this threshold as far as possible and thus best responds to the *total* costs of price exaction. In this way, decisions as to whether and how to conduct the price exaction in the criminal process can be understood as closely resembling their civil analogue in form, but characterized by severe problems in gathering the information regarding both economic and widely dispersed moral costs required to define the lowest threshold and so permit the 'rational' prosecution of the greatest proportion of cases. It is the difficulty of extracting this information and bringing it to bear upon those directly responsible for the decision to prosecute that has shaped the evolution of complex and necessarily imperfect structures of incentives and authority in the English and American criminal processes.

In both Britain and the United States, the power to initiate prosecution is effectively vested in a public official who is bound by strict constraints on material expenditure but who exercises substantial discretion both in the selection of cases to be pursued and the precise charges to be brought in them[5]. In England and Wales this official is the Chief Constable of the local police, and in the Magistrates' Courts, where the vast majority of criminal cases are heard (*see*, for example, Jackson, 1972b, p. 178), it is his own police officers and assisting staff solicitors who are responsible for prosecutions in the name of the Crown. For those more serious offences that must be prosecuted in the Crown Courts, the organization of the English Bar requires that the police retain an independent barrister, briefed by the police solicitor, to represent the Crown. But here too it is the Chief Constable who determines, within broad limits, the specific charges against the defendant[6] and whose budget must bear the economic cost of prosecuting them (Jackson, 1972a, p. 164).

In American jurisdictions the police and prosecutorial functions are administered separately, although the investigatory activities of the two agencies are necessarily closely co-ordinated and prosecutorial policy strongly influences the deployment of the police. Moreover, the absence of an independent trial bar permits the public prosecutor to employ his own legal staff in the prosecution of all cases, wherever heard. But these structural differences are of far less significance than the fundamental organizational similarity between the two systems, the combination within a single authority of charging discretion and budgetary constraint in the conduct of prosecutions[7].

Prosecutorial decisions in both countries appear generally responsive to two distinct, though not irreconcilable, considerations of policy. There is, of course, the pressure of the caseload, the need to resolve as many offences as possible, preferably with a conviction of some kind, so that the various agencies of law enforcement may be seen by the community to be doing their job well[8]. At the same time, however, prosecutors are encouraged to 'individualize' the criminal sanction, tailoring dispositions to reflect the personal characteristics of each offender and the totality of circumstances surrounding each offence. This requires more than the simple maximization of prosecutorial 'output'; the prosecutor is asked instead to seek in every case the outcome he believes best serves the law enforcement interests of the whole community[9].

These concurrent objectives can be accommodated within the price exaction framework through a straightforward model of prosecutorial decision-making[10]. Let us assume the existence of a distinct prosecutorial utility function for each case in the agency's caseload. This function depicts the degree to which the prosecutor's objectives are satisfied in each case and relates the satisfaction or utility he derives from each case to the punishment price exacted from the defendant. As suggested by the individualization objective, we posit the existence of a particular sentence, say P_O, which represents the outcome that, in the prosecutor's necessarily subjective view, equates the punishment price to the social cost generated by the offence in question. The problem of caseload pressure motivates the assumption that, for punishments less than P_O, prosecutorial utility rises with increasing punishment, although at a decreasing rate. That is, each successive unit of punishment imposed upon the defendant adds a smaller positive increment to the prosecutor's utility. In this way, the relative importance of the conviction itself, of imposing *some* measure of punishment upon the offender, is emphasized[11].

Punishment prices, of course, can be exacted only upon a conviction, be it by plea of guilty or after a full trial. Where a plea agreement of some kind is involved, and where the prosecutor is confident that it will be honoured by the court at the time of sentencing, the punishments in the individual utility functions are known to him with substantial certainty before the fact. At trial, the uncertainty of conviction confronts the prosecutor with an *expected* utility instead, which depends both upon the sentence anticipated upon conviction and the probability that the defendant will be found guilty. In either case, however, the prosecutor can increase his *a priori* utility by investing some part of the material resources at his disposal in the pursuit of each case. Where trials are necessary, expenditures for case-strengthening efforts, such as witness interviews, legal research and searches for additional evidence, can be seen as ways of purchasing positive increments in the probability of conviction and, through it, expected utility. Where guilty pleas are concerned, the effect is much the same. Given that the defendant's willingness to agree to plead guilty is highly responsive to his estimate of conviction probability, a prosecutor who increases this probability in a given case clearly strengthens his bargaining position[12].

It thus seems reasonable to suppose that the prosecutor will attempt, given the sequential nature of the cases before him and his inevitably limited ability to gather and employ the requisite information, to allocate his scarce resources to these cases so as to maximize the sum of the individual *a priori* utility functions, inducing favourable guilty pleas where he can and generating increased conviction probabilities where defendants insist upon full trials. As a result, the prosecutor will, wherever possible, select of his own volition that mode of conviction which entails the smallest *economic* cost of price exaction, just as did Coke, the private decision-maker in our tort example[13].

Suppose, for instance, that in a particular case the prosecutor, at a cost of £200 in preparation expenditures and barrister's fees, can create a 50 per cent probability of conviction at a trial in which the anticipated sentence is twenty years' imprisonment, so that the expected punishment involved is 10 years in prison. If the expenditure of £125 on preparation would persuade the defendant to plead guilty in return for a certain punishment of ten years, then even a prosecutor neutral to the risks of trial will clearly choose the cheaper mode of price exaction and save the remaining £75 for the pursuit of another case. Further, if the prosecutor is risk-averse with respect to punishment, as our behavioural assumptions imply, he will continue to choose the plea for some range of punishment *less* than the expected trial sentence of ten years rather than submit to the vagaries of the trial[14].

Although it captures the essential elements of the decision to prosecute in both England and the United States, a particularly interesting problem arises when this abstraction is considered alongside the actual organizational arrangement of English and American prosecutions. At issue is the relative diffusion of decision-making authority in the two systems. In the American criminal process, power over all the necessary legal determinations encompassed by the model is effectively concentrated in the office of the public prosecutor. Apart from his virtually unchecked discretion with respect to charge, statutorily defined constraints on the trial court's choice of sentence for various offences and the deference traditionally shown by the trial court to his sentence recommendations[15] combine to give the prosecutor an effective power to fix, and thus to negotiate, the actual sentence to be imposed upon a plea of guilty. Where the distance between the prosecutor's wishes and his ability to see them fulfilled is this short, our simple model can be applied almost without qualification.

The Chief Constable's reach, however, is not so great. While he does control the conduct of cases directly in the Magistrates' Court, he must rely upon the services of an independent and potentially 'uncooperative' barrister in the Crown Court. Moreover, although jurisdictional limitations empower magistrates to impose sentences of no greater than one year's imprisonment[16], Crown Court judges sentence quite freely at common law and under statute and are unencumbered by prosecutorial recommendations. For serious offences, then, the powers required to implement the preferences of our abstract prosecutor are in practice vested in three individuals, the Chief Constable himself, the prosecuting barrister and the sentencing judge. For our model to be of positive value in such an environment, the degree of implicit co-ordination between these agents, or the confluence of personal interests amongst them, must be very great indeed.

This is in fact precisely what we observe. The descriptive literature on induced guilty pleas in England repeatedly cites the close, 'fraternal' working relationship that exists between the Bar, from which counsel for both sides are drawn, and the judiciary[17], and the common training and outlook they share (Thomas, 1978, pp. 175–176). The 'Liberal Bureaucratic' values that pervade the entire English criminal process[18], and effectively combine an apparently genuine concern for individualized justice with a conscious sensitivity to matters of economic cost and administration, are very much like those held by American prosecutors (Miller, 1969, pp. 154–172) and by the omnipotent prosecutor in our own behavioural model. They permit the smooth operation of a system of induced pleas without centralized authority despite the ostensibly adversarial nature of the criminal process and the independence of the judge.

It is the pervasiveness of these values that makes possible the large scale inducement of guilty pleas upon which both the English and American criminal processes have come to depend. Certainly, the structural differences between the two systems have required that superficially different means to secure these pleas be developed. In both cases, the trial judge is forbidden to participate actively or directly in negotiations regarding the plea[19] and retains the formal power over sentence. But the American prosecutor's ability to fix the punishments of those who plead guilty enables him to bargain explicitly and concretely with defendants over the actual severity of their sentences, rendering the court's sentencing authority largely nugatory. The organization of English prosecutions makes overt bargaining of this kind impossible, for the trial court's power to sentence is real rather than nominal. Nevertheless, pleas *are*, within the bounds established by the Court of Appeal, systematically induced in two ways[20]. The prosecutor's charging discretion permits explicit negotiation with the defendant over the specific charges to which he will plead guilty; the defendant is technically acquitted of whatever charges he has not so admitted[21], and if the court accepts a plea to a lesser offence in such cases, its sentence must be appropriate to this offence rather than a greater one that might originally have been charged[22]. Alternatively, the court may reduce the sentence of those who plead guilty; where such 'discounts' are routine, predictable and made known to defendants prior to plea, they amount to implicit but real plea agreements[23]. With respect to the inducement of pleas, then, structural considerations are matters of form rather than substance. The essential element of the induced plea, the effective grant of a more lenient sentence to defendants who agree to plead guilty, is as well woven into the English criminal process as it is into the American.

10.2.2 Burdening the right to trial: the defendant's choice and the problem of risk preference

We turn now to the problem posed to the defendant by this organizational arrangement. For simplicity of exposition, let us assume that the cost of legal representation and case preparation actually borne by the defendant can be neglected[24]. Then the defendant will agree to a guilty plea if he perceives the cost to him of the sentence received upon the plea as less than the expected disutility of the trial prospect and its associated sentence. That is, he will plead if

$$L(S_p) < qL(S_v)$$

where L is a function that measures the defendant's disutility for any given punishment; S_p is the sentence associated with a guilty plea; S_v is the sentence expected to result from a guilty verdict at trial; and q is the defendant's *a priori* estimate of the probability of conviction at trial.

A number of English writers (*see*, for example, Baldwin and McConville, 1977, pp. 108–109; Bottoms and McClean, 1976, pp. 234–235) have argued that the imposition of a harsher sentence upon a defendant found guilty at trial than upon one who pleads guilty amounts, *per se*, to penalizing the exercise of the right to trial. But this strong position rests upon an inapposite comparison of sentencing outcomes in two cases observed at the conclusion of all proceedings in each, after the defendants involved have made their choices with respect to plea and the consequences of those choices have been revealed. The decision to exercise any right cannot be burdened *ex post*; as our own formulation suggests, the relevant comparison is between two defendants *before* the decision by either as to plea, while the choice is still open to them. For this perspective, particular defendants may indeed find that a true 'price' has been placed on the right to trial, but the questions of when this is the case, and just how great the burden has been when it is, are rather more difficult.

Consider first a risk-neutral defendant, one to whom the disutility of a particular sentence rises in direct proportion to its length, so that each successive unit of punishment adds an equal increment of personal cost. Suppose he knows that his chances of being convicted at trial are 50 per cent and that the sentence he will receive if convicted is 10 years, so that viewed *ex ante*, the expected sentence at trial is five years' imprisonment. If the prosecutor offers this defendant a certain five year sentence in exchange for a guilty plea, the choice between bargain and trial is a matter of indifference to him because the *a priori* costs associated with each are the same. Even if the defendant goes to trial, and loses, and the judge, pronouncing the 10 year sentence, remarks, 'If you had pleaded guilty, I would have given you five years', there should be no question of impropriety[25]. The defendant has not 'paid a price' for the exercise of his right to trial; he has simply chosen to participate in a 'lottery' with two possible outcomes rather than accept a certain outcome of equal *a priori* value. Indeed, were the prosecutor to offer seven years rather than five, the trial prospect would be decidedly more attractive, much like paying £1 to buy a 50 per cent chance of winning £3 and an equal chance of winning nothing. Thus, no burden is placed on the defendant's choice whenever $S_p \geqslant qS_v$, even where S_v exceeds S_p, for the consideration offered in exchange for a guilty plea then merely reflects the uncertainties of litigation. The trial prospect represents at worst an actuarially fair gamble for the defendant, and the imposition of the longer sentence S_v upon conviction is simply the result of a losing play in a fair, or more than fair, game.

The problem of preserving the defendant's free choice arises when, given a particular probability of conviction, the sentence offered by the prosecutor falls below the expected value of the trial prospect. As we have seen, this might in some cases simply result from risk-aversion on the part of the prosecutor[26]. But it may instead represent an attempt by the prosecutor to shift, in effect, the economic costs of the price exaction to the defendant and so to deter him from insisting upon a trial. This latter interpretation is especially difficult to escape where the prosecutor seeks to influence the defendant's choice not by lowering S_p, but rather by 'overcharging', increasing S_v well beyond the actual social costs involved in the alleged criminal activity[27]. In either case, as the plea offered diverges increasingly from the expected sentence at trial, the defendant's attitude toward risk becomes a correspondingly more important factor in his decision than the 'objective' probability of conviction, raising the spectre of a significant incidence of guilty pleas by factually innocent but risk-averse defendants.

To illustrate, consider two defendants, Madison, a gambler, and Adams, who is more prudent, each facing a 50 per cent chance of conviction and a 10 year sentence if found guilty at trial. Madison's preference for risk implies that each successive year of imprisonment represents a positive but decreasing increment of disutility; for him, the 10 year term imposes less than twice the disutility of a five year term. In order to seek an acquittal, Madison would reject an offer of five years' imprisonment (the expected trial sentence), and would continue to reject offers of *less* than five years until the prosecutor proposed the prison term that was, in Madison's eyes, half as painful as the 10 year sentence. He would, that is, prefer the trial lottery unless offered a bargain considerably better than the actuarial value of the trial prospect. Adams, on the other hand, regards the 10 year term as more than twice as costly as the five year sentence, for the pain of confinement rises at an increasing rate for each additional year. His risk-aversion would lead him to accept even sentences greater than the expected trial sentence of five years, perhaps seven or eight years, to avoid the possibility of the ten year term.

Now, while Madison would reject a prosecutorial offer of five years which Adams would accept without hesitation, the sentencing discount associated with guilty plea might be so great, say a two year term, that even Madison would be persuaded to relinquish his right to trial and agree to plead guilty. If Adams were so risk-averse that he would have accepted a seven year term rather than face the risk of 10, would an offer of two years be so powerful an inducement as to overbear his will, entirely apart from his factual guilt or innocence? For an extremely risk-averse defendant, moreover, even a plea agreement representing only the expected sentence at trial poses this problem. Given the sense of voluntary behaviour underlying models of economic 'rationality', none of these agreements would be seen as coerced, for each party was at least as satisfied with the agreement as with the alternatives. But the law's view has generally been more subtle[28], and in both the English and American courts, it is on this ground of volition and coercion that the propriety of induced pleas has been argued.

10.3 External aspects of the price exaction procedure: moral cost considerations

10.3.1 The role of appellate courts

The organizational forms discussed thus far are, in their nature, able to account only partially for the costs involved in imposing the punishment price. The combination of budgetary constraints, broad charging discretion and, in the English case, the sentencing leniency routinely shown to those who plead guilty, provide the prosecution with both the incentive and the opportunity to reduce the purely *economic* costs of price exaction as much as possible. But once the prosecutor decides upon a particular course of action, the budgetary mechanism alone is insufficient to bring the *moral* costs associated with various price exaction procedures to bear upon his selection of one mode of conviction or another. Thus, even if negotiated or induced guilty pleas were to generate moral costs, specifically those created by the risk of systematically erroneous convictions (given the relaxation of safeguards inherent in the full criminal trial), that outweighed the economic savings involved, their incidence might remain very high because nothing compels the prosecutor to account for moral costs that do not impinge upon his budget. In this sense, the prosecutor has no incentive to allocate his budget in such a way as to address all the community's interests in choosing a mode of price exaction.

It is here that the appellate courts play an important corrective role[29]. The potential existence of significant moral costs borne by members of the community at large, not party to the price exaction procedure itself, is first signalled by the claims of one or more individual defendants that their own guilty pleas were entered involuntarily as a result of the inducements or pressures confronting them. To the extent that the courts see this inherently subjective claim as general and prototypical, they attempt to 'objectify' it by testing it against their own subjective evaluation of the degree of 'unfairness' entailed in the procedures at issue, a determination based largely upon judicial perceptions of widely shared values of criminal justice and notions of 'reasonable' behaviour. Within the price exaction framework, this process can be interpreted as an effort to evaluate the uncounted moral costs of the challenged procedure and, where these are seen to exceed the savings in economic expenditure that motivated it, to foreclose this aproach and direct the criminal process to an alternative mode of conviction that more successfully addresses the full costs, both economic *and* moral, of price exaction.

It must be recognized that this process of structural evolution in the price exaction mechanism is not an 'optimizing' process. The strictly limited ability of appellate courts to make accurate assessments of the moral costs associated with various procedural alternatives precludes any suggestion of 'optimal' decisionmaking. Decisions that might be seen as optimizing under hypothetical conditions of perfect information may be rendered suboptimal or even dysfunctional given the potential for error introduced by these informational constraints. Nevertheless, the price exaction analysis does suggest that, as a *positive* matter, the judicial resolution of these questions can be taken as a rough measure of the relative magnitude of the economic and moral costs involved as perceived by those bodies charged with estimating them. They represent the implicit value judgments and assumptions of fact that underlie the common English and American preference for 'bargain justice'.

10.3.2 The negotiated guilty plea in the United States Supreme Court

Although the problem had been addressed previously and somewhat fitfully in the lower federal courts[30], the Supreme Court did not begin serious consideration of the negotiated plea until 1968. In *United States v Jackson*[31], the Court indirectly spoke to their propriety in striking down a provision of the Federal Kidnapping Act[32] that permitted the death penalty to be imposed only after a full trial by jury, rather than upon a guilty plea. 'The inevitable effect of any such provision,' said the Court, 'is, of course, to discourage assertion of the Fifth Amendment right to demand a jury trial. If the provision had no other purpose or effect than to chill the assertion of constitutional rights by penalizing those who choose to exercise them, then it would be patently unconstitutional.'[33] The Court conceded that in this instance the government might have had another legitimate purpose in mind, mitigating the severity of the death penalty by commending the decision to the trial jury. But '[w]hatever might be said of Congress' objectives, they cannot be pursued by means that needlessly chill the exercise of basic constitutional rights. The question is not whether the chilling effect is "incidental" rather than intentional; the question is whether that effect is unnecessary and therefore excessive.'[34]

Implicit here is the suggestion that sentencing concessions that go beyond the uncertainties of litigation might be 'patently unconstitutional' as well[35], for as we have argued, the very purpose of such inducements is to discourage defendants from insisting upon costly trials. But the trial procedure is not the only source of cost that the defendant might impose upon the state. Where the defendant invokes a statutory right to appellate review of his conviction, the state is forced not only to bear the costs of contesting the appeal but, should the attack be successful, to retry or negotiate with the defendant or abandon its prosecution of the case. Just as in the case of plea negotiations, the exercise of this right can effectively be deterred by the threat of a substantially more severe sentence for those whom the state must reconvict after a successful appeal. In *North Carolina v Pearce*[36], however, the Court reinforced the *Jackson* result by holding this practice unconstitutional as well. 'It...would be a flagrant violation of [due process] for a state trial court to follow an announced practice of imposing a heavier sentence upon every reconvicted defendant for the explicit purpose of punishing the defendant for having succeeded in getting his original conviction set aside.' Once the state chooses to establish a right of appellate review, it is 'without right to...put a price on an appeal. A defendant's exercise of a right of appeal must be free and unfettered....[I]t is unfair to use the great power given to the court to determine sentence to place a defendant in the dilemma of making an unfree choice.'[38]

Yet when the Court did confront the question of negotiated pleas squarely in *Brady v United States*[39], it ignored the implications of *Jackson* and *Pearce* and upheld the general practice of plea bargaining in its most common forms against a claim that such pleas were inherently involuntary. Stressing the 'mutuality of advantage'[40] to prosecutor and defendant that underlies the negotiated plea, the Court endorsed offers of leniency 'to a defendant who in turn extends a substantial benefit to the State.'[41] It condemned as involuntary only those pleas produced by threats of physical harm or by mental coercion 'overbearing the will of the defendant'[42]. The definition of such overbearance in terms of risk-aversion considerations is not made clear, but there is a suggestion that prosecutorial overcharging or judicial abuse of the sentencing power might render such a plea involuntary[43]. The Court made clear that it *was* sensitive to the hazards of plea negotiations. If it could have been shown that a particular bargaining tactic, or the negotiation process itself, 'substantially increased the likelihood that defendants, advised by competent counsel, would falsely condemn themselves'[44], the Court would have had serious doubts about the case.

> But our view is to the contrary and is based on our expectations that courts will satisfy themselves that pleas of guilty are voluntarily and intelligently made by competent defendants with adequate advice of counsel and that there is nothing to question the accuracy and reliability of the defendants' admissions that they committed the crimes with which they are charged.[45]

This expectation that false pleas by competently advised defendants will be rare may itself rest on a belief, shared by a former Solicitor General of the United States[46], that preliminary screening of cases by the police, the prosecution and, in some cases, the grand jury, will ensure that no defendants actually faced with the decision to accept or reject a plea agreement are, in fact, innocent of the offence in question.

While the *Brady* Court would not go so far as to acknowledge explicitly the reason for this apparent retreat from *Jackson* and *Pearce*[47], Chief Justice Burger did so almost casually the following term in *Santobello v New York*[48]:

> '[P]lea bargaining' is an essential component of the administration of justice. Properly administered, it is to be encouraged. If every criminal charge were subjected to a full-scale trial, the States and the Federal Government would need to multiply by many times the number of judges and court facilities.

As the Chief Justice suggests, moreover, the obvious reason for this reliance upon negotiated pleas is not in fact contrary to the language of *Jackson*. For the Court did not hold in that case that *all* procedures designed to deter the exercise of the right to trial were forbidden; rather, the central question is whether a particular procedure 'is *unnecessary* and therefore excessive'. The Court appears persuaded, not without reason, that where the fulfillment of the constitutional guarantee of a day in court for every defendant would dramatically increase the economic claims of criminal justice on ever scarcer social resources, 'the promise must be tempered if society is unwilling to pay its price'[49]. Relative to the economic costs of providing a full trial for every defendant accused, of course, the actual costs to the states and the federal government of contesting appeals and reconvicting successful appellants are in practice very small. Indeed, one suspects that were the American criminal process someday to be threatened with suffocation by potential appellants as it has already been by prospective trial defendants, the procedures struck down in *Pearce* would become as 'necessary' as the very similar tactics upheld in *Brady*. But within the price exaction framework, these cases can be read as an implicit evaluation that the moral costs associated with the attempt to burden the right of appeal outweigh the economic savings it would entail, but that the vastly greater economic costs involved in the case of negotiated pleas compel the opposite result.

It would, I think, be mistaken to think that the Court has not been aware of this implicit cost accounting, or that its members experienced no uneasiness over it. In *Bordenkircher v Hayes*[50], the Court considered the propriety of a prosecutor's threat to reindict a defendant under the state's habitual offender statute, which carried a mandatory life sentence, should he refuse the offer of a plea agreement on a charge of uttering a forged cheque for $88.30. Although the prosecutor's right to invoke this statute under state law was unchallenged and there was sufficient evidence to support the indictment, the issue was posed in terms of prosecutorial 'vindictiveness', suggested by language in *Pearce*: 'Due process of law, then, requires that vindictiveness against a defendant for having successfully attacked his first conviction must play no part in the sentence he receives after a new trial.'[51]

In upholding the defendant's life sentence under the recidivist statute after his insistence upon a trial, the Court said:

> To punish a person because he has done what the law plainly allows him to do is a due process violation of the most basic sort, and for an agent of the State to pursue a course of action whose objective is to penalize a person's reliance on his legal rights is 'patently unconstitutional'. But in the 'give-and-take' of plea bargaining, there is no such element of punishment or retaliation as long as the accused is free to accept or reject the prosecutor's offer.[52]

The distinction the Court attempted to draw here is clearly a very problematic one, for it chose the wrong hypothetical defendant upon which to base its analysis. It is not the defendant that accepts the offer that is retaliated against in the plea bargain, it is those, like Hayes, that *refuse* the offer and are sentenced accordingly after trial that must pay the penalty for exercising their rights. There is no inducement to plead without the example of the Hayeses to place before recalcitrant bargainers. The Court itself seemed to recognize the futility of distinguishing *Pearce*, for it soon conceded that 'by tolerating and encouraging the negotiation of pleas, this Court has necessarily accepted as constitutionally legitimate the simple reality that the prosecutor's interest at the bargaining table is to persuade the defendant to forgo his right to plead not guilty.'[53]

10.3.3 The induced guilty plea in the Court of Appeal

In contrast to the open, occasionally agonized, approach of the American Supreme Court, the Court of Appeal's endorsement of the systematic inducement of guilty pleas has been indirect and implicit. To be sure, the Court of Appeal has repeatedly and in emphatic terms attacked overt discussions between the trial judge and defence counsel over the precise sentencing concessions to be awarded a defendant who enters a plea of guilty. But at the same time, the Court has clearly established 'procedures which can produce results akin to those produced by direct plea bargaining' (Cross, 1975, p. 103) and taken some care to preserve those procedures during its periodic denunciations of negotiated pleas. The result, as we shall argue, has been to create a system of plea inducement in which the transfer of essential information is specifically impeded and which may, therefore, often operate so as to defeat its own purpose.

The keystone of the English structure is the well-settled principle that a defendant's plea of guilty ought in general to mitigate the sentence he receives, ostensibly in recognition of the contrition evinced by the plea (*see* Thomas, 1979, pp. 50–52). In *Harper*[54], for example, the Court reduced a sentence of five years' imprisonment after a trial in which the defendant had alleged improper behaviour by the police.

> This court feels it quite improper to use language which may convey that a man is being sentenced because he has pleaded not guilty, or because he has run his defence in a particular way. It is, however, of course proper to give a man a lesser sentence if he has shown genuine remorse, amongst other things by pleading guilty.[55]

While the wisdom of such a policy can be questioned[56], if the element of contrition is genuine and in fact the source of the defendant's plea, this 'sentencing discount' involves no logical contradiction. But this rationale was immediately weakened substantially by the Court in the companion case of *de Haan*[57]. There, the fact of the defendant's guilty plea itself, without any independent showing of remorse, was held to *require* the granting of leniency, 'for that is clearly in the public interest'[58]. In practice, moreover, both the mandate and the example of *de Haan* appear to guide the practice of sentencing judges, who routinely award the discount to those who plead guilty without even a *pro forma* attempt to establish the defendant's motives[59]. In such circumstances, the logic of *Harper* is severely undermined, a point not lost upon defendants faced with the necessity of choosing a plea (Bottomley, 1973, p. 122).

Against this background, the Court first confronted the induced plea and its relationship to the sentencing discount in *Turner*[60]. Charged on complex issues of fact with theft, Turner at first persisted in a plea of not guilty despite the urgings of his own counsel and briefing solicitor. Just as the trial was to begin, however, he relented and changed his plea to guilty in response to his counsel's 'personal opinion'[61], formed on the basis of a private meeting with the trial judge, that such a plea was likely to result in a non-custodial sentence rather than the prison term anticipated upon conviction at trial. Turner appealed, claiming that he was thus deprived of a free choice as to plea, and the Court agreed. In remanding the case for a *venire de novo*, it offered some observations on the 'vexed question of so-called "plea bargaining"'[62].

The Court explicitly forbade judicial statements to the effect that a specific discount would be awarded on the basis of a guilty plea[63]. Yet at the same time, it reiterated the propriety of the discount itself and specifically charged defence counsel with the 'duty' to inform the accused of the fact of its existence[62]. Beyond this, 'when it is felt to be really necessary'[64], the Court appeared to encourage private discussions between both counsel and the trial judge of matters that might be 'of such a nature that counsel cannot in the interest of his client mention them in open court,'[62] including the desirability of a guilty plea to a lesser charge.

As we have seen, the overt participation of the trial judge in plea negotiations is generally proscribed in the United States as well and is, in any case, unnecessary where the sentencing discount is regularly granted and its extent can reliably be communicated to the defendant. Hence the ambiguity of the *Turner* directions, which seem simultaneously to forbid the inducement of guilty pleas and to sanctify the institutional arrangements by which it can be carried out effectively. This apparent contradiction was made explicit but left quite unresolved by the Court in *Cain*[65]. There, the trial judge sent for both counsel during the trial and made clear to them that if the appellant persisted in what he saw as a futile defence he would be sentenced very severely, but that a changed plea of guilty would be favourably received and make 'a considerable difference'[66]. Applying *Turner*, the Court found Cain's subsequent guilty plea involuntary and ordered a new trial. But the Court went on to suggest that where defence counsel was unfamiliar with the trial judge and his sentencing practice, private discussions aimed at 'obtaining guidance' as to what sentence the judge had in mind so that his client might properly be advised were indeed within the *Turner* guidelines.

> It was trite to say that a plea of guilty would generally attract a somewhat lighter sentence than a plea of not guilty after a full dress contest on the

> issue. Everybody knew that it was so, and there was no doubt about it. Any accused person who did not know about it should know it. The sooner he knew the better.[67]

With *Cain*, as one commentator has aptly written,

> The law seems to have got into a very confused and puzzling state. The accused ought to know that a plea of guilty will attract a lighter sentence than he would receive after conviction on a plea of not guilty .... Yet, where precise information is available, he is to be denied it: so that, if the accused decides to plead not guilty, he will or may do so on a false premise and one which — in the circumstances of the present case — his counsel knows to be false.[68]

A terse and somewhat cryptic Practice Direction[69], issued shortly after *Cain*, did little to resolve the tensions inherent in *Turner*. Indeed, the Court has continued to disclaim the form of plea agreements while carefully preserving their substance on a series of opinions[70] that border on the disingenuous. In *Atkinson*[71], for example, the appellant was convicted at trial of handling stolen goods and sentenced to six months' imprisonment. At a hearing conducted well before the trial, the judge suggested in open court to Atkinson's counsel that 'if he decides to change his plea [to guilty] we can dispose of it all today, and he would be out in the sunshine.'[72] As the Court of Appeal itself noted, '[t]hat was a clear indication, which no doubt was faithfully conveyed to the appellant, that if he pleaded guilty there would be no question of his going to prison.'[72] But Atkinson persisted in his plea of not guilty and, as sentence was passed, the judge recalled this earlier episode:

> And I observed that I there indicated that...I had it in mind sending this man to prison. But he has not pleaded guilty, has he? And the position of a man who pleads guilty is one thing, because he can say, 'Well, I am sorry. I am showing, by pleading guilty, I am not going to put the public to further expense.' A man who is found guilty, having denied it, is in a far different position, is he not?[72]

In allowing the appeal, the Court appeared to make its position on such procedures clear:

> Plea-bargaining has no place in the English criminal law....Our law having no room for any bargain about sentence between court and defendant, if events arise which give the appearance of such a bargain, then one must be very careful to see that the appearance is corrected.... [S]uch useful devices as a pretrial review must not be used by the court to

> indicate to an accused man that he may be treated one way if he pleads not guilty but in another way if he pleads guilty.[73]

But remarkably, on the facts of this case, the Court also said:

> Of course the trial judge was not striking any bargain with the defence. He was indicating the difference in sentence that a man can on occasions secure in his favour by a plea of guilty.... Although the learned judge no doubt had no intention of making a bargain with the defence as to plea, it may well have appeared to the appellant that he was being offered the relief from a sentence of immediate imprisonment if he should decide to plead guilty.[74]

In this way, the Court reiterated its general approval of the sentencing principles set forth in *Harper* and *de Haan*, and went on to sanction both open and private communications between judge and counsel within 'the limits set in *R v Turner*'[73]. Where it clearly lay within the power of the Court to eliminate the sentencing discount itself and to close the channel through which, inevitably, information regarding the extent of that discount in particular cases will be sought, the Court's refusal to do either necessarily renders its pronouncements on 'plea bargaining' somewhat hollow (cf. Baldwin and McConville, 1979, pp. 202–208). However 'damaging to the face of justice'[75] the inducement of guilty pleas may be, the Court appears, like its more candid American counterpart, to have found that damage worth bearing in light of the economic savings achieved by those pleas.

Once this underlying value judgment has been made, however, the full benefit of a system of induced guilty pleas can be realized only where essential information is allowed to flow freely within it[76]. As a result, the Court's continuing refusal to make precise information about the sentencing discount available to defendants prior to their decision as to plea serves only to frustrate the purpose of the discount itself. As we have argued (*see* section 10.2.2), the defendant will relinquish his right to trial where the expected cost to him of the trial prospect exceeds that of the proposed plea agreement, that is, where

$$L(S_p) < qL(S_v)$$

In these terms, the effect of the Court's policy is to create substantial uncertainty in the defendant's mind about the value of the variable S_p. Suppose, for example, that counsel is able to tell a particular defendant that a conviction at trial would mean a sentence of 10 years, but only that 'some reduction' is likely to follow a guilty plea. When the defendant asks how great this reduction will be, counsel's reply must necessarily be seen as merely an estimate; 'four years', therefore, must be understood by the defendant as 'four years, but possibly less'. Now, if the defendant would in fact have accepted a plea offer of six years, but gone to trial if the term offered were any greater than this, the uncertainty surrounding the decision would result in a trial (and its attendant costs) even if the judge fully intended to impose a sentence of six years following a guilty plea.

More generally, the uncertainty implied by the Court's policy requires that any estimate S_p, be it correct or not, made by a defendant prior to plea must be *increased* by some amount, say h, to reflect the possibility that the estimate is too low. If

$$L(S_p) < qL(S_v) < L(S_p + h)$$

that is, if the expected cost to the defendant of the trial prospect is greater than that of a 'certain' agreement at S_p but less than that of an 'uncertain' one, an uncertain defendant will elect a trial, even though the judge was in fact prepared to sentence him in such a way as would otherwise have induced a guilty plea. When this occurs, the potential welfare gains to both prosecution and defence that would have accompanied the guilty plea are never realized. The 'price' of an induced plea is increased, as relatively lower values of S_p must be offered to secure an agreement. The prosecution thus pays a premium because of the uncertainty forced upon defendants by the Court's policy and, if this uncertainty is sufficiently great, *no* agreements will be struck despite the desire of all sides to see them completed.

Deary[77] suggests that the 'real sense of grievance' engendered by uncertainty of this kind may require adjustment of sentence to reflect the reasonable expectations of defendants induced to plead guilty. But if, as the commentator in that case argues, '[it cannot] be treated as a decision that "plea bargains" will be enforced by the Court of Appeal,'[78] the problems created by the Court's anomalous position will persist. I have argued elsewhere that rules or policies that deny individuals necessary information in just this way can only be seen within the price exaction framework as transient (Adelstein, 1981). As a positive matter, then, I would suggest instead that *Deary* represents a first step toward the reconciliation of the Court's position regarding information transfer with its larger policy regarding induced pleas themselves.

10.4 A direction for further research

The principal purpose of this chapter has been to consider the development of the English system of induced guilty pleas and the nature of the value judgments that support it from the particular vantage point offered by the price exaction analysis. From a more general perspective, however, this comparative study can itself be seen as a kind of 'experiment', an attempt to test the usefulness of the framework as a theoretical basis for understanding the evolution of structural and organizational forms within the criminal process (cf. Adelstein, 1981, pp. 196–198). But this first step has necessarily ben a short one, for the common sources and close historical relationship between the English and American criminal processes have generally caused their similarities to dominate their differences and thus left relatively little scope for significant comparative analysis.

The real value of the framework, I believe, lies in its potential for illuminating the parallel evolution of systems of criminal price exaction characterized by different historical experience and substantial variance in the structure of basic institutions. Consider, for example, the degree of independent authority vested in the public prosecutor in the selection and pursuit of individual cases, an element that, in principle, distinguishes the Anglo-American criminal process from the 'inquisitorial' or 'mixed' systems of Europe. Substantial and largely unchecked prosecutorial discretion in these areas is a pervasive part of the Anglo-American system, but continental law tends to favour a rule of compulsory prosecution (or 'principle of legality') in cases of serious crime, monitored by a process of judicial review of decisions not to prosecute (*see*, for example, Langbein, 1977, pp. 87–89, 100–105, 111–115). But all these systems must somehow deal with the problem of selecting which offences to prosecute, and how, when the available human and material resources are insufficient to provide every defendant with a full criminal trial. As we have seen, the Anglo-American response has been to resort to some kind of plea agreement, a course made possible only by the freedom of prosecutors and courts to adjust the charges against a particular defendant to correspond with the terms of the agreement. On the European side, the legality principle forecloses this approach, but continental systems have in fact developed organisational forms consistent with mandatory prosecution that address the problem of case selection in the face of limited resources. The German forms of *Strafbefehl* and *Opportunitätsprinzip*, for example, are qualitatively different from their Anglo-American analogues of plea agreements and substantial prosecutorial discretion (ibid., generally, pp. 87–111), and close attention must be paid to the reasons for and effects of these differences. But analysis within the price exaction framework also makes clear that they serve many of the same purposes and arise for many of the same reasons, and much can be learned from this as well.

From a still wider perspective, it is clear that, in addition to the fundamentally different approach to economic analysis it implies, comparative study of this kind must also draw heavily upon the skills and analytical approach of legal scholarship. Perhaps the most important contribution of the price exaction framework will be the essential place it creates for legal analysis and a recognition of the much larger role that must be played by legal analysis in the emerging field of economics and law.

Notes to chapter ten

1 This essay is a product of an academic year spent by the author as Visiting Fellow, Centre for Socio-Legal Studies, Wolfson College, Oxford. I am deeply grateful to the staff of the Centre for their friendship and intellectual support during this most enjoyable year, and to Wesleyan University and the British Social Science Research Council for the financial support that made it possible.

2 Pollock and Maitland (1968, p. 451) trace the English practice to the time before the line separating crime from tort had been sharply drawn:

'The deed of homicide is thus a deed that can be paid for by money. Outlawry and blood-feud alike have been retiring before a system of pecuniary compositions.... From the very beginning...some small offences could be paid for; they were "emendable". The offender could buy back the peace that he had broken. To do this, he had to settle not only with the injured person but also with the king.... A complicated tariff was elaborated. Every kind of blow or wound to every kind of person had its price, and much of the jurisprudence of the day must have consisted of a knowledge of these preappointed prices.'

3 See, generally, Adelstein (1979b). The incorporation of nonmaterial and moral effects into discussions of economic efficiency has been suggested elsewhere in the legal literature. See, for example, Michelman (1967, pp. 1173, 1214–1218); Calabresi and Melamed (1972, pp. 1111–1112); and University of Pennsylvania Law Review (1974). Compare the earlier and more traditional discussion of Cohen (1940).

4 It is most important to emphasize the positive nature of the concept of moral cost. These effects are postulated solely to capture a real social phenomenon that has been reflected in Western attitudes toward crime and punishment for centuries. But to argue that such costs exist and play a central role in the criminal process is not to imply approval or justification for a given instance of them. Thus, for example, that a statutorily illegal act by a person of one race or nationality may often generate greater moral cost than an otherwise identical act by a person of another does not provide ethical support for the intolerance that makes it so, but it may help to explain the unequal punishments observed in the two cases. More generally, the positive magnitude of these moral costs appears quite variable and highly sensitive to the specific details of each criminal act. The identities of victim and offender and the particular circumstances that surround a given offence are, in practice, principal determinants of the 'gravity' or 'seriousness' of the offence and thus of the punishment to be imposed upon the offender. It is, moreover, this individualization that eliminates the possibility of competitive forces that might otherwise facilitate the organization of explicit markets in these effects. See Adelstein (1978b, pp. 793–796).

5 Although private prosecution remains a fundamental principle of English criminal procedure, its role is largely symbolic rather than practical. In Hertfordshire, for example, during a three month period in 1969 only 81 of 9341 prosecutions (less than one per cent) were brought by private citizens. See Wilcox (1972, pp. 3–4); Jackson (1972a, pp. 155–158).

6 *Metropolitan Police Commission, ex parte Blackburn*, [1968] 2 QB 118; Williams (1956).

7 On prosecutorial discretion with respect to the charging decision, see *Powell v Katzenbach*, 359 F (2d) 234 (DC Cir. 1965), cert. denied 384 US 906 (1966); *United States v Cox*, 342 F (2d) 167 (5th Cir. 1965), cert. denied 381 US 926 (1965); Cox (1976, pp. 394–403). From the perspective of price exaction, this charging discretion is the means by which the prosecutor seeks to adjust the punishment imposed upon the offender to his perception of the largely moral costs associated with the criminal offence. Since these costs are themselves borne by a large number of persons that are not direct participants in the price exaction process, the punishment sought by the prosecutor necessarily reflects his own subjective and often imperfect estimate of these social costs. As we have suggested, the need for a 'principal-agent' relationship of this kind creates severe problems of information gathering and introduces a

substantial potential for error into the prosecutorial decision-making process that is not present where costs are concentrated in specific individuals who retain the responsibility for decisions based upon them.

8 With respect to the United States, see Cox (1976, pp. 413–415). On comparable English pressures, see Jackson (1972b, pp. 80–82); Bottomley (1973, p. 108).

9 American practice is reported in Miller (1969, pp. 161–165) and Newman (1966, pp. 112–130). The English policy is considered in Jackson (1972b, pp. 88–93) and Wilcox (1972).

10 These arguments are developed more formally and in much greater detail in Adelstein (1978a).

11 For punishments exceeding P_O, we need make no specific assumptions concerning the shape of the prosecutor's utility function. Thus, the value of the function (the degree to which the prosecutor is satisfied) may fall when punishment exceeds P_O, reflecting the prosecutor's sense that P_O is in fact the most appropriate outcome. Alternatively, it may remain constant or rise slightly beyond P_O to account for the value of these more severe sentences as bargaining chips in negotiations with other defendants.

12 We consider the defendant's problem more fully in section 10.2.2. Insofar as pretrial detention may be a less costly means of 'softening' defendants and inducing guilty pleas than investigation or trial preparation, prosecutors may resort to this tactic as well. See, for example, Blumberg (1970, p. 59). 'Bail bargaining' along these lines appears to be quite common in England. See Bottoms and McClean (1976, pp. 200–204); Heberling (1978, pp. 101–103). The Court of Appeal took judicial notice of this practice in *Northam*, (1967) 52 Cr App R 97, 100.

13 Note that the remaining economic costs of price exaction, such as the cost of apprehending suspected offenders, are substantially independent of whether the conviction follows a guilty plea or a full trial.

14 This is a consequence of the assumption of diminishing marginal utility of punishment. The difference between the expected sentence at trial and the smallest acceptable certain punishment below it represents the prosecutor's 'risk premium', the value to him, in units of punishment, of removing the uncertainty inherent in the trial.

15 This deference is increasingly being institutionalized in law. See, for example, the relevant rule in the American federal courts: '(e) Plea agreement procedure... (3) *Acceptance of a Plea Agreement.* If the court accepts the plea agreement, the court shall inform the defendant that it will embody in the judgment and sentence the disposition provided for in the plea agreement.' *Federal Rules of Criminal Procedure* 11 (e) (3) (1976).

16 Magistrates' Courts Act 1952, s.108. This sentencing constraint creates a strategic incentive for defendants to have their guilty plea entered in the Magistrates' Court wherever possible. See Heberling (1978, p. 97).

17 See, for example, Heberling (1978, p. 96); Baldwin and McConville (1977, pp. 84–85, 111). One writer has described the English system of induced pleas as a 'delicate mutual back-scratching system' Parker (1971, p. 408).

18 See Bottoms and McClean (1976, pp. 228–235): 'The Liberal Bureaucratic Model holds ... that the protection of individual liberty, and the need for justice to be done and to be seen to be done, must ultimately override the importance of the repression of criminal conduct.... [But] the liberal bureaucrat is a practical man; he realises that things have to get done, systems have to be run. It is right that the defendant shall have substantial protections; crime control is not the overriding value of the criminal justice system. But these protections must have a limit. If it were not so, then the whole system of criminal justice, with its ultimate value to the community in the form of liberal and humane crime control, would collapse. Moreover, it is right to build in sanctions to deter those who might otherwise use their "Due Process" rights frivolously, or to "try it on"; an administrative system at State expense should not exist for this kind of time-wasting.... [T]he values of the Liberal Bureaucratic Model are everywhere to be found in the actual operation, and even in some of the formal rules, of the English courts.... All these rules help to smooth administrative operation of the system, while leaving open to the defendant his formal rights — a classic statement of the Liberal

Bureaucratic position.' (pp. 229–231).

19 The American federal courts are governed by *Federal Rules of Criminal Procedure* 11 (e) (1) (1976); see also the discussions in *Scott v United States*, 419 F (2d) 264 (DC Cir. 1969) and *United States ex rel Elksnis v Gilligan*, 256 F Supp. 244 (S.D.N.Y. 1966). On the English side, see *Turner*, [1970] 2 QB 321 and *Atkinson* [1978] 2 All ER 460.

20 On induced pleas in the English criminal process generally, see Thomas (1978); Heberling (1978); Baldwin and McConville (1977); Bottoms and McClean (1976, pp. 104–134); Jackson (1972b, pp. 163–171).

21 Criminal Justice Act 1972, s.17.

22 Cf. *Kennedy*, [1968] Crim LR 566.

23 On the legitimacy of the sentencing discount, see, for example, *Harper*, [1968] 2 QB 108, a case we discuss more fully in section 10.3.3. The extent of the discount in practice is the subject of Baldwin and McConville (1978).

24 In both the United States and England, the vast majority of defendants who require representation have counsel provided for them at public expense. Compare, for example, President's Commission (1967, pp. 152–161) with Jackson (1972b, pp. 133–142). This simplifying assumption is relaxed in the model developed by Adelstein (1978a).

25 Cf. *Scott v United States*, 419 F (2d) 264, 277–278 (DC Cir. 1969).

26 Note that where this is the case, prosecutors will bargain most readily with defendants whose guilt is in substantial doubt, precisely those, it can well be argued, who most deserve the formalities of the trial procedure. Trials will thus be likely in only the most perfunctory cases, where the defendant's guilt is easily proved and the prosecutor has no reason to concede anything.

27 This practice apears to be more common in the United States than in England. Compare, for example, President's Commission (1967, pp. 9–13) with Baldwin and McConville (1977, pp. 111–112).

28 Thus, in considering a fifteen-year-old boy's station-house confession, Justice Frankfurter argued: 'It would disregard standards that we cherish ... to hold that a confession is "voluntary" simply because the confession is the product of sentient choice. "Conduct under duress involves a choice." [C]onduct devoid of physical pressure but not leaving a free exercise of choice is the product of duress as much so as choice reflecting physical constraint.' *Haley v Ohio*, 332 US 596, 606 (1948) (Frankfurter J, concurring) (Quoting *Union Pracific R Co v Public Service Commission*, 248 US 67, 70 (1918)).

29 This argument, and the empirical and epistemological issues surrounding it, are discussed in detail in Adelstein (1981, pp. 154–198).

30 See, for example, the tortuous history of *Shelton v United States*, 242 F (2d) 101 (5th Cir.), *rev'd en banc on rehearing*, 246 F (2d) 571 (1957), *rev'd per curiam on confession of error*, 356 US 26 (1958).

31 390 US 570 (1968).

32 18 USC s.1201 (1976) (amended 1972). The 1972 amendment struck out the provision at issue in *Jackson*.

33 390 US at 581.

34 Ibid. at 582 (citations omitted).

35 Indeed, there were suggestions at the time that *Jackson* had sounded the death knell for the negotiated plea. See, for example, the argument of the New Jersey Supreme Court in *State v Forcella*, 245 A (2d) 181 (N.J. 1968).

36 395 US 711 (1969).

37 Ibid. at 724.

38 Ibid. at 724, quoting *Worcester v Commissioner*, 370 F (2d) 713, 718 (1st Cir. 1966).

39 397 US 742 (1970).

40 Ibid. at 752.

41 Ibid. at 753.

42 Ibid. at 750.

43 Ibid. at 751 n.8.

44 Ibid. at 758.

45 Ibid. at 758. Adelstein (1978a) suggests that, apart from the effects of risk-aversion, the passage of time may play an important role in the decision to plead guilty. To the extent that this factor influences all defendants, there is a suggestion that innocent defendants may indeed be induced to plead guilty by the structure of the bargaining system itself.

46 See Griswold (1969, p. 314). English commentators have expressed a similar view with respect to the English criminal process. See, for example, Heberling (1978, p. 103).

47 'Of course, that the prevalence of guilty pleas is explainable does not necessarily validate those pleas or the system which produces them.' 397 US at 752–753.

48 404 US 257, 260 (1971).
49 *Scott v United States*, 419 F (2d) 264, 278 (DC Cir. 1969).
50 434 US 357 (1978).
51 395 US at 725.
52 434 US at 363.
53 Ibid at 364. In dissent, two Justices argued that this tactic was precisely the sort of 'vindictiveness' forbidden by *Pearce*. But the moment for these arguments was in *Brady*, not here; once the plea bargaining system has been vindicated, as the majority implies, it cannot be denied the single procedure that makes it work. One senses here that the real issue is submerged, for what makes Hayes' case so poignant and motivates the dissenters' passion is that his life sentence was triggered by the passing of a bad cheque for less than $90. This may indeed be a miscarriage of justice, but if it is, the real source is the harshness of the recidivist statute itself, an issue which was not raised in the case, rather than the bargaining tactics of the prosecutor.
54 [1968] 2 QB 108. See also *Davis* [1965] Crim LR 251; *Flynn* [1967] Crim LR 489.
55 [1968] 2 QB at 110.
56 Consider the discussion in *Scott v United States*, 419 F (2d) 264, 270–271 (DC Cir. 1969).
57 [1968] 2 QB 108.
58 Ibid. at 111. See also *House* [1978] Crim LR 173, decided in 1974, 1186/C/73, in which a sentence was reduced from seven to five years to reflect a guilty plea and 'for this reason only'.
59 See Baldwin and McConville (1978, pp. 117–118): '[T]he defendant who pleads guilty in the Crown Court is almost never asked by the judge if he wishes to say anything before sentence is passed.... There can be no doubt ... that if the courts had engaged in a more searching inquiry in the cases that we examined, they would have been rarely satisfied that the defendant was genuinely contrite.'
60 [1970] 2 QB 321.
61 Ibid. at 324.
62 Ibid. at 326.
63 Ibid. at 327.
64 Ibid. at 326–327.
65 The Times (London), 23 February 1976, at 11. Reported [1976] Crim LR 464.
66 The Times, ibid., at 11.
67 Ibid. (Widgery LCJ).
68 [1976] Crim LR 465.
69 'The decision in *R v Cain* has been subject to further consideration by the Court of Appeal. In so far as it is inconsistent with *R v Turner* the latter decision should prevail.' [1976] 1 WLR 799.
70 See, for example, *Grice* [1977] 66 Cr App R 167; *Llewellyn* (1978) 67 Cr App R 49; and similar cases discussed Baldwin and McConville (1979).
71 [1978] 2 All ER 460.
72 Ibid. at 461.
73 Ibid. at 462.
74 Ibid. at 461–462.
75 *Atkinson* [1978] 2 All ER 460, 463.
76 These points are discussed in detail in Adelstein (1978b, pp. 809–816).
77 [1977] Crim LR 47.
78 Ibid. at 48.

References

ADELSTEIN, R. (1978a), The plea bargain in theory: a behavioral model of the negotiated guilty plea, *Southern Economic Journal*, **44**, no. 3, 488–503.

ADELSTEIN, R. (1978b), The negotiated guilty plea: a framework for analysis, *New York University Law Review*, **53**, no. 4, 783–833.

ADELSTEIN, R. (1979a), Informational paradox and the pricing of crime: capital sentencing standards in economic perspective, *Journal of Criminal Law and Criminology*, **70**, no. 3, 281–298.

ADELSTEIN, R. (1979b), The moral costs of crime: prices, information, and organisation, in *The Costs of Crime*, (C.M. Gray, ed.) Sage, London, 233–255.

ADELSTEIN, R. (1981), Institutional function and evolution in the criminal process. *Northwestern University Law Review*, **76**, no. 1, 101–198.

BALDWIN, J. and McCONVILLE, M. (1977), *Negotiated Justice*, London: Martin Robertson.

BALDWIN, J. and McCONVILLE, M. (1978), The influence of the sentencing discount in inducing guilty pleas, in *Criminal Justice: Selected Readings*, pp. 116–128 (J. Baldwin and A. Bottomley, eds.), London: Martin Robertson.

BALDWIN, J. and McCONVILLE, M. (1979), Plea bargaining and the Court of Appeal, *British Journal of Law and Society*, **6**, no. 2, 200–218.

BLUMBERG, A. (1970), *Criminal Justice*, Chicago: Quadrangle.
BOTTOMLEY, A. (1973), *Decisions in the Penal Process*, London: Martin Robertson.
BOTTOMS, A. and McCLEAN, J. (1976), *Defendants in the Criminal Process*, London: Routledge and Kegan Paul.
CALABRESI, G. and MELAMED, A. (1972), Property rules, liability rules, and inalienability: one view of the cathedral, *Harvard Law Review*, **85**, April, 1089–1128.
COHEN, M. (1940), Moral aspects of the criminal law, *Yale Law Journal*, **49**, no. 6, 987–1026.
COX, S. (1976), Prosecutorial discretion: an overview, *American Criminal Law Review*, **13**, no. 3, 383–434.
CROSS, R. (1975), *The English Sentencing System*, 2nd ed., London: Butterworths.
GRISWOLD, E. (1969), Criminal procedure, 1969 — is it a means or an end?, *Maryland Law Review*, **29**, no. 4, 307–319.
HEBERLING, J. (1978), Plea negotiation in England, in *Criminal Justice: Selected Readings*, pp. 95–105, (J. Baldwin and A. Bottomley, eds.) London: Martin Robertson.
HOLMES, O. (1963), *The Common Law* (M. Howe, ed.) Boston: Little Brown.
JACKSON, R. (1972a), *The Machinery of Justice*, 6th ed., Cambridge University Press.
JACKSON, R. (1972b), *Enforcing the law*, rev. ed., London: Penguin.
LANGBEIN, J. (1977), *Comparative Criminal Procedure: Germany*, Minneapolis: West.
MICHELMAN, F. (1967), Property, utility, and fairness: comments on the ethical foundations of 'just compensation' law, *Harvard Law Review*, **80**, no. 6, 1165–1258.
MILLER, F. (1969), *Prosecution: The Decision to Charge a Suspect with a Crime*, Boston: Little Brown.
NEWMAN, D. (1966), *Conviction: The Determination of Guilt or Innocence Without Trial*, Boston: Little Brown.
PARKER, G. (1971), Copping a plea, *Justice of the Peace and Local Government Review*, **135**, 408–409.
POLLOCK, F. and MAITLAND, F. (1968), *The History of English Law, Volume II*, 2nd ed., Cambridge University Press.
POSNER, R. (1973), An economic approach to legal procedure, *Journal of Legal Studies*, **2**, no. 2, 399–458.
PRESIDENT'S COMMISSION on Law Enforcement and the Administration of Justice (1967), *Task Force Report: The Courts*, Washington: Government Printing Office.
THOMAS, D. (1979), *Principles of Sentencing*, 2nd ed., London: Heinemann.
THOMAS, P. (1978), Plea bargaining in England, *Journal of Criminal Law and Criminology*, **69**, no. 2, 170–178.
UNIVERSITY OF PENNSYLVANIA LAW REVIEW (1974), Just compensation and the assassin's bequest: a utilitarian approach, **122**, April, 1012–1032.
WILCOX, A. (1972), *The Decision to Prosecute*, London: Butterworths.
WILLIAMS, G. (1956), Discretion in prosecuting, *Criminal Law Review*, 222–231.

CHAPTER ELEVEN

Judicial responses to exchange rate instability[1]

Roger A. Bowles and Christopher J. Whelan

11.1 Introduction

In recent years, the value of sterling, in terms of both its domestic and international purchasing power, has become increasingly unstable. The advent of such instability has had a variety of consequences. One such consequence has been pressure for reform of the law relating to foreign currency (*see*, for example, Mann, 1971). The pressure began to arise when foreign plaintiffs came to find themselves incurring serious losses resulting from the rapid depreciation of their claims as sterling fell sharply against other currencies. Traditionally, English judges had confined themselves to making awards in sterling but the judiciary came to perceive a conflict between their traditional view of sterling as the centre of the universe and the basic principles of civil law requiring adequate compensation of victims. The resolution of this conflict is not quite complete, as will be argued later.

The primary focus of this particular essay is however upon the evolution of the new set of rules and on some of the difficulties that this process encountered. The judiciary play an important role in the reform of the law but it is rather difficult to read the relevant judgments without sometimes being assailed by doubts as to how far they themselves are aware of all the consequences of their decisions.

The approach adopted here does not follow the conventional methodology of economics, even though this area does raise a number of questions to which such methodology could be addressed. It would be possible, for example, to investigate the likely effects on the behaviour of prospective contractors of the switch from one rule to the other and whether the resulting set of contracts is, in an efficiency sense, superior. Rather, our attention is limited to making selective comments upon the internal consistency of the arguments used in different cases, and the work may thus be viewed as falling in the more traditional vein of legal analysis. Nevertheless, it will be argued that instances arise in which it is useful to pursue some of the arguments about the consequences of legal changes with the aid of some simple economics.

11.2 The law before 1975

Until the *Miliangos* decision in 1975[2], arbitrators and courts followed two clearly established rules relating to judgments involving foreign currencies[3]. The first, the *sterling rule*, provided that awards of damages in English courts had to be expressed in pounds sterling. The second, the breach-date conversion rule (Mann, 1971, p. 363 *et seq*), was a corollary of the first, and concerned the date at which an obligation to pay some foreign currency should be converted into pounds sterling. It provided that the rate of exchange for conversion should be the one ruling at the time of breach. For a debt, this would be at a rate of exchange on the day when the debt became due and payable[4]; for a contract, it would be the rate of exchange applying on the date the contract was broken[5]; and for a tort, it would be the rate of exchange on the date of the tortious act[6].

The supremacy of sterling derived from what is known as the *nominalist principle*, namely that obligations to pay sums of money are satisfied by payment of the nominal amount of the obligation: that is, the face value. The notion that sterling is taken to be constant in value[7] resulted, in terms of foreign money obligations, in unusually distorted judicial expressions of the world. The underlying principle that 'A pound in England is a pound whatever its international value'[8], led Lord Denning to the following statement in 1956: 'A man who stipulates for a pound must take a pound when payment is made, whatever the pound is worth at that time. Sterling is the constant unit of value by which in the eye of the law everything else is measured. Prices of commodities may go up or down, other currencies may go up and down, but sterling remains the same.'[9]

The second rule, the breach-date rule, followed on almost automatically. As Lord Denning explained, 'So long as sterling is regarded as stable whilst other currencies go up and down, it would seem that justice is best done by taking the rate of exchange at the date of the breach.'[10] It would be wrong to assume that Lord Denning was unaware of exchange rate instability, for he expressly referred to the fact that sterling had depreciated and had been devalued, that it had departed from the gold standard, and that there had been much inflation.

According to Dr. F.A. Mann, whose 1971 book *The Legal Aspect of Money* remains the authoritative study on the subject, the breach-date rule undoubtedly arose 'from much misunderstanding and many accidents' (Mann, 1971, p. 336). In particular, he wondered if the rule would have been different if, at the time when the courts were first confronted with the problem, it had been sterling rather than foreign currency which suffered the depreciation (ibid.).

Mann wrote in 1971, but felt that his book was 'not the place for melancholy reflections about the vicissitudes of the judicial process and the evolution of the law.' (Ibid.). Since he wrote, however, judicial attitudes have altered radically, probably for the reasons indicated by Mann: it became increasingly difficult to regard the pound as stable while virtually all other currencies appreciated.

The impetus for a move away from the sterling rule towards a rule that took more account of the international value of sterling can be argued to derive from two different sources. These two sources can usefully be introduced by reference to some early remarks that Lord Denning had made in defence of the sterling rule approach. He had argued that if a foreign creditor 'chooses to sue in our courts rather than his own, he must put up with the consequences'[10] and added that the sterling rule 'is better suited to a commercial community. Any other rule would mean that the sum payable would depend on the delays of parties or of courts. That cannot be right.'[10]

These two assertions require closer examination, for they seem to constitute quite a powerful case for the nominalist sterling approach. The suggestion that an injured party seeking to recover for debt or damages from a party of different nationality has a choice of country in which to pursue legal action is of course perfectly valid. It can however be pointed out, first, that plaintiffs will only have a small range of possible countries to choose from and, secondly, that if plaintiffs find English rules unattractive relative to those applied elsewhere, the English courts will be avoided and those in other countries will be used more intensively. Whilst Lord Denning was apparently unconcerned about this, it may be argued that such a position is not in the interests of those lawyers and others whose incomes depend heavily on the volume of litigation being brought in English courts. Indeed, the attempt to maintain London as a centre for the arbitration of international disputes is reflected in a number of reforms and in particular the early stimulus for reform of the treatment of foreign currency obligations by London arbitrators, which culminated in the passage in 1979 of the Arbitration Act.

The second of Lord Denning's assertions seems to be mistaken. Reliance on the nominalist principle is just as likely to make the sum payable dependant on the delays of parties or courts as any other rule. It is simply that the incentive for delay takes a different form. Under the nominalist rules, defendants had strong incentives to delay in order to reduce the real costs of meeting the claims against them, whilst under less rigid or certain rules (which now exist and are discussed below), the defendant will wish to settle quickly or slowly depending upon the view he takes about the future course of exchange rates and interest rates. The plaintiff, however, no longer has any immediate interest in the speed with which matters are conducted, since the real value of his claim is now held constant. It is difficult therefore to accept the view of Lord Denning that the nominalist principle was the only way to prevent delaying tactics.

The force of these criticisms became increasingly significant as the international value of sterling declined. It seems natural therefore to look next at the advent of exchange rate instability as it affected the value of sterling. *Table 11.1* indicates that the weakness of sterling vis-à-vis the US dollar began in 1967 but that since the exchange rate was allowed to float in 1971, there has been a recent strengthening of sterling. The period 1961–66 was characterized by an exchange rate of around $2.80 to the pound and the period 1967–70 by a lower rate of around $2.40 following the balance of payments crisis of 1967 and the resulting devaluation. From 1971 onwards the pound's value varied much more, and in particular lost ground very rapidly over the period 1974–76 (during which time it fell by 27.5 per cent), some of which it regained over the following years 1977 and 1978.

Table 11.1 *Spot exchange rates 1966–79.* (Source: *International Financial Statistics, IMF)*

Year	*France* FF/£	*Germany* DM/£	*Switzerland* SF/£	*USA* $/£
1966	13.816	11.096	12.072	2.790
1967	11.813	9.625	10.410	2.407
1968	11.798	9.538	10.258	2.384
1969	13.343	8.858	10.366	2.401
1970	13.214	8.733	10.332	2.394
1971	13.333	8.341	9.992	2.552
1972	12.034	7.519	8.862	2.348
1973	10.938	6.280	7.536	2.323
1974	10.438	5.659	5.965	2.349
1975	9.076	5.306	5.302	2.024
1976	8.461	4.022	4.172	1.702
1977	8.968	4.012	3.812	1.906
1978	8.504	3.719	3.296	2.035
1979	8.940	3.851	3.514	2.224

Note: Figures refer to the exchange rate ruling at the *end* of each year.

Rather more spectacular than the volatility of the sterling/US dollar exchange rate have been the movements of exchange values of the stronger European currencies, which are also illustrated in *Table 11.1*. This is of particular relevance because much of the case law involves these currencies[11].

Having outlined the earlier law and the circumstances in which pressure for its reform grew, we look next at the changes in the law that have taken place and subsequently at some of the difficulties to which these changes have given rise.

11.3 The law since 1975

11.3.1 Miliangos

It is a fundamental principle of the law of damages both before and after 1975, that an injured party is entitled to *restitutio in integrum* that is, as far as possible, to be restored to the condition that he was in before the damage arose (*see* Atiyah, 1971). As Lord Eldon stated in 1805, if a debtor fails in his promise to pay £100 'wherever the creditor sues him, the law of that country ought to give him just as much as he would have had if the contract had been performed'[12]. Under the sterling and breach-date rules, creditors had to suffer the losses that ensued from any depreciation of sterling between the date of breach and the date of judgment.

Referring to the sterling rule, Mann (1971, p. 373) stated that 'Many of the reasons which, from time to time, were advanced were so tenuous that they need no attention.' It is ironic, however, that some of the first signs of judicial unease over the rules came from Lord Denning. In 1970, he stated that 'the common law rule on this subject is most unsatisfactory,'[13] but the other two judges in the case felt bound by precedent.

The possibility of a change, of going against the clearly established rules of precedent, followed the 'constitutional convention' in 1966, when the House of Lords declared that they were no longer bound by their own previous decisions[14]. However, it was not until 1975 that the House reversed their previous ruling. In *Miliangos v George Frank (Textiles) Ltd*[15], a majority of their Lordships held that actions for the recovery of debt could be expressed in foreign currencies, and that the rate of conversion into sterling of the amount of foreign currency awarded should be at the rate of 'the date when the court authorizes enforcement of the judgment in terms of sterling.'[16] Although the House affirmed the decision reached below by the Court of Appeal[17], which itself relied on an earlier decision it had made[18], their Lordships made it clear that the Court of Appeal should not have deviated from the clear precedent of earlier House of Lords decisions. Thus, reform of the law by the judiciary had to await first, the 1966 declaration, and secondly, a suitable case to be appealed to the House of Lords. Since *Miliangos*, the judiciary have extended the rule to cases of damages for breach of contract and for tort[19].

It should be added here that the sterling rule was a rule of English procedure, the function of which is not to do justice, but to provide machinery for the enforcement of rights (Mann, 1971, p. 373). In *Miliangos*, Lord Wilberforce stated that 'it must surely be wrong in principle to allow procedure to affect, detrimentally, the substance of the creditor's rights.'[20] While the extension of the rule in *Miliangos* to cases of damages for tort or breach of contract occurred because 'it is undesirable that the rule of procedure should be retained for a claim for damages (whether in tort or for breach of contract) while departed from in a case of debt,'[21] the reason for any alteration in procedure was put down to the exchange rate instability[22].

The decision in *Miliangos* 'revolutionised'[23] the law. It has been greeted with enthusiasm by legal commentators on both sides of the Atlantic. Thus, Mann (1976, p. 167) has praised 'the openly progressive and reforming spirit displayed in fields of international commerce which for many decades has been burdened by poorly reasoned precedent. Riordan (1978, p. 422) went even further: 'To trace the juridical development of this new rule reveals a most enlightening example of two key tenets of the reform and modernization process of the common law: first, that the law should reflect the fundamental (commercial) realities of the day, and second, that the judge has a major role to play in keeping the law in step with those realities.'

11.3.2 The Despina R and SEAS[24]

Having established that judgments can be expressed in foreign currencies, the main problem for arbitrators and judges is: in which currency are losses to be expressed[25]? In *Despina R*, two ships collided. Damages of 85 per cent of the loss and damage of the other ship had been agreed by the owners of the *Despina R*. The expenses of repair had been incurred in four currencies, while the plaintiff conducted his business in US dollars. Lord Wilberforce suggested that in tort cases of this kind there were three possible solutions: the first is to take the currency in which the expense or loss was immediately sustained: the 'expenditure currency'; the second is to take the currency in which the loss was effectively felt or borne by the plaintiff, having regard to the currency in which he generally operates or with which he has the closest connection: the 'plaintiff's currency'; and the third is to take the sterling equivalent at the time that the losses occurred or at some other date: the 'sterling rule'.

The *SEAS* case involved a breach of contract. As in *Despina R*, liability was admitted, and the question was once again, in which currency should the loss be measured[26]? The possible solutions included those available in the tort case: the expenditure currency (cruzeiros) or the plaintiff's currency (French francs, used to obtain the cruzeiros), but an additional solution in a case of contract was the currency of the contract or charterparty (US dollars).

In both appeals Lord Wilberforce opted for the plaintiff's currency. He reached this conclusion by applying the normal principles governing the assessment of damages: in cases of tort, *restitutio in integrum* and reasonable forseeability; in cases of breach of contract, *restitutio in integrum* having regard to what was in the reasonable contemplation of the parties at the time of contracting. In both cases before him, Lord Wilberforce rejected the sterling solution: in tort, 'to give a judgment in the currency in which the loss was sustained produces a juster result than one which fixes the plaintiff with a sum in sterling taken at the date of the breach or of the loss.'[27] Moreover, where a plaintiff through normal business conduct uses his own currency to obtain other currencies in which the loss is sustained, the loss to him is really in his own currency[28]; in contract, the currency selected should be that 'which most truly expresses his loss', thus 'the essential question is what was the loss suffered by the respondents?'[29] In both cases, Lord Wilberforce would 'not approve of a hard and fast rule'[30] in tort to the effect that the plaintiff's currency should be always selected, or in contract that the contract currency would be necessarily appropriate unless there was a 'decisive interpretation'[31]; he preferred 'a flexible rule in which account must be taken of the circumstances in which the loss arose, in which the loss was converted into a money sum, and in which it was felt by the plaintiff.'[32]

11.4 Some difficulties

While the changes in the law have been welcomed as sensible and desirable, there are three aspects of the implementation of the new rules that may give rise to concern. In the first place, some conceptual difficulties are raised by the principle of *restitutio in integrum* in this context; secondly, under the new rules, courts are faced with the problem of selecting an appropriate rate at which to calculate interest on damages; and further, this discretion, together with the existence of flexible rules governing the choice of currency, leads to a measure of uncertainty.

11.4.1 restitutio in integrum

In a rather literal sense, the damage resulting from a tortious act or breach of contract may be established largely by identifying the immediate harm that has befallen the victim or plaintiff. If *A* does not receive the promised payment of $100 for goods delivered, it seems fairly clear that *A* has 'lost' $100 and should be able to reclaim it. Equally if *B* damages *A*'s ship in such a way that *A* has to incur reasonable expenses of $250 to repair it, there does not seem to be any problem in arguing that *A* has 'lost' $250 that *A* should be able to recover from *B*. Unfortunately, life is not quite as simple as these examples may suggest, as we will now show. In order to clarify our argument, we deal separately with cases of contract and cases of tort.

Contracts are entered into when both parties think that they can thereby increase their wealth. The perceptions of the parties about the increase in wealth resulting from making the contract will depend in part upon the rules that the parties agree upon (or assume will be applied) in the event of the breakdown of the contract. Thus a person that views a proposition as initially attractive may refrain from entering a contract if he thinks that it might fail and that the consequences of such failure for his own position would be unpleasant. The terms agreed in the contract will therefore reflect the prevailing set of rules, and so one could argue for example that under the nominalist principle parties delivering goods would charge a premium in the price they set that takes allowance of the losses they may expect to incur if the buyer defaults in payment. As far as our discussion of legal doctrines is concerned, it could be argued that the *restitutio in integrum* principle becomes slightly ambiguous when viewed in such a light, since the '*integrum*' can itself be thought of as being determined by the set of rules in force. It should of course also be remembered that the parties to the contract may be expected to calculate the costs of recovery in the event of breakdown by reference to the rules that prevail in the country in which they expect recovery to be pursued, a matter over which they may have some discretion. When calculating the losses that a given set of rules will generate, parties have to make guesses about the strategy that the other side will follow, so that if there is likely to be an incentive for a party defending an action to delay, this has to be taken into account. One particular consequence of this is that if the rules that are to be applied are unclear, or if for example they allow extensive discretion to the court, then parties may be more reluctant to enter into contracts than they would be otherwise, particularly if they have an aversion to risk. It can therefore be argued that the uncertainty that now prevails about whether the court will rely upon the plaintiff's currency rule or some other rule, may have the effect of deterring the formation of contracts that might otherwise occur.

In the case of torts it has become conventional for economists to argue that the degree of care exercised by participants in potentially hazardous activities (like motoring or sailing ships) will reflect the costs associated with injury (Calabresi, 1970; Hirsch, 1979, ch. 7). That is, the legal rules will themselves have some deterrent effect. To the extent that the nominalist principle, in times of inflation and exchange rate weakness may reduce the ability of a plaintiff to recover all of his 'losses', we might expect prospective plaintiffs to view such a rule as increasing their costs. At the same time however participants in such activities will find their costs as prospective defendants correspondingly lowered, so that for example the cost of third party insurance falls. The net effect of the imposition of the nominalist rule could therefore be regarded as affecting the costs of different sorts of insurance; it becomes cheaper to injure others but means lower recoveries for injuries to oneself. People worried about this state of affairs may simply respond by buying first party insurance designed to compensate for the reduction in the volume of damages they can recover from third parties. Again, however, if there is uncertainty about the exact set of rules that the court will apply and if the legal costs associated with this uncertainty are high, then individuals may respond by exercising more care than is 'optimal' in the sense that they may take additional safety precautions even though in terms of aggregate costs such precautions may be counter-productive. Viewed in the light of the overall effects then, the choice between the nominalist approach and the contrasting approach recently introduced can be seen to be a less straightforward matter than has been suggested elsewhere (Riordan, 1978; Mann, 1976). The form in which costs are experienced has changed, but the aggregate level of costs may be either higher or lower. It may be argued however that whichever way this dispute is settled, there remains a more technical, but nevertheless serious, source of possible inconsistency in the way in which the courts apply the new rules. Taking the court's objective to be to restore to the plaintiff the losses that he has experienced as a direct result of the tortious action or breach of contract, there arises the difficulty of the rate of interest that is to be applied in calculating the interest payable on the debt or damages for the period between breach (or occurrence of damage) and judgment, and the question of choice of currency.

11.4.2 Interest

In an era of high nominal interest rates, plaintiffs stand to lose heavily from any delay that occurs between the harm being experienced and an award or settlement being made. The judiciary attempt to offset such prospective losses by allowing a claim for interest to be paid on the sum at stake. It is clearly of central importance that the judges choose an appropriate rate at which to calculate such claims, for if the 'wrong' rate is used plaintiffs will be systematically over-compensated or under-compensated. Furthermore, use of the 'wrong' rate creates incentives for one or other of the parties to delay proceedings. If the rate were 'too low' defendants could regard delay as a cheap form of buying extended credit, while if it were 'too high' the plaintiff could regard it as an unusually attractive method of saving.

The choice of interest rate (and in particular the choice between applying English and foreign interest rates) becomes a more interesting matter when it is observed that an inverse relationship may normally be expected to prevail between exchange rate changes and interest rate differentials. Countries with currencies that are expected to be weak over future months or years have to offer higher interest rates than other countries if they are to attract international funds. Thus it is that countries whose currencies prove in the event to be losing value will generally be characterized by high interest rates and vice versa.

The important implication of the existence of an inverse relation between exchange rate changes and the level of interest rates prevailing in the relevant countries is that the higher interest rates may be expected to offset to some extent adverse movements in exchange rates. Indeed this must be so, for international speculators and investors will place their funds in the most lucrative location, and competition to attract such funds will force central banks to offer interest rates that reflect any pessimism that international investors feel about the likely course of future exchange rates. Investors may of course make incorrect guesses about future exchange rates, but such errors simply mean that interest rate differentials may not fully reflect the changes that actually occur in exchange rates.

The systematic relation between exchange rates and interest rates has the important consequence for the legal problems at issue that the court must be sure to identify the relevant interest rate. If a plaintiff lives in Switzerland and sets out to recover damages or debt in Swiss Francs the appropriate rate at which to calculate any interest on the damages or debt will be that which prevails in Switzerland. This indeed was the course of action followed in the *Miliangos* case. In *Miliangos (No. 2)*, where the choice of interest rate was discussed, Bristow J in reaching his decision that Swiss interest rates should be applied remarked:

> In my judgment the plaintiff should be treated *mutatis mutandis* in the same way as he would have been had he been awarded judgment in sterling, and had he then borrowed sterling in England pending judgment so as not to be out of his money.[33]

To have awarded English interest rates (which were considerably, and predictably, higher than those prevailing in Switzerland over the relevant period) would have been to overcompensate the plaintiff. Either the plaintiff is to be treated as if he were investing on the English market (and thus earning high interest rates to offset the prospect of depreciation in the international value of his currency) or as if he were investing on a foreign market and thus earning lower interest rates.

In order to illustrate the prospective importance of the choice of interest rate it is apposite to observe from *Table 11.2* that there was a significant difference between interest rates in Switzerland and the UK at the time relevant to the *Miliangos* case.

Table 11.2 *Discount Rates in Switzerland and UK 1973–1975* (Source: *The Economist*)

Year	*1973*		*1974*				*1975*		
Quarter	*3*	*4*	*1*	*2*	*3*	*4*	*1*	*2*	*3*
Switzerland	4.5	4.5	5.5	5.5	5.5	5.5	5.0	4.5	3.5
UK	11.5	13.0	12.5	11.8	11.5	11.5	10.0	10.0	11.0

Simple calculations show that application of the appropriate Swiss rate to the debt of SF 416 144.20 (which corresponded to about £60 000 at the time of the hearing at first instance) between the date from which interest was to be calculated (31 October 1971) and the judgment date (4 December 1974) would lead to an award of interest of the order of £15 000. Application of the UK Minimum Lending Rate on the other hand would lead to an award of around £30 000, that is to say, double the appropriate amount. Elementary as these arguments may appear, they have on occasion since *Miliangos* been overlooked.

This contention is well illustrated by reference to a case we have discussed elsewhere (Bowles and Whelan, 1979b). In this case, *Helmsing Schiffahrts*

GmbH & Co. KG v Malta Drydocks Corporation[34], the plaintiffs were German shipowners who contracted through the second and third defendants for the building of two ships by Malta Drydocks Corporation. The price was expressed in Maltese pounds, which had been agreed as the currency of account, and the claim was 'justifiably'[35] made in that currency. The only remaining issue for the Commercial Court was choice of the appropriate currency in which to express judgment and of the rate of interest to be applied. Kerr J was faced with a choice of three possible rates: English, German and Maltese. The sum of 105 000 Maltese pounds, which should have been paid to the plaintiffs in 1972, was eventually paid in 1976. As a result, the plaintiffs had to borrow in Germany in the interim at German commercial borrowing rates, which at that time were said to be approaching 15 per cent per annum. Kerr J decided to differ from the rule which Bristow J had adopted, and held that over the period in question the plaintiffs were entitled to interest payable in Maltese pounds, but based on prevailing commercial borrowing rates in Germany. Certainly, the case before him was more complicated than the *Miliangos* case in that the currency in which judgment would have been made, Maltese pounds, was not the currency of the plaintiffs. But Kerr J, in his attempt to fully compensate the plaintiffs seems to have erred in the procedure that he followed in his calculations.

Two plausible lines of argument may be followed in the calculations. The first entails the assumption that the plaintiffs, had they received the money that they were due when it became payable, would have held it in an account in Germany. Had they done so, or been treated as having done so, the appropriate procedure would have been to convert the sum payable in 1972 in Maltese pounds into German currency at the exchange rate ruling at the time, and to then apply German interest rates for the period 1972–76 over which the plaintiffs had forgone use of the funds. The second line of argument is that the funds would have been held in an account in Malta over the period in question. In this event the calculation would have proceeded by applying Maltese interest rates over the period to the basic sum expressed in Maltese pounds. The amount of principal and interest could then have been converted, if required, into German currency at the rate of exchange prevailing at the time of judgment.

The method of calculation followed by Kerr J conformed to neither of these two methods but represented what we have described elsewhere as a 'conceptually unsatisfactory hybrid' (Bowles and Whelan, 1979b, p. 240). By continuing to express the basic sum in Maltese pounds when applying German rates Kerr J suppresses the influence of the change in the exchange rate between the currencies over the period. A Maltese investor would certainly not expect to be offered German interest rates by his national bank or anyone else on a Maltese pound account just as a German investor would not earn Maltese interest rates on a Deutsche Mark account.

11.4.3 Uncertainty

Returning to the more general issue of the relation between interest rates and exchange rates, it is possible to derive the impact of interest rate differentials upon the size of interest payable on damages in recent times. There are various ways in which this could be done, although the essentials of the calculations remain the same, namely to isolate the increase in the amount that is to be payable as a result of exchange rate deterioration and the offsetting amount that is due to the existence of an interest rate differential. The possibility that this offsetting amount may be large means that exchange rate instability will not itself be the only factor to take into account when decisions are being made about the currency in which losses are to be expressed.

Table 11.3 *Net advantage of the sterling rule for French, Swiss and American plaintiffs over 2 year periods, 1966–79*

Period	*USA* $\varnothing us$	*France* $\varnothing f$	*Switzerland* $\varnothing sw$
1966–68	–0.1345	–0.1126	–0.1110
1967–69	–0.1505	–0.1327	–0.1209
1968–70	+0.0404	+0.1659	+0.0896
1969–71	+0.0335	+0.1212	+0.0787
1970–72	+0.0854	–0.0140	+0.0131
1971–73	–0.0020	–0.1275	–0.1368
1972–74	–0.0863	–0.2225	–0.2766
1973–75	+0.0100	–0.0928	–0.2596
1974–76	–0.1235	–0.3046	–0.2595
1975–77	–0.3528	–0.1958	–0.3240
1976–78	+0.0799	+0.0063	–0.1274
1977–79	–0.2158	–0.0147	–0.1895

Notes: The figures are calculated by applying equation (7) of the appendix to data taken from *International Financial Statistics*. They refer to the number of pounds sterling by which plaintiffs in the different countries would have been better off under the sterling rule rather than under the plaintiff's currency rule, per pound, over each period.

One method that produces results that can be relatively easily interpreted is to calculate the net advantage or disadvantage that application of the sterling rule rather than the plaintiff's currency rule would generate for plaintiffs. That is, we take a sum of £1 at the beginning of year one and calculate the sterling sum that application of the two different rules would generate by the end of, say, year two. The sum generated by the sterling rule is simply the basic sum of £1 plus interest (calculated as in the courts at simple rather than compound rates). The sum generated by the plaintiff's currency rule is calculated by exchanging the £1 into the plaintiff's currency at the rate ruling at the start of year one, adding interest calculated at the simple rate prevailing in the plaintiff's country and converting the total generated back into sterling at the exchange rate ruling at the end of year two. An algebraic account of these two alternative procedures appears in the appendix to this chapter.

Table 11.3 illustrates the net effect of applying the sterling rule rather than the plaintiff's currency rule for a succession of the two year periods between 1966 and 1979. It shows that for the most part the deterioration resulting from a fall in the value of sterling exceeds the gain resulting from UK interest rates being relatively high, at least in the case of comparisons between the UK and France and the UK and Switzerland. Comparison in the case of the USA suggests that roughly half the time the sterling rule would generate larger sums for the plaintiff than would the plaintiff's currency rule.

The observation has the important implication that the new rule is not a universal panacea for foreign plaintiffs and suggests that given a choice, they might frequently opt for the sterling rule. In his dissenting judgment in *Miliangos*, Lord Simon argued that 'the foreign creditor will have the benefit of movement of the exchange rates either way: if sterling is appreciating, he will sue in sterling; if it is depreciating, he will sue for the foreign money. This strikes me as highly unjust to the English debtor, as well as importing an undesirable element of monetary speculation into English litigation.'[36]

The apparent uncertainty that a choice of currency engenders was not adequately answered by Lord Wilberforce. In *Miliangos* he argued that 'the relevant certainty which the rule ought to achieve is that which gives the creditor neither more nor less than he bargained for.'[37] In his speech in the *SEAS* and *Despina* cases when faced with a choice of currency however, he merely pointed out that the plaintiff must prove his case and show that use of a particular currency must be reasonably foreseeable if damages were to be awarded in that currency[38]. But lingering uncertainties remain. Thus, in the *SEAS* case, at first instance, Goff J held that since he could not imply from the contract an agreement to pay damages in US dollars (which was also the plaintiff's currency), he held that the award should be made in the currency in which the loss was incurred, that is, Brazilian cruzeiros, the expenditure currency[39]. Yet on appeal, both the Court of Appeal[40] and the House of Lords opted for the plaintiff's currency, which, they held, best expressed the losses incurred.

Lord Wilberforce in *Despina R* was content to observe that 'there should be no automatic and invariable rule to this effect: if, in the circumstances, he fails to satisfy the court or arbitrators, they may give judgment or award in whatever other currency represents his loss.'[41] The need, ultimately, to rely on a judicial response itself creates further uncertainty.

11.5 Behaviour of defendants

The relation between interest rates and exchange rates has been shown to have implications for the calculation of the sum required to restore the direct losses of plaintiffs. It is clear that the choice between the different rules will also have consequences for the behaviour of defendants. Rational defendants face some quite interesting calculations if they are to minimize the discomfort they are themselves to suffer in meeting any award made by the courts. This behaviour is of relevance, since it may affect the decisions that individuals make about the terms on which to enter into contracts. It is also of relevance once the individual is 'locked in' to a situation in which a breach of contract or a tort has occurred, since it may affect negotiations and any settlement that occurs out of court.

For the sake of simplicity let us take the following example. An English party causes harm to an American party in 1979 that the former estimates at about £1000, there being no serious question about liability. At that time, £1 = $2, and the Englishman anticipates being successfully sued in the English courts but decides nevertheless to contest the claim. Since the Exchange Control Regulations have recently been abolished[42], the English party anticipating application of the plaintiffs currency rule has a number of possible courses of action open to him, namely:

(1) buy 2000 US dollars immediately on the spot market and invest them in US securities;
(2) buy forward the number of dollars necessary to meet the claim that will finally be made (including interest);
(3) buy no dollars and continue to operate purely in sterling;
(4) some combination of (1) to (3).

Had he expected application of the sterling rule, then there would have been no reason to buy any dollars at all. In the context of the plaintiff's currency rule, the situation is more complex. If the defendant had knowledge of the date at which the claim was to be settled and reliable information about both UK and US interest rates over the period, then he might be expected to reason as follows. Actions (1) and (2) are both essentially 'certain' methods of generating the sum of dollars that will ultimately be needed: the defendant would thus immediately reject the more expensive of these options. Action (2) is the riskiest method, since a depreciation of sterling, not totally offset by a UK interest rate advantage, will make the meeting of a dollar claim relatively expensive. It is also possible, however, that sterling may appreciate or its depreciation be more than offset by an interest rate differential so that holding sterling in the interim and buying spot dollars at the date of judgment might be the cheapest possible solution. The most likely view that defendants in this position will take is that they would like to eliminate some, but not all, of the risk. If it is assumed that defendants are risk-averse and that to remain in sterling would on average reduce the costs of meeting the claim (as compared with the lower of (1) and

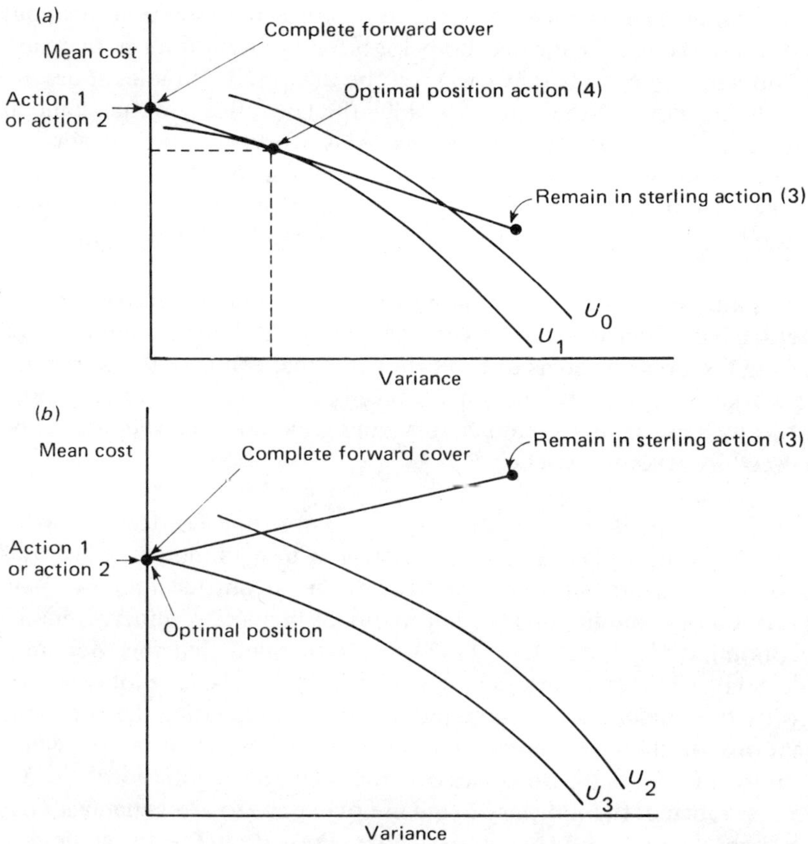

Figure 11.1 *Mean-variance analysis of defendant behaviour under the plaintiff's currency rule: (a) when sterling is expected to be strong; (b) when sterling is expected to be weak*

(2)), then defendants could be expected to buy some dollars, but not as many as they anticipated finally spending. If sterling was expected to prove a morc costly method of meeting the claim on average, then the defendant could be expected to cover the whole of his expected liability *ab initio* by buying current or forward dollars, whichever were the cheapest for his purposes. These two cases are illustrated by *Figures 11.1(a)* and *11.1(b)* respectively.

11.6 Conclusions

The series of recent developments in the English law relating to judgments in foreign currencies has given rise to some interesting difficulties, as has been outlined above. In making an assessment about whether the reforms that have taken place have as yet led to a satisfactory solution or about whether the judiciary are the best body for bringing about reform, there are some important questions that remain to be answered. Prominent among these is the question of the extent to which the law reflects, or has come to reflect, conditions prevailing in the everyday world to which it applies. Whilst this is recognized by the judiciary, it may give rise to reservations about the extent to which the judiciary themselves are capable of fully apprehending all the issues. Lord Wilberforce is surely right in arguing:

> But if I am faced with the alternative of forcing commercial circles to fall in with a legal doctrine which has nothing but precedent to commend it or altering the doctrine so as to conform with what commercial experience has worked out, I know where my choice lies. The law should be responsive as well as, at times, enunciatory, and good doctrine can seldom be divorced from sound practice.[43]

At the same time however it is interesting to note that Lord Simon, in his dissenting speech, argued that a matter such as foreign money obligations demanded 'the contribution of expertise from far outside the law — on monetary theory, public finance, international finance, commerce, industry, economics.'[44] While Mann (1976, p. 168) stated that this view may involve 'some slight exaggeration', it is submitted that the case for experts is proved by the inadequacy of most judges in comprehending the economic implications of their judgments and by the ensuing uncertainty, which profoundly influences the processes of settlement and negotiation[45].

The resistance of the judiciary to the use of experts to assess damages has been widely documented (*see*, in particular, Prevett, 1972). In the field of foreign money obligations, judges do not apear to have taken expert advice on how foreign exchange markets operate or how foreign interest rates work. It is difficult therefore to resist the view that on occasion the correct rule or decision is reached by incorrect or incomplete argument and that on other occasions mistakes are made[46].

The judicial process may itself be ineffective as a means of law reform. In 1971, Mann argued (p. 371), regarding the problem of the sterling and breach-date rules, that if the rules of procedure were not altered, 'a satisfactory solution cannot now be achieved except by legislation.' He repeated this view even after the *Miliangos* decision, which he praised. He regarded the sorting out of undecided questions by further litigation as 'an invidious method, for it would be expensive, slow and productive of uncertainty.' He concluded, 'let us protect private parties against the vicissitudes of litigation.' (Mann, 1976, p. 168).

The costs of litigation are well-known to be high. Court hearings use up large amounts of the time of highly paid workers, although in the present context any such costs have to be compared with the costs of the legislative process. These latter may also be high, for they too will involve the input of legal and other expertise. Reliance upon the adversarial system may have the effect of slowing down the process of law reform because the plaintiff who is risk-averse may be very reluctant to press a claim that would require a new ruling. The successful plaintiff does not receive any 'bonus' for winning, even though his actions may raise the sums negotiated in out-of-court settlements by others in a similar position and even though pursuing his own cause opens him up to considerable uncertainty.

It is apposite in conclusion to consider the implications of the English experience for countries that retain rules of a pre-*Miliangos* kind. One such country is Canada, where s. 11 of the Currency and Exchange Act 1970 restricts judgments to Canadian dollars[47]. The suggestion that Canada should follow on the heels of the judicial response in England (*see* Riordan, 1978) is in danger of overlooking the difficulties that have been encountered in the cases since *Miliangos*.

Whilst an evolutionary force of some kind that reduces the life expectancy of bad rules as compared with good rules may be at work, the very considerable inertia of the common law system and the other obstacles referred to above, mean that judicial responses to complex problems may on occasion lack vision.

Notes to chapter eleven

1 An earlier version of this chapter was presented at the SSRC Law and Economics Seminar held at Hertford College Oxford in January 1980. We would like to thank participants in the seminar, particularly the discussant M.J. Elliott, for helpful comments.

2 *Miliangos v George Frank (Textiles) Ltd*, [1976] AC 443; see Bowles and Phillips (1976).

3 These were established in *Celia (SS) (Owners) v SS Volturno (Owners) (The Volturno)*, [1921] 2 AC 544, and *Re United Railways of Havana and Regla Warehouses Ltd*, [1961] AC 1007.

4 *Re United Railways, op. cit.*

5 *Ottoman Bank v Chakarian (No. 1)*, [1930] AC 277.

6 *The Volturno, op. cit.*; these rules were 'settled and beyond doubt': *MacGregor on Damages* (1972), p. 341.

7 *Philips v Ward*, [1956] 1 WLR 471, 474 *per* Lord Denning MR.

8 *The Baarn (No. 1)*, [1933] P 251, 265, quoted in Mann (1971), p. 85.

9 *Treseder-Griffin v Co-operative Insurance Society*, [1956] 2 QB 127, 144. Lord Denning repeated this view in the House of Lords: *Re United Railways, op. cit.*, p. 1069.

10 *Re United Railways, op. cit.*, p. 1069.

11 Moreover, reform of the law in 1975 was preceded by Article 106 of the Treaty of Rome which obliged English Courts to give judgment in the currency of a member state if that was the currency of the contract: see *Schorsch Meier GmbH v Hennin*, [1975] QB 416.

12 *Cash v Kennion*, 11 Ves 315, quoted in Mann (1971), p. 369.

13 *The Teh Hu*, [1970] P 106, 124 per Lord Denning MR in dissent.

14 *Practice Statement (Judicial Precedent)*, [1966] 1 WLR 1234.

15 [1976] AC 443.

16 Ibid., p. 468 *per* Lord Wilberforce.

17 [1975] QB 487.

18 *Schorsch Meier*, op. cit.

19 For example, *Jean Kraut AG v Albany Fabrics Ltd.*, [1977] QB 182; *Owners of MV Eleftherotria v Owners of MV Despina R*; and *Services Europe Atlantique Sud*

(*SEAS*) *of Paris v Stockholms Reteriaktiebolag SVEA of Stockholm*, [1979] AC 685.
20 [1976] AC 443, 465.
21 *The Despina R,* op cit., p. 704 *per* Lord Russell of Killowen.
22 *Miliangos,* op cit., p. 463 *per* Lord Wilberforce.
23 *George Veflings Rederi A/S v president of India* [1979] 1 WLR 59, 62 *per* Lord Denning MR; *Barclays Bank International Ltd v Levin Brothers (Bradford) Ltd,* [1977] 2 QB 270, 282 *per* Mocatta J.
24 Op. cit.; see Bowles and Whelan (1979a).
25 [1979] AC 685, 696 *et. seq. per* Lord Wilberforce.
26 Ibid., p. 702.
27 Ibid., pp. 696–97.
28 Ibid., p. 697.
29 Ibid., p. 701, adopting the words of Lord Denning MR in the present case, [1979] QB 491, 514.
30 Ibid., p. 698.
31 Ibid., p. 701.
32 Ibid., p. 703.
33 *Miliangos v George Frank (Textiles) Ltd, (No. 2),* [1977] QB 489, 497.
34 [1977] 2 Lloyd's Rep 444.
35 Ibid., p. 448.
36 [1976] AC 443, 482.
37 Ibid., p. 466.
38 [1979] AC 685, 697, 698, 699.
39 [1977] 3 WLR 176.
40 [1978] 2 WLR 887.
41 [1979] AC 685, 699.
42 On exchange controls generally, see Shuster (1973).
43 [1976] AC 443, 464.
44 Ibid., p. 481.
45 See, for example, Phillips and Hawkins (1976); Phillips, Hawkins and Flemming (1975).
46 For a discussion of this contention in the related context of mortgage contracts, see Bowles (1977), which examines *Multi-Service Bookbinding Ltd and others v Marden,* [1978] 2 WLR 535.
47 RSC 1970 cC–39.

References

ATIYAH, P.S. (1971), *An Introduction to the Law of Contract*, Oxford: Clarendon Press.

BOWLES, R.A. (1977), *The Linking of Mortgages to Foreign Currency Indices*, unpublished, University of Nottingham.

BOWLES, R.A. and PHILLIPS, J. (1976), Judgments in foreign currencies: extension of the Miliangos rule, *Modern Law Review*, **39**, no. 4, 196–201.

BOWLES, R.A. and WHELAN, C.J. (1979a), Judgments in foreign currencies: extension of the Miliangos rule, *Modern Law Review*, **42**, no. 4, 452–458.

BOWLES, R.A. AND WHELAN, C.J. (1979b), The currency of suit in actions for damages, *McGill Law Journal*, **25**, no. 2, 236–243.

CALABRESI, G. (1979), *The Costs of Accidents: A Legal and Economic Anjalysis*, New Haven, Conn: Yale University Press.

HIRSCH, W.Z. (1979), *Law and Economics: An Introductory Analysis*, London: Academic Press.

MANN, F.A. (1971), *The Legal Aspect of Money*, 3rd ed., Oxford: Clarendon Press.

MANN, F.A. (1971), Case note of Miliangos, *Law Quarterly Review*, **92**, 165–168.

McGREGOR on *Damages* (1980), 4th ed., London: Sweet and Maxwell

PHILLIPS, J. and HAWKINS, K. (1976), Some economic aspects of the settlement process: a study of personal injury claims, *Modern Law Review*, **39**, no. 5, 497–515.

PHILLIPS, J., HAWKINS, K.O. and FLEMMING, J. (1975), Compensation for personal injuries, *Economic Journal*, **85**, no. 337, 129–134.

PREVETT, J.H. (1972), Actuarial assessment of damages: the Thalidomide case, *Modern Law Review*, **35**, 140–155, 257–267.

RIORDAN, B. (1978), The currency of suit in actions for foreign debts, *McGill Law Journal*, **24**, 422–441.

SHUSTER, M.R. (1973), *The Public International Law of Money*, Oxford: Clarendon Press.

Appendix 11.1

Comparison of the rules for calculating damages

A party to a contract (subsequently the plaintiff) expects to receive an amount W in his own currency at date t_0, at which time the exchange rate, giving the number of units of his own currency that may be bought with one unit of sterling, is e_{t_0}. The defendant fails to pay on the date specified and is sued by the plaintiff. Judgment is given at date t_1 by which time the exchange rate is e_{t_1}. In the days prior to the *Miliangos* decision, the court would make an award of A_1 units of sterling, where:

$$A_1 = W/e_{t_0} \tag{1}$$

The value of this award to the plaintiff is measured by the number of units of his own currency that this will buy. This amount is obviously

$$e_{t_1}A_1 = W\, e_{t_1}/e_{t_0} \tag{2}$$

and thus in the event that the plaintiff's currency is appreciating against sterling, the plaintiff will lose out since $e_{t_1} < e_{t_0}$, which implies that the $e_{t_1}A_1$ that he receives is less than the original amount W.

In order to facilitate a comparison of this original sterling rule with the recently-adopted plaintiff's currency rule, take the interval between the initial date t_0 and the day on which the court sets down judgment to comprise T equal periods. The exchange rate at the day of judgment is given as e_T, whilst the interest rate in the plaintiff's currency is r_t^P in period t and in sterling is r_t^{UK} in period t. The traditional sterling rule generates a total award A_2 of:

$$A_2 = \frac{W}{e_{t_0}}(1 + \sum_{t=t_0}^{T} r_t^{UK})\, e_T \tag{3}$$

The plaintiff's currency rule on the other hand generates an award A_3 of:

$$A_3 = W(1 + \sum_{t=t_0}^{T} r_t^P) \tag{4}$$

where both awards are measured in terms of units of the plaintiffs currency. If the plaintiff were given a choice between the two rules we could expect him to adopt a decision rule under which he chooses the sterling rule if A_2 exceeds A_3 but not otherwise. That is to say that he would choose the sterling rule in those cases where the following inequality was satisfied:

$$A_2 - A_3 > 0$$

i.e.

$$(1 + \sum_{t=t_0}^{T} r_t^{UK}) e_T / e_{t_0} > (1 + \sum_{t=t_0}^{T} r_t^{P}) \qquad (5)$$

Clearly, this decision depends purely upon the relationship between interest rate differentials and exchange rate changes and is invariant with respect to the size of award.

A convenient way to express the impact of exchange rate changes net of interest rate differentials is to define a new variable ∅ where:

$$\varnothing \equiv (A_2 - A_3)/W \qquad (6)$$

The variable ∅ measures the net advantage per unit of sterling of applying the sterling rule rather than the plaintiff's currency rule. Denoting the mean interest rate in England over the T periods beginning at t_0 by $r^{\mathbf{UK}}$ and the mean interest rate in the plaintiff's currency over the same period by $r^{\mathbf{P}}$, equations (3), (4) and (6) can be combined to give:

$$\varnothing = (1 + Tr^{\mathbf{UK}})\, e_T/e_{t_0} - (1 + Tr^{\mathbf{P}}) \qquad (7)$$

The plaintiff's choice of rule will be governed by whether, over the period at issue, ∅ is positive or negative. *Table 11.3* in this chapter includes calculations of ∅ under a variety of conditions.

PART FOUR

Public law

The essay by Hirsch is concerned with the evolution of landlord–tenant laws in England and the United States, and with the welfare implications of these laws for tenants in both countries. From his theoretical and empirical analysis the author concludes that the strengthening of tenants' legal rights in the post-war period does not appear to have benefited tenants in the way the new laws were intended to do.

Fenn investigates legal rule-making in unemployment compensation schemes, with particular reference to rules relating to the disqualification of claimants due to their dismissal from employment through misconduct. Drawing a parallel between misconduct rules and contributory negligence, the analysis shows that recent developments in labour law in the UK have increased the incentive for employers to facilitate the enforcement of the misconduct rule, particularly at times of depressed demand for the employers' products.

Feldman and Kay argue that most tax avoidance opportunities are provided by the difficulties involved in arriving at legally operational interpretations of the economist's preferred definition and measurement of income. They contrast these problems with the relative ease of devising expenditure taxes that are hard to avoid.

CHAPTER TWELVE

Landlord–tenant relations law

Werner Z. Hirsch

12.1 Introduction

American property law is rooted in English common law. How, then, have landlord–tenant laws evolved in the two countries since the end of World War II, and what have been their effects, particularly on the welfare of tenants in England and the United States? These are the issues of concern to this chapter.

The traditional landlord–tenant relationship, originally weighted heavily in favour of the landlord, has been greatly modified since the end of World War II. In both countries, courts and legislations, partly in recognition of severe housing shortages, have created and extended the rights of residential tenants. Regulations that have emanated from the courts and legislatures have generally been in the form of habitability, rent control, just-cause eviction and age discrimination laws. They all have one important common feature. Each and every one of these measures places additional burdens on landlords, and all too often little attention is paid to the likely reaction to these burdens of landlords and investors in housing. Depending on a housing market's demand and supply conditions, landlords, for example, may respond to such increased costs by absorbing the costs and operating at a lower profit, by passing the costs on in the form of higher rent, by abandoning the building or by any combination of these. Clearly, the second and the third alternatives are detrimental to the welfare of low-income tenants.

This chapter is written in the spirit of Judge Skelly Wright who declared in 1972. 'We cannot expect judges to solve the housing dilemma, but at least they should avoid affirmative action which makes it worse.'[1] In line with this admonition, I will first summarize a number of landlord–tenant laws. Then I will engage in a limited analysis of some welfare implications, employing microeconomic, and sometimes econometric, techniques. I would like to emphasize that the welfare analysis only examines selected welfare dimensions.

However, before we engage in this effort, I would like to point to two parallel undertakings of the mid-1970s in the United Kingdom and in the United States. In 1975 the Law Commission (Law Com. No. 67) handed to the Lord High Chancellor its proposed *Codification of the Law of Landlord and Tenant* who in turn on 11 June 1975 laid this *Report on Obligations of Landlords and Tenants* before Parliament (Law Commissioners, 1975). The Report proposes *inter alia* that particular obligations of landlords and tenants be divided into two classes — mandatory obligations that cannot be varied or excluded and variable obligations that can be varied or excluded by agreement of the parties. The important mandatory obligations included the tenant's right to exclusive possession of the premises and their quiet enjoyment; the tenant's mandatory obligation to pay rent, to protect the premises and to disclose his identity; as well as the landlord's obligations to disclose his identity.

The Law Commission also recommended that tenancy for a term of less than seven years be governed by an overriding covenant obliging the landlord to repair the structure and interior of a dwelling. In tenancies of a furnished dwelling for a term not exceeding 20 years there should be an implied, but variable, covenant by the landlord to keep the entirety of the premises in repair. In tenancies over 20 years and in the absence of expressed agreement, the entire responsibility for repairs of the premises should be imposed on the tenant.

On May 21, 1976, the American Law Institute adopted *Restatement of the Law: Property 2d — Landlord* and *Tenant* (American Law Institute, 1976). According to its section on habitability, a court could hold that a landlord had breached a covenant of habitability even though he had an agreement with a tenant on a month-to-month basis that clearly indicated that both landlord and tenant were fully aware of housing code violation. Remedies available to tenant include rescission, damages, rent abatement and rent withholding. Moreover, tenants are protected against retaliatory eviction.

12.2 Habitability laws

12.2.1 Nature of laws

Before World War II, most of the American states retained the common law rule that landlords owed no duty to deliver and maintain habitable housing. Thus they subscribed to the doctrine of *caveat emptor*. Moreover, the lessee's covenant to pay rent was considered independent of the lessor's covenant to provide habitable housing. After World War II many American cities enacted housing codes, which, however, were rarely enforced. Courts and legislators responded by providing a number of remedies allowing tenants to initiate code enforcement.

In the United States remedies took the form of repair-and-deduct, rent withholding and receivership laws (Hirsch, Hirsch and Margolis, 1975). They were supplemented by anti-retaliatory eviction laws. Developments in the United Kingdom were similar to those in the United States.

The repair-and-deduct remedy constitutes a self-help measure. It allows the tenant, upon his own initiative, to repair his defective premises and deduct the repair charges from his rent, after the landlord has been notified of the defect and has failed to act within a reasonable time. This remedy is limited to minor defects and represents for the landlord the least costly code enforcement mechanism.

Rent withholding can rely on an escrow method or rent abatement. In the first case, the tenant pays rent into a court-created escrow account. Rental income is withheld from the landlord until violations are corrected. Three states (Illinois, Michigan and New York) (ibid., p. 1107) even authorize rent withholdings by the state Welfare Department or some other agency. An alternative is rent abatement, which permits a tenant to remain in possession of premises without paying rent, or paying a reduced amount, until housing defects are remedied. The condition of the premises constitutes a defence either to an action of eviction or to an action for rent. Since the actual differences between withholding and abatement are very small, they will be treated together.

Receivership involves appointment by the court of a receiver who takes control of the building and who corrects hazardous defects, after a landlord has failed to act within a reasonable period. If large scale repairs that cannot be financed through rental payments are needed, some statutes permit the receiver to seek additional loans. In so doing, old first liens are converted into new second liens, imposing particularly heavy costs on the lender and, therefore, ultimately on the landlord. Rent is deposited with the court-appointed receiver until the violation is corrected. As long as the tenant continues to pay rent into escrow, the landlord cannot evict for non-payment.

Of these three remedies, receivership is the most potent for assuring habitable housing and at the same time the most costly to the landlord. All rental income to the landlord is stopped, because all tenants in the building, not only the aggrieved ones, pay rents into escrow. Moreover, the landlord loses control over his building to a receiver who may be enthusiastic about fixing-up the building, possibly even above minimum standards established by housing codes. Finally, contrary to most repair-and-deduct and withholding laws, receivership is usually initiated by the government, which is backed by large legal resources.

The three major remedies are often supplemented by laws that can reinforce them — retalitory eviction, for instance, which is designed to protect tenants from being penalized by landlords for complaining against housing code violations. Such laws usually freeze rents for 90 days after compliance.

In the United Kingdom there exist various laws providing for compulsory improvements and repair. For example, the Housing Act of 1974 in Part VIII provides powers to compel landlords to provide a bathroom and other standard amenities on request from a tenant (Hadden, 1978). This requirement, which had existed since 1964, was intended by the 1974 Act to include repairs associated with the provision of standard amenities, and also to permit local authorities to act without a formal request from a tenant. In response to representation from a tenant, local authorities inform the owner and then inspect the premises and finally prepare a schedule of work and an estimate of costs. Under certain circumstances steps are initiated by the local authority as a result of house-to-house inspection. At any time within six weeks the owner may appeal to the county court on the ground that the notice is invalid, for example that the expense involved is unreasonable or that the standard of repairs required is unreasonable in relation to the age, character and locality of the house. Once the notice has become operative, the owner has a further six months to decide whether or not to serve a purchase notice on the local authority. If no action of any kind has been taken by the owner on the expiration of the six month period, the local authority may then serve a formal reminder asking whether the owner intends to carry out the work. Should this not produce a satisfactory response, the local authority may then serve further notice stating that it intends to carry out the work in default, and after a further 21 days may do so. Alternatively, it may wait until the full 12 months have expired and then act in default, though it must still give the owner 21 days notice of its intention to do so. In either instance, the cost of the work may then be recovered from the owner, subject to further provision of an appeal against the amount claimed.

Procedures for compelling owners to carry out repairs on their property have been successfully instituted under the Public Health Act of 1936 and 1961. Large authorities are reported to issue hundreds or thousands of formal and informal notices per year under these statutes compared to tens or hundreds under the Housing Act. Compulsory repair under the Public Health Act requires a finding of a statutory nuisance. As such it must either be prejudicial to the health of an occupier of the house in question or a nuisance that is a danger or an annoyance to adjoining occupiers or other people in the area. It appears that the Public Health Act has been mainly used to require owners to remedy relatively inexpensive defects.

12.2.2 Welfare effects of habitability laws

In order to estimate some welfare effects of the various habitability laws, it is necessary to estimate a rental housing demand and supply system. Habitability laws are included among the explanatory variables so as to permit estimation of the extent to which both the demand and the supply function tend to shift upward in the presence of particular laws. To the extent that such laws are enforced and lead to improved repair and maintenance, the tenants' well-being is enhanced, and an upward shift of the demand function will occur. On the supply side, habitability laws can affect maintenance and repair decisions. Together with the potential legal costs, they can lead to an upward shift of the supply function. Welfare conclusions can be derived by comparing the vertical shift of these two functions.

Estimation of the rental housing demand and supply system is complicated by the nature of housing, a complex commodity with both stock and flow characteristics. Since the flow of housing services does not easily lend itself to measurement, we will use a hedonic approach to housing services. It provides a method for measuring the distinctive characteristics of a dwelling and permits the expression of these characteristics as a single quantity that reflects the market's consensus about their relative importance. The larger this quantity, that is the larger the flow of housing service units associated with a given dwelling, the higher is the quality. Landlords who comply with habitability laws and invest in repair and maintenance, thus, provide enlarged quantities of housing services and better housing quality.

This concept of flow of housing services permits us to view rent as the value of a dwelling that stems from the quantity of characteristics — housing service units — its contents and their prices. Under certain assumptions about the competitiveness of the housing market, a hedonic approach can therefore help estimate implicit or shadow housing service prices and quantities, which can then be used for the estimation of housing demand and supply functions.

In the hedonic price approach, the dependent variable — monthly gross rent including utilities (*R*) — is regressed against five quantity variables (*QUAN*) and four classes of quality variables[2]:

$$R = \mathrm{f}(QUAN, INDW, NEHDA, NEHDB, PUBSP) \quad (1)$$

Housing characteristics are grouped into quantity characteristics (*QUAN*); number of rooms, age of building, number of bathrooms, presence of air conditioning and use of rented parking: and four classes of quality characteristics; quality inside the dwelling (*INDW*) — similar to the 'Dwelling Unit Quality' variable of Kain and Quigley (1970), neighbourhood quality that relates to physical characteristics of area (*NEHDA*) — similar to the 'Quality of Proximate Properties' and 'Basic Residential Quality' variables used by Kain and Quigley, neighbourhood quality that relates to public services provided in the area (*NEHDB*), and the quality of public space inside the building (*PUBSP*). Thirty-three housing quality variables are used. Variable definitions and sources are given in appendix 12.1.

Rent is expected to have a positive relation with each of the five quantity variables, and a negative relation with each of the four (lack of) quality variables, since the index number assigned to a dwelling increases with its shortcomings, i.e. as its quality declines.

Rent equations were estimated for each of 70 geographical regions in the United States in both semilog and linear form[3]. The rent equations in semilog form for 70 geographic regions, located by 34 Standard Metropolitan Statistical Areas (SMSAs) and covering 25 states plus the District of Columbia, has a coefficient of determination (R^2) ranging from 0.15 in Westmoreland County, Pennsylvania, to 0.73 in Montgomery County, Maryland[4]. Among the quality groups, the Inside Dwelling Quality (*INDW*) performs best both in terms of signs and statistical significance, followed by Public Space Quality (*PUBSP*), Physical Neighborhood Quality (*NEHDA*), and Public Services Neighborhood Quality (*NEHDB*). In a very few cases the last two variables, while statistically significant, have a wrong sign. Of the five quantity variables, number of rooms performs best, followed by age of building, number of bathrooms, presence of air conditioning and renting of parking. The whole set of nine variables is found to be significantly different from zero at a 95 per cent level (one-tailed test) for all regions except Kane County, Illinois. Altogether the magnitudes of the net regression coefficients are found to be consistent among all geographic regions.

From the 70 hedonic rent equations, rental housing price and quantity indices were computed by specifying a standard bundle of housing services and using hedonic values to calculate the cost of the standard bundle in each region. In order to obtain quantity indexes we defined an average price vector for the entire sample size and coupled that with the mean values of housing characteristics purchased in each geographic region. The price index of any one region can thus be formulated as the sum of the cross-product terms between the estimated hedonic values of that region and the fixed bundle of housing attributes. The quantity index of a given region is a price-weighted average of the quantities purchased. The prices in this index are the hedonic values averaged across geographic regions. The index is formulated as the sum of the cross-product term between the means of the estimated hedonic values of the entire sample size and the mean value of housing attributes purchased by a representative region.

With the aid of the estimated implicit or shadow housing prices and quantities, demand and supply functions are estimated. The functional form of the demand function can be expressed as

$$P_I = g(Q_I, L_I, Y_I, T_I, B_I) \tag{2}$$

where P_I = price index of region I; Q_I = quantity index of region I; L_I = law variables of region I; Y_I = incomes variables of region I; T_I = taste variable of region I; B_I = price of non-housing commodities variable of region I.

In relation to the status of habitability laws, dummy variables were used to distinguish housing locations with active habitability laws from those without such laws — one if an active law is present and zero if not. The dummy variables not only reflect presence or absence of a habitability law, but also, wherever possible, status of enforcement. The issue of enforcement may have been less complicated than under most circumstances, since the case filing pattern of our study of New York

(Hirsch, Hirsch and Margolis, 1975, pp. 1135–1136) and that of Mosier and Soble (1973) of Detroit is very similar. In both instances, shortly after a habitability law appeared on the scene, many cases were filed during the first few years, hitting a peak after 5–6 years. By far the largest number of habitability laws studied by us relative to 1974–75 were passed in the preceding 4–6 years. Moreover, during those years most states had very active legal aid attorneys assisting indigent tenants. Therefore, enforcement was uniformly stringent.

Therefore, we introduce three law variables in the form of dummy variables[5]:

REPAIR — identifies states with repair and deduct laws in 1974;
EWHOLD — identifies states with both witholding laws and retaliatory eviction laws in 1974;
RECEIV — identifies states with receivership laws in 1974.

All three laws, if enforced, impose costs on landlords and therefore are expected to be positively correlated with price. As an income variable, we use median family income of renters in 1974–75 (*FAMINCO*) and expect it to be positively correlated with price. As a taste variable we introduced mean annual rent payments by indigents as a percentage of median family SMSA income in 1974–75 (*OREUT*). This percentage testifies to some extent to households' preference for housing compared to other goods and services. A positive correlation with price is expected. In the absence of data on non-housing prices for our 34 SMSAs — the Bureau of Labor Statistics cover only 12 of them — we have used, following de Leeuw and Ekanem (1971), a price level proxy (*PRICELEV*)[6]. Housing is an important item in consumer's budgets, and we do not know whether its price varies directly with the general price level or inversely with it. In the former case, the correlation would be positive and in the latter negative.

The functional form of the supply function can be expressed as

$$P_I = \mathrm{h}(Q_I, L_I, K_I)^7 \qquad (3)$$

where P_I, Q_I and L_I have the meaning as in equation (2) and K_I = vector of cost of production variables in region I, i.e. *PERPTAX* = per capita property tax in \$000s in 1974–75, *LAND* = per square foot land value of dwellings in 1974 and *CONWAGE* = hourly wages of building helpers and labourers in 1974[8]. We expect the quantity, law and production cost variables to be all positively correlated with price.

In order to estimate demand and supply function, a two-stage least squares method is employed. The first stage is designed to find an instrumental variable that correlates with the dependent variable, but has zero correlation with the disturbance term. Then the instrumental variables are used in the second stage to estimate supply and demand equations. Since the system is overidentified, we are not able to obtain a unique set of structural parameters from the reduced form parameters. Of the four possible sets of structural equations we have selected that which gives results consistent with our underlying hypotheses, i.e. demand function $P = f(Q)$ and supply function $P = h(Q)$. Moreover, price (P) varies more than quantity (Q). Several functional forms were tried in estimation; an inverse semilogarithmic form gave the best results. The results of the semilog formulation are presented in *Table 12.1*.

Table 12.1 *Regression results for demand and supply functions for 70 geographical areas; inverse semilog with log price as dependent variable*

	DEMAND		*SUPPLY*	
	Coefficient	*t-stat.*	*Coefficient*	*t-stat.*
INTERCEPT	4.143	17.20*	3.118	6.57*
QUAN(b)	–0.0069	–4.87*	0.0079	3.25*
EWHOLD	0.022	0.98	0.072	1.43
RECEIV	0.046	2.05**	0.156	3.27*
REPAIR	–0.0026	–0.14	0.019	0.43
PRICELEV	0.0093	1.96**	(*a*)	–
FAMINCO	0.063	3.19*	(*a*)	–
OREUT	0.0034	11.79*	(*a*)	–
PERPTAX	(*a*)	–	0.561	2.40*
CONWAGE	(*a*)	–	0.035	1.28
LAND	(*a*)	–	0.168	3.75*

*Significant at 0.01 one-tailed test level ($t_{1.60} = 2.39$). **Significant at 0.05 one-tailed test level ($t_{1.60} = 1.67$). (a) Variable not entered. (b) Estimated from first stage.

The demand function performs well. All variables, except *REPAIR* which is not statistically significant, have the right signs. Three variables—quantity (*QUAN*), income (*FAMINCO*) and taste (*OREUT*) — as well as the constant are found to be statistically significant at the 99 per cent confidence level (one-tailed test); the receivership law variable (*RECEIV*) and the price level variable (*PRICELEV*) are statistically significant at the 95 per cent confidence level (one-tailed test). The other two habitability law variables are not statistically significant.

Also, the supply function performs well. All variables have the right signs. Four variables — quantity (*QUAN*), receivership law (*RECEIV*), tax (*PERPTAX*) and land value (*LAND*) — are found to be statistically significant at the 99 per cent confidence level (one-tailed test). The constant is also significant 99 per cent confidence level (one-tailed test). The other two habitability law variables — *REPAIR* and *EWHOLD* — are not statistically significant.

Thus, of the three laws, only receivership laws have statistically significant effects on both the housing demand and supply functions of low-income renters.

With the aid of the demand and supply functions thus estimated, we can evaluate specific habitability laws as to their welfare effects on demanders and suppliers of rental housing. For example, if tenants were unaffected by a habitability law, i.e. the regression coefficient in the demand function relating price to the presence of a particular habitability law were statistically insignificant, no demand curve shift would have occurred. If, however, the regression coefficient were statistically significant and positive, the presence of a habitability law would have increased the value tenants attach to their apartment. In a similar manner a statistically significant positive habitability law coefficient in the supply function indicates that the presence of a law on average increases the cost of an apartment. Welfare effect evaluation requires comparison of the relative magnitudes of vertical shifts of demand and supply functions with respect to the presence of a particular habitability law. If, for example, a significantly larger upward shift were found to occur in the demand function associated with the presence of a given habitability law than in the supply function, we could conclude that the valuation by renters of improved housing exceeded the accompanying rent increase, and vice versa.

The empirical analysis reveals that only receivership laws have statistically significant effects on both the demand and supply function. With the aid of *Table 12.1* we can conclude that a supply curve shift due to the presence of receivership laws is about three and one-third times as great as the demand shift. Applying a test developed by Fisher to three-stage least square regression results, a F-statistic of 10.94 is estimated[9]. It testifies to the fact that the receivership regression coefficients in the demand and supply equations are statistically different at the one per cent level. (The critical value of $F(1,124)$ is 6.84 at the one per cent level).

The other two habitability laws, i.e. withholding and repair-and-deduct laws, do not have statistically significant welfare effects, even though the supply function regression coefficient in relation to withholding laws (*EWHOLD*) has both the correct sign and is statistically significant. In terms of the test developed by Fisher, the coefficients in the demand and supply functions are not statistically different.

In summary, of the three types of habitability laws available to tentants, only receivership, in 1974–75, had a statistically significant effect on both demanders and suppliers of low-cost rental housing in 34 large SMSAs with more than one-quarter of the United States population. Its presence was found to be associated with a statistically significant increase in rental expenditures incurred by indigent tenants not matched by benefits. Thus, to the extent that habitability laws are mainly designed to improve the welfare of indigent tenants, they have failed, at least in the sample studied. Receivership laws may even have been counterproductive in the United States. The likely reason is that the regulations imposed on landlords were not accompanied by government income transfers to indigent tenants, a step that would have permitted the tenants to pay for improved housing.

Habitability laws are likely to have distinctly different effects on indigent tenants living in council housing in the United Kingdom. Housing authorities are empowered to charge 'reasonable rents', which do not make a profit on the housing account (except for a working balance). 'Reasonable rents' are not defined by statute, but the courts have held that reasonable rents must preserve a balance between the interests of the tenants and those of the taxpayers as a whole, and also that the rents of dwellings, or groups of dwellings, must be set at a reasonable level, i.e. neither exceptionally high or low. These limits are admittedly wide, and authorities who wish to do so can at their discretion fix rent levels so that all or most of their expenditure, net of subsidies, is met from rents or, alternatively, at the other extreme so that a large part of it is charged to the rates (property taxes), if they so prefer.

The important point is that for many tenants rent increases are matched in part or totally by increased welfare payments. Tenants benefit often from one of two systems of assistance: one is the system of rent rebates administered by the housing authorities themselves with the help of a 75 per cent grant from central government, and it applies mostly to low wage earners; and the other is the system of social security payments administered by the central government Department of Health and Social Security, which applies mainly to those not in the work force. Those receiving a rent rebate usually have to meet 40 per cent of any rent increase, the remaining 60 per cent being rebated. Those receiving social security payments usually get the entire rent increase paid for them. The assistance is usually adjusted from the beginning of the increase, which is generally decided upon sometime in advance, at budget meetings, and there has to be a statutory notice to tenants of four weeks before any increase can be implemented. Consequently, assistance adjustments can follow rent increases with little, if any, lag.

Thus the government income transfer to indigent tenants that follows shortly after rent increases have been initiated, should permit many indigent tenants to benefit from habitability laws in the United Kingdom.

12.2.3 Secular effects on housing stock quality

All countries worry about a threatening deterioration of their housing stock. The United States has been fortunate in that the number of substandard rental housing has declined since 1960; the question is what role, if any, habitability laws have played in this positive development.

In order to ascertain whether habitability laws have contributed to the shrinkage of substandard rental housing in the United States, a housing model was built and implemented with the aid of time series data (*see* Hirsch and Cheung-Kwok Law, 1979; Davis, Eastman and Chang Hua, 1974; Davis, Eastman and Chang Hua, 1975; Hansen, Lapp and Quin, 1975). The model centres on the concept of substandard housing, which can be defined in a number of ways that differ mainly in comprehensiveness. For example, if we define only dilapidated housing as substandard we are more restrictive than if we include all units that are classified as dilapidated plus those classified as deteriorating units lacking some or all plumbing facilities. The available data allowed four different substandard rental housing concepts. Their definitions and implementation are presented in appendix 12.2. The four different concepts of substandard housing—L_1, L_2, L_3 and L_4—are used as dependent variables in the estimating equations.

In the case of L_1, only those rental units classified as dilapidated in 1960 are regarded as substandard. L_1 is positive 32 out of 39 times, with +3.4 per cent the mean and 2.78 the standard deviation, i.e. rental housing deteriorated between 1960 and 1974–75 by an average of 3.4 per cent.

Variable L_2 combines renter-occupied dilapidated units with renter-occupied deteriorating units lacking some or all facilities. By this expanded definition of substandard rental housing in 1960, 19 observations of L_2 are negative and 20 positive, with the mean −1.43 per cent and the standard deviation 5.04, indicating an increase in the quality of rental housing between 1960 and 1974–75 of 1.43 per cent.

L_3 offers the broadest definition of low-quality rental housing. Specifically, low-quality rental housing in 1960 is here defined as the sum of units listed as dilapidated and those listed as deteriorating, whether they do or do not have plumbing facilities. All but one of the observations are negative and show an increase in the quality, with the mean –12.4 per cent and the standard deviation 6.4.

The case of L_4 provides consistency in definition, in that in both periods substandard housing units are those rental units that lack some or all plumbing facilities. All 39 SMSAs show an increase in housing quality. The mean value is −17.0 per cent and the standard deviation is 10.6.

Thus, except by the very narrow definition of L_1, there was substantial skrinkage in substandard housing between 1960 and 1974–75. As expected, the improvement increased the broader the definition of substandard housing in 1960. However, even under the consistent definition of substandard housing in terms of absence of plumbing facilities, housing shows large improvement.

Independent variables that are hypothesized to explain changes in substandard rental housing between 1960 and 1974–75 can be separated into three classes — supply-related variables, *S*; demand-related variables, *D*; and law variables, *K*. In short,

$$L = \mathrm{f}(S,D,K). \qquad (4)$$

As a supply-related variable we selected the percentage increase of low-cost rental units built after 1960 and renting for less than $100 a month in 1974–75 (*Z*). Since the private sector has not been supplying low-cost rental housing, Z reflects the extent of government intervention to produce better housing accommodation for low income families. We would expect that as government intervention increases, more low-cost rentals would be built and the shrinkage of low-quality rental units would be greater. The expected sign of the coefficient is negative.

Three demand-related variables are included: percentage change in the number of poor families living in SMSA from 1960 to 1974–75 (Y), percentage change of per capita income between 1960 and 1974–75 (I), and ethnicity (B).

Finally two habitability law variables were included: the presence of repair and deduct laws (K_1) and of receivership laws (K_2).

Thus, the model that was implemented can be expressed as follows:

$$(L_1, L_2, L_3, L_4) = \mathrm{F}(Z, Y, I, B, K_1, K_2) \tag{5}$$

We would expect the relation between the percentage of substandard housing (L) and Z, I, K_1 and K_2 to be negative and between L and Y and B to be positive.

An ordinary least squares regression was estimated, relating each of the four dependent variables to the six independent variables for the 39 SMSAs. Results are presented in *Table 12.2*. The model performs well for all four definitions of the dependent variables. R^2 ranges from 0.3130–0.05687 and in all cases the F-statistics for the whole equation are statistically significant at a 95 per cent confidence level. All variables, except for two cases of Y and K_1, consistently have the expected signs. However, in the four cases the regression coefficient is not statistically significant. Z is statistically significant at the 95 per cent confidence level (one-tailed test) in all formulations but L_4. Y is statistically significant at a 95 per cent level (one-tailed test) when the dependent variable is L_4. B is significant in all cases but L_1, I is significant at the 95 per cent level when the dependent variable is L_4.

Thus, as one would expect, if a relatively large percentage of new low-cost rentals are supplied, whether through public or other action, the stock of substandard housing declines. Great care is needed in interpreting the three demand-related variables. The correlation coefficients among the three are quite large, indicating a substantial degree of multicolinearity[10].

Receivership laws have statistically significant effects on the shrinkage of substandard housing in an SMSA, regardless of how substandard is defined. The broader the 1960 definition of substandard rental housing, the larger the shrinkage. Thus the net regression coefficient increases from 0.014 in terms of L_1, to 0.023 in terms of L_2, and to 0.033 in terms of L_3. The coefficient is largest, i.e. 0.046, when L is consistently defined as absence of plumbing facilities. It makes sense that landlords would be less inclined to act in accordance with a receivership law if their property was merely deteriorating rather than dilapidated or lacking plumbing facilities.

Table 12.2 *Dependent variables related to the six independent variables for the 39 SMSAs*

	Intercept	*Z*	*Y*	*B*	*I*	K_1	K_2
L_1	0.0904	−0.5826	−0.0613	0.3847	−0.0375	−0.0010	−0.0141
t	(1.83)*	(2.18)*	(0.37)	(1.08)	(0.75)	(0.12)	(1.47)**
Beta		[−0.38]	[−0.082]	[0.25]	[−0.16]	[−0.018]	[−0.25]
	$R^2 = 0.3130$	$F = 2.43$***					
L_2	0.0786	−1.1656	0.0374	1.0181	−0.0486	0.0015	−0.0232
t	(1.05)	(2.88)*	(0.15)	(1.89)*	(0.64)	(0.12)	(1.59)**
Beta		[−0.42]	[0.028]	[0.37]	[−0.12]	[0.015]	[−0.23]
	$R^2 = 0.5195$	$F = 5.77$***					
L_3	−0.0009	−1.1181	−0.0384	1.1608	−0.0902	0.0062	−0.0331
t	(0.01)	(1.90)*	(0.11)	(1.48)**	(0.82)	(0.33)	(1.57)**
Beta		[−0.32]	[−0.022]	[0.33]	[−0.17]	[0.049]	[−0.26]
	$R^2 = 0.3729$	$F = 3.17$***					
L_4	−0.3675	−0.3892	1.8834	2.2023	−0.3580	−0.0022	−0.0456
t	(2.46)*	(0.48)	(3.80)*	(2.04)*	(2.35)*	(0.09)	(1.57)**
Beta		[−0.067]	[0.66]	[0.38]	[−0.41]	[−0.010]	[−0.21]
	$R^2 = 0.5687$	$F = 7.03$***					

**Significant at 0.05 one-tailed test level. **Significant at 0.10 for one-tailed test level. ***Significant at 0.05 two-tailed test level. t-value is given in parenthesis. Beta (in square brackets) is the standardized net regression coefficient.*

As hypothesized above, a stiff habitability law like receivership imposes heavier costs on landlords than do repair-and-deduct laws and therefore is more likely to be honoured. The empirical results are consistent with this hypothesis, since in no case do repair-and-deduct laws have a statistically significant effect on the shrinkage of substandard rental housing. That a repair-and-deduct law, by its very nature, cannot induce landlords to cure the absence of plumbing facilities is confirmed by the regression results.

In conclusion, between 1960 and 1974–75 in the presence of receivership laws, the stock of substandard rental housing, *ceteris paribus*, decreased by on average 1.4 4.6 per cent, depending on how substandard is defined. Thus, if we want to decrease the relative prevalence of substandard rental housing in metropolitan areas, we should seek enactment and enforcement of laws that extend the warranty of habitability in a decisive manner. Specifically, receivership laws rather than repair-and-deduct laws should be enacted. In fact, this would merely require the extension of an existing trend in the United States. We should remember that habitability laws were initially promulgated not so much for the purpose of contributing to the shrinkage of substandard housing, as to assist low-income tenants. Yet, as we showed above, the welfare of low-income tenants may not be improved by an extension of the warranty of habitability, although the amount of substandard housing in SMSAs has been reduced.

12.3 Rent control laws

12.3.1 Nature of laws[11]

In the United Kingdom, rent control was enacted by Parliament shortly after the outbreak of World War II. The Rent and Mortgage Interest Restrictions Act of 1939 applied to rent controls as well as security of tenure of existing buildings as well as to those buildings constructed and let subsequently. Rents were fixed at September 1939 levels. Although the price level rose rapidly between 1939 and 1948, i.e. by over 75 per cent and in the following decade by about 45 per cent, rent control was enforced strictly and real returns on rented property declined precipitiously.

The Rent Act of 1957 provided for 'block' decontrol of dwellings with rateable values about £40 in London and £30 elsewhere, and for 'decontrol by movement' of dwellings below these limits, i.e. when vacancy occurred subsequent lettings were outside the scope of the Rent Act. The maximum rents of lettings subject to the Act were to be twice the gross value for rating purposes, i.e. twice the 1939 rental value when landlord was responsible for repairs and exterior decoration and tenant for interior decoration. The rent increase permitted would have averaged two-thirds to three-quarters of the rent previously paid. While this increase was large, it should be compared with a two-and-a-half-fold increase in average earnings between 1939 and 1957 and a one-and-a-half-fold increase in the general price level. While the Act included provisions allowing 'block' decontrol to be extended to dwellings of lower rateable value, in 1959 the government gave a pledge not to use this power.

The 1961 and 1964 Housing Acts provided local authorities with stronger powers to compel landlords to make repairs and undertake improvements. The Protection from Eviction Act of 1964 and the Rent Act of 1965 reintroduced security of tenure for most tenants renting unfurnished dwellings. The Rent Act of 1965 provided for a new system of determining rents for protected tenancies that were not subject to control under the 1957 Act. It provided for the rent of protected tenancies to be assessed by reference not to a historic norm but to a balanced market at the time of determination, it permitted revision at regular intervals of the rents so determined, and it provided for special machinery to determine rents. In 1972 rent allowances that related to family circumstances, income and rent were introduced. Moreover, in 1969, 1972, 1974 and 1975, as part of general counter-inflation policy, temporary steps were taken to restrict rent increases.

A report by the Department of the Environment concluded in 1977 that '. . . between 1960 and 1975 . . . [it] is unlikely that the number of dwellings built or converted for letting by private owners exceeded 100 000.'[12]

In the United States, a number of cities and states have enacted rent control laws (Baar, 1977). In addition to New York City, which has had rent controls for many years starting with the end of World War II, more than 110 New Jersey municipalities adopted rent control ordinances during the first half of the 1970s. Massachusetts, Cambridge, Brooklyn, Summerville and Lynn passed rent control ordinances in the 1970s. During the same period Maryland had a rent control law, which, however, expired on 1 July 1974. In June 1973 Maine adopted a local option law, and in November 1973 Congress passed a law authorizing the District of Columbia to adopt rent control. Pursuant to the Federal Act, the District of Columbia Council promulgated rent control regulations in 1974.

In California, real estate prices skyrocketed in the late 1970s and a number of local jurisdictions (including the City of Los Angeles and the County of Los Angeles) adopted rent control ordinances. The Los Angeles City Ordinance has the following features:

(1) Apartments built after March 1979 are exempt from controls. So are luxury units, which for one-bedroom apartments are defined as those renting for more than $420 a month.
(2) Rents can be raised to any level on units that tenants voluntarily vacate or from which they are legally evicted.
(3) Landlords can unilaterally decide to make capital improvements and pass those costs on to renters over a five-year period. They can also evict tenants in order to perform certain major improvements inside apartments, and then charge the new tenants any rent they wish.
(4) Seeking to avoid a large and expensive bureaucracy of rent-control administrators, the ordinance left enforcement of the law entirely to tenants through civil action.
(5) A 'just-cause' eviction clause limits landlords' ability to oust renters.
(6) Annual rent increase cannot exceed seven per cent.
(7) Landlords who have financial problems because of the high price for which they purchased the property are denied the case-by-case relief that is authorized for landlords with actual operating problems.

Rent control ordinances differ substantially between various jurisdictions. For example, in New York City landlords are allowed annual rent increases of 5 – 8.5 per cent and can raise rents an additional 15 per cent on vacated apartments. There, landlords have capital-improvement protection as in Los Angeles, but they cannot make nonessential improvements inside an apartment without tenants' consent nor evict tenants to perform the work. Moreover, rent-control administrators can initiate action against landlords. However, most of these ordinances are mainly designed to protect low income tenants.

12.3.2 Welfare analysis

While rent control laws differ in detail, they all have in common the fact that they reduce the freedom of landlords to set rent levels. Thus, while the actual cost of providing housing services is likely to increase, particularly during periods of inflation, rent control ordinances can prevent landlords from passing on appropriate parts of these cost increases to tenants. The imposition of rent controls under such circumstances is presented in *Figure 12.1* (*see also* Olsen, 1972). Specifically, the two axes are rent (R) and

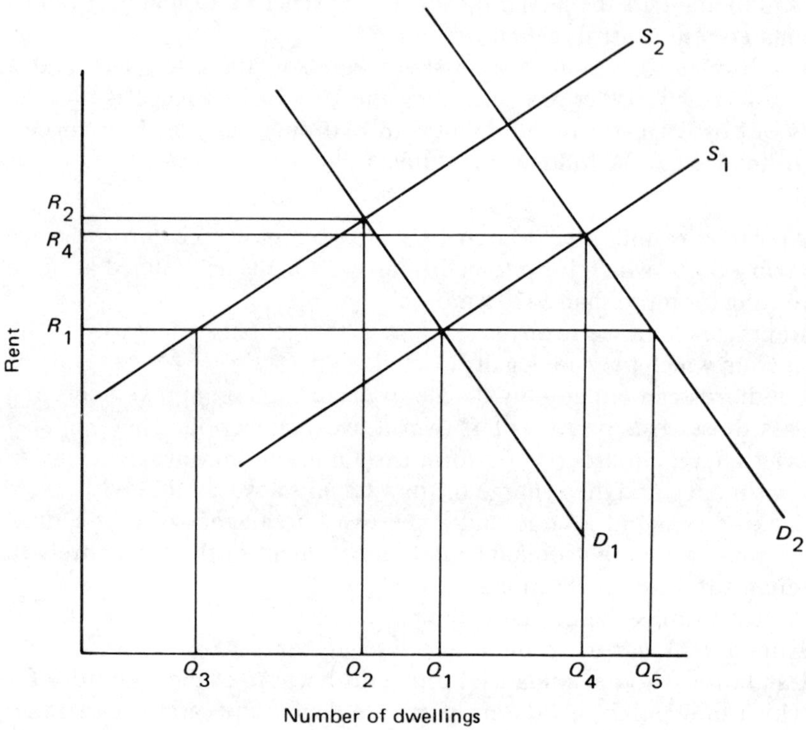

Figure 12.1 *Rent control laws*

number of dwellings (Q). Before the imposition of rent control on low-cost apartments, at equilibrium the number of dwelling units was Q_1 and their rent was R_1. As a result of, for example, increases in the price of input factors, whether repair and maintenance costs, utilities or property taxes, the supply function shifts to the left from (S_1) to (S_2). Without a change in demand, a new equilibrium would be reached at Q_2 and R_2. Rent control would prohibit landlords from charging the rent that they would otherwise have sought, i.e., their rent will be below R_2. In the most extreme case where no rent increase is permitted, landlords would supply $Q_1 - Q_3$ fewer dwellings than would be demanded in the short run. In the long run, rent control is likely to have a chilling effect on investors and therefore curtail the supply of housing. Thus, cumulative declines in low-cost dwellings could be anticipated, accompanied by housing shortages.

Some empirical estimates of the likely side effects are possible. Based on the econometric study of large metropolitan areas in the United States reported earlier, the long-run price elasticity of housing supply related to land prices was found to be 0.20. Thus, for example, a 10 per cent increase in the price of land per year would tend to increase rents by 6.5 per cent. If no rent increases were permitted, supply would be reduced by 2.4 per cent of low-cost housing units, and if only half of that increase were permitted the shortage would be 1.2 per cent.

The effects of rent control can also be examined from the demand side. For example, because income in a given low-cost rental housing market increases over time, the demand function tends to shift to the right from D_1 to D_2. If we assume that in the short run the supply of low-cost housing rental units cannot change, a new equilibrium would be reached at a rent of R_4 and number of dwelling units, Q_4. (*See Figure 12.1*). Rent control does not permit this new price for housing units to be attained. For example, if no increase in rents is permitted, then a shortage of $Q_5 — Q_1$ dwelling units will result. Landlords not permitted to raise rents may reduce repair and maintenance, i.e. the quality of housing. Alternatively, they may withdraw dwellings from the market. This can be done by converting apartments into condominiums, convalescent homes, homes for aged, co-operatives, etc. They may even be forced to abandom their properties because of the artificial imbalance between costs and rents.

Using again the same econometric study of large metropolitan areas, some empirical estimates can be offered. The income elasticity for low-cost housing was found to be +0.98 for 1974–75. In an uncontrolled rental market in the presence of an annual per capita income increase of 8.0 per cent, for example, and on the assumption that the short-run supply of low-cost housing does not increase, annual rent increases of about 8.0 per cent could be expected. If rent control were to be imposed and were to permit no increase whatsoever, an 8.0 per cent shortage of low-cost rental units could be expected. If, on the other hand, rent increases were held to half of the expected 8.0, i.e. 4.0 per cent per annum, a shortage of about 4.0 per cent would result. These shortages would be cumulative as long as income increases year by year.

Developments in the United Kingdom since the passage of the Rent Act apear consistent with the above analysis. In 1951, 52 per cent and in 1957 44 per cent of all housing in England and Wales was rented from private landlords (Department of Environment, 1977a, 1977b). By 1976, private rentals had dropped to 15 per cent. (Owner-occupied housing increased from 31 per cent in 1951 to 55 per cent in 1976). Moreover, during this period privately-owned rental housing deteriorated rapidly; much was demolished.

Many tenants moved to public housing at enormous expense to British taxpayers. (2.2 million households lived in public housing in 1951 and 10 million in 1976). The quality of rental housing in the United Kingdom plummeted along with its availability. Today, a much larger percentage of privately rented housing is dilapidated than of any other type of housing. In 1976, for example, the government found only one per cent of public housing and three per cent of owner-occupied housing to be unfit dwellings, whereas 16 per cent of privately rented housing was deemed unfit (Department of Environment, 1977a). Thus, while we do not maintain that all rental housing stock deterioration or all the decline in private rented housing (from 6.4 million in 1951 to 2.6 million in 1976), is due to rent control, it appears to be a major contributor.

What if we exclude construction from rent control? Most local California ordinances have done so, as had the Hong Kong Rents Ordinance of 1921 (Cheung, 1975). We must remember that investors compare a large number of alternative opportunities in a variety of locations before reaching their ultimate decision. In this process, they seek out the investment that offers the highest possible return for their capital over a number of years, the return (or profit) being the difference between total expected receipts and costs. Jurisdictions that control rents in any manner increase the risk and cost of investors and therefore induce potential investors to seek other investment opportunities.

It is important to realize that rent control laws can have a deleterious effect on low-income tenants and we now examine the reasons for this. Even in a jurisdiction in which average vacancy rates are extremely low, these rates can be quite high in poor neighbourhoods. For example, in the late 1970s, while vacancy rates in much of well-to-do West Los Angeles, California, were about two per cent, they were not much below eight per cent in poor Southeast Los Angeles. In the presence of rent control ordinances that permit annual rent increases of a fixed percentage (in Los Angeles it is seven per cent), landlords are tempted to seek these authorized increases for fear that new future ordinances may freeze rents at the lower rate. Vacancy rates in higher income areas will tend to be exceedingly low for three reasons: presence of excess demand due to below-market rents, negligible new construction in the face of rent control laws, and increased rental demand resulting from population growth. Prospective tenants, who, in the absence of rent control would have paid higher rents than those paid by present tenants, are forced to turn to substitutes, most often, housing in low-income areas. In addition, low-income families seeking to move into higher income areas — for example to obtain better jobs — will be prevented from doing so by the low vacancy-rates in the more expensive neighbourhoods. As a result, more and more prospective tenants are bidding for the same stock of housing in lower income areas and are reducing vacancy rates. This upward shift in demand will enable landlords to ask for the full permissable rent increase. Thus, while many low-income tenants are likely to have benefited in the past from generally high vacancy-rates in their neighbourhoods, many of them now are exposed to annual rent increases. Moreover, under rent control landlords are reluctant, if not financially unable, to provide proper upkeep of low-cost housing. One major consequence is that an increasing portion of existing low-cost housing will be abandoned or taken out of the housing stock for other, more profitable purposes.

In the United States there has been a debate about the relative merits of locally-imposed compared to statewide rent control. Some of the considerations are as follows. If any one City imposes rent control, its upper-middle income and upper-income tenants are unlikely to put up with ill-maintained and ill-repaired apartments. They will continue to demand good housing and to be willing to pay for it. Thus, many of the affluent will simply leave the controlled city. Their departure will shrink the property tax base, damaging the city's fiscal health. One result of such an exodus will be heavier fiscal burdens heaped on the remaining residents — who in turn will seek to move out. Those who will stay are those least able to move, and many of them will tend to be poor and in need of major government assistance. As argued above, investors will shun the rent control jurisdiction as well, further damaging its fiscal health.

In addition to producing a shortage of rental units for low-income groups and providing a negative incentive for housing maintenance, rent control is also likely to create difficult enforcement problems which, in all cases, lead to a greatly enlarged bureaucracy. Moreover, as New York City has shown, as have French and Italian cities, rent controls once imposed are politically difficult to lift, and therefore generate many long-term ill-effects on the tax base, quantity and quality of housing stock, etc.

For all these reasons, it is very likely that rent control ordinances, even those designed to especially aid low-income groups, are often counter-productive. In the long run they are likely to hurt poor tenants rather than help them.

12.4 Just-cause eviction laws

12.4.1 Nature of law

In the United States a few local and state governments have begun the experiment with just-cause eviction statutes to assure tenants of continued tenancy. Under such laws tenants can only be evicted for just cause, which is explicitly stipulated in the legislation. For example, such statutes in New Jersey delineate a limited number of legal grounds, which constitute the sole basis for eviction:

(*a*) Failure to pay rent;
(*b*) Disorderly conduct;
(*c*) Wilful damage or injury to the premises;
(*d*) Breach of expressed covenants;
(*e*) Continued violation of landlord's rules and regulations;
(*f*) Landlord wishes to retire permantly; or
(*g*) Landlord wishes to board-up or demolish the premises because he has been cited for substandard housing violations and it is economically unfeasible for him to eliminate the violations[13].

A just-cause eviction law applying solely to senior citizens was passed by the California Assembly in the 1973–74 legislative session, but died in the Senate[14]. It listed six grounds, similar to the New Jersey ones, for evicting a tenant 60 years of age or older who had been in continuous possession of a dwelling for five years.

On the local level, universal just-cause eviction ordinances have also been enacted, usually very similar to the New Jersey one. For example, in 1979 the City of Los Angeles passed such an ordinance in conjunction with its rent control law, which permits rent increases whenever a voluntary vacancy occurs. Under such a rent control law, it is essential that tenants are protected against capricious eviction.

12.4.2 Welfare analysis

A just-cause eviction law applicable to all tenants increases the security of tenancy. Within the hedonic price approach discussed earlier, security of tenancy is just another economic commodity traded between landlords and tenants. The demand function for apartments with just-cause eviction guarantees is higher, i.e. further to the right, than that without such guarantees, *ceteris paribus*. Thus, the law by protecting tenants enhances their utility.

While just-cause eviction laws increase the welfare of tenants, they also impose costs on landlords. Specifically, such laws reduce landlords' rights and thereby flexibility, and place greater risk upon them. For example, they reduce landlords' options to evict tenants in order to remodel their facilities for another class of tenants. Moreover, legal costs are likely to increase. As a consequence, the rental housing supply function shifts to the left in the presence of universal just-cause eviction laws, *ceteris paribus*.

In *Figure 12.2*, the effect of the imposition of a universal just-cause eviction law is illustrated. Rent (R) is one axis and number of dwellings (Q) the other. Prior to the imposition of the law, landlords face demand function D_1 and supply function, S. They lease Q_1 dwellings at R_1 rent. The benefits that result from just-cause eviction laws can be represented in an upward shift of the demand function from D_1 to D_2, which for simplicity's sake is assumed to be parallel. Costs imposed by the law on landlords may be viewed as the insurance they can purchase against the hazards that ensue from the law. This insurance is assumed to amount to *A–C*, and accordingly the new demand function, reflecting both benefits to tenants and costs to landlords, will be D_3. (Note that in this case costs exceed benefits.)

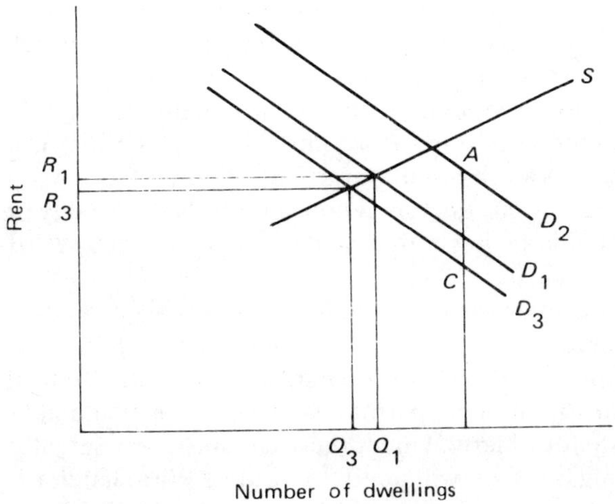

Figure 12.2 *Universal just-cause eviction law*

As can be seen in *Figure 12.2*, the just-cause eviction law has a chilling effect on landlords, who consequently supply fewer dwellings, Q_1–Q_3, at a somewhat lower rent, R_1–R_3. The decline in the number of dwellings supplied in the face of universal just-cause eviction laws can be explained as the law forcing landlords to supply an additional economic commodity — security of tenancy. Since rent increases to compensate for the additional costs are not permitted, landlords will seek to reduce costs by cutting back on other housing services, particularly repair and maintenance. As a consequencc, buildings will deteriorate and sooner or later reach a stage at which they are abandoned. Should habitability laws not permit reduced maintenance, financial considerations will stimulate conversion of apartment houses to condominiums, co-operatives, convalescent homes, etc., all steps that reduce the supply of low cost rentals.

The case discussed so far and presented in *Figure 12.2*, is only the first of three possible cases. In a second case, the cost to the landlord is smaller than the increased value to the tenant. The result usually will be more dweliings, however, at a higher rent. In a further case, law-induced benefit and cost increases are about equal. As a consequence, all parties are left in the same welfare situation as before, i.e. no change either in the number of dwellings or their rent.

A just-cause eviction law, rather than protecting all tenants and being universal, can be written so as to apply only to a particular group of tenants. Landlords then face two classes of renters, those protected by just-cause legislation and those who are not. Separation of these two groups is not difficult when they are identifiably defined, and enforcement is facilitated by the prohibition of sub-letting. For example, aged tenants are likely to have distinctly different rental housing demand characteristics compared to young tenants. The difference stems from the fact that aged tenants seek relatively easy access to various private and public facilities, and are particularly concerned about a pollution-free environment as well as personal safety. These preferences in part are derived from the physical vulnerability of the aged, who by and large are risk-averse. As a consequence of these considerations the rental housing demand elasticity of aged tenants can be expected to be lower than that of young tenants, *ceteris paribus*.

Discriminatory just-cause eviction laws singling out the aged tend to induce landlords not to rent to senior citizens. Also, landlords will tend to be reluctant to build apartment houses with characteristics that appeal particularly to the aged, or to remodel apartments in a manner that makes them especially attractive to the elderly. Under these circumstances, greater segregation in the housing market will tend to result. With landlords increasingly reluctant to rent to older people, the latter will tend to end up in the least desirable places, and it is altogether likely that such laws will prove to be counterproductive. By and large, the same effects will result from any discriminatory just-cause eviction law, regardless of who is singled out for preferential treatment.

12.5 Age discrimination laws

12.5.1 The law

The state of New Jersey passed legislation specifically barring housing discrimination against children as early as 1898, but such laws gained prominence in the United States only during the 1970s. That discrimination against families with children is a serious problem is beyond doubt. Thus, for example, the Orange County Fair Housing Council estimated in 1978 that children are prohibited in 70 per cent of all rental housing units in California. Even if this estimate is high, the fact that in 1978 about 45 per cent of all California households were renters, would compel us to view this type of discrimination as a serious social problem.

Arguments against such discrimination include the serious impact on family stability as well as a deep psychological effect on children. Moreover, since most negro and Mexican-American families have many children, child discrimination might be disguised racial discrimination and no doubt contributes to such discrimination.

Yet, there is another side to child discrimination. Certain families claiming rights to peace and quiet prefer not to live among children. Elderly tenants in particular object to facing the likelihood of tripping over tricycles and toys in hallways and other common premises. Finally, landlords maintain that children are destructive and necessitate repair and maintenance expenses substantially larger than are required where buildings and grounds are used only by adults.

In the United States remedies have been offered by local and state governments. Since land use control has been delegated by most states to local governments, their agencies have dealt with this problem in an attempt to promote public health, safety, welfare and morals. The cities of San Francisco, Los Angeles and Berkeley, California have passed ordinances prohibiting discrimination against families with minor children in the rental or leasing of residential property. Units with a certain minimum floor area and buildings serving exclusively persons 62 years of age and older are exempted from the requirements of the ordinance. Penalties for violation are specified and the ordinance is subject both to annual review and to automatic expiration. Anti-child discrimination ordinances also exist in Everett, Washington and Howard County, Maryland.

Local governments have used exclusionary zoning (often in the form of large-lot zoning for single family homes as well as bedroom restrictions in multiple family dwellings) to reduce the number of families with many children that settle in their midst. Courts have not taken a clear-cut position towards the exclusionary zoning device, but in *Molino v Mayor and Council of Borough of Glassboro*, the court struck down such zoning[15].

Local jurisdictions also have exercised control over the ability of families with children to obtain housing through their definitions of what constitutes a 'family' and their say about what classes of individuals are permitted to live together in one dwelling. *Moore v City of East Cleveland* deals with such a case[16].

By early 1979 at least six states had statutes that prohibited discrimination in housing against families with children. These states include: Arizona, Delaware, Illinois, Massachusetts, New Jersey and New York. The states of Montana and New Hampshire as well as the District of Columbia prohibit discrimination on the basis of age. In California state law prohibits 'arbitrary' discrimination[17]. However the courts upheld the right of landlords to discriminate against male children over five years of age[18].

In *Riley v Stoves* a covenant barring children under the age of 21 from a mobile home community for retirees was found constitutional by an Arizona appeal court[19]. In 1975 the Arizona state legislature enacted a law that prohibits rental of a dwelling to a family with children if a covenant restricting children is in effect[20].

The position of the federal government in relation to anti-child discrimination in unclear at this time. The Fair Housing Act and the Age Discrimination Act avoid direct reference to discrimination against children in housing[21]. However, the National Housing Act of 1950 has a provision that requires landlords to certify that they do not discriminate against families with children in housing built with federally insured mortgage loans[22].

12.5.2 Welfare analysis

To the extent that anti-age discrimination laws are implemented, and as mentioned earlier there is little evidence to this effect, their implications for landlords would be similar to those of all other laws that impose additional costs on landlords. While under such conditions the short-run effects on tenants with children are likely to be positive, the long-run effects are much less clear. Moreover, it is also unclear how the welfare gains of tenants with children will compare with the welfare losses incurred by other tenants. However, except in rare circumstances, anti-age discrimination laws are ineffective and thus their actual welfare effects are likely to be very small.

12.6 Conclusions

These are anxious times for tenants and landlords in both the United States and the United Kingdom. Ever since the end of World War II, property law has been undergoing profound changes. The general direction of the change in the two countries has been very similar. Tenants have been awarded new rights; landlords, in what is basically a zero-sum game, have had some rights taken away. This tilting in favour of tenants has been accomplished through the extension of the warranty of habitability, through rent control, just-cause eviction provisions and anti-discrimination laws.

While these changes in landlord–tenant relation laws were designed to benefit indigent tenants in particular, they do not appear in most instances to have done so. Habitability laws, especially, appear to have been counter-productive in the United States although perhaps not in the United Kingdom where they are often accompanied by income transfers.

In general, since the changes in landlord—tenant relationships in the United Kingdom were nationwide and started in a major way almost 35 years ago, their effects have had time to manifest themselves. The virtual disappearance of a private market for rental housing, although brought about by a variety of factors, is no doubt mainly due to the tilt in favour of tenants.

In the United States, the newly evolving relationship between landlord and tenant has been more gradual and more diffuse, since under federalism many of the public decisions are made by independent local and state authorities. A strong and vigourous private rental housing market persists in the United States, although in some jurisdictions more and more restrictions are being imposed on landlords. In Los Angeles, California, admittedly an extreme case, landlords in 1981 were encumbered by a state-wide extension of the warranty of habitability as well as local rent control, just-cause eviction and child discrimination ordinances. As a result, rental housing in Los Angeles is rapidly approaching the status of a public utility. This present status may turn out to be only the first step on the road leading to the disappearance of private rental housing, a road the United Kingdom has travelled before us.

Notes to chapter twelve

1 *Robinson v Diamond Housing Corp.*, 463 F (2d) 853, 871 (D.C. Cir. 1972).

2 For detail see Hirsch (1979).

3 Reasons for selecting the semilog (with the dependent variable in log-form) over the linear form include the following: the semilog transformation rectifies the heteroskedasticity that is common to most cross-section analyses, long-time tenants often receive discounts, large families often pay more than smaller ones for the same dwelling, racial minorities often pay more for the same dwelling due to prejudice, and the semilog form provided a slight improvement in R^2 compared to the linear form.

4 The estimation of rent equations by hedonic price techniques faces many of the classical problems associated with composite commodities. A major problem relates to the conditions under which a vector of goods (in this case attributes) can be treated as a single commodity and when a single price for the composite can be expressed as a function of prices of the attributes in the vector. Basically, the quantity of the composite can be measured in terms of a base bundle only if the attributes have fixed marginal prices that equal average prices. How can we test whether this condition is met? There are two routes to ensure the fixity of marginal attribute prices. The first requires non-joint production of attributes and constant returns to scale in the market. Since non-joint production is the exception to the rule, the second route is of greater interest. Accordingly, if there is joint production of attributes and constant returns to scale in the market, and preferences for housing attributes (q) and for other goods (x) are of the form $f_i[g(q,x_1),x_2]$, where g is linearly homogeneous, then marginal attribute prices will be fixed.

We gave tested for the linearity of the hedonic price relationships in the range of our data, and a number of econometric tests have satisfied us of the adequacy on our linear specification.

Specifically, a quadratic hedonic price function was estimated and an F-test based on the percentage change in the sum of the squared residuals undertaken. For the large majority of equations, linearity could not be rejected.

A second test was undertaken to look across markets. It was designed to see whether prices of attributes stay more or less fixed across sites. Cross-city price indices were compared and differences were not found to be statistically significant.

5 Presence of withholding and retaliatory eviction laws were combined, since withholding is tenant initiated and costly to landlord, which is not the case in relation to the other two remedies.

6 We used the percentage of renters in an area with an annual family income of \$5000 or more as a proxy. This proxy was found to be highly correlated with the areas' median family income of all households and with the Consumer Price Index of select SMSAs ($r = 0.84$). See deLeeuw and Ekanem (1971).

7 Since hourly wages of building helpers and labourers (*CONWAGE*) basically are the same throughout a given SMSA, they can be applied to the entire SMSA. However, property taxes and land values do vary over the SMSA. While we would have

preferred separate data for each data point, we had to use SMSA data.

8 Ideally, altogether separate data for construction cost and for repairs and maintenance cost should enter the supply function. The best data available for the first variable are the Boeckh Construction Cost Index and for the second variable, wages of building helpers and labourers (*CONWAGE*). The two are highly correlated (r=0.74). Since Boeckh is more highly correlated with *PERPTAX* (r=0.55) and *LAND* (r=0.29) than is *CONWAGE* with *PERPTAX* (r=0.37) and LAND (r=0.05), *CONWAGE* was selected over Boeckh for inclusion in the supply function.

9 The Fisher test for a significant difference between the *RECEIV* coefficients in the inverse semilog supply and demand equations requires calculating the *F*-statistic given by

$$F = \frac{(u'u - u^{*\prime}u^*)/(trM - trM^*)}{u^{*\prime}u^*/trM^*}$$

where: $u'u$ = sum of squared residuals in restricted regression; $u^{*\prime}u^*$ = sum of squared residuals in unrestricted regression; $trM = (T_1+T_2-p-2q)$; $trM^* = (T_1+T_2-2p-2q)$; T_1 = no. of observations in demand equation; T_2 = no. of observations in supply equation; p = no. of restricted explanatory variables in each equation; q = no. of unrestricted explanatory variables in each equation.

The *F*-statistic is distributed as *F* with ($trM-trM^*$) and trM^* degrees of freedom. (Fisher, 1970).

In our model $T_1 = T_2 = 70$, $p = 1$ and $q = 7$, $u'u = 0.827142$ and $u^{*\prime}u^* = 0.760076$. Making the substitutions we have

$$F = \frac{0.067066/1}{0.760076/124} = 10.94.$$

Although our sample size is 70, the test basically assumes a sample size approaching infinity.

10 In the presence of a high degree of multicolinearity it is impossible to identify the independent effects of each of the three variables upon the dependent variable. Since there is no *a priori* reason to drop any of the three variables from the equation, they are included in the statistical analysis with the understanding that the estimated coefficients are likely to be biased. We therefore will refrain from interpreting *Table 12.2* as suggesting that increasing the income of renters has no statistically significant effect on the shrinkage of substandard rental housing. Nevertheless all three demand-related variables are statistically significant at the 95 per cent one-tailed level when L_4 is the dependent variable.

11 Department of Environment, *Housing Policy* (1977).

12 *Ibid.*, p. 67.

13 N.J. Stat. Ann. 2A, 18–53 (West Supp. 1974).

14 A.B. 1202 (1973–1974 Regular Session), California Assembly.

15 116 NJ Super 195, 281A (2d) 401 (1971).

16 431 US 494, 52 LEd (2d) 531, 97 S Ct 1932 (1977).

17 Cal Ann Civ Code s 51 (Deering Supp. 1977).

18 *Flowers v John Burnham and Company*, 21 Cal App (3d) 700, 704, 98 Cal Rptr 644, 645 (1971).

19 22nd Ariz App 223, 526, P (2d) 747 (1974).

20 Ariz. Rev. Stat. Ann. s 33–1317 B.S. 33–303B (Supp. 1975).

21 USC 3601 *et seq.* and 42 USC 6101 *et seq.*

22 National Housing Act, s. 207 (b) and 903 (a).

References

AMERICAN LAW INSTITUTE (1977), *Restatement of the Law: Property 2d — Landlord and Tenant*, vol. 1, St. Paul, Mn: American Law Institute Publishers.

BAAR, K.K. (1977), Rent control in the 1970s: the case of the New Jersey Tenants' Movement, *Hastings Law Journal*, **28**, no. 3 631–683.

CHEUNG, S.N.S. (1975), Roofs or stars: the stated intents and actual effects of a rent ordinance, *Economic Inquiry*, **13**, no. 1, 1–21.

DAVIS, O.A., EASTMAN, C.M. and CHANG HUA (1974), The shrinkage in the stock of low-quality housing in the central city: an empirical study of the U.S.

experience over the last ten years, *Urban Studies*, **12**, 221–224.
DAVIS, O.A., EASTMAN, C.M. and CHANG HUA (1975), Reply to the comment by Hansen, Lapp, and Quinn: substandard housing, *Urban Studies*, **12**, 221–224.
DEPARTMENT OF ENVIRONMENT (1977a), *Housing Policy*, Technical Volume Part III, ch. 9, London: HMSO.
DEPARTMENT OF ENVIRONMENT (1977b), *Housing Policy: A Consultative Document*, Cmnd 6851, 14, London: HMSO.
DEPARTMENT OF ENVIRONMENT (1977a), *Housing Policy*, 56, Technical Volume, part I, London: HMSO.
DELEEUW, F. and EKANEM, N.F. (1971), The supply of rental housing, *American Economic Review*, **91**, December, 806–817.
FISHER, F.M. (1970), Test of equality between sets of coefficients in two linear regressions: an expository note, *Econometrica*, **38**, 361–366.
HADDEN, T. (1978), *Compulsory Repair and Improvement*, Oxford: Centre for Socio-Legal Studies.
HANSEN, R.A., LAPP, F. and QUINN, H.S. (1975), Substandard housing in central cities: a comment, *Urban Studies*, **12**, 219–220.
HIRSCH, W.Z., HIRSCH, J.G. and MARGOLIS, S. (1975), Regression analysis of the effects of habitability laws upon rent, *California Law Review*, **63**, no. 5, 1097–1142.
HIRSCH, W.Z. and CHEUNG-KWOK LAW (1979), Habitability laws and the shrinkage of substandard rental housing stock, *Urban Studies*, **16**, no. 1, 19–28.
HIRSCH, W.Z. (1979), *Law and Economics: An Introductory Analysis*, New York: Academic Press.
KAIN, J.F. and QUIGLEY, J.M. (1970), Measuring the value of housing quality, *Journal of the American Statistical Association*, **65**, June, 532–547.
THE LAW COMMISSION (1975), *Codification of the Law of Landlord and Tenant — Report on Obligations of Landlords and Tenants*, London: HMSO.
MOSIER, M.M. and SOBLE, R.A. (1973), Modern legislation, metropolitan court, miniscule results: a study of Detroit's landlord tenant court, *University of Michigan Journal of Law Reform*, no. 1, **7**, 8–80.
OLSEN, E.O. (1972), An econometric analysis of rent control, *Journal of Political Economy*, **80**, no. 6, 1081–1100.

Appendix 12.1

Variable descriptors

Variable name or number		*Description*	*Source*
1974	*1975*		
RENT		Monthly gross rent including electricity, *gas, oil and/or coal*	Year 1 and 2 *SMSA Annual Housing Survey*, 1974–75, US Department of Housing and Urban Development and US Bureau of Census
H001	H006	Age of building	
H044	H033	Number of rooms	
H059	H063	Number of bathrooms	
H078	H081	Air conditioning	
H121	H157	Rented parking	
INDW		Inside Dwelling Quality	
H045	H034	Working electrical wall outlets	
H051	H053	Complete kitchen facility	
H058	H062	Complete plumbing facility	
H073	H076*	Number of rooms without heat	
H075	H078	Number of heating breakdowns	
H079	H082	Type of air conditioning	
H087	H089	Basement in house	

Variable name or number 1974	1975	*Description*	*Source*
NEHDA		Physical Neighborhood Quality	Year 1 and 2 *SMSA Annual Housing Survey*, 1974–75, US Department of Housing and Urban Development and US Bureau of Census
H170	H207*	Noise bothersome	
H173	H218	Airplane noise a bother	
H176	H208*	Traffic bothersome	
H179	H217	Odours bothersome	
H182	H213*	Trash, litter bothersome	
H184	H214	Abandoned structures	
H187	H215	Rundown houses	
H191	H216*	Industry bothersome	
H193	H209	Streets need repair	
H214	H233	Deteriorating housing on street	
NEHDB		Public Services Neighborhood Quality	
H206	H223	Inadequate shopping	
H208	H225	Inadequate police	
H210	H227	Inadequate fire protection	
PUBSP		Public Space Quality	
H043	H033	Passenger elevator	
H215	H236	Light fixtures in hall	
H217	H238	Bad stairways	
OREUT		Mean annual rent and utility payments as percentage of median family income	
FAMINCO		Median Renter Family Income in $000s	
PRICEL		Price Level Proxy	
PERPTAX		Per Capita Property Tax in SMSA in £000s, 1974 and 1975	*Local Government Finances in Selected Metropolitan Areas and Large Counties*, US Bureau of the Census, 1974–75, 1975–76
LAND		Per square foot Land Value of Dwellings in SMSA, 1974	*Data for States and Selected Areas on Characteristics of FHA Operations Under Sec. 203*
CONWAGE		Hourly average union rates of building helpers and labourers, 1974	*Handbook of Labor Statistics*, Bureau of Labor Statistics, 1977

* The 1975 Survey modified the 1974 definitions of variables related to physical neighbourhood characteristics. For example, the 1974 variables H169 (any street noise), H170 (noise bothersome) and H171 (noise objection move) were combined into a single 1975 variable, i.e., H207 — any street noise.

Appendix 12.2

Four substandard rental housing concepts

Definitions for available 1960 and 1974–75 data are not entirely consistent. In the 1960 Census of Housing, the category 'Substandard Housing' consists of two parts: units 'lacking some or all facilities' (bath, toilet and hot water) but not 'dilapidated'; and units that are 'dilapidated' and may or may not lack facilities.

Data for the end of the period under consideration come from the Annual Housing Survey of Metropolitan Areas, 1974 and 1975. In the survey, tenants were asked to rank their dwellings in one of four categories. The lowest category was poor, and it is this category that is being used for the end of the period under consideration. However, there is one set of data for 1960 and for 1974–75 that defines substandard housing in an identical manner, i.e.units lacking some or all plumbing facilities.

We will use four dependent variables differing mainly in the way sub-standard rental housing is defined at the beginning of the period under consideration;

$$L_1 = \frac{P_E - D_B}{RH_B} \tag{6}$$

$$L_2 = \frac{P_E - E_B}{RH_B} \tag{7}$$

$$L_3 = \frac{P_E - F_B}{RH_B} \tag{8}$$

$$L_4 = \frac{G_E - G_B}{RH_B} \tag{9}$$

where P_E is the number of renter-occupied units rated as 'poor' at end of period under consideration; RH_B the total number of renter-occupied units at beginning of period under consideration; D_B the total number of renter-occupied units classified as either 'dilapidated' or lacking plumbing facilities or both, at the beginning of the period under consideration; E_B the total number of renter-occupied units lacking some or all facilities at the beginning of the period under consideration; F_B the total number of renter-occupied units classified as 'dilapidated' plus that classified as 'deteriorating'; G_E the total number of renter-occupied units classified as lacking some or all plumbing facilities at the end of period under consideration, and G_B

the total number of renter-occupied units classified as lacking some or all plumbing facilities at beginning of period under consideration.

The table below illustrates the different definitions of substandard rental housing at the beginning of the period, i.e. 1960.

Rental units	*Sound*	*Deteriorating*	*Dilapidated*
With all plumbing facilities	1	3	5
Lacking some or all plumbing facilities	2	4	6

Hence,

$$D_B = 5 + 6$$
$$E_B = 4 + 5 + 6$$
$$F_B = 3 + 4 + 5 + 6$$
$$G_B = 2 + 4 + 6$$

CHAPTER THIRTEEN

The law and economics of the misconduct rule of unemployment insurance

Paul T. Fenn

13.1 Introduction

The public provision of financial compensation for contingent losses has become an increasingly important area of state intervention for most developed economies, and as such has been mirrored by a rapidly growing body of public law. The growing body of the statutes and the importance of the rules contained therein, have led in recent years to a developing interest in both legal and economic analysis in this area. Whereas economists have been preoccupied with the impact of benefit levels, eligibility criteria and financing rules on individual and corporate behaviour, lawyers have concentrated on the scrutinization of the legislation and the case-law with a view to critical appraisal of the way in which the legal rules have been interpreted in the light of their given purpose. This chapter is an attempt to take one aspect of legal rule-making in the area of unemployment compensation, and to examine it from both legal and economic perspectives in the hope that the whole will be greater than the sum of the parts.

The aspect in question is that relating to the disqualification of claimants for unemployment benefit as a result of their dismissal from employment through misconduct. Disqualifying rules of this nature are common to a wide variety of unemployment compensation schemes (Woodsworth, 1977), although this essay will mainly confine itself to the law as it stands in the UK. Benefit disqualification can, of course, arise for a number of reasons other than the claimant's misconduct, but the issues involved can differ widely in each case (Fenn, 1980). The working of the misconduct rule has the advantage of illustrating the nature of the relationships between employees, employers and insurance officials. The interests of these parties can sometimes conflict, and analysis of their behaviour within the framework provided by the legal rules sheds some light on both short and long term movements in labour market aggregates.

This chapter is divided into three sections and a conclusion. The first section deals with the historical development and subsequent legal interpretation of the misconduct rule. The second section examines the adaptive behaviour of employers, and the third presents an empirical analysis of benefit disqualifications for misconduct in the UK from 1960 to 1976, a period during which there were a number of statutory developments affecting the relationship between employer and employee.

13.2 The misconduct rule: objectives and interpretation

The misconduct rule as we know it today dates back to the first appearance of unemployment insurance on the statute book, in part two of the National Insurance Act 1911. Although this Act was without real precedent, it is interesting to note that the earlier Workmens' Compensation Act of 1897 included provision for the removal of employers' no-fault liability where the employee was guilty of 'serious and wilful misconduct'[1]. Undoubtedly this clause was seen as a means by which the contributory negligence principle of the fault system could be retained in some form. The background to the 1911 provisions is, however, more appropriately seen in terms of the conflict between popular concern over 'malingering', and the desire of the Board of Trade team of civil servants to produce a workable, actuarially fair, system of social insurance. The popular mood was captured by Beatrice Webb:

> The unconditionality of all payments under unemployment insurance schemes constitutes a grave defect. The State gets nothing for its money in the way of conduct, and it may even encourage malingerers.[2]

At the same time, the architects of the 1911 scheme, Beveridge and Llewellyn Smith, were proposing to limit it to a relatively small number of industries that were particularly prone to seasonal and cyclical fluctuations in employment[3], and to ensure by means of actuarially calculated contribution requirements and benefit levels that the insurance risks were spread evenly over time. Winston Churchill, then President of the Board of Trade, referred to this actuarial process as 'the magic of averages'[4], and was convinced that its proper use would obviate the need for disqualification clauses relating to employees' conduct:

> I do not feel convinced that we are entitled to refuse benefit to a qualified man who loses his employment through drunkenness. He has paid his contributions; he has insured himself against the fact of unemployment, and I think it arguable that his foresight should be rewarded irrespective of his dismissal, whether he lost his situation through his own habits of intemperance or through his employer's habits of intemperance. I do not like mixing up moralities and mathematics.[5]

Largely through the efforts of Llewellyn Smith, however, the misconduct clause was included in the 1911 Act, although Gilbert (1966) has argued that this was on actuarial and not moral grounds — it was felt that the risk was incalculable. Such an interpretation does not seem to square with Llewellyn Smith's declared belief (1910, p. 513) that the risk of losing employment through 'bad work, irregular attendance, or drunken habits' *ought* to remain with the individual employee, in order that the 'national character' should not be impaired. It appears that morality and mathematics were inextricably linked from the very beginnings of unemployment insurance in the UK.

In fact, for the brief period before the 1914–18 war during which the 'experimental' scheme was working in the environment for which it was intended, the analogy with private insurance was reasonably acceptable. Strictly, the analogy was with some form of group insurance in which a single premium is set for a number of people whose level of risk is roughly comparable, at a level that equalizes the expected present values of premiums and benefits[6]. Hence the risk involved was narrowed by confining the scheme to trades where unemployment was considered to be of a temporary, seasonal or cyclical, nature — in this way the risks were seen to be fairly predictable and short-term, so that 'group insurance' implied transfers between contributors and beneficiaries, which evened out over the cycle. Similarly, the imposition of a misconduct clause disqualifying certain people from benefits can be seen as an attempt to remove that particular variation in the risk due to the future behaviour of the insured.

Such problems involve the principles of 'adverse selection' and 'moral hazard', potentially features of all types of insurance. Both arise as a result of an unequal distribution of relevant information between the insurer and the insured. In the first case, adverse selection results from the inability of the insurer to determine some relevant characteristic of the insured at the time the insurance contract is entered into — hence the possibility that the insurer will find himself covering a disproportionate number of high risk cases. Moral hazard, on the other hand, arises when the insured has the power to alter his future behaviour in response to insurance in such a way that cannot be effectively monitored by the insurer. In this way the risk itself is increased by the insurance. The presence of either or both of these problems may result in market failure. Neither the degree of loss-spreading nor the level of care on the part of the insured will be optimal. This argument has consequently been used to justify the introduction of compulsory public provision of insurance in certain areas (Arrow, 1963; Akerlof, 1970). Whether such provision is likely to produce a welfare improvement has been subject to some debate (Pauly, 1968, 1974; Arrow, 1968). However, the principles involved were clearly recognized in the early debate on unemployment insurance. The government, as we have seen, dealt with the 'adverse selection' of insureds through its exclusion of certain trades. Moreover, the requirement of a minimum contribution record of 26 weeks was a means of effectively excluding many of the casual, high risk employees through ensuring that their insurance 'purchases' were limited. The problem of 'moral hazard' was reduced by setting the benefit level (seven shillings initially) substantially below the average level of earnings in the covered trades — a form of 'co-insurance' — and by requiring a 'waiting period' of one week before benefit was paid — a form of 'deductible' (*see* Baily, 1979). The introduction of the misconduct rule appears to suggest that the legislators were not satisfied that these controls were sufficient. By monitoring the behaviour of insured employees it was possible to impose a further penalty on those who had voluntarily increased the risk of dismissal as a result of their 'laziness, drunkenness or carelessness'.

Since then, unemployment insurance has grown, both in the UK and elsewhere, to cover a wide range of differential risks, and has come to cope with widespread unemployment of an unpredictable and lasting nature. To many commentators, these developments imply that such schemes should no longer be seen as analogous to private insurance (Peacock, 1952; Pechman *et al.*, 1968), although Burns (1956, p. 34) has suggested that, if the analogy is to be with private group insurance,

> ... the difference is largely a matter of scale, namely the extent of the coverage, the liberality of the benefits and the range of the risks assumed by private enterprise and by government.

It is interesting, therefore, to examine the way in which the National Insurance adjudicators have interpreted the misconduct rule in the light of its legislative origins and subsequent developments. In the UK, however, there seems to have been a marked reluctance on the part of the National Insurance Commissioners to attribute any clear purpose to the rule. Possibly the closest they have come to it is given in the Commissioner's decision reported in R(U)17/54, where it was said that the restricted disqualification period of six weeks for misconduct was

> a limited application of the principle of insurance law that the insurer is not responsible for losses which the insured person voluntarily brings upon himself.

The implication in this case is that there should be an element of wilfulness or intent behind the claimant's act or omission, if disqualification is to follow. It is after all a principle of insurance law that negligence of the assured alone does not exempt the insurer from liability, as one of the objectives of insurance is to protect the insured from the consequences of negligence (Ivamy, 1979, p. 282). However, much of the case law in the UK does not appear to fit the principle implied by R(U)17/54. The best illustration of this is given in R(U)8/57, where an employee had been prosecuted for but acquitted of embezzlement, but it was held that there was evidence of 'serious carelessness', and that this was all that was required for disqualification. More recently, in R(U) 2/77, it has been reiterated that misconduct will include 'some types of carelessness ...', and the main criterion for disqualification is that the conduct should be

> causally but not necessarily directly connected with the employment, and having regard to the relationship of employer and employee and the rights and duties of both, can fairly be described as blameworthy, reprehensible and wrong.

In general, then, it seems that the rule has been interpreted in the UK as a means of excluding from benefit those whose standard of conduct renders them unfit or unsuitable for a job, irrespective of the degree of wilfulness or intent[7]. Interestingly, this is in contrast to the interpretation of the equivalent rule under American law. The oft-cited *Boynton* case is quite clear on this matter;

> the term 'misconduct' is limited to conduct evincing such wilful or wanton disregard of an employer's interest as is found in deliberate violations or disregard of standards of behaviour which the employer has the right to expect of his employee....on the other hand mere inefficiency, unsatisfactory conduct, failure in good performance as the result of inability or incapacity, ... are not to be deemed 'misconduct' within the meaning of the statute.[8]

Sanders (1955) cites this and other cases as evidence in support of his contention that the misconduct disqualification, which is common to all US state unemployment insurance schemes, is designed to protect against the hazard of self-induced compensatable unemployment (the seeking of the insured event). Disqualification is based on evidence of a *deliberate* disregard of the employer's interest or the employee's obligation to his employer, where the latter is equated with the 'going' standard of conduct at the plant, warehouse or office. Hence cases of misconduct typically involve excessive absenteeism, intoxication during working hours, insubordination, refusal to perform assigned work and so on.

Both British and American unemployment insurance schemes consequently appear to lay considerable emphasis on standards of conduct on the part of the employee. In Britain, however, the standard of conduct expected is judged independently of the employee's state of mind, so that disqualification for misconduct can, in some circumstances, arise out of faulty workmanship, inefficiency or negligence. Ogus and Barendt (1978) have put this down to the 'grave problems of proof' involved with issues of *mens rea*, leading to the establishment of suitability criteria as 'objective' standards of conduct for each worker. Hence there is an obligation placed on each insured employee to meet this standard of conduct, and a breach of this obligation that leads to dismissal implies that the employee 'has lost his employment through his own avoidable fault'[9]. In this way the British system imputes a degree of voluntary behaviour following a breach of accepted norms of conduct, whereas the American system apparently requires proof that the breach was deliberate. While the latter approach reflects more closely the roots of unemployment insurance in private group insurance, in which wilful misconduct is seen as a breach of the contract but negligence is not, the former approach is nearer in spirit to the notion of contributory negligence in tort law, in which the plaintiff's behaviour is assessed in relation to that which might have been expected from a 'reasonable' man. The difference between the two approaches may simply be a reflection of different attitudes towards social 'insurance'. At some stage, the analogy with private group insurance can wear thin. The degree of interpersonal loss-spreading is extended from that which a private insurance company would find financially prudent, to that which the community considers desirable. The system then becomes one of no-fault compensation. The misconduct rule remains as an important contribution to the minimization of the 'primary costs' (Calabresi, 1970) of unemployment. A clearer recognition of the purpose of the rule helps both in explaining much of the case law in this area, and in justifying its continuing existence. As Burns (1956) has pointed out in a more general context, confusion between the aims of insurance and those of income security can be more than a problem of semantics.

13.3 Dismissal for misconduct: optimizing behaviour where the law is given

Emphasis on 'acceptable' standards of conduct is, as we have seen, characteristic of both British and American systems of unemployment insurance adjudication. There is, apparently, a standard of conduct that the employer has a right to expect from an employee. The final arbiter of this standard is not the employer himself but the adjudicating officials. Hence dismissals on the grounds of misconduct have not led to disqualification when the offence is held to be insufficiently reprehensible (R(U)2/60). Mere inefficiency does not normally amount to misconduct, if it is shown that the employee is working to his fullest capacity (R(U)34/52). Moreover, recent legislative developments in the UK have emphasized the employee's right to 'fair' treatment: in the absence of proven misconduct, the employer must demonstrate that the dismissal was either on grounds of the employee's capability or qualifications, or as a result of the redundancy of his job. Failure to do so leaves the employer liable for legal remedies.

As a result of this development it is arguable that employers' awareness of the legal interpretation of misconduct has increased. Decisions with respect to dismissal will undoubtedly be constrained by reference to the inferred norms of conduct. All of which is not to say that an employee's transgression of these 'objective' norms will automatically result in his dismissal. There are many other factors influencing an employer's propensity to dismiss. Whatever it is that a firm is maximizing it will be subject to a number of constraining factors, only one of which is the law. In times of inadequate product demand, for example, the extent to which a smaller workforce will maximize profits (or minimize losses) will depend in part on the relevant revenue and cost conditions, and in part on the 'adjustment costs' associated with moving to a lower level of employment. On the one hand, the latter will include the loss of any investment the firm may have made in terms of training the employee, and on the other hand, they will include any compensation the firm is required to pay to the dismissed employee subsequently. The firm would therefore dismiss if the employee's expected future marginal product (including that due to the firm's investment in training) fell below his expected future wages by more than the amount of compensation that would be payable. It follows that the firm will be less likely to dismiss an employee for a given fall in marginal product, the higher his level of training and the higher the expected compensation.

Under British law, an employer can be liable for compensation to a dismissed employee in three ways. First, an employee can sue his employer for common law damages for wrongful dismissal. Secondly, he may be able to claim compensation (if not reinstatement) for unfair dismissal payable under the Trade Union and Labour Relations Act 1974. Thirdly, an employer is liable for 59 per cent of any redundancy payment for which the employee qualifies under the Redundancy Payments Act 1965. The employer can consequently only escape liability if he can demonstrate that the dismissal was due to the employee's misconduct or to his incompetence, and that he, the employer, 'acted reasonably in treating it as a sufficient reason for dismissing the employee.'[10] In any other circumstances compensation of one form or another will be payable[11].

By defining the circumstances under which employers have the right to dismiss without providing compensation, the law can be seen to enforce what is basically a long-term contingent claims contract, where the contingencies are specified in the statutes and in the case law[12]. In this way, only nonperformance on the employee's part either through his misconduct or through his incompetence will be sufficient to release the employer from his contractual obligations. Placing the burden of proof of a breach on the employer (as in redundancy or unfair dismissal) rather than on the employee (as in the tort of wrongful dismissal) can be seen as implicit recognition of the employer as the best informed party.

It follows that the emphasis placed on the circumstances that lead to dismissal, and the penalties imposed where employers have exceeded their legal rights, will presumably induce employers to take more care over who they dismiss and for what reasons. Moreover, declarations made by employers to insurance officers with respect to the reasons for termination are admissible as evidence in Industrial Tribunals in which questions of unfair dismissal are settled[13]. The implication is that the legislative moves towards clarifying employers' rights in recent years have effectively engaged employers in policing the disqualification rules of unemployment insurance. In a way that is analogous to the experience rating of the payroll tax in the US (*see* Marston, 1975, p. 16), making employers liable for compensation that can be escaped if the dismissal was due to the employee's misconduct provides cost-minimizing employers with an incentive to report fully and accurately when such circumstances are present.

What determines the standard of conduct that will be sufficient to avoid dismissal? Clearly it is *not* simply the standard that is revealed through the case law as that which would count as 'misconduct'. If product demand is high and alternative labour is scarce, it may be optimal for the employer to accept a lower standard of conduct, or simply to devote fewer resources to monitoring employee behaviour (*see* Alchian and Demsetz, 1972). If, on the other hand, product demand is low, employers may wish to dismiss for relatively trivial breaches of discipline, which might not count as misconduct as the law has defined it. Because the interpretation of the law is not certain, the full extent of the employer's liability will not be known *ex ante*, so that the employer's decision-making process will be one of optimizing where the statutes are given, but where the outcome of the legal process, in addition to the behaviour of product demand, are subject to uncertainty.

The average standard of conduct of dismissed employees depends therefore on the outcome of this decision-making process. For a given level of 'blameworthy, reprehensible and wrong' behaviour, we might expect more dismissals for misconduct during periods in which the level of product demand is low, and fewer when demand is high. In this context, it is interesting to quote Calvert (1979, p. 153):

> One suspects that in R8/60(4B), where the employers frankly stated that if it had not been for a shortage of work they would have given the claimant another chance, it might have avoided confusion to have found that there was no 'misconduct' at all, but rather that in a short-time situation, the employer chose to dispense with the services of an employee whose conduct was less satisfactory than that of others.

In sum, the relationship between employer and employee has increasingly become the subject of legal regulation, and this development might be expected to have repercussions for unemployment insurance eligibility. On the one hand, the willingness of employers to report the circumstances surrounding dismissal and to screen out appropriate cases of 'misconduct', may have increased. On the other hand, the extension of employee rights in this area may have affected employers' propensity to terminate contracts where the evidence is not clear cut. Moreover, this propensity will tend to fluctuate over time in relation to variations in demand. We test some of these hypotheses in the following section, 13.4.

13.4 Disqualification for unemployment benefit as a result of misconduct: some evidence

Figure 13.1 shows the number of disqualifications for unemployment benefit in the UK at quarterly intervals from 1960 to 1976, together with the number of unfilled vacancies reported by Local Employment Offices over the same period. The latter series is taken as a useful indicator of the cyclical fluctuation in aggregate demand in the UK economy. *Figure 13.1* also shows the dates from which the provisions of the Redundancy Payments Act 1965 and the Industrial Relations Act 1971 become effective.

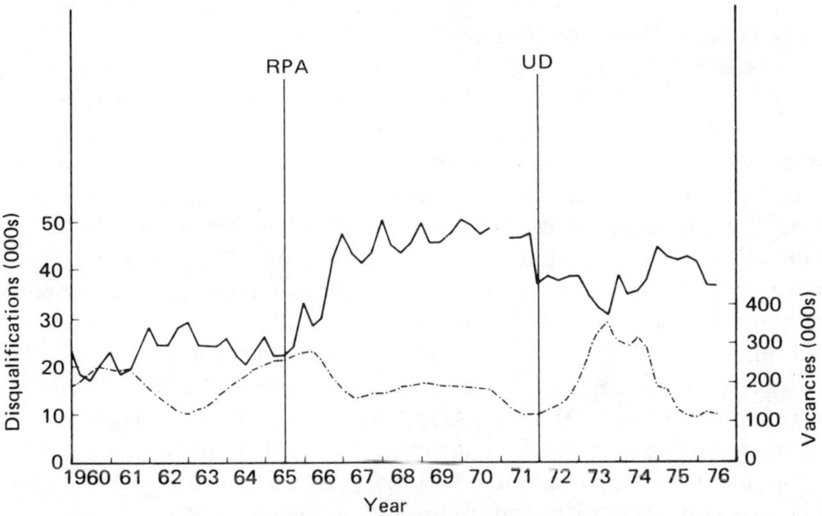

Figure 13.1 *Disqualifications for misconduct, and unfilled vacancies, 1960–1976. RPA and UD are the effective dates of the Redundancy Payments Act 1965 and Industrial Relations Act 1971 respectively. —— represents disqualifications; –·–·–* represents unfilled vacancies.

The 1965 Act provided for lump sum payments to employees dismissed on the grounds of redundancy. The amount paid depends on the employee's age, length of service and his earnings, in accordance with schedule I of the Act. The employer makes the initial payment and is then entitled to a rebate from the Redundancy Fund, which is made up of contributions from all employers. Since 1977 this rebate has been assessed at 41 per cent of the total payment. In assessing the impact of the 1965 Act, Mukherjee (1973, p. 88) found that:

> On the basis of crude estimates it appears that not much more than £2 million a year was being paid out by employers to redundant workpeople in the 5 or so years preceding the severance payment legislation. Yet in the first full year of implementation of the Act, the amount of money paid out was greater than £26 million.

Although the proportion of total labour costs represented by such redundancy payments was not high, the relative increase in employers liability following the Act was marked. Whether the increase was sufficient to induce a change in employers' propensity to dismiss is doubtful, but, as pointed out above, proof of incompetence or misconduct as the factor determining dismissal removes the obligation to pay, providing the employer with an incentive to report fully any such circumstances. It is quite possible, therefore, that we might observe an increase in the proportion of dismissals that are reported as due to misconduct, and consequently an increase in the number of disqualifications after 1965.

The Industrial Relations Act 1971 provided for compensation to be paid by an employer to an unfairly dismissed employee in the event of no re-engagement. If re-engagement is recommended by a tribunal but not complied with by the employer, compensation can be reduced. In many cases, an award of compensation is agreed before a tribunal hearing as a result of the Department of Employment conciliation process. In 1973, compensation was awarded in 2904 cases, with some £0.9 million paid out (Jackson, 1975). This compares with £66.6 million in redundancy payments in the same year. Although unfair dismissal applications have increased considerably since 1973 as a result of reductions in the qualifying period of employment, the number of compensated cases (approximately 15 000 in 1977) remains far below that of redundancy payments. In spite of this, a survey of employers in manufacturing industry in 1977 found that the aspect of employment legislation to have had the most widespread effect on employers has been unfair dismissals requirements (Daniel, 1978).

The same survey found that only 42 per cent of employers claimed that unfair dismissals legislation had no effect on their behaviour, compared with 77 per cent for the Redundancy Payments Act. Moreover, it was suggested that unfair dismissal measures have reduced rates of dismissal, 'particularly in establishments where levels were relatively high prior to the legislation'.

If we turn again to *Figure 13.1*, first impressions are of a definite rise in the number of disqualifications from late 1965 onwards and a possible decline after 1971. However, these apparent shifts are superimposed on a seasonal and cyclical pattern, evidently related to fluctuations in demand. The appropriate way of revealing the separate contributions of each of these factors is through the statistical technique of multiple regression, with misconduct disqualifications as the dependent variable. The resulting equation was estimated as:

$$\text{Ln}\,\frac{M_t}{E_t} =$$

$$\underset{(0.08)}{-2.275^{*}\cdot \text{Ln}V_t} \underset{(0.06)}{-0.002\cdot S_{\text{I}}} \underset{(0.06)}{-0.06\cdot S_{\text{II}}} \underset{(0.06)}{-0.08\cdot S_{\text{III}}} \underset{(0.05)}{+0.563^{*}\cdot RPA} \underset{(0.06)}{-0.06\cdot UD}$$

in which the coefficient of determination, $R^2 = 0.76$, the Durbin–Watson statistic, $DW = 1.59$, * = significant at 5% level, and where $\frac{M_t}{E_t}$ represents the proportion of total employees (E_t) who are disqualified from unemployment benefit for misconduct in period t, V_t is the number of unfilled vacancies in period t, S_{I} to S_{III} are seasonal dummy variables for the first three quarters of each year respectively, and *RPA*, *UD* are shift variables representing the impact of the Redundancy Payments Act and the Industrial Relations Act respectively. The coefficients of each of these variables can consequently be viewed as the separate contribution of each to the overall probability that a given employee will be dismissed for misconduct and subsequently disqualified from benefit[14]. The two significant findings, therefore, are that an increase in aggregate demand (as proxied by the level of vacancies) reduces the probability of a misconduct dismissal, and that the Redundancy Payments Act appears to have increased it. There is further tentative evidence that the probability is higher in winter months than in summer, and that there was a slight reduction in the probability following the 1971 legislation.

In general these findings do appear to substantiate our argument that dismissals for misconduct depend not on some exogenous standard of employee behaviour, but rather on employers' tolerance of such behaviour, which will tend to vary with the state of trade, both seasonally and cyclically. Secondly, the evidence of a large increase in misconduct dismissals following 1965 is not matched by any evidence of an equivalent increase in aggregate dismissals in that period, which seems to imply an increase in the proportion of dismissals reported as due to misconduct[15]. Thirdly, the small decline in misconduct dismissals following the 1971 Act (which is not statistically significant) could reflect a reduction in the dismissal rate for some small employers as found in Daniel's study. It should be noted, however, that these findings depend crucially on the assumption that dismissals reported by employers to insurance officers as being due to misconduct will normally lead to disqualification, and that any discretion held by insurance officers in this matter is negligible and/or random. Variation over time in officials' appetite for enforcement is not unknown (Grubel, Maki and Sax, 1975), but scope for discretion in this particular area would appear to be minimal.

13.5 Conclusion

In section 13.2 of this paper the misconduct rule of unemployment insurance was characterized as a provision that owed much to its origin in an analogy with the 'wilful misconduct' principle of private insurance, and indeed much of the case law, particularly in the US, is at least partially consistent with this view. However, the modern 'pay-as-you-go', nonfunded scheme of unemployment benefit has weakened the appeal of this analogy. Much emphasis has been placed by adjudicators on employers' rights to 'acceptable' standards of conduct, comparable with the common law notion of 'due care'. Breaches of such standards are interpreted as evidence of fault, and the claimant is refused benefit for a limited period. The misconduct on this reasoning is essentially similar to the principle of contributory negligence.

In common law, the incentive to establish contributory negligence is on the part of the tortfeasor. In unemployment insurance, where compensation is not normally payable by the employer who is responsible for the dismissal, there is less incentive for him to demonstrate any contributory fault. Hence the party who has access to the relevant information at least cost, will not necessarily gather it. We have shown in section 13.3 that recent developments in labour law in the UK, by extending employees' rights and by holding employers liable for compensation in certain circumstances, have effectively increased the incentive for employers to 'police' the misconduct rule. At the same time, the law is only one factor in any decision to dismiss and the findings of section 13.4 have emphasized the extent to which the careless employee is at the mercy of the market. To paraphrase Winston Churchill, although both employer and employee can be made to suffer for 'habits of intemperance', it is the employer who remains the licensee.

Notes to chapter thirteen

1 Section 1(c).
2 Beatrice Webb. *Our Partnership* (1948). quoted in Fulbrook (1978), p. 137.
3 Trades covered were building, construction of works, shipbuilding, engineering, construction of vehicles, iron-founding and certain kinds of sawmilling.
4 Hansard, 26 HC Deb (25 May 1911) col. 509.
5 *Notes on Malingering*, 6 June 1909 in the Beveridge Papers, quoted in Gilbert (1968) pp. 271–2.
6 Gilbert (1966) refers to this as 'lateral' insurance, as opposed to individual, 'lineal' insurance.
7 This interpretation of the case law is confirmed by Ogus and Barendt (1978), p. 109, in which they refer to the 'suitability theory' of the misconduct disqualification.
8 *Boynton Cab. Co. v Neubeck* 237 Wis 219, 296, NW 636 (1941).
9 R(U)8/57.
10 Trade Union and Labour Relations Act 1974, s.24.
11 It is also possible, although not usual, for an employee to sue for damages for breach of contract, given the provisions of the Contracts of Employment Act 1972.
12 See Williamson, Wachter and Harris (1978) for a discussion of alternative modes of employment contracting.
13 The relevant enquiry form is UB 85, which is automatically sent to each employer the claimant has had in the seven weeks prior to the claim.
14 The functional form is formally equivalent to a mean supply of offence function, where potential offenders are given by E_t.

See Ehrlich (1973) for a similar specification.

15 One possible explanation for this phenomenon, which we do not discuss here, is that the real increase in benefit levels following the introduction of the Earnings Related Supplement to unemployment benefit in 1966 lessened the financial burden of unemployment, and may therefore have resulted in less concern over standards of conduct on the part of most employees. See Fenn (1980) for a full discussion of this issue: the evidence seems to suggest that the rise in misconduct disqualifications predates the National Insurance Act 1966.

References

AKERLOF, G. (1976). The market for lemons: qualitative uncertainty and the market mechanism, *Quarterly Journal of Economics*, **84**, no. 3, 488–500.

ALCHIAN, A. and DEMSETZ, H. (1972), Production, information costs and economic organisation, *American Economic Review*, **62**, no. 5, 777–795.

ARROW, K.J. (1963), Uncertainty and the welfare economics of medical care, *American Economic Review*, **53**, 941–969.

ARROW, K.J. (1968), The economics of moral hazard: further comment, *American Economic Review*, **58**, no. 3, part 1, 537–539.

BAILY, M. (1978), Some aspects of optimal unemployment insurance, *Journal of Public Economics*, December.

BURNS, E.M. (1956), *Social Security and Public Policy*, New York: McGraw-Hill.

CALABRESI, G. (1970), *The Costs of Accidents*, New Haven, Yale University Press.

CALVERT, H. (1979), *Social Security Law*, 2nd ed. London: Sweet and Maxwell.

DANIEL, W.W. (1978), The effects of unemployment protection laws in manufacturing industry, *Department of Employment Gazette*, June.

EHRLICH, I. (1973), Participation in illegitimate activities: a theoretical and empirical investigation, *Journal of Political Economy*, **81**, no. 3, 521–564.

FENN, P.T. (1980), Sources of disqualification for unemployment benefit 1960–1976, *British Journal of Industrial Relations*, **18**, no. 2, 240–253.

FULBROOK, J. (1978), *Administrative Justice and the Unemployed*, London: Mansell.

GILBERT, B.B. (1968), *The Evolution of National Insurance in Great Britain*.

GRUBEL, H.G., MAKI, D. and SAX, S. (1975), Real and insurance induced unemployment in Canada, *Canadian Journal of Economics*, **8**, no. 2, 176–193.

IVAMY, E.R. HARDY (1979), *General Principles of Insurance Law*, 4th ed., London: Butterworths.

JACKSON, D. (1975), *Unfair Dismissal*, Cambridge University Press.

LLEWELLYN SMITH, H. (1910), Economic security and unemployment insurance, *Economic Journal*, **26**, no. 80, 510–529.

MARSTON, S.T. (1975), The impact of unemployment insurance on job search, *Brookings Papers on Economic Activity*.

MUKHERJEE, S. (1973), *Through No Fault of Their Own*, MacDonald, London.

OGUS, A. and BARENDT, E. (1979), *The Law of Social Security*, London: Butterworths.

PAULY, M.V. (1968), The economics of moral hazard: a comment, *American Economic Review*, **58**, no. 3, part 1, 531–537.

PAULY, M.V. (1974), Overinsurance and the public provision of insurance: the roles of moral hazard and adverse selection, *Quarterly Journal of Economics*, **88**, no. 1, 44–54.

PEACOCK, A.T. (1952), *The Economics of National Insurance*, London: William Hodge.

PECHMAN, J.A., AARON, H.J. and TAUSSIG, M.K. (1968), *Social Security: Perspectives for Reform*, Washington DC: Brookings Institution.

SANDERS, D.H. (1955), Disqualification for unemployment insurance, *Vanderbilt Law Review*, **8**, no. 1, 307–337.

WILLIAMSON, O.E., WACHTER, M.L. and HARRIS, J.E. (1975), Understanding the employment relation: the analysis of idiosyncratic change, *Bell Journal of Economics*, **6**, no. 1, 250–280.

WOODSWORTH, D.E. (1977), *Social Security and National Policy*, McGill and Queen's University Press.

CHAPTER FOURTEEN

Tax avoidance

J. Feldman and J. A. Kay

14.1 Introduction

It is widely thought that tax avoidance is an aberration about which little systematic can be said. In this chapter, we argue that it results from the difficulty of giving legal expression to economic concepts. We analyse the sources of these difficulties and present a systematic taxonomy of avoidance schemes. We argue that it is the definition and measurement of income, in both personal and corporate sectors, that provides the majority of avoidance opportunities. Income is a concept that has proved elusive of agreed definition by economists, and the obstacles to giving it effective legal form have proved even greater.

It is conventional to distinguish (legal) avoidance from (illegal) evasion. The incidence of evasion has received some recent attention from economists: see for example Allingham and Sandmo (1972), Christiansen (1980). The essence of the distinction is that evasion depends on the concealment of facts; avoidance occurs when the facts of a transaction are admitted but the outcome differs from the intention of the relevant legislation. This distinction is sharper in the UK, where Revenue assessment prevails, than in the US system, which prefers self-assessment. In a broad sense, one avoids tax when one consumes untaxed tea rather than taxed whisky. However, common usage of 'avoidance' implies a degree of artificiality. The untaxed transaction has much the same effect as the taxable transaction: only the tax charged differs. This distinction between artificial avoidance and other kinds is not a precise demarcation line: the line between evasion and avoidance is clearer but there is still one important area in which it is blurred. That is where the tax treatment of a transaction depends on the motive for undertaking it, so that distortion shades into misrepresentation that shades into falsehood. A typical problem here is the treatment of business expenses, where deductibility usually depends on the objective of the expenditure — something that can be known only to the potential taxpayer, and not always to him.

In general, however, the extent of evasion depends on the efficiency of collecting and reporting mechanisms; the extent of avoidance depends on the efficiency of taxing statutes in giving practical effect to legislative intention. There are three principal tasks that such statutes are required to perform. First, there is the problem of characterization: defining 'income', 'whisky', 'capital transfers' or whatever is the intended subject of the tax. Secondly, there is the problem of measurement: it is necessary to compute the amount of income, the volume of whisky, the value of capital transfers. Thirdly, there is a problem of identification: it is necessary to specify the individual or organization that is responsible for paying a tax. This is only significant when different individuals are subject to tax at different rates. This is always the case, to some degree, because there are limits to the territorial jurisdiction of any taxing legislation. It becomes more serious when, as is usually the case, some residents — such as charities — are exempt from the tax; and more serious still when progressive tax schedules impose different rates of tax for each individual taxpayer based on his overall circumstances.

It is also important to stress that the extent of both avoidance and evasion depends on rates of tax and the incentives that these provide. The attempt to legislate rates of tax rising to 98 per cent — as in the UK until 1979 —makes both inevitable. We prefer to avoid the moral issues raised — but in relation to avoidance, and perhaps evasion also, we share the view of the minority of the 1955 Royal Commission on taxation: 'the existence of widespread tax avoidance is evidence that the system, not the taxpayer, stands in need of radical reform.' (para. 33).

14.2 Origins of tax avoidance

In this chapter, we shall refer to the experience of tax legislation and tax avoidance in both the UK and the USA. There are important differences between the types of avoidance devices most commonly used in the two countries. These result from differences in the structure of tax administration that in turn arise from differences in the time and manner in which income taxes were introduced.

Britain imposed income tax in 1799 and was the first country in the world to do so. The tax itself was resented, and the unprecedented intrusion into the personal affairs of individuals that it implied was resented even more. As a result, the codification devised by Addington in 1803 was based on two related principles; namely, separate schedules of taxation for different kinds of income and deduction of tax at source. Under the schedular system, separate assessments were made for different kinds and sources of income, so that at no time was a complete picture of the financial affairs of any particular individual required or obtained. At the same time, the primary burden for supplying information and collecting tax was imposed on the payer of income rather than the recipient. Necessary to the smooth running of this system was the imposition of the tax at a single flat rate on all kinds of income of all taxpayers.

The historical rationale of this system has long since vanished. It is instructive to note that there was originally no schedule for taxing employment income since it was inconceivable that anyone who was an employee would have status or resources such as to render him liable for tax; the provisions for taxing income from employment are a development of the original rules for taxing the emoluments of certain crown offices. Once income tax became progressive, it required considerable ingenuity to levy it without actually measuring the total income of any individual. But this feat is still (more or less) accomplished; it is still the case that a British taxpayer never sees a single assessment of his income from all sources and normally nor does his tax inspector. The structure of 1803 still governs the administration of the British tax system.

In the US, by contrast, income tax was introduced in 1913 and was from the start conceived as a progressive tax on the total income of individuals. Income in the United States is defined as broadly as possible; the general rule is that everything is included unless one specific statute excludes it. For example, the current regulations, which have the force of law, say 'Gross income includes income realized in any form, whether in money, property, or service. Income may be realized, therefore in the form of services, meals, accommodations, stock, or other property, as well as in cash.' The compartmentalization of income and of legislation that the schedular system implies in the UK simply does not arise in the USA. The same has tended to be true of tax avoidance devices. Tax avoidance in Britain has most often been concerned with exploiting the rules of some particular schedule to obtain more advantageous treatment of some item of income. Tax avoidance in the US has largely been devoted to the artificial generation of losses in one area of activity that can be used as a set-off against income usually without regard to whether it arises from the same or another area.

This difference is increased in significance by differences between the two countries in constitutional procedures. In Britain, the power of the executive in relation to the legislature is very much greater than in the US. Tax policy is determined in broad outline by the Treasury and in detail by the administering departments. The influence of Parliament on the content of legislation, by convention even more limited in relation to taxation than in other areas of government policy, is in practice negligible. In the US, on the other hand, Congress can both reject substantive proposals that the administration brings to it and initiate tax legislation of its own, and it regularly does. Against this should be noted the greater freedom of the US Internal Revenue Service (IRS) to make detailed regulations for operating and implementing the system within the overall framework of legislation imposed on it. The powers of the Inland Revenue to make administrative rules are much more limited.

The effect of the greater power of Congress relative to the executive is to increase the influence of special interest groups relative to the integrity of a rational tax structure. Thus American tax legislation is full of unsystematic concessions in response to self-interested lobbyists to an extent unknown in the UK, where the political process is better able to resist such pressures. These areas provide fertile ground for avoidance devices. On the other hand, the IRS can respond more flexibly to the exploitation of the fine shades of definition or defective administrative detail than can the British Inland Revenue. These constitutional differences reinforce the differences in character between the tax avoidance industries on the two sides of the Atlantic.

These contrasts should not be exaggerated. It is notable that recent British avoidance schemes — of which the commodity carry scheme is the most notorious example — have tended to be more American in character, with artificial transactions generated to shelter unrelated income; though it is also true that these have attracted a degree of disapprobation much greater than more conventional avoidance gambits. The House of Lords' decisions in *Ramsey and Rawling* (1981 STC 174, HL), in which schemes were struck down on the grounds that the sequence of transactions lacked commercial reality, represent a major setback to the use of artificial devices. The American approach represents an aggressive challenge to the authority of the state, which attracts relatively aggressive responses. The British have traditionally relied on stretching the rules and exploiting niceties of definition, with gentle Revenue intervention to restrain excess. It is possible that his contrast reflects differences in social attitudes that extend well beyond taxation. It is also possible that these differences are diminishing.

14.3 Tax avoidance and the definition of income

In both the UK and the US the major part of tax revenue is derived from taxes on personal or corporate income. The majority of tax avoidance devices also relate to personal or corporate income. We therefore begin with an examination of the problems of legislating an income tax.

The most appropriate definition of income is itself the subject of debate in both economics and accounting, and when an economist and accountant came together they had no difficulty in putting together a volume of — inevitably inconclusive — debate on the subject (Parker and Harcourt, 1969). But the most widely accepted definition is probably that of Hicks: 'income is the maximum value which [a man] can consume during a week, and still expect to be as well off at the end of the week as he was at the beginning.' (Hicks, 1946, p. 172). The majority of practical problems in the determination of income for tax purposes arise from the attempts to implement two of the concepts of that definition; the word 'expect' and the phrase 'well off'. There is a subsidiary group of problems that arise from the difficulty of interpreting the word 'consume'; these are, in the main, the issues already noted of distinguishing business and personal expenditure and will not be discussed further in this essay.

It is obvious from the beginning that expectations are incapable of precise definition, objective measurement or equitable assessment; and it is not surprising that this area of the definition is a primary source of problems. Indeed economists advocating an approach to tax policy based on an economic concept of income have quickly retreated from the implications of this aspect of the Hicksian definition and have generally preferred the Haig–Simons approach; 'personal income may be defined as the algebraic sum of (a) the market value of rights exercised in consumption and (b) the change in the value of the store of property rights between the beginning and end of the period in question.' (Simons, 1938, p. 50).

A significant change of tense occurs as we move from one definition to the other. The Hicksian definition looks forward — hence the role of expectations. The Haig–Simons definition looks back — after expectations have become, or have not become, realizations, and hence capable of measurement and practical implementation. Haig–Simons measures not what a man (or woman, or corporation) could expect to spend in some future period, but what he could in fact have spent in some past period. If expectations always materialized there would of course be a simple equivalence between the two concepts, but in an unpredictable world there will be substantial divergencies.

Thus the Haig–Simons modification removes a principal problem in implementing the Hicksian concept. The difficulty is that the Hicksian definition is in fact closer to most people's 'common sense' interpretation of income, and as a result Haig–Simons advocates have had little success in putting forward their definition as a basis for legislation or judical interpretation. It implies that changes in the paper value of the same collection of assets, or windfall receipts, add to taxable capacity in just the same way as do earnings from employment or dividends from shares. It is possible to argue that they do, or that people should behave as if they do. But it is clear that this does not correspond to the perceptions of those who receive windfalls or benefit from unrealized capital appreciation, or to the opinions of those who frame or interpret tax legislation.

It is therefore necessary to distinguish between accretions to wealth that are income and taxable as such, and others that are capital gains and taxable as such, if at all. British legislation provides virtually no assistance on the basis of this distinction and we have to examine case law. This issue was much discussed by the 1955 Royal Commission on Taxation, who surveyed decisions with particular reference to what they called the 'badges of trade', the presence or absence of which determined whether a particular profit on resale of an asset was trading income — subject to income tax — or something else on which no tax was levied. The Commission's list of the 'badges of trade' included the nature of the goods, the length of time held, the frequency of transaction, the work done on the assets, the reason for the sale and the reason for the whole transaction.

The problem of distinguishing income from capital gains is a major difficulty of characterization. It is a difficulty that British tax law does not attempt to tackle. It has therefore become a primary source of opportunities for tax avoidance and has spawned an extensive body of anti-avoidance legislation.

The second area of Hicksian income definition that appeared as an immediate source of problems was the expression 'well off'. Contained within this are problems of both measurement and identification. The measurement problems is obvious. In principle, an annual income tax requires annual valuation of all assets. Even if all assets were like listed securities, with market prices published daily in the financial newspapers, this would be a considerable administrative burden. But there are few kinds of asset for which market prices are readily available, and a wide range for which markets are thin or non-existent. This not only compounds the administrative problem of valuation, it would lead to tax demands that the individuals concerned lacked the financial resources to meet. Hence the general principle is to defer recognition of changes in asset values until realization occurs.

The difficulty here is not simply that the implicit assumption underlying it is not true; it is compounded by the fact that realization is an operation that is frequently under the control of the taxpayer. Thus a range of avoidance gambits are devices for deferring realization. At this point, the problems of measurement and of identification interact. The reason is that under an income tax regime that corresponded closely to an economic concept of income, it would be necessary to assign all income that accrued to an institution as if it were passed through to the individual who was the ultimate beneficiary. This is difficult, but the difficulty would not matter in practice if everyone was taxed at the same rate since it would then be possible to levy tax on the institution at the uniform rate of all individuals. Since income tax is in fact levied at different rates on different individuals, the approaches adopted are to levy tax on the institution at some average rate or to defer collection of tax until some ultimate realization takes place, or some combination of the two. We shall show below how these *ad hoc* procedures give extensive scope for avoidance devices.

14.4 Tax avoidance in practice

We have argued that avoidance opportunities result from difficulties of legal definition; that these difficulties take the form of problems of characterization, measurement and identification; and we have shown how these problems are particularly acute in relation to the expressions 'expect' and 'well off' in the Hicksian definition of income. We shall now consider how specific avoidance devices have exploited these opportunities. Our analysis suggests that an appropriate response to tax avoidance would be to refine the legal definition of income to minimize the area of difficulty or doubt, and if this did not prove effective to shift the tax base towards a concept more capable of satisfactory legal expression. In practice, however, the usual reaction has been to attack the mechanics of specific avoidance devices. Since this does not remove the underlying problem, it is to be expected that the same difficulty will occur in a different guise, and this is precisely what has happened. It is no surprise that the best known British inventor of avoidance schemes in recent years, Roy Tucker, has commented that his principal source of inspiration for new schemes was reading old anti-avoidance legislation. The same thing is true in the United States: there is no more fertile source of clever avoidance ideas than Joint Committee reports about legislation designed to correct avoidance.

A primary problem of characterization is that of distinguishing income from capital gains. We have suggested how this arises from the difficulty of achieving by legislation anything that corresponds to the word 'expect' in the Hicksian definition of income. The conversion of income into less heavily taxed capital gain has therefore become a central gambit in tax avoidance.

Traditional, and somewhat crude, mechanisms for exploiting this are the practices of 'bond-washing' and 'dividend stripping'. These rely on the existence of taxpayers with different marginal rates of tax. Bond-washing exploits the fact that interest and dividends on securities are paid at intervals — typically six-monthly. Consider a bond that yields 10 per cent per annum and is priced at 100. As the six-monthly interest date comes closer, the price of the bond will rise — say from 100 to 104. For any such bond, there is a date on which it goes 'ex-dividend' — the person who holds it on that date is the person entitled to receive the coming interest payment, and a subsequent purchaser is not entitled to the dividend. When the bond goes ex-dividend its price will therefore fall back to 100.

It is therefore efficient to ensure that a bond that is normally held by a (say) 50 per cent taxpayer is held by a non-taxpayer on the day it goes ex-dividend. The holder of the bond sells the bond the previous day for 104 and repurchases it a day later for 100. Doing this every six months be obtains a tax-free return of 4 per six-monthly period, or 8 per cent. The non-taxpayer makes a loss of 4 on each transaction, but this is more than offset by the interest payment of 5 that he receives. The bond-holder has raised his net annual return from 5 per cent (after 50 per cent tax) to 8 per cent, so that the marginal rate he pays is not 50 per cent but 20 per cent; his associate makes a profit of two and the Revenue loses five. The scheme is advantageous for any price of the bond on the day before it goes ex-dividend that lies between 102½ and 105. Which level within these limits it reaches depends on the relative number of taxpayers and non-taxpayers. If the majority of participants in the market are taxpayers at 50 per cent, then 'associates' will be in short supply and the rewards they gain bid up, so that the cum-dividend price of the bond will be close to 102½; if non-taxpayers are relatively numerous the price will approach 105. (Because indifference curves between income and capital gains are straight lines for sophisticated taxpayers, the limit theorem does not yield a determinate equilibrium even if the numbers of participants on both sides of the market are large.)

Anti-avoidance legislation to deal with bond-washing began in Britain in 1927, which a provision (in relation to higher rates of tax only) that raised an additional charge to tax if liability had been reduced substantially below that which would have arisen if interest had been paid as it accrued. This provision proved insufficient; in particular, it reduced the attractions of the scheme to the higher-rate taxpayer but not to his associate. The position of associate was advantageous, not only to non-taxpayers but also to professional dealers in securities for whom capital losses are deductible against other income and who would therefore derive a (taxable) profit (of one in the example above) by holding the security for a day. A further strengthening of the legislation in 1937 therefore provided that if an agreement was made to sell and repurchase a security, and the outcome was that the interest payable on it accrued to someone else, then that interest would be treated as the taxable income of the original owner. However, this failed to cover the possibility that the original owner might simply sell the right to receive the interest, without selling the security itself. This loophole was closed in the 1938 Finance Act.

Imposing restrictions on agreements to buy and resell proved inadequate. It was possible to engage in bond-washing without an explicit agreement for purchase and resale, since there was in fact no difficulty in finding willing buyers and sellers at predictable market prices. In 1959 more comprehensive rules were introduced for dealing with bond-washing, which sought to identify situations where purchases and sales of securities were made within a short period during which an interest payment became due. Where these conditions are identified, a set of rules is prescribed, complex in both structure and application, for determining the relevant tax treatment. Finally, a number of transactions of this kind were brought within the scope of a very general 1960 provision that gave the Revenue power to undo the effects of some kinds of security transactions.

We have discussed bond-washing in some detail because it illustrates a number of the general characteristics of tax-avoidance schemes and legislation. First, the source of the problem is the inability of the legislator to give effect to the underlying economic concept. In terms of the Hicksian definition of income, capital gains that result from the accrual of predictable interest due but not yet paid have the character of income. If these gains *were* taxable income, the problem of bond-washing would disappear immediately. While it would not be impossible to achieve this result, there are some difficulties is distinguishing capital gains arising from this source from other capital gains, which tax legislation treats differently, and for this or other reasons these gains are not treated as income. This creates the opportunity for tax avoidance. (For securities with less than five years to maturity, the UK practice is to quote the element of accrued interest in the sale of purchase as a component separate from the price. Even in these cases, accrued interest is treated as capital rather than as income.)

Secondly, the legislative response is not to get to the heart of the problem, but to attack the mechanisms of the avoidance scheme. In this example the central problem is, as we have seen, genuinely difficult to solve, but in addition tax administrators tend to eschew fundamental principles, preferring to make minimal responses to identified problems. This may not be as decisive a factor where legislators are involved, but tax avoidance is more generally the problem of administrators. A consequence of this approach is that the anti-avoidance provisions do not work very well. As the development of bond-washing illustrates, when one particular group of schemes is outlawed, it is often possible to construct more complicated and less efficient schemes that have similar effect. A further set of anti-avoidance provisions is invoked, with slightly greater success and substantially greater complexity. The final exasperated outcome is the buttress of a rather vague and general provision that leaves doubt in the minds of honest and dishonest taxpayer alike; the sum of the resulting legislation is complex in appearance and uncertain in effect. The third characteristic of this saga that should be noted, is that the anti-avoidance measures deal only with a small group of highly artificial schemes. In none of the cases discussed was there any shred of a motive other than tax avoidance attached to the activity. But in the much wider range of cases in which the *principle* of this avoidance scheme is exploited but only in conjunction with a bona-fide commercial transaction, nothing is done. Even in the case of short-dated government stocks, where accrued interest is quoted as a separate component of the price of a security, the interest accrued is treated as capital rather than as income. In consequence, the conversion of taxable income into tax-free capital gain remains a central device for reducing the tax-burden on investment income.

Schemes for transforming income into capital gains are common in the US also. Commodity straddles have been a common form of these plans in recent years. An investor buys a long future contract for (say) June corn, and sells at the same time a short contract for August corn. He hopes that during the immediate term both prices will decline, perhaps because more corn is being harvested. He then closes out the long position, suffering a short-term loss that can be deducted from unrelated income. At the same time, he buys another long contract for September corn; this second purchase has the effect of locking-in his gain in the short contract or 'leg' of the straddle. Later, when the long-term capital gains holding period expires, the investor can realize the profit in the second set of contracts. The effect of this simple straddle is to transform ordinary income into long-term capital gain.

The nature of the IRS attack on this kind of scheme illustrates the frustrating, and we suggest impossible, task facing tax collectors confined to traditional definitions and measurements of income. The IRS has sought to challenge these schemes because they lack any economic risk, and hence lack any 'business purpose' unrelated to tax savings. The principal response of the tax shelter industry has been to develop slightly more sophisticated versions of the same schemes. The current favourite is one using treasury bills. An investor suffers a short-term loss in certain government securities, which are by a special statute deductible from ordinary income, and at the same time the investor realizes a long-term gain in a futures contract involving the slightly different government stock. This version depends on the special statute that was originally designed to encourage people to invest in government securities, obviously as a way to raise money for the federal treasury.

The promoters of treasury bill schemes have yet to solve legitimately one lurking problem. Interest rates are hard to predict. Sometimes these schemes run the risk of turning long-term gains into ordinary income; the expected loss in treasury bills can turn into a short-term profit if market interest rates decline, and the expected gain in the short-futures contract can then become a long-term capital loss. So far, the typical solution is to indulge in a little bit of frankly illegal tax fraud. The transactions are often done after-the-fact in a rigged market, and the investor never really owns the required treasury bills themselves. Eventually we would expect that the IRS will wake up to this difficulty.

The result of all this is not entirely a perversion. Congress started out with a device to encourage investments of a desired nature. What could have a more attractive and powerful lobby than the federal treasury! The overall effect of the statute that allows losses on treasury bills to be deductible from ordinary income (instead of being capital losses) may be consistent with the original legislative goals. Certainly it encourages both real and artificial transactions in treasury bills. However, a fundamentally irrational concession undermines the basis of tax legislation in other areas.

The transformation of income into capital gain is an example of how tax avoidance can be achieved by exploiting difficulties of characterization. Difficulties of identification arise when the tax avoider can alter the identity of the recipient of income without altering the identity of the beneficiary. Both the US and UK encourage two kinds of these schemes: charitable contributions, and transfers of property to children or elderly relations. While capital transfer taxes in the UK and gift taxes in the US place some limitations on the size of gifts one can make to parents or children, the basic plan works easily. One can simply give some income-producing property, such as bonds, to a child or to a parent, and the income arising from that investment will accrue to the low-rated relation rather than to the higher-rated donor. There are some obvious constraints. The gift must be a real transfer, usually for a long term. The income must not be used to finance legal obligations of the donor. Thus, a gift of property in the US to pay for essential food and shelter for a child, when the provision of food and shelter is a legal obligation of the parent, will not result in a transfer of taxable income away from the parent. US tax legislation favours charitable gifts much more strongly than is the case in Britain, though the difference is diminishing — such a gift represents a transfer of assets from a taxpaying donor to a charity, which enjoys a specially granted tax-free status. The usual fringes of abuse occur when the donor continues to enjoy the transferred property. For example, should a full charitable deduction be allowed for a gift of a painting to a museum when the donor continues to have the use of the painting for four months every year? The general rule is to reduce the deemed value of the gift proportionately.

Identification schemes are equally popular within purely business contexts. For example, the payment of a high franchise fee, perhaps with a promissory notes, creates a deduction for the payer and corresponding income for the payee. That is, if someone pays MacDonalds $150000 a year for the right to sell hamburgers under golden arches, the amount paid is a business deduction for the franchisee, and at the same time it is income to MacDonalds. But MacDonalds may not mind having this income deemed to it: it may have other means of sheltering its income. For example, suppose MacDonalds in turn licenses it rights from a parent franchisor situated in a tax haven. It then could make a corresponding payment to its off-shore parent, and take a domestic deduction. The parent would recognize taxable income, but at a lower rate.

Measurement schemes or issues generally accompany identification issues, and they occur only in the context of problems of identification or characterization or both. If an item is taxable for one party at the same rate as that at which it is deductible for another, there is no advantage in securing an artificially high or low value for the transaction. Benefit is only obtained if the two parties are taxed at different rates, or if the tax treatments of the two sides of the transaction differ. Thus a general problem is to determine how much income or gain is shifted to a low-tax recipient. For example, the outright gift of a sum to a charity presents no special measurement problem if the value is not open to any dispute. But suppose the gift is of very uncertain value, perhaps only recently acquired by the donor at a great discount. There is a popular bible-donation scheme in the US in which bibles are acquired for $15 each with the bibles carrying certified appraisals showing their fair market values to be $60. A friendly religious institution agrees to accept the bibles as a gift, and to give a receipt showing the higher valuations. The sixty-dollar valuations are supported by sales records showing that identical bibles are widely sold, on a door-to-door basis, for $60 each.

Measurement issues can combine both identification and characterization problems. One popular US scheme involves the claiming of investment tax credit, which is a direct credit against unrelated taxes rather than a deduction from income, for art reproduction masters. These masters are used to make lithographs. A similar scheme involving lithograph masters is widely sold in the UK to take advantage of capital allowances, which operate as deductions against unrelated income. In the US schemes, an investor pays $10 000 in cash plus a promissory note for $190 000 for an art master. He then claims an investment tax credit based on the equipment value of $200 000, with the sum allegedly in turn reflecting his purchase price. However, the promissory note was 'non-recourse'; it was only liable for repayment from profits earned from reproductions using the art masters. The IRS could argue that the valuation (i.e. measurement) of $200 000 is grossly inflated. Similar schemes in both the US and the UK are sold using master gramophone recordings instead of lithograph masters, with identical tax issues. These schemes involve questions of characterization of whether (in this case) there really was an expense of $200 000, and similarly of identification of whether there was a real payment of the total purchase price of the lithograph or recording to the seller. In both cases, the sellers would probably seek to avoid tax liability on the gain attributed to sales at the high prices by a contrived further purchase — another identification issue — from a tax-free entity.

14.5 Is tax avoidance inevitable?

In section 14.3 of this chapter we began with an economic definition of income and examined the problems that arose in translating that concept into a working set of legislative rules. If the proposal to introduce an income tax were a new one, and an examination of this kind was undertaken, it probably would be concluded that an income tax, whatever its theoretical merits, was impracticable. It is not clear to us, in the light of the discussion of section 14.4, that experience has shown that this judgment is wrong.

A major reason why this conclusion is resisted is that there is one major area, covering the overwhelming majority of taxpayers and the larger part of tax revenue, in which income tax works relatively well. This is the area of income from employment. The reason the tax works well is that there is for each employee a single transaction at the end of each week or month and it is that transaction which yields the tax base. There is little problem of definition; and since every payslip has a name and an amount on it there is no problem of identification or of measurement. The tax works in a straightforward manner because its base is cash flow. The forms of employment income that do pose problems for tax determination are precisely those where there is income but no cash flow — deferred remuneration of all kinds (primarily pensions) and fringe benefits. It is because the relationship between economic income and cash flow is much more tenuous in other areas that income tax works much less satisfactorily in relation to self-employment and investment income.

This suggests that more effective tax legislation could be achieved if a systematic cash flow base was adopted (as argued by Andrews, 1974). This would relate tax liability directly to the flow of cash to an individual — from his employer, his investments or his business transactions — rather than to an approximation to calculations of hypothetical accrued income. A similar conclusion can be reached from a different direction by observing that of the three awkward expressions contained in the Hicksian income of definition — expect, well-off and consume — two disappear if the tax base is expenditure rather than income and only the (limited) ambiguity surrounding the word 'consume' remains. The cash flow income tax of Andrews is, as he acknowledged, exactly equivalent to the expenditure tax of Kaldor (or Hobbes) (Kaldor, 1955; Hobbes, 1651).

It is certainly the case that avoidance is not a major problem for existing expenditure taxes. A recent manual of tax avoidance, or tax planning as it is euphemistically called, (Chapman, 1980) stresses its comprehensiveness by noting that it includes one chapter (out of 54) on VAT — 'there is even a section on value added tax, a tax which most would regard as unplannable'.

Why is this? Part of the reason is clearly that rates of VAT, in Britain and elsewhere, have generally been much lower than rates of income tax, so that incentives for tax avoidance are much less. But this does not mean that such incentives are non-existent. An alternative explanation (suggested by Butt, 1979) emphasizes the difference in collecting procedures, suggesting that indirect taxes pose many fewer problems than do direct taxes because they are collected from a few large organizations rather than a multiplicity of individuals. The importance of this difference is somewhat exaggerated, since the bulk of income tax revenue is collected from large employers just as the bulk of value added tax is collected from large retailers. But the argument also overlooks the relevance of the distinction between avoidance and evasion in this context. Avoidance, we argued, was a function of the tax base; evasion was a function of collection procedures (section 14.1). Using indirect taxation rather than direct alters the collection mechanism — and so may affect evasion opportunities — but if the economic base on which the tax is levied is the same the scope for avoidance is the same whether collection is by direct or indirect means.

We cannot argue that any tax system — or any tax system levied in a country in which we would wish to live — could be immune from problems of tax avoidance. But it does not follow from that that all tax systems are affected equally by it. The tax systems of the US and UK have suffered considerably by relying heavily on income-based taxes. Income is an economic and accounting concept to which it has proved impossible to give effective and objective legislative content. We have referred extensively in this paper to Hicks' definition of income. Hicks' conclusion, after a lengthy discussion of his definition and others, was that income and capital were 'bad tools, which break in our hands.' (1939, p. 177). In the hands of tax legislators, they have indeed broken.

References

ALLINGHAM, M.G. and SANDMO, A. (1972), Income tax evasion: a theoretical analysis, *Journal of Public Economics*, **1**, no. 3, 323–338.

ANDREWS, W.O. (1974), A consumption type or cash flow personal income tax, *Harvard Law Review*, **87**, no. 6, 1113–1195.

BUTT, D.M.B. (1979), The target for tax reform, *British Tax Review*, **no. 3**, 168–177.

CHAPMAN, A.L. (ed.) (1980), *Tax Planning*, London: Tolley Publishing.

CHRISTIANSEN, V. (1980), Two comments on tax evasion, *Journal of Public Economics*, **13**, no. 3, 389–394.

HICKS, J.R. (1946), *Value and Capital*, Oxford University Press.

HOBBES, T. (1651), *Leviathan*, London: Andrew Cooke.

KALDOR, N. (1955), *An Expenditure Tax*, London: Allen and Unwin.

PARKER, R.H. and HARCOURT, G.C. (1969), *Readings in the Concept and Measurement of Income*, London: Cambridge University Press.

REPORT of the Royal Commission on the Taxation of Profits and Income (1955), (The Radcliffe Report), Cmnd 9474, London: HMSO.

SIMONS, H.C. (1938), *Personal Income Taxation*, Chicago University Press.

Index